T0212723

Lecture Notes in Computer Science   9455

Commenced Publication in 1973
Founding and Former Series Editors:
Gerhard Goos, Juris Hartmanis, and Jan van Leeuwen

Editorial Board

David Hutchison
  Lancaster University, Lancaster, UK
Takeo Kanade
  Carnegie Mellon University, Pittsburgh, PA, USA
Josef Kittler
  University of Surrey, Guildford, UK
Jon M. Kleinberg
  Cornell University, Ithaca, NY, USA
Friedemann Mattern
  ETH Zurich, Zürich, Switzerland
John C. Mitchell
  Stanford University, Stanford, CA, USA
Moni Naor
  Weizmann Institute of Science, Rehovot, Israel
C. Pandu Rangan
  Indian Institute of Technology, Madras, India
Bernhard Steffen
  TU Dortmund University, Dortmund, Germany
Demetri Terzopoulos
  University of California, Los Angeles, CA, USA
Doug Tygar
  University of California, Berkeley, CA, USA
Gerhard Weikum
  Max Planck Institute for Informatics, Saarbrücken, Germany

More information about this series at http://www.springer.com/series/7409

Ian Cleland · Luis Guerrero
José Bravo (Eds.)

Ambient Assisted Living

ICT-Based Solutions in Real Life Situations

7th International Work-Conference, IWAAL 2015
Puerto Varas, Chile, December 1–4, 2015
Proceedings

 Springer

Editors
Ian Cleland
University of Ulster
Londonderry
UK

José Bravo
University of Castilla-La Mancha
Ciudad Real
Spain

Luis Guerrero
Universidad de Costa Rica
San Jose
Costa Rica

ISSN 0302-9743   ISSN 1611-3349   (electronic)
Lecture Notes in Computer Science
ISBN 978-3-319-26409-7   ISBN 978-3-319-26410-3   (eBook)
DOI 10.1007/978-3-319-26410-3

Library of Congress Control Number: 2015953781

LNCS Sublibrary: SL3 – Information Systems and Applications, incl. Internet/Web, and HCI

Springer Cham Heidelberg New York Dordrecht London
© Springer International Publishing Switzerland 2015
This work is subject to copyright. All rights are reserved by the Publisher, whether the whole or part of the material is concerned, specifically the rights of translation, reprinting, reuse of illustrations, recitation, broadcasting, reproduction on microfilms or in any other physical way, and transmission or information storage and retrieval, electronic adaptation, computer software, or by similar or dissimilar methodology now known or hereafter developed.
The use of general descriptive names, registered names, trademarks, service marks, etc. in this publication does not imply, even in the absence of a specific statement, that such names are exempt from the relevant protective laws and regulations and therefore free for general use.
The publisher, the authors and the editors are safe to assume that the advice and information in this book are believed to be true and accurate at the date of publication. Neither the publisher nor the authors or the editors give a warranty, express or implied, with respect to the material contained herein or for any errors or omissions that may have been made.

Printed on acid-free paper

Springer International Publishing AG Switzerland is part of Springer Science+Business Media
(www.springer.com)

Preface

Aging demographics and declining health in older adults are predicted to put unaffordable pressures on care systems. Innovation is therefore required in order to cope with these societal challenges.

The aim of ambient assisted living (AAL), through the use of intelligent products and the provision of remote care services, is to extend the time in which older people can live in their home environment by increasing their autonomy and assisting them in carrying out activities of daily living. These solutions include innovative concepts to ensure person-centered care. They consider the growing importance of both formal and informal caregivers across public and private sectors and seek to deliver sustainable care services and to maximize the opportunity for technologies to support care.

This volume presents cutting-edge research in the development and testing of AAL solutions to support older adults to live independently for longer. The contributions have been curated from submissions to IWAAL 2015, the 7th International Work-conference on Ambient Assisted Living, which was held December 1–4, in Puerto Varas, Patagonia, Chile.

This specialized conference, now in its seventh year, focuses specifically on the opportunities to utilize ICT to improve quality of life and support autonomy. IWAAL approaches this problem from a technology, human, and business perspective, therefore covering a range of important topics including: self-management/self-care, health monitoring, context awareness, personalization, social integration, knowledge management, integration and interoperability, exploitation strategies, and commercialization. This volume includes 28 articles from internationally recognized researchers from 15 countries. Following the review process we had an acceptance rate of 77 % for long papers. A total of 100 reviews were undertaken to reach these decisions. We would like to thank all the authors who submitted their work for consideration and also the reviewers who provided detailed and constructive reviews, all in a timely manner.

Finally, we would like to express our sincere gratitude to our colleagues for their hard work in the organization of this event, particularly Sergio Ochoa from the University of Chile and Jose Bravo from Castilla-La Mancha University. We would also like to thank all the members of the Program Committee for their time and contributions.

December 2015

Ian Cleland
Luis Guerrero
José Bravo

Organization

General Chair

Jose Bravo — University of Castilla-La Mancha, Spain

Local Organizing Chair

Sergio F. Ochoa — University of Chile, Chile

IWAAL Program Committee Chairs

Luis Guerrero — University of Costa Rica, Costa Rica
Ian Cleland — University of Ulster, UK

Publicity Chair

Jesús Fontecha Diezma — University of Castilla-La Mancha, Spain

Web Master

Iván González Díaz — University of Castilla-La Mancha, Spain

Steering Committee

Xavier Alaman, Spain
Jose Bravo, Spain
Jesus Favela, Mexico
Juan Manuel García Chamizo, Spain
Luis Guerrero, Costa Rica
Ramon Hervas, Spain
Rui Jose, Portugal
Diego López-De-Ipiña, Spain
Chris Nugent, UK
Sergio F. Ochoa, Chile
Gabriel Urzáiz, Mexico
Vladimir Villarreal, Panama

Organizing Committee

Nelson Baloian, Chile
Javier Bustos, Chile
Francisco Gutiérrez, Chile
Valeria Herskovic, Chile
José Pino, Chile
Gustavo Zurita, Chile
Tania Mondéjar, Spain
Iván González, Spain
Justyna Kidacka, Spain

Program Committee

Bessam Abdulrazak	University of Sherbrooke, Canada
Xavier Alamán	UAM, Spain
Mariano Alcañiz	UPV - LabHuman, Spain
Rosa Arriaga	Georgia Institute of Technology, USA
Luis Carriço	University of Lisbon, Portugal
Filippo Cavallo	The BioRobotics Institute, Italy
Wei Chen	Eindhoven University of Technology, The Netherlands
Giuseppe de Pietro	ICAR - CNR (Italian National Council of Research), Italy
Giuseppe Depietro	ICAR - CNR (Italian National Council of Research)
Rachael Dutton	Accord Group, UK
Jesus Favela	CICESE, Mexico
Antonio Fernández-Caballero	Univerity of Castilla-La Mancha, Spain
Pascual Gonzalez	University of Castilla-La Mancha, Spain
Terje Grimstad	Karde AS, Norway
Luis Guerrero	Universidad de Costa Rica, Costa Rica
Maria Haritou	National Technical University of Athens, Greece
Riitta Hellman	Universitetet i Åbo (Turku), Finland
Valeria Herskovic	Pontificia Universidad Católica de Chile, Chile
Martin Jaekel	Zurich University of Applied Sciences, Switzerland
Alan Jovic	University of Zagreb, Croatia
Martin Kampel	Vienna University of Technology, Austria
Bernhard Klein	Singapore-ETH Centre, UK
Lenka Lhotska	Czech Technical University in Prague, Department of Cybernetics, Czech Republic
Jens Lundström	Halmstad University, Sweden
Oscar Mayora	CREATE-NET, Italy
Paolo Melillo	University of Bologna, Italy
Francisco Moya	University of Castilla-La Mancha, Spain
Elena Navarro	University of Castilla-La Mancha, Spain

Panagiota Nikopoulou-Smyrni	Brunel Univesrity, UK
Chris Nugent	University of Ulster, UK
George Okeyo	University of Ulster, UK
George Papadopoulos	University of Cyprus, Cyprus
Leandro Pecchia	University of Warwick, UK
Rainer Planinc	Vienna University of Technology, Austria
Marcela Rodríguez	UABC, Mexico
Ali Salah	Bogazici University, Turkey
François Siewe	De Montfort University, France
Jonathan Synnott	University of Ulster, UK
Monica Tentori	CICESE, Mexico
Gabriel Urzáiz	Universidad Anahuac Mayab, Mexico
Vladimir Villarreal	Technological University of Panama, Panama
Andreas Voss	University of Applied Sciences Jena, Denmark

Additional Reviewers

Ian Cleland, UK
Phillip Hartin, UK
Timothy Patterson, Canada
Colin Shewell, UK
Joe Rafferty, UK

Contents

Behaviour Analysis and Activity Recognition

Sensing for Health and Wellbeing

Human Interaction and Perspectives in Ambient Assisted Living Solutions

Ambient Assisted Living for Tele-Care and Tele-Rehabilitation

An Android Telecare Prototype for a Low-SES Seniors Living Facility: A Case Study

Fáber Danilo Giraldo[(✉)], Santiago Granada Montes,
and Yonattan Pineda Olarte

System and Computer Engineering, University of Quindío, Armenia, Colombia
{fdgiraldo,sgranadam,ypinedao}@uniquindio.edu.co

Abstract. Colombia is experiencing an important demographic growing trend, where the *aging* phenomena is more evident between the current populations. Most of the elders are affected by social situations. In addition, a lack of Telecare technology to support caring processes is exposed. In order to explore the introduction of Telecare approaches for elders in Colombia, a software prototype for a real low-SES Seniors Living Facility was developed. The main contribution of this work is the application of Human-Computer Interaction (HCI) [8] principles and user-centered design (UCD) practices to formulate an Android software application for elders, taking into account all the challenges at this level of interaction, the kind of population under certain scenarios in Colombia, and also the creation of positive perceptions of the final software considering aspects of emotions, reliability of service and optimal user experience [4].

Keywords: Telecare prototype · Elders · User-centered design · HCI

1 Introduction

According to [10], 8 % of the world population is 65 years or more, and it is expected that in 20 years this percentage increases to 20 %. Many of these people are even older than 80 years.

The United Nations Population Fund (UNFPA) for Colombia describes an important demographic transition, where 60-year old people reached around 10 % of the total of population in 2012, with an evident aging of the population in some of the most important cities in Colombia [9]. The UNFPA report also exposes some of the difficulties that old people in Colombia must face, such as the low proportion of people having pensions, few job opportunities for elders, high levels of poverty, high dependency burdens (children and elders carers), negative image of the worth of elders in society, and lower educational levels in this sector of the population. The UNFPA report promotes strategies for the efficiency, effectiveness and transparency of the overall health system for elders, emphasizing care programs based on previous experiences about preparation for aging in other contexts (Europe, Far East and North America).

The progressive increase of the population in Colombia, especially the group of elders, is a challenge for the government regarding the development, quality of

© Springer International Publishing Switzerland 2015
I. Cleland et al. (Eds.): IWAAL 2015, LNCS 9455, pp. 3–8, 2015.
DOI: 10.1007/978-3-319-26410-3_1

life, and the compliance with the rights and social inclusion in the country. The main causes of the increment of aging population in Colombia are the increasing life expectancy, declining mortality, control of infectious and parasitic diseases, declining fertility rates and migration processes. Quindío is one of the regions of Colombia most affected by the phenomenon of aging population[1] [2].

2   Context of the Research

This research was performed over a specific senior living facility in the department of Quindío in Colombia. This facility serves to a very vulnerable population that consists of adults over sixty years; most lack nancial resources, some of them are abandoned by their families, and others do not have parents. Currently this low-SES seniors living facility has a total population of 40 elders between internal and external patients. External patients refer to some elders who have an identified family but prefer to be in the old peoples home, even living in this place.

In our project small Telecare prototypes based on technologies such as Android and Java applications were incrementally developed. A strategy of software development practices using the IBM Rational Unified Process (RUP) [3] and User Centered Design (UCD) [1] was employed. These practices guaranteed the development of the functionality and interaction features. Due to the particular characteristics of elders, the interaction itself became the main challenge of our research proposal.

3   Android Telecare Prototype

An Android app was implemented for the elders; the associated tasks model for this app is shown in Fig. 1 using a Concurrent-Task Tree (CTT) diagram [7]. When the TeleCare prototype starts, it exposes the login user interface (Fig. 2A), which has the photo and the name of each elders. After this, a pain user interface (Fig. 2B) is displayed. This is the main UI of the prototype; it displays four images each one corresponding to *headache*, *sore throat*, *stomach pain* and *chest pain*; each image is only a representation of an abnormal symptom. Each image has an edge of one color so that elders can differentiate images and limits.

If an elder has some of the above symptoms, he/she chooses the image to identify the abnormal situation, and the application sends the alert notifications to carers and family. We use special figures to indicate to the elders the successful delivery of the alert to carers and family. If the alert was successfully sent, the prototype displays a pop-up window with a green *OK* image to give some comfort to the elder. This is accompanied by a sound message: *"you will be taken care of very soon"*. This window is displayed for 5 s. When any abnormal situation

---

[1] In an official report of the Health Ministry of Colombia, Quindío was ranked as the third place in Colombia with the highest proportion of elders regarding the total population.

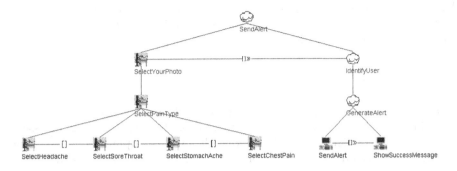

Fig. 1. CTT model for the Android Telecare prototype.

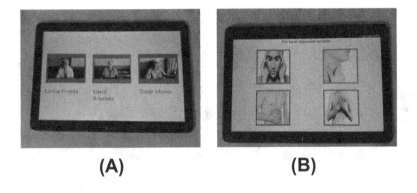

(A)   **(B)**

Fig. 2. Login and main user interface of the app (in Spanish).

Fig. 3. Notifications for successful/unsuccessful message delivery (in Spanish).

in the alert delivery is detected, a red X image appears with a sound message that indicates: *"please try again"*. It is used to indicate to the elder that he/she must re-send the alert due to any communication problem (network and/or cloud platform problems that send notifications) (Fig. 3).

4   Validation

A preliminary validation procedure was performed with real users in the senior living facility (Figs. 4 and 5[2]). The main goal of these exercise was to assess the level of interaction of the elders with the Android application, adjusting the prototype according to the problems and observations reported by elders. A formal procedure to select the elders participants was applied for the validation. We used the inclusion criterion from the JH Downton classification table [5]. This instrument is used by nurses to classify the physical condition, mental state, activity performed and mobility of patients.

Fig. 4. Interaction of elders with the Telecare prototype.

This validation was critical due to the particular features of the elder participants; they have not previously interacted with any technology (some of them only with an analogical radio). Most of the participants had high levels of illiteracy, and others had visual and mental restrictions.

At the beginning of the procedure each adult was asked about the meaning of each image. The elapsed time since the login until the generation of the alert was taken for every participant (see Table 1). This validation included questions regarding the experience of interaction with the application. Even if the interaction times reported were high for a typical Android app, these show an usage of the application without a substantial difficulty, considering that the participants interacted for the first time with a Tablet/Smartphone device.

Regarding the questions of *how was your experience and what is the importance of the application?*, some obtained answers were:

---

[2] The pictures from both figures have permissions of elders that participanted in the validation.

Fig. 5. Elder participants in the validation process.

Table 1. Interaction times reported.

Older adult	Interaction time reported for finding each pain				Average
	Headache	Stomach ache	Sore throat	Chest pain	
1	18.4 s	15.8 s	16.3 s	17.6 s	**17.0 s**
2	20.0 s	26.7 s	10.4 s	10.6 s	**16.7 s**
3	28.7 s	22.4 s	21.1 s	19.2 s	**22.8 s**
4	13.7 s	16.0 s	15.1 s	16.6 s	**15.3 s**
5	20.4 s	19.3 s	16.6 s	13.0 s	**17.3 s**
6	14.8 s	19.2 s	24.7 s	20.0 s	**19.6 s**
7	22.6 s	17.7 s	11.8 s	13.1 s	**16.3 s**
8	10.5 s	9.0 s	11.1 s	8.9 s	**9.8 s**
9	17.3 s	19.7 s	23.6 s	18.6 s	**19.8 s**
10	13.3 s	13.8 s	11.5 s	11.6 s	**12.5 s**
11	25.1 s	27.2 s	25.3 s	23.7 s	**25.3 s**
12	16.9 s	17.9 s	29.0 s	21.7 s	**21.3 s**
13	17.3 s	15.4 s	19.3 s	14.3 s	**16.5 s**

- *It is very nice, very useful because our families do not know anything about us very often.*
- *It is important because the emergency system is not working currently.*
- *I feel so protected by the application.*
- *Interesting because it helps to guide me.*

5 Conclusions

In this work, we reported the implementation and preliminary validation of a Telecare prototype application for a senior living facility in Colombia. We use principles from HCI and user-centered design to implement a software solution with a high interaction level for elders. The incorporation of devices as tablets and smartphones evidenced a high benefit and an appropriate interaction level for the elders.

As further work, we plan to implement an important component to manage mental health issues that affect elders. According to [6], more than 20 % of elders 60 years or more suffer some mental or neural disorder (excluding those manifested by headache), and the 6.6 % of the disability in this range is attributed to mental disorders in the nervous system. Dementia and depression are the most common neuropsychiatric disorders in this group, with a representative impact in the department of Quindío.

References

1. Abras, C., Maloney-Krichmar, D., Preece, J.: User-centered design. In: Bainbridge, W. (ed.) Encyclopedia of Human-Computer Interaction, 37th edn, pp. 445–456. Sage Publications, Thousand Oaks (2004)
2. Ministerio de Salud de Colombia. Envejecimiento en colombia (2012) (in Spanish)
3. Kruchten, P.: The Rational Unified Process: An Introduction, 2nd edn. Addison-Wesley Longman Publishing Co. Inc., Boston (2000)
4. Lallemand, C., Gronier, G., Koenig, V.: User experience: a concept without consensus? Exploring practitioners perspectives through an international survey. Comput. Hum. Behav. **43**, 35–48 (2015)
5. Midlov, P., Ekdahl, C., Olsson Moller, U., Kristensson, J., Jakobsson, U.: Predictive validity and cut-off scores in four diagnostic tests for falls - a study in frail older people at home. Phys. Occup. Ther. Geriatr. **30**(3), 189–201 (2012)
6. World Health Organization: Mental health and older adults, September 2013
7. Paternò, F.: ConcurTasktrees: an engineered notation for task models. In: Diaper, D., Stanton, N.A. (eds.) The Handbook of Task Analysis for Human-Computer Interaction. LEA, Mahwah (2003)
8. Rosinski, P., Squire, M.: Strange bedfellows: human-computer interaction, interface design, and composition pedagogy. Comput. Compos. **26**(3), 149–163 (2009). A Thousand Pictures: Interfaces and Composition
9. Sandino, O.: Envejecimiento en colombia: Tendencias demográficas y seguridad económica (2009) (in Spanish)
10. Valencia, M.I.B.: Envejecimiento de la población: un reto para la salud pública. Rev. Colomb. Anestesiol. **40**(3), 192–194 (2012). (in Spanish)

A Method to Develop Interactive Environments to Support Occupational Therapies

Héctor Cardona Reyes[1](✉), Jaime Muñoz Arteaga[1],
Juan Manuel González-Calleros[2], and Francisco Acosta Escalante[3]

[1] Universidad Autónoma de Aguascalientes,
Av. Universidad #940,
20131 Aguascalientes, AGS, Mexico
{k6550g,jmauaa}@gmail.com
[2] Universidad Autónoma de Puebla,
Av. San Claudio Y 14 Sur,
Puebla, PUE, Mexico
juan.gonzalez@cs.buap.mx
[3] Universidad Juárez Autónoma de Tabasco,
Av. Universidad S/N,
86040 Villa Hermosa, TAB, Mexico
francisco.acosta@ujat.mx

Abstract. Physical therapy is not limited to a simple rehabilitation procedure; this paper proposes a method for production of interactive environments in order to support the recovery process for people with temporary physical disability. The proposed method preconizes the rehabilitation as a set of ordered steps, taking into account best practices in occupational therapy coming from several actors involved in the rehabilitation process such as patients and specialists, but also those involved in the production and design of interactive environments. Then the proposed method is composed of models to design different levels of interaction that must be taken into account to produce interactive environments for users with different levels of ability/disability; these environments could represent an accessible mean with low cost and current trend of technology.

Keywords: Interactive environments · Disability · Occupational therapy · Activities of daily living · Rehabilitation and MDA approach

1 Introduction

According to the World Health Organization (WHO), more than one billion people worldwide live with some form of disability [1]. There are various techniques and methods that are part of physical therapy, one of them are the Activities of Daily Living (ADL) [2]. Reed and Sanderson [3] and Romero [4] consider the activities of daily living such as tasks that a person could be able to do to take care of themselves independently, including personal care, communication and movement. In addition, people with physical disabilities requires treatments for better develop their physical

© Springer International Publishing Switzerland 2015
I. Cleland et al. (Eds.): IWAAL 2015, LNCS 9455, pp. 9–15, 2015.
DOI: 10.1007/978-3-319-26410-3_2

therapy in a way that is useful, affordable, with low cost and available resources that may lead to restoring mobility, freedom and independence. This work proposes a method for production of interactive environments as a solution that meets the specifications of specialists in occupational therapy regulating the process of recovery of people in rehabilitation through activities of daily living and capitalizes good practices presented, and involves various actors involved in the rehabilitation process such as patients and specialists.

2   Related Work

The literature there are several works on rehabilitation, Table 1 shows some works that address the rehabilitation support through the use of technology.

Table 1. Related work that support rehabilitation through virtual environments.

Work	Domain
[6]	Design model
[5]	Interactive system
[8]	Serious games, videogames, virtual reality
[7]	Interface design

However, the related works presented do not provide information on the process of production, if they form a multidisciplinary team for its development, it is also unknown or not available the best practices that can be of support to other patients and specialists. So this work proposes a method for producing interactive environments incorporating the above aspects and could be a solution to regulate the process of recovery of people in rehabilitation.

3   Problem Outline

Define a method for designing interactive environments required deal with the following problems: It lacks of techniques to capitalize on the knowledge provided by experts and documented practices available in rehabilitation issues; It lacks of a user-centered software for solving specific user needs; It is necessary a method to capitalize some best practices and foster rehabilitation for systematic production of interactive environments according to the needs of people with disabilities; There are several multidisciplinary areas and several roles should be take into account, such as specialists, designers, analysts, programmers, and end users in the production process of interactive environments; It is important to consider the adaptability of interactive environments to different user contexts. In the next section the proposed design interactive environments, as a support method is approached rehabilitation.

4   Method to Develop Interactive Environments

This work proposes a method for the development of interactive environments based on a model approach, as shown in Fig. 1. The method starts with the definition of skills based on real situations such activities skill, sensory, problem solving through movements and activities that recreate situations of daily life or work (occupational therapy) [2, 9]. Furthermore it is based on clinical practice guidelines (CPG) [10]; which they are recommendations grounded in the best available evidence in order to contribute to the quality and effectiveness of care.

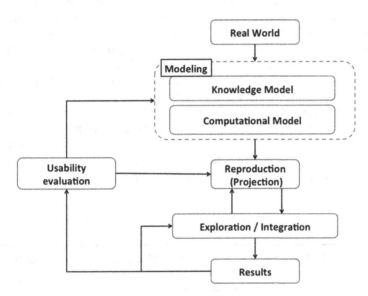

Fig. 1. Method for developing interactive environments to be used for occupational therapies, adapted from [9]

The identification of real world situations can create a representation of the activities that will be necessary to model, i.e. generate a knowledge model to know the user characteristics with disabilities, defining their skills and limitations, this can generate a computational representation of the environment in 2D or 3D considering the user functional limitations identified in the knowledge model. According to the type of occupational activity and user requires a model that captures the requirements and information to permit that can only be used by users with a certain level of functionality. Once established parameters and model entities actions are taken into account substantial information to the specialist and the patient to allow the assessment and classification for feedback will allow to obtain data on the acceptance of the design model inserted into the prototype environment caused and whether or not it is a representation of the user mental model. Next section explains in detail each stages of method throughout a case study about the motor rehabilitation of hand muscles.

5 Case Study

This section discusses the implementation of interactive environments in young adults with disabilities who receive OT for hand rehabilitation in the System for the Integral Development of the State Family Aguascalientes, Mexico (DIF) [11]. The DIF has a Physical Therapy Unit with different modules where there are different devices that facilitate the rehabilitation of patients [15]. This case study had the participation of patients and experts attending the Unit of Physical Therapy, patients here have different conditions in terms of age, disability and type of treatment to follow. On of the purpose to develop this case study was to assist the recovery of patients receiving rehabilitation of the hand through the use of interactive environments besides checking each of the stages performed in the method design for interactive environments proposed.

Real world stage: In this phase a group of five volunteers, aged: 9, 50, 58, 63, 68 years, with diagnoses including surgery sequel, hand dystrophy and primarily cerebrovascular events. Two specialists in physical rehabilitation within a 30-minute session lead treatment for these patients, which is to conduct activities through occupational therapy to regain mobility in her hands. The objective in this stage was to identify the evaluation of the patient's functionality to provide a definition of the desired patient's cognitive abilities and know the limitations of potential users.

The modeling stage: The specialist determines a set of movements founded on the documented techniques occupational therapy [12], these movements are divided into two types, movements of the fingers and thumb movements, as shown in Table 2.

Table 2. Some hand movements for occupational therapy [12]

Type of movement	Action to take	Image
Mobility of fingers	With the tip of the thumb, try to touch the yolk of each of the other fingers.	
Thumb opposition	Bring the heel to the base thumb finger, starting and ending index little finger	

This permits us to define a model user tasks and interactions to be simulated within the interactive environment as well as the variables and indicators for expert and patient feedback.

The computational model helps determine the platform, modeling languages and elements taking into account the needs of the user, with it 2D and 3D scene objects for interactive environment are determined. In this sense a diagram of tasks [13] is performed based on knowledge to assign physical hand therapy for this group of patients. As shown in Fig. 2.

Projection stage: The projection allows determining the correspondence according to the presenting problem and target users. Physical therapy specialist involved in the design process validates interactive environment that effectively produced interactive

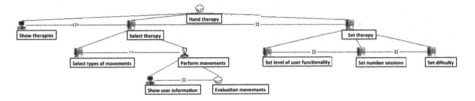

Fig. 2. Specification of therapy for hand rehabilitation in terms of user task.

environment, have the required feedback and is right under the required treatment and occupational therapy activities.

Exploration and Integration stage: During this phase basic instructions are given to patients for use of the interactive environment, the virtual scenarios and 3D objects in the scene are described, as shown in Fig. 3. A session of 20 min on average was established for each patient where performed the tasks set by the interactive environment and the information obtained in this session allow information that goes from the perception of patients to a new way of carrying their recovery through the use of technology to shape how these environments help to assist the rehabilitation process and information for feedback. Interactive environments used allow the rehabilitation specialist and the user have a guide feedback and monitoring of rehabilitation sessions [9].

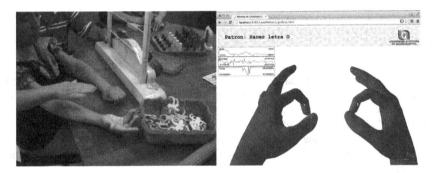

Fig. 3. Hand rehabilitation through an occupational therapy at DIF in Aguascalientes, Mexico (left), and computer assisted hand rehabilitation (right).

Results stage: The results define new variables that allow feedback model this can ensure as far as possible the appropriate model to assist the rehabilitation process of the user. Which will be of great importance to the feedback process. These results provide feedback to the expert and patient in order to know the current situation in terms of mobility of the hands. It is noteworthy that allowed interactive environments exposed the patient to know new forms of interaction for their rehabilitation session.

Evaluation stage: At the conclusion of the exploration phase, a questionnaire based usability scenarios [14] was applied, in order to measure user satisfaction in relation to the usability of interactive environments. This questionnaire was conducted through observation, it is important to mention that users with disabilities is not easy to apply a questionnaire, in many cases professional assistance is required, so it is important to define new strategies for usability evaluation for these users.

6 Conclusions

This work highlights the importance of having a model-based method, which allows through its phases, designing interactive environments that are a support for the rehabilitation of people with disabilities [15]. This method considers the established practice used by rehabilitation specialists to carry the context of an interactive environment, and provides feedback to both the patient and the professional therapy. The case study in DIF patients served as a starting point to test the proposed method and follow up on the issues raised. It allowed to obtain results for feedback from experts and patients, in addition to observing a cognitive effect of improved perception of objects in relation to the member in rehab. Finally, the proposed method allows interactive environments adapt to the needs of users and experts, giving users have a support in their rehabilitation process.

Acknowledgements. The authors appreciate the economic support given by CONACYT to current research and thank to physical therapy specialist Anita Aranda Chavarria from DIF Aguascalientes for her help to conduct the case study presented in this paper.

References

1. Organización Mundial de la Salud, Discapacidad y salud, Nota descriptiva N°352, Septiembre de 2013, (Citado el 29 de agosto 2014). http://www.who.int: http://www.who.int/mediacentre/factsheets/fs352/es/
2. Moruno, P.: Definición y clasificación de las actividades de la vida diaria. En P. Moruno y D. Romero (eds.) Actividades de la vida diaria. Masson, Barcelona (2006)
3. Reed, K.L., Sanderson, S.: Concepts of Occupational Therapy. Williams & Wilkins, Baltimore (1980)
4. Romero, D.M.: Actividades de la vida diaria. Anales de Psicología **23**, 264–271 (2007)
5. Cuppens, E., Raymaekers, C., Coninx, K.: A model-based design process for interactive virtual environments. In: Gilroy, S.W., Harrison, M.D. (eds.) DSV-IS 2005. LNCS, vol. 3941, pp. 225–236. Springer, Heidelberg (2006)
6. Zhang, S., Hu, H., Zhou, H.: An interactive internet-based system for tracking upper limb motion in home-based rehabilitation. Med. Biol. Eng. Comput. **46**, 241–249 (2008)
7. Karunanithi, M., Sarela, A.: A home-based care model of cardiac rehabilitation using digital technology. In: Yogesan, K., Bos, L., Brett, P., Gibbons, M.C. (eds.) Handbook of Digital Homecare. BIOMED, vol. 2, pp. 329–352. Springer, Heidelberg (2009)
8. Burke, J., McNeill, M., Charles, D., Morrow, P., Crosbie, J., McDonough, S.: Optimising engagement for stroke rehabilitation using serious games. Vis. Comput. **25**, 1085–1099 (2009)
9. Sanchez, J.: A model to design interactive learning environments for children with visual disabilities. Educ. Inf. Technol. **12**, 149–163 (2007)

10. Secretaria de la Salud, 2015, Catálogo Maestro de Guías de Práctica Clínica (CMGPC), (Citada: 30 de marzo 2015). http://www.cenetec.salud.gob.mx: http://www.cenetec.salud.gob.mx/contenidos/gpc/catalogoMaestroGPC.html
11. Sistema para el Desarrollo Integral de la Familia Aguascalientes, DIF, (Citada: 10 octubre 2014). http://www.aguascalientes.gob.mx/dif/
12. Traumatología Hellín, Ejercicios de mano y muñeca, (Citada el 10 de octubre 2014). http://traumatologiahellin.wordpress.com/ejercicios/ejercicios-de-mano-y-muneca/
13. Paternò, F.: ConcurTaskTrees: an engineered notation for task models. In: The Handbook of Task Analysis for Human-Computer Interaction, pp. 483–503. Lawrence Erlbaum Associates, Mahwah (2003)
14. Lewis, James R.: IBM computer usability satisfaction questionnaires: psychometric evaluation and instructions for use. Int. J. Hum. Comput. Interact. 7(1), 57–78 (1995)
15. Bravo, J.L., Tordesillas, M.J., Padrón, M.A., Jerez, N.A., González, V., Blanco, A.: Plataforma Accesible en el Marco de la Rehabilitación Físico-Cognitiva. In: Décima Conferencia Iberoamericana en Sistemas, Cibernética e Informática (CISCI 2011). 8th Simposium Iberoamericano en Educación, Cibernética e Informática. 19 de Julio al 22 de Julio de 2011. Orlando, Florida, USA

Troyoculus: An Augmented Reality System to Improve Reading Capabilities of Night-Blind People

Adrián Fernandez[1], Paul Fernandez[1], Gustavo López[2(✉)],
Marta Calderón[1], and Luis A. Guerrero[1,2]

[1] Escuela de Ciencias de la Computación e Informática,
UCR, San Pedro, Costa Rica
{fadrian59, pafb5051}@gmail.com,
marta.calderon@ucr.ac.cr,
luis.guerrero@ecci.ucr.ac.cr
[2] Centro de Investigaciones en Tecnologías de la Información y Comunicación,
UCR, San Pedro, Costa Rica
gustavo.lopez_h@ucr.ac.cr

Abstract. Our goal in this project was to develop an augmented reality system, called Troyoculus, to help night-blind people improve their reading capabilities. We developed two prototypes, one based on Oculus Rift and other based on a smartphone. We tested both prototypes using three variables: distance between the subject and the reading target, amount of light in the reading area, and font size. Two subjects participated in the testing. Results show an average improvement of at least 6 % points in reading performance and a maximum improvement of 43 % points using Oculus Rift at 12 lux. Test results of both prototypes were better than when subjects were not using any device.

Keywords: Augmented reality · Night-blind · Head-mounted displays · Vision enhancement

1 Introduction

Application of technology to help visually impaired people has been extensively studied over the years [1, 2]. However, there are several types of visual impairments without medical treatments and we think that technology could be applied to help people that suffer these impairments.

Vision impairment refers to a vision disability resulting in little or no useful vision [3]. The medical community has identified a wide variety of disease conditions and anatomical anomalies that lead to low vision and blindness. Low vision and legally blind definitions are based on measurements of a person's visual acuity and visual field [4]. One of these impairments is night-blindness. Night-blindness is a disease in which a person can see with large amounts of light but cannot see when light sources are reduced.

In this paper, we present a technological device that uses Augmented Reality (AR) to help night-blind or low vision people. We do not intent to provide a vision

© Springer International Publishing Switzerland 2015
I. Cleland et al. (Eds.): IWAAL 2015, LNCS 9455, pp. 16–28, 2015.
DOI: 10.1007/978-3-319-26410-3_3

enhancement device for all purposes. Our goal is to help people that suffer night-blindness or similar diseases.

We created a system called Troyoculus and developed two versions of our system. The first prototype used an Oculus Rift, a webcam, and an XBOX 360 controller. The second prototype used a smartphone and a case (CardBoard EasyLife) to attach it to the user's head.

We performed two evaluations with both prototypes. Each evaluation was performed with a different subject. Subject 1 (male) suffers several vision impairments including: Retinitis pigmentosa, corneal ectasia, myopia, and strabismus. Subject 2 (male) suffers: Retinitis pigmentosa, Keratoconus (right eye), and ocular albinism. Both, subject 1 and 2 are night-blind.

Each evaluation was performed by testing both prototypes at different distances and amounts of light. It consisted of a visual acuity test using Snellen based charts [5].

The structure of this paper is as follows. Section 2 shows related work, Sect. 3 describes Troyoculus. Section 4 details the tests performed with Troyoculus and Sect. 5 shows the results of such evaluation. Finally, Sect. 5 shows some conclusion of this research.

2 Related Work

Visual impairments affect the reading capabilities of people that suffer them. Several efforts have been conducted in the application of technology to help visual impaired people. The first efforts on this field were applied by increasing font size in printed documents. Moreover, researchers found that large margins, colors, characters per line, and other factors were also important [6].

Other researchers studied the application of magnification aids for people with low vision [7, 8]. In their research, Bowers, Meek, and Stewart [7] used specialized magnification glasses, instead of regular use glasses. Since glasses were for reading, they used near-viewing glasses. Authors concluded that magnification aids improve user's reading rate. This is our base to take advantage of the Troyoculus zooming feature.

Another study try also to improve the mobility of people with low vision by night vision goggles [9], which show that altering the image shows the person can get some improvement to their conditions.

Several image enhancement algorithms are available in literature [10, 11]. However, most of them were defined for general purposes without considering special characteristics of users. In this research we tried to combine image enhancement and the special requirements of our visually impaired users.

3 System Description

Our system is called Troyoculus. The name is a combination of the name of the person who inspired the system and the first prototype that was build using an Oculus Rift.

Troyoculus uses graphical displays and interfaces that capture real world images and processes them to improve night-blind people reading capabilities.

| 1) Image captured by the camera | 2-3) Duplicated image and self-illumination | 4) Bright excess filter applied |

Fig. 1. Example of an image processing using Troyoculus

Figure 1 shows an example of the process with a book page. Both prototypes use the same five steps. However, the Oculus-based prototype requires a camera and the smartphone-based uses the embedded camera. In the Oculus Rift version, zoom is available for the user to adjust the image before reading.

The self-illumination filter does not actually cast light; it provides a source of indirect light and recalculates brightness and contrast. The optimal settings for self-illuminated surfaces depend on the lighting conditions and desired effects.

Original brightness and self-illumination filter can cause bright excess. To solve this problem, a bright excess filter is applied, setting a yellow screen over the self-illuminated image. Figure 2 shows the process of our application.

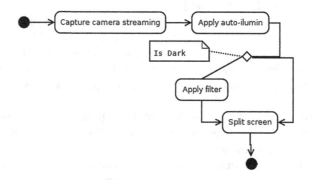

Fig. 2. Prototype sequence diagram

3.1 Oculus Rift Based Prototype

Oculus Rift [12] is a Virtual Reality (VR) headset designed for video games. It uses tracking technology to provide 360° head tracking and it allows stereoscopic 3D view by using parallel images for each eye.

Our Oculus Rift based prototype uses a webcam to take images from the user perspective, processes them, and shows them on the Oculus Rift screen. The user can zoom in the images using an XBOX 360 controller.

To perform the processing in this prototype, we used a laptop. However, a microcontroller could also have been used for this purpose. Figure 3 shows the Oculus Rift based prototype.

Fig. 3. Oculus Rift Prototype

3.2   Smartphone Based Prototype

For the second prototype, we decided to use a smartphone because it provides an embedded camera and processing capabilities. Both features give mobility to the device, and some smart phones provide a better screen resolution than the Oculus Rift.

To attach the smartphone to the user's head, we used Easy Life VR headset. Easy Life headset has 10.8 in. of length, 7 in. of width, and 1.2 in. of height. Figure 4 shows an image of our second prototype.

The smartphone used was a Samsung Galaxy S5 Active [13]. It has a Quad-core 2.5 Krait 400, 2 GB of RAM and a display of 5.1 in. with a resolution of 1080 × 1920.

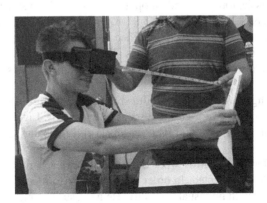

Fig. 4. Smartphone Prototype

Both prototypes were developed to improve the user's reading capabilities in different settings. The main difference between them is that the first one has more flexible configuration because the computer offer better processability and easy communication with external devices, while the second prototype improves the system usability because works without wires and the user can move around with this. Next section shows the system's evaluation.

4 Evaluation

We performed two different evaluations. The first one was a preliminary test with experts to assess possible secondary effects, and with subjects to seek for any signs of discomfort while using AR devices. The second evaluation was the prototype testing using a visual acuity test. Settings for this test are detailed in Sect. 4.2.

4.1 Preliminary Tests

The first evaluation performed with the Oculus Rift based prototype was an expert assessment of secondary effects. For this purpose, we presented the device to an optometrist and an ophthalmologist. Both tried it and agreed that the possibility of secondary effects of using Troyoculus was null.

Afterwards, we tested the Oculus Rift based prototype with the subjects. To do this, we used available applications for the Oculus Rift and they were asked to report dizziness or nauseas. Preliminary evaluations with subjects were positive as they did not experience any secondary effects.

4.2 Prototype Testing

We designed a test with three variables: distance between the subject and the reading target, font size, and amount of light in the reading area. Distance between the subject and the reading target was set at 20 cm and 40 cm. These distances were suggested by the consulted experts (optometrist and an ophthalmologist). Font size was the standard for vision acuity tests: 72, 42, 30, 26, 14, 10, 8, 6 and 5 points. Figure 5 shows both charts used during testing. Charts were modified to fit this format; original version had more space between letters and between lines. The used charts got 3–72 point letters, 4–42 point letters, and 5 letters of the rest. A random function was used to pick the letters in the charts.

The amount of light was set due to infrastructure availability. We did not want to use focal lamps. Therefore, we used fluorescent ceiling lights. Light measurement was performed using Phidgets Precision Light Sensors [14]. Lights during the tests were set at 12 and 300 lux.

In total, 36 different scenarios were defined. Before each run a chart for vision acuity test was randomly selected. In order to evaluate performance, we tested the first prototype with a male with no visual disability. He got a success rate of 100 % in all the scenarios.

Evaluation was conducted in several stages. To establish the baseline, the first test was performed at 20 cm and 40 cm. Each distance setting was tested at 12 lux and 300 lux, all without helping devices.

Next, Oculus Rift based prototype was tested. Zoom was adjusted by the subject. After the adjustment, the test was conducted at 40 cm with 300 lux, after that at 20 cm with 300 lux. Light was adjusted and 40 cm and 20 cm tests were tested again.

Finally the same process was followed with the smartphone based prototype. Results were gathered. Several days after, the test was executed again with the second subject.

Fig. 5. Charts used for the vision acuity test.

5   Results and Discussion

Two subjects participated in the Troyoculus test, in a laboratory scenario changing three variables: distance, font size and amount of light.

5.1   First Subject Results

Subject 1 (male) suffers several vision impairments including: Retinitis pigmentosa, corneal ectasia, myopia, and strabismus. Table 1 shows his baseline results.

The baseline was established performing the visual acuity test without helping devices. Our first testing subject reached a success rate of 42 % when reading from a distance of 40 cm at 300 lux. When tested at 12 lux, his success rate descended to only 8 % (i.e., he was able to read only two out of the three 72 font size letters).

Baseline results were just as expected, low light causes worst performance when reading. The closer the reading target was, the better the results were. In the closer setting, the amount of light caused a reduction of 43 %points.

When the target was at 40 cm the reduction was smaller. However it caused the user to reach only an 8 % performance. The best result was achieved at a distance of 20 cm at 300 lux with a success rate of 64 %. At 20 cm and 12 lux, he only reached a success rate of 21 %.

Table 1. Results of evaluation without any helping device (subject 1)

Distance		40 cm		20 cm	
Amount of light		300 lux	12 lux	300 lux	12 lux
Font size	72	100 %	67 %	100 %	100 %
	42	100	0	100	50
	30	80	0	100	40
	26	100	0	100	0
	14	0	0	80	0
	10	0	0	20	0
	8	0	0	80	0
	6	0	0	0	0
	5	0	0	0	0
Success rate		42 %	8 %	64 %	21 %

With the baseline established, we conducted the test of 36 scenarios with the same subject, but this time using the Oculus Rift based prototype (Table 2 shows the results). In this scenario our testing subject reached a success rate of 49 % when reading at 40 cm and 300 lux, and of 56 % at 20 cm and 300 lux.

The Oculus Rift based prototype improved our subject's reading capability at 12 lux. At 40 cm, he got a success rate of 44 % and of 64 % at 20 cm. Despite not all results obtained with the test using the Oculus Rift based prototype were better than the baseline, improvement was significant when working at low luminance (12 lux).

The last test we performed with the first testing subject was using the smartphone based prototype. We ran the same test (36 scenarios) with this aid device. Table 3 shows the results of this test.

The testing subject had exactly the same performance at 40 cm and 300 lux with the smartphone based prototype and the Oculus Rift based prototype, a success rate of 49 %. At 40 cm and 12 lux, the performance with the smartphone was a slightly better than with the Oculus Rift, raising from 44 % to 47 %.

Table 2. Results of evaluation using the Oculus Rift based prototype (subject 1)

Distance		40 cm		20 cm	
Amount of light		300 lux	12 lux	300 lux	12 lux
Font size	72	100 %	100 %	100 %	100 %
	42	100	100	100	100
	30	100	100	100	100
	26	100	100	100	100
	14	40	0	80	100
	10	0	0	20	20
	8	0	0	0	40
	6	0	0	0	20
	5	0	0	0	0
Success rate		49 %	44 %	56 %	64 %

Table 3. Results of evaluation using the smartphone based prototype (subject 1)

Distance		40 cm		20 cm	
Amount of light		300 lux	12 lux	300 lux	12 lux
Font size	72	100 %	100 %	100 %	100 %
	42	100	100	100	100
	30	100	100	100	100
	26	100	100	100	100
	14	40	20	80	100
	10	0	0	80	0
	8	0	0	80	0
	6	0	0	100	0
	5	0	0	40	0
Success rate		49 %	47 %	87 %	56 %

The main difference between the two prototypes was at 20 cm and 300 lux, as with the smartphone the testing subject was able to read at least one letter of each font size, and he reached a success rate of 87 %. At 20 cm and 12 lux the testing subject reached a success rate of 56 %, eight percentage points under the result achieved with the Oculus Rift based prototype.

Aggregate results are shown in Fig. 6. As it was expected, the success rate was higher at 300 lux than at 12 lux. However, at 12 lux a significant improvement can be seen between the baseline test results and the aided test results.

It is important to highlight that all results obtained with the test using the smartphone based prototype were better than the baseline (no aiding device). At 40 cm overall results show a better performance when using the smartphone based prototype than when using the Oculus Rift based one.

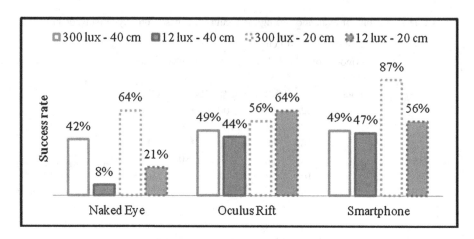

Fig. 6. Aggregate results (subject 1)

At 20 cm and 12 lux the testing subject had a better performance when using the Oculus Rift based prototype (64 %) that when using the smartphone (56 %). However, at 300 lux the Oculus Rift interfered with the testing subject reading ability as the result was lower than the one obtained in the naked eye test.

These contradictory results may be caused by two factors. The first one is the Oculus Rift bad screen resolution, which makes the subject watch little black dots on the screen. These dots could not be a problem to recognize big objects but they are when working with little objects such as letters.

The second factor is the difference between the charts used. Then, it is possible that the one used for the Oculus Rift test contained letters more difficult to differentiate.

5.2   Second Subject Results

All tests were conducted with the second subject. Subject 2 (male) suffers of: Retinitis pigmentosa, Keratoconus (right eye), and ocular albinism. This section shows his results. The baseline test showed that his vision is lower than 20/200 (i.e., he could not read any letter). For the second test, subject 2 used the Oculus Rift based prototype. Table 4 shows the results obtained.

Oculus Rift based prototype results show a significant improvement in the subject's vision capabilities because now he could read 20 % of the 30 font size letters (i.e., he could read one letter) at 12 lux and 20 % of the 26 font-size letters at 300 lux.

All subject 2 results with Oculus Rift are promising as he could see at least slightly. When compared with his baseline, all improvements are significant. Similar to subject 1, the best results with subject 2 were obtained at 20 cm and 300 lux, when he could read even a 10pt font size letter, and got a success rate of 100 % for the 26 font-size at 12 lux. Table 5 shows the results of the smartphone based prototype test.

Even though the subject could not read any letter at 40 cm and 12 lux, these results still show an improvement in the vision of the subject. In the particular case of subject 2,

Table 4. Results of evaluation using Oculus Rift based prototype (subject 2)

Distance		40 cm		20 cm	
Amount of light		300 lux	12 lux	300 lux	12 lux
Font size	72	100	100	100	100
	42	50	100	100	100
	30	100	20	100	100
	26	20	0	80	100
	14	0	0	40	0
	10	0	0	20	0
	8	0	0	0	0
	6	0	0	0	0
	5	0	0	0	0
Success rate		30 %	24 %	49 %	44 %

Table 5. Results of evaluation using smartphone based prototype (subject 2)

Distance		40 cm		20 cm	
Amount of light		300 lux	12 lux	300 lux	12 lux
Font size	72	33,33	0	100	100
	42	0	0	25	25
	30	0	0	0	0
	26	0	0	0	0
	14	0	0	0	0
	10	0	0	0	0
	8	0	0	0	0
	6	0	0	0	0
	5	0	0	0	0
Success rate		4 %	0 %	14 %	14 %

results using the smartphone prototype were worse than using the Oculus Rift based prototype.

This may be because the zooming feature of the Oculus Rift based prototype allows the subject to adjust the image when needed. This makes clear that is necessary to include a zooming feature in the smartphone prototype, which is an interesting result. However, out of the scope of the test was that subject 2 tested the smartphone based prototype while walking and showed improvement in sight. This leads us to think that Troyoculus could be applied for more than just reading.

Figure 7 shows the aggregate results obtained for the subject 2. Subject 2 could not read anything without helping device. However, when using the Oculus Rift based prototype he could read almost 40 % of the chart. When using the smartphone based prototype, he could read 8 % of the chart.

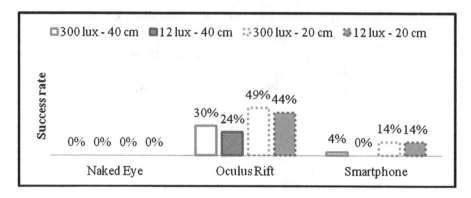

Fig. 7. Results subject 2

The difference between 300 lux and 12 lux with the Oculus Rift based prototype is not significant, just six percentage points. The smartphone showed a really poor performance at 40 cm, since subject 2 only reached a success rate of 4 % at 300 lux and no improvement over the naked eye test at 12 lux.

The Oculus Rift based prototype still has a better performance than the smartphone. However, both devices improve the subject's vision.

5.3   General Results

General results showed that, in all scenarios, our system helped night-blind subjects to read. Figure 8 shows average results of the two subjects. It is clear that the lower the light, the more our system helps users.

Amount of Light. At 12 lux average results show an improvement over the baseline of 40 % points for the Oculus Rift based prototype, and 22 % point for the smartphone based prototype. When using stronger sources of light results showed an improvement of 20 % points for the Oculus Rift based prototype, and 12 % points for the smartphone based prototype.

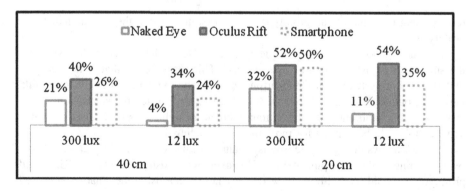

Fig. 8. General results

Distance. Average results show significant improvement at 20 cm and 40 cm. As it was expected, better results were achieved at 20 cm than at 40 cm. Average results showed an improvement of 23 % points at 40 cm when using the Oculus Rift based prototype, and 13 % points with the smartphone based prototype. At 20 cm average results showed an improvement of 32 % points with Oculus Rift and 21 % points when using the Smartphone respectively.

6 Conclusion and Future Work

An augmented reality system to improve reading capabilities of Night-Blind people was proposed and tested with visually impaired users. Results were promising as the testing subjects reading abilities improved when using Troyoculus, without suffering any secondary effects.

Results show that performance achieved depends on both the degree of visual impairment of the person using the Troyoculus and the quality of images generated. Since our target population suffers a visual disease which cannot be corrected nor cured, any improvement in their reading performance may be valuable for them.

The zooming feature available only in the Oculus Rift based prototype made a significant difference in the performance achieved by subjects during tests. Future work to include this feature in the smartphone based prototype is also necessary.

To improve the obtained results, it is necessary to go through various aspects. The first one is to find a way to generate sharper images. The next one is to include a second camera for generating a real stereoscopic vision and improving the visual field of the user.

Testing the new features they will be held in a larger population to have better results validated.

References

1. Fuglerud, K.S.: The barriers to and benefits of use of ICT for people with visual impairment. In: Stephanidis, C. (ed.) Universal Access in HCI, Part I, HCII 2011. LNCS, vol. 6765, pp. 452–462. Springer, Heidelberg (2011)
2. Ghali, N.I., Soluiman, O., El-Bendary, N., Nassef, T.M., Ahmed, S.A., Elbarawy, Y.M., Hassanien, A.E.: Virtual reality technology for blind and visual impaired people: reviews and recent advances. In: G, T., Hassanien, A.E. (eds.) Advances in Robotics and Virtual Reality. ISRL, vol. 26, pp. 363–385. Springer, Heidelberg (2012)
3. Armstrong, H.: Advanced IT education for the vision impaired via e-learning. J. Inf. Technol. Educ. **8**, 243–256 (2009)
4. Lancioni, G., Singh, N.: Assistive Technologies for People with Diverse Abilities. Springer, New York (2014)
5. Snellen, H.: Probebuchstaben zur Bestimmung der Sehscharfe. Van de Weijer, Utrecht (1862)
6. American Foundation for the Blind.: Tips for making print more readable http://www.afb.org/info/living-with-vision-loss/reading-and-writing/making-print-more-readable/235

7. Bowers, A., Meek, C., Stewart, N.: Illumination and reading performance in age-related macular degeneration. Clin. Exp. Optom. **84**(3), 139–147 (2001)

8. Lusk, K.: The effects of various mounting systems of near magnification on reading performance and preference in school-age students with low vision. Br. J. Vis. Impairment **30**(3), 168–181 (2012)

9. Hartong, D.T., Jorritsma, F.F., Neve, J.J., Melis-Dankers, B.J.M., Kooijman, A.C.: Improved mobility and independence of night-blind people using night-vision goggles. Invest. Ophthalmol. Vis. Sci. **45**(6), 1725–1731 (2004)

10. Yang, S., Cui, W., Zhang, D.: Night vision image enhancement based on double-plateaus histogram. In: Shen, G., Huang, X. (eds.) ECWAC 2011, Part I. CCIS, vol. 143, pp. 74–79. Springer, Heidelberg (2011)

11. Lee, J.-W., Lee, B.-H., Won, Y., Kim, C.-H., Hong, S.-H.: Real-time night visibility enhancement algorithm using the similarity of inverted night image and fog image. In: Kim, K.J. (ed.) Information Science and Applications. LNEE, vol. 339, pp. 1045–1052. Springer, Heidelberg (2015)

12. Oculus VR. https://www.oculus.com/

13. Samsung Galaxy S5. http://www.samsung.com/latin/consumer/mobile-devices/smartphones/galaxy-s/

14. Phidgets, Inc 1127_0 - Precision Light Sensor. http://www.phidgets.com/

Contextualizing Tasks in Tele-Rehabilitation Systems for Older People

Arturo C. Rodriguez[1], Cristina Roda[1], Pascual González[2],
and Elena Navarro[2(✉)]

[1] Computer Science Research Institute (I3A), Albacete, Spain
{Arturo.Rodriguez,Cristina.Roda}@uclm.es
[2] Computing Systems Department,
University of Castilla-La Mancha, Albacete, Spain
pgonzalez@dsi.uclm.es, elena.navarro@uclm.es

Abstract. Nowadays, one of the most important issues in developed countries is the progressive aging of the population. Thus, governments are irrevocably forced to invest more and more money to take care of their citizens. Regarding healthcare, the attention is focused on those aspects derived from the physical and cognitive problems associated to older adults. Fortunately, fields of research, such as *Gerontechnology*, are showing promising results for improving quality of life of older people. These works have given rise to remarkable advances in tele-rehabilitation due to the appearance of new technologies and a better understanding of users and their diseases. However, to optimize the development process of these new systems and to take into account user's features and the surrounding environment, existing modeling languages must evolve. Tele-rehabilitation systems cannot behave in the same way with every user and under every condition, rather they must be able to adapt themselves to the user needs, according to the condition of the environment. In this work, a context meta-model is presented which allows analysts to specify users' features, devices and the environment, as well as relevant states for the system. Moreover, the relationship between context and task model is also addressed by a CSRML-based task meta-model.

Keywords: Gerontechnology · Tele-rehabilitation · Task model · Context model · CSRML · MDA · Context data state · Task contextualization

1 Introduction

The increase in average life expectancy and the low birth rate in developed countries are causing a progressive aging of population. For instance, a study [1] of the National Institute of Demographic Studies of France shows how the pyramid of population have evolved towards a more uniform distribution in the last 100 years, which implies an older population growth. The European Commission Information Society and Media [2] has also highlighted this problem and warns that the situation is becoming unsustainable. The demographic changes and the increase of chronic diseases force healthcare systems around Europe to make a higher investment.

© Springer International Publishing Switzerland 2015
I. Cleland et al. (Eds.): IWAAL 2015, LNCS 9455, pp. 29–41, 2015.
DOI: 10.1007/978-3-319-26410-3_4

New fields of research, such as *Gerontechnology* [3], can be a part of the solution to this problem. Gerontechnology aims to develop products, environments and services for improving quality of life of older people in terms of physical and cognitive problems and providing them with new opportunities in their personal life.

A direct consequence of this field is the advance in tele-rehabilitation systems. *Tele-rehabilitation* can be defined as [4] "the application of telecommunication, remote sensing and operation technologies, and computing technologies to assist with the provision of medical rehabilitation services at a distance". However, these advances must be accompanied of improvements in the development process. The definition of new languages or the modification of existing ones are becoming a real need when talking about modeling such systems and taking these models as part of the development process.

It is of vital importance to take into consideration *context information* while modelling a tele-rehabilitation system for older people at design-time. Monitoring context information allows a system to be aware of changes in (i) the *environment* that surrounds it (e.g. changes regarding illuminance or noise levels); (ii) the *devices* that are integrated into it (e.g. the temperature of a device); and (iii) the *users* (e.g. their heart rate, EEG or corporal temperature) that interact with it.

Interaction between older people and computers is sensible to all these changes, thus a tele-rehabilitation system should be able to self-adapt, taking into account these changes, in order to facilitate a friendly interaction. Furthermore, systems that involve *physical rehabilitation* for older people should guarantee an adequate healthcare service. In this sense, it would be highly recommended to provide these systems with mechanisms for adapting their behavior according to, for instance, the heart rate of the patient. This is one of the most critical parameters regarding older adults because, as Palatini et al. state [5], *an elevated heart rate is a risk factor for cardiovascular death in older men*. This work focuses in context modeling and how the context affects to the tasks performance. As a result, a context meta-model and an extension of a Task meta-model, based on CSRML (Collaborative Systems Requirements Modelling Language), are proposed. After this introduction, Sect. 2 presents a review of previous work in context modeling, its relation with task modeling and a new proposal of context meta-model. Then, in Sect. 3, a Case Study is presented to support our proposal. Finally, conclusions and future work are described in Sect. 4.

2 Towards a New Context Meta-Model for Contextualizing Tasks

Tele-rehabilitation services are considered a good example of the new-look systems that make use of emerging technologies, such as gesture or voice recognition. This kind of systems requires many context information. Therefore, suitable languages that allow analysts and designers to define and model this information are becoming critical. Dey [6] defines context as "any information that can be used to characterize the situation of an entity. An entity is a person, place, or object that is considered relevant to the interaction between a user and an application, including the user and applications themselves". Dey's definition is widely accepted, although Soylu et al. [7] find it too generic. Taking into account Dey's definition of context, it can be stated that a *context model* represents the information of the context that surrounds the system as well as of the system itself.

Over the last few years, numerous studies about context modeling have been proposed and, in spite of the variety of context interpretations and how they are modeled, some common aspects arose from them, namely *environment, devices* and *user*. For example, an initial proposal [8] focused on concerns, like Location and the ability to detect nearby devices. On the other hand, Rodden et al. [9] included new concepts to context modeling, identifying five dimensions of context: Infrastructure context, Application context, System context, Location context and Physical context. However, all these proposals do not offer a language to model the context. UsiXML [10] tackles the context modeling as part of a model-driven user interface development process. It proposes a meta-model that is instantiated for specifying the entities that are relevant for the system at hand, as well as their capabilities and their interaction zones. However, UsiXML does not provide support for modeling dynamic context information (i.e. information that changes at runtime). On the contrary, the aim of this context meta-model is to describe the structural context information of the system. Another context meta-model was proposed by Vale and Hammoudi [11] that was applied to context-aware development within a model-driven development process. This meta-model is based on ontological concepts and describes the context at two abstraction levels that correspond to M2 and M1 layers within Model-Driven Architecture (MDA). Despite these two levels of abstraction, context information in M1 is restricted to four concepts: Time, Location, Device and Profile. The use of just four concepts makes the description of context too specific, hampering a more detailed specification of other dimensions related to the user or the environment. Moreover, it also ignores the actual relationship between dynamic pieces of information and devices needed to measure them. This is an important issue that Schmidt had already stated in [12]. Hence, most of the existing proposals for modeling context are influenced by the type of application for which they have been defined because of the difficulties encountered while attempting to standardize a meta-model that should cover all possible dimensions of context.

As mentioned above, some concepts as *environment, user* and *device* are recurrent in the literature. They can be considered as *context elements* in a context model. Moreover, in many cases, these elements are modeled by describing their *capabilities* or set of features. However, Tele-rehabilitation systems must be aware of context information that changes at runtime. This makes necessary to include the following concepts: (i) *context data*, that represent features of a *context element* that changes dynamically and (ii) *state* of a context data, that represent current value, condition or range of values within which the context data is. In order to address this problem, in this work a context meta-model is proposed, shown in Fig. 1, whose main elements are the following:

- *ContextModel.* Represents an instance of the context model.
- *ContextElement.* It is used to specify an element whose description is relevant for the system. It can be a *User*, a *Device* or the *Environment*.

- *Capability.* It is used to specify a set of features related to a context element. For instance, GPS capability of a mobile Device, vital signs of a User, or ambient conditions. The features that define a Capability are called *ContextData*.
- *ContextData.* It represents features of the context that change at runtime, and this change directly affects the system itself. For instance, the value associated to the feature Heart Rate, regarding the Capability Vital Signs for a concrete User, should change over time as the heartbeat of the user is constantly changing. This dynamic information is not directly related to Literals, but to States.
- *State.* It is employed to establish a value, range of values or condition of dynamic data. When the current value (measured at runtime) of the dynamic data matches that State (i.e. it matches a concrete value or condition) or it falls within a range of values, the system behavior will be affected at runtime. This concept is similar to the *Input Range* defined by Schmidt [12].
- *AtomicState.* It is used to denote a condition that cannot be decomposed. An atomic condition is always related to a concrete ContextData. For instance, the ContextData "Heart Rate" may be related to a range or condition relevant to the system, such as GREATER_THAN 180 bpm.
- *CompositeState.* It is used to specify complex conditions that are composed of two or more Conditions related by means of logical operators. For instance, LOWER_THAN 180 bpm AND GREATER_THAN 120 bpm.

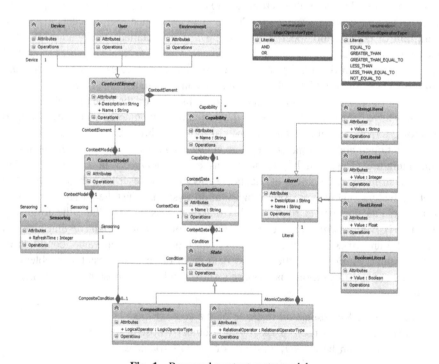

Fig. 1. Proposed context meta-model

- *Sensoring.* It is to specify relationships between context information and the device that measures it. By means of the *RefreshTime* attribute, it can be also specified the frequency of measurement.
- *Literal.* It is used to specify types, values and measurements for specific context data (e.g. IntLiteral: 180 bpm).

2.1 Contextualizing Task Models

As aforesaid, the context meta-model shown in Fig. 1 enables analysts to specify the agents that are a part of the system and interact with it, their attributes, and the conditions of those attributes that will affect the system behavior. Once these conditions have been specified, a relationship between tasks and context conditions may be established in order to identify what context conditions may affect the triggering of a concrete task.

As aforementioned, in the older people tele-rehabilitation field, a detailed description of *user* is crucial, as well as the specification of the *environment* conditions that affect the interaction tasks. Moreover, the context also directly influences on *how* tasks are carried out. While reviewing literature, we may find out classical *task meta-models*, as for instance *ConcurTaskTrees* (CTT) [13]. It is used to specify the tasks of a system independently of both the platform and the interaction modality. CTT allows analysts to hierarchically specify the system tasks and the temporal relationships among them. However, in later steps of the development lifecycle, it may be desirable to *contextualize the task model* (i.e. to add context information to the task model, such as the context situations that may trigger a concrete task or the agents that perform it) in order to determine how these tasks have to be carried out and how the system should react under specific context conditions from the interaction point of view. For example, a tele-rehabilitation system may decide to initiate a system task (e.g. Reduce Exercise Intensity) according to a high heart rate of the user, or change how it provides the user with feedback (e.g. change from acoustic to haptic interaction modality in a noisy environment). Therefore, a contextualized task model may give rise to more precise interaction models within a model-driven development process.

Context information must be measured by *sensors* or devices that make up the system but, at the same time, become *actors* with a concrete *role* that may need to communicate, collaborate or coordinate between them and the system in order to carry out some interaction tasks. In a context-aware system, sensors can be seen as agents that interact with the system and other agents to perform concrete tasks. Hence, two main conclusions can be drawn:

1. It is necessary to model these interaction tasks taking into account the agents involved.
2. It is necessary to differentiate individual tasks (i.e. those tasks that are carried out by a single agent, human or not, that interacts with the system) from collaborative/coordination/communication tasks (i.e. those tasks that need more than one agent to be carried out while interacting with the system).

This leads us to conclude that the task taxonomy used in the classic task meta-models is not expressive enough, and thus new categories are needed in order to address these two conclusions. A more recent proposal, namely CSRML [14], incorporates new concepts to specify, within its *Task Refinement Diagrams*, collaboration, coordination and communication tasks of agents and system. CSRML is an extension of the $i*$ framework [15] for the specification of collaborative systems, extending the meaning of some of its elements. For instance, in CSRML, an Actor playing a Role can participate in individual or collaborative tasks and can be responsible for the accomplishment of a particular goal. Therefore, CSRML provides support to the special requirements of CSCW (Computer Supported Cooperative Work) systems. For this reason, this work presents an extension of the CSRML facilities for task modelling. As can be observed in Fig. 2, a new meta-class called *ContextDataState* has been included. This meta-class enables analysts to establish a relationship with a condition of the context model. Note that Fig. 2 shows a partial view of the extension of the CSRML task meta-model. Some concepts that are not related to the aim of this paper have been omitted for better understanding. A task can be related to several context conditions which means that the task will start if the context matches with the definition of any of the context conditions. In the following section, a case study is presented in order to show how a tele-rehabilitation system can be modeled using the meta-models proposed in this section.

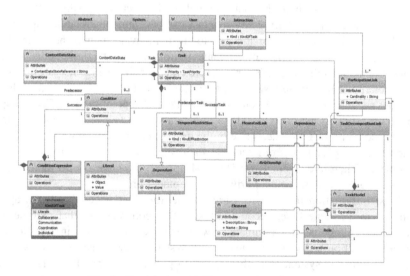

Fig. 2. Partial view of CSRML task meta-model

3 Case Study: Contextualized Tasks in Tele-Rehabilitation Systems for Older People

In this section, we present a case study of a Tele-rehabilitation system for older people in order to show how tasks can be contextualized. The tele-rehabilitation system to be modeled is currently under development by the LoUISE research group [16]. This system allows therapists to create customized rehabilitation exercises for each specific older adult in order to provide him/her a *bespoke therapy*. At the same time, the system can be aware of context and adapt itself to user needs at runtime. In this case study, we are going to model the *Upper Limb Rehabilitation* (ULR) task, which refers to rehabilitation exercises that involve the upper extremities of older people's body. Notice that this task is modeled using the basic elements offered by CSRML, as well as the additional ones for contextualizing tasks.

Figure 3 shows the CSRML *Responsibility Diagram* (RD) of our case study. This diagram is used to specify the *actors* that are going to be involved in the system; the *roles* each actor may assume; and finally, the role responsible for the accomplishment of each task. Figure 3 illustrates that the ULR task is specified as an *abstract* task (i.e. a task that can be decomposed into more concrete tasks). The RD also depicts that are six actors involved: *User, Computer, Noise sensor, Illuminance sensor, Heart Rate sensor,* and *Skin Conductance sensor*. The User actor plays the *Patient* role in the Tele-rehabilitation system; the Computer actor plays the *UI Adaptor* and *Virtual Therapist* roles, depending on the task it is performing; the Noise sensor actor acts as the *Environment Noise sensor* role; the Illuminance sensor actor has the *Environment Illuminance sensor* role; the Heart Rate sensor actor plays the *Heart Rate stress sensor* role; and finally, the Skin Conductance sensor actor plays the *Skin Conductance stress sensor* role. Furthermore, this figure also displays that the Virtual Therapist role is the head of the ULR task, so it is in charge of assuring an adequate realization of the ULR task.

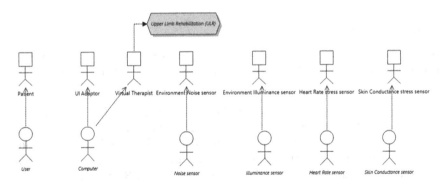

Fig. 3. Responsibility diagram of the *Upper Limb Rehabilitation* task, using CSRML

Once the roles related to each system actor have been defined, the abstract ULR task can be described in more detail, showing all the tasks that make it up. In CSRML, this is done by means of the *Task Refinement Diagram* (TRD) which is used to specify tasks, and the roles responsible for performing each task. In addition to abstract tasks, CSRML also distinguishes between *non-interaction* and *interaction tasks*. The former are tasks carried out by an agent (human or not) or by the system, without any interaction with other agents or the system. The latter are tasks carried out by agents and the system, involving interaction between them to perform the task. Moreover, non-interaction tasks can be decomposed into two different types of tasks: *user* and *system tasks*, depending on who is involved in them. Thus, if they are performed by a human agent, they are called *user tasks* (i.e. cognitive tasks, decision processes), otherwise, they are called *system tasks* (i.e. performed by a non-human agent or by the system itself). Regarding interaction tasks, CSRML defines four types of tasks:

- *Individual task.* It is a task performed by a single actor (not the system).
- *Collaboration task.* It is a task carried out by two or more actors, with different or the same roles, in a collaborative way (i.e. the task could not be done without the explicit participation of each actor). Among these actors, we may find the system and/or agents, both humans and non-humans.
- *Communication task.* It is a task performed by two or more actors, with different or the same roles, to exchange some information. As in the previous case, among these actors, we may find the system and/or agents, both humans and non-humans.
- *Coordination task.* It is a task performed by two or more actors, with different or the same roles, that proceed in a coordinated way. As previously, among these actors, we may find the system and/or agents, both humans and non-humans.

Figure 4 depicts the contextualized TRD regarding the ULR task. This ULR task is decomposed into several subtasks: *Start ULR*, *Execute ULR*, *Adapt interface* and *Stop ULR*. Except the first one, Start ULR, which is an individual task that involves the patient interacting with the system to indicate his intention of initiating the Upper Limb rehabilitation, the remaining subtasks are also abstract so that they will be explained next, describing how some of them can be contextualized.

3.1   Execute ULR

This task is related to the execution of all the exercises including in the Upper Limb rehabilitation and it is also decomposed into three different subtasks, executed in a concurrent way:

1. *Move UL* is an individual task performed by the Patient. It involves he has to move his Upper Limbs while the system is recording his movements;
2. *Monitor stress* is an abstract task that describes the monitoring of the patient's stress while he is doing rehabilitation movements. For this aim, first, it must be gathered the stress information from Skin Conductance and Heart Rate stress sensors, in a coordinated way; and second, it must be detected the stress level thanks to the collaboration between these type of sensors (they provide the stress information) and the Virtual Therapist which is in charge of interpreting this information from the sensors and determining the corresponding stress level for the patient;
3. *Adapt ULR* is an abstract task performed by the Virtual Therapist. It specifies the adaptation of the ULR exercises to provide a bespoke therapy to the patient by changing the number of repetitions and/or the target area limit. The target area is represented as a rectangle that the Patient's limbs under rehabilitation should reach while doing a particular rehabilitation exercise.

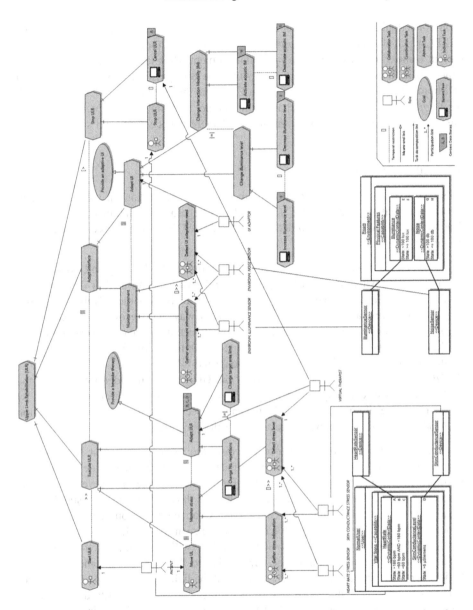

Fig. 4. Contextualized Task Refinement Diagram of the *Upper Limb Rehabilitation* task, using CSRML

Regarding the contextualization of this task, the Patient role is associated with the User using the system in order to be aware of his vital signs. This information is relevant to adapt the ULR exercises. Moreover, the roles Skin Conductance stress sensor and Heart Rate stress sensor are related to the Skin Conductance sensor device and the Heart Rate sensor device, respectively. In this sense, the task *Adapt ULR* has been contextualized with three particular context conditions, as seen in Fig. 4: B, C, and D, which will affect the triggering of such task when they become true within the current context. For instance, in a particular moment while the Patient is performing a concrete ULR exercise, his Heart Rate would be 80 bpm (i.e. it is between 60 and 180 bpm) so it satisfies context condition B. Hence the system could decide to launch the *Adapt ULR* task in order to change the number of repetitions of such exercise, in this case it would be reduced, given that the Patient is becoming a bit stressed.

3.2   Adapt Interface

This task is related to the adaptation of the interface depending on the environment information, namely the interface is adapted with regard to the lighting and the noise. The Adapt interface task is also decomposed into two different subtasks, concurrently executed:

1. *Monitor environment* is an abstract task to monitor the lighting and noise of the environment where the Patient is performing the ULR exercises. For this aim, first, the system *Gathers environment information* from Environment Noise and Environment Illuminance sensors, in a coordinated way, and second, it *Detects a UI adaptation need* thanks to the collaboration between this type of sensors and the UI Adaptor. This is in charge of interpreting this information from the sensors and determining whether it is necessary to adapt the UI.
2. *Adapt UI*, an abstract task performed by the UI Adaptor. It is defined to adapt the User Interface regarding the lighting and noise levels to provide an adaptive UI by changing the illuminance level (Increasing or Decreasing it) and/or the Interaction Modality (IM) (Activating or Deactivating the acoustic IM).

Regarding the contextualization of this task, the roles Environment Noise sensor and Environment Illuminance sensor are related to the Noise sensor device and the Illuminance sensor device, respectively. Furthermore, there are several subtasks (Increase illuminance level, Decrease illuminance level, Activate acoustic IM and Deactivate acoustic IM) that have been contextualized with four concrete context conditions: F, E, H and G, respectively, as can be seen in Fig. 4.

As in the previous task, these context conditions will determine whether these four tasks, regarding the adaptation of the UI, will be finally done. For instance, while the Patient is performing a concrete ULR exercise, if the lighting level is 60 lux (it satisfies context condition E: Illuminance < 100 lux) and the noise level is 120 db (it satisfies context condition G: Noise > 100 db), then the system could decide to *Decrease illuminance level* and *Deactivate acoustic IM*. These tasks are related to context conditions E and G, respectively, to adapt the UI to the current environmental conditions.

3.3   Stop ULR

This can be done by the Patient him/herself (*Stop ULR* individual task) or by the Virtual Therapist (*Cancel ULR* system task). With respect to the contextualization of this task, only one of its subtasks has been contextualized with the context condition A (HeartRate > 180 bpm): *Cancel ULR*. In this sense, this context condition trigger such task when it is satisfied. For example, while a Patient is performing a concrete ULR exercise, if his Heart Rate becomes 190 bpm, then the context condition A would be satisfied as the value for the Heart Rate is greater than 180. Hence, the system could decide to do the *Cancel ULR* task in order to stop the exercise since the current condition is becoming too stressful for the Patient.

4 Conclusions and Future Work

In the last few years, new technologies have opened new doors to improve our quality of life. These technologies are especially useful in fields such as Gerontechnology. However, these advances must include new languages that allow us to optimize the development process of Tele-rehabilitation systems. This kind of systems highly rely on the context because they need of the user information, environment conditions and the different agents that participate in doing the tasks. Classic task meta-models lack of a detailed description of concepts, such us collaboration, coordination or communication that are critical in Tele-rehabilitation systems. In order to tackle these issues, a meta-model for specifying dynamic context information has been defined as an extension of the task modeling facilities of CSRML. This extension includes expressive power to specify include relationships with the Context Model so that analysts can contextualize the task models. These relationships enable to define and execute transformations, in a model-driven development process, that can use context information to obtain more accurate interaction models.

A case study has been also presented in this paper to show how our proposal can be used to model context information and how a task model, based on CSRML, can be contextualized. A tele-rehabilitation system has been presented that allows therapists to create rehabilitation exercises to be performed by older people. Concretely, it has been shown how a kind of exercises, ULR ones, can be modeled as a CSRML task. As shown, CSRML provides support for several types of tasks, including those related to the specification of collaborative systems. Furthermore, it has been also seen the contextualization of some tasks with regard to the monitoring of some vital signs of the patient, such as Heart Rate and Skin Conductance, and of some environmental aspects, such as Lighting and Noise. This contextualization of tasks facilitates the achievement of several goals of our system (e.g. provide a bespoke therapy and an adaptive UI). They are needed as the system is designed to be aware of some context conditions that could trigger some tasks at runtime, namely those tasks related to the adaptation of the ULR task to each specific patient and to the adaptation of the UI itself. Moreover, any type of device within our tele-rehabilitation system, such as the Heart Rate sensor, the Skin Conductance sensor, the Illuminance sensor and the Noise sensor can be easily modeled with CSRML by means of actors with a specific role. In this way, the ULR task can be also contextualized in terms of which tasks are performed by which devices. This can be done thanks to the specification of relationships between devices and their corresponding roles. These are in turn related to some particular tasks since the TRD in CSRML provides support for specifying what roles will carry out what tasks.

Therefore, our proposed context meta-model provides useful mechanisms to easily specify context data regarding the *user*, the *environment* and the *devices* (also including those that act as *sensors*), as well as significant *states* associated to these context elements that will provoke some changes in the system behavior at runtime. In Tele-rehabilitation, the specification of such states related to, e.g. the patient's vital signs, is considered a must to provide him/her with a secure therapy, especially for older people.

As future work, one of the next necessary steps is the evaluation of this proposal by analysts and designers within a model-driven development process. This evaluation is currently being designed. On the other hand, there are other context dimensions that may be interesting to include in the context modeling. For instance, the static features regarding different devices, environment and users may be useful for documenting and analyzing the system context of use. Furthermore, the available interaction modalities can be seen as part of the context too. Finally, a tool based on Microsoft DSL-Tools technology is currently under development in order to support these languages.

Acknowledgements. This work was partially supported by the Spanish Ministry of Economy and Competitiveness/FEDER under TIN2012-34003 grant, and through the FPU scholarship (FPU12/04962) also from the Spanish Government.

References

1. Pison, G.: 1914–2014: A century of change in the French population pyramid. Inst. Natl. d'Études Démographiques. 509, (2014)
2. European Commission Information Society and Media: ICT for Health and i2010: Transforming the European healthcare landscape towards a strategy for ICT for Health., Luxembourg (2006)
3. Fozard, J.L., Rietsema, J., Bouma, H., Graafmans, J.A.M.: Gerontechnology: creating enabling environments for the challenges and opportunities of aging. Educ. Gerontol. **26**, 331–344 (2000)
4. Boucenna, S., Narzisi, A., Tilmont, E., Muratori, F., Pioggia, G., Cohen, D., Chetouani, M.: Interactive technologies for autistic children: a review. Cognit. Comput. **6**, 722–740 (2014)
5. Palatini, P., Casiglia, E., Julius, S., Pessina, A.C.: High heart rate: a risk factor for cardiovascular death in elderly men. Arch. Intern. Med. **159**, 585–592 (1999)
6. Dey, A.K.: Understanding and Using Context. Pers. Ubiquitous Comput. **5**, 4–7 (2001)
7. Soylu, A., de Causmaecker, P., Desmet, P.: Context and adaptivity in pervasive computing environments: links with software engineering and ontological engineering. J. Softw. **4**, 992–1013 (2009)
8. Schilit, B.N., Theimer, M.M.: Disseminating active map information to mobile hosts. IEEE Netw. **8**, 22–32 (1994)
9. Rodden, T., Cheverst, K., Davies, N.: Exploiting contet in HCI design for mobile systems. In: MobileHCI (1998)
10. UsiXML Consortium: UsiXML, USer Interface eXtensible Markup Language (2007)
11. Vale, S., Hammoudi, S.: Context-aware model driven development by parameterized transformation. In: CEUR Workshop Proceedings, pp. 121–133 (2008)

12. Schmidt, A.: Implicit human computer interaction through context. Pers. Technol. **4**, 191–199 (2000)
13. Paternò, F., Paternò, F., Mancini, C., Mancini, C., Meniconi, S., Meniconi, S.: ConcurTaskTrees: a diagrammatic notation for specifying task models. In: Proceedings of the IFIP TC13 International Conference on Human-Computer Interaction, pp. 362–369 (1997)
14. Teruel, M.A., Navarro, E., López-Jaquero, V., Montero, F., González, P.: A CSCW requirements engineering CASE tool: development and usability evaluation. Inf. Softw. Technol. **56**, 922–949 (2014)
15. Castro, J., Kolp, M., Mylopoulos, J.: A requirements-driven development methodology. In: Dittrich, K.R., Geppert, A., Norrie, M. (eds.) CAiSE 2001. LNCS, vol. 2068, pp. 108–123. Springer, Heidelberg (2001)
16. Roda, C., Rodríguez, A., López-jaquero, V., González, P., Navarro, E.: A multi-agent system in ambient intelligence for the physical rehabilitation of older people. In: 13th Conference on Practical Applications of Agents and Multi-Agent Systems (PAAMS 2015), Salamanca, Spain, pp. 113–123 (2015)

Pilot Evaluation of a Collaborative Game for Motor Tele-Rehabilitation and Cognitive Stimulation of the Elderly

Gilberto Borrego[1(✉)], Alberto L. Morán[1], Arturo LaFlor[1],
Victoria Meza[1], Eloísa García-Canseco[1], Felipe Orihuela-Espina[2],
and Luis Enrique Sucar[2]

[1] Facultad de Ciencias, Universidad Autónoma de Baja California,
UABC, Ensenada, Mexico
{gilberto.borrego,alberto.moran,arturo.laflor,mmeza,
eloisa.garcia}@uabc.edu.mx
[2] Instituto Nacional de Astrofísica, Óptica y Electrónica,
Tonanzintla, Puebla, Mexico
{f.orihuela-espina,esucar}@inaoe.mx

Abstract. In this paper the design, development and preliminary evaluation of a serious videogame for the motor rehabilitation of upper limb and cognitive stimulation of the elderly are presented. The game includes features that allow (i) performing collaborative therapy exercises between two patients, (ii) remote configuration of the session therapy, and (iii) monitoring/analyzing of the session results by the therapist. A pilot evaluation with 7 older adults and an expert therapist, suggest that the game is perceived as stimulating, useful, usable and even funny, while providing an effective way to support/monitor the patient, and to adjust the therapy programs.

Keywords: Serious game · Tele-rehabilitation · Collaborative software

1 Introduction

Older adults are a sector of the population that takes increasing importance due to its growth projections for the coming years. This highlights the increased incidence of diseases related to cognitive impairment and cerebral-vascular accidents in this population. Serious games are a promising approach to provide non-pharmacological treatments, in the aim to meet and maintain the cognitive state and physical fitness of the elderly through activities for cognitive stimulation, and physical activation an rehabilitation [1–3]. In particular, multiplayer serious games have been used to this purpose and to addressing the potential social isolation and demotivation caused by their condition [4–6]. In this work, the results of the design, construction and pilot evaluation of a serious videogame for upper limb motor rehabilitation, physical activation and cognitive stimulation of the elderly are presented. The serious game extends one of the games of the virtual platform, designed for upper limb rehabilitation, in order to adapt it for its in-home use by including the following features: remote

© Springer International Publishing Switzerland 2015
I. Cleland et al. (Eds.): IWAAL 2015, LNCS 9455, pp. 42–48, 2015.
DOI: 10.1007/978-3-319-26410-3_5

configuration, monitoring, evaluation and adaptation of the therapy by the therapist as the patient performs it. Also, the game allows the realization of collaborative therapy exercises between two patients to address the motivational area and the patients who stay at home. Our pilot evaluation results suggest that the videogame is perceived as being fun, stimulating, useful and usable, while providing effective mechanisms to monitor and support the patient, and to reconfigure the therapy programs.

2   A Platform for Motor Therapy and Cognitive Stimulation

The Gesture therapy virtual platform is a low-cost tool for use in the patient's home, originally developed for virtual rehabilitation of the upper limb [7]; it is currently being reused as an alternative interaction mechanism for cognitive stimulation and physical activation of the elderly with good results [8, 9]. The platform uses a distinctive gripper which controls the avatar of the user and which monitors the strength of finger pressure as patients perform the therapy. Therapy content is provided by means of a set of serious games that encourage repetitive movements through beneficial exercises for rehabilitation and physical activation; and pose activities that stimulate cognitive abilities of the older adults in a single-user environment. Currently, Gesture Therapy doesn't have mechanisms to monitor the patients and to adjust the therapy remotely (tele-rehabilitation); and the benefits of two-player games are not exploited. In the next section we describe our proposal to include a two-player game and tele-rehabilitation features to the Gesture Therapy platform for in-home use.

3   Collaborative Environment Description

Use Scenario. The use case starts when John, the therapist, configures the therapy for his patients Alice and Bob, using the Web application on his PC. Therapy configuration includes selecting the activity (i.e. the BalloonsRescuer game), and setting its parameters (e.g. duration and interval between balloons). Subsequently, Bob (or a relative) starts the virtual therapy platform from his home and communicates with Alice to ensure his presence in the collaborative game; either via audio call or chat. Then Bob starts the videogame, it receives the therapy configuration parameters from the server, and then it shows Bob's avatar (i.e. a hand). Bob has to wait for Alice to join him. Once Alice enters to the game at her home PC, it shows Bob's configuration with which she will play and she could starts the game for both. During the game, John, the therapist, can see in a Web page how both patients are playing. When the game finishes, it sends the session results (scores) to the server. Thus John can see the patients' results and even reconfigure their therapy program based on their recent performance. This scenario is shown through a diagram in the Fig. 1.

The Patients' Serious Game. The BalloonsRescuer serious game was developed using Unity 4.5 in 2D mode. The main objective of the game is to avoid that the balloons fall to the ground. Balloons fall every few seconds for a specified time (both parameters are configurable). To save a balloon the user has to "touch it" or "hit it" three times with his "fist". The fist moves from left to right and vice versa in the scenario (see Fig. 2). With each touch or hit, the balloon color and gesture change. If a balloon falls to the ground, it turns gray and explodes. The score game shows: the countdown time and the counting of saved and fallen balloons and balloons hits. The game ends at the conclusion of the specified time.

Telerehabilitation. This is done through a Web application directed to the therapist. With this application he can manage his patients and their files, manage the configuration of their therapies (e.g. duration, type of movement, etc.). Also, the therapist can consult the results of past game sessions through tables and graphs; and he can see the video of an ongoing session in (quasi) real time through a video streaming service if two players are online and performing their therapy.

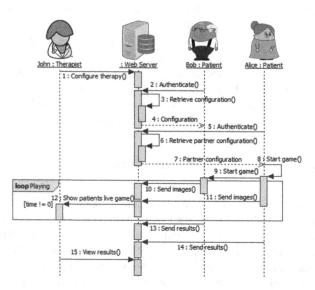

Fig. 1. Sequence diagram of the main scenario of use. The therapist configures the therapy for both patients. The game receives the configuration once the patients are authenticated. They play, and the therapist sees the game progression and receives the game results.

Collaborative Game and Service Architecture. The Web application has three parts: presentation (HTML, CSS and Javascript), logic and data access (accessed by a Web 2.0 service). Video streaming is done by the StreamingServer by taking multiple screenshots of the game per second and transmitting them to the server through a Web socket. All these components (except the presentation) were developed using .NET Framework 4.5 and SQL Server 2008. This architecture is presented in Fig. 3.

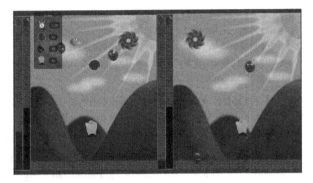

Fig. 2. The BalloonsRescuer videogame. First the balloon is green, with the 1st hit it turns yellow, with the 2nd hit it turns red, and with the 3rd one it turns blue and flies away to the sky.

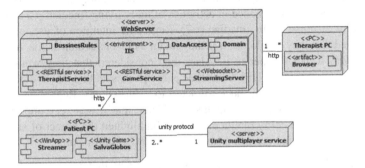

Fig. 3. Deployment diagram of the Web application and the videogame. The patient's PC hosts the game and the streaming application. The unity server is used to implement the two-player game. The WebServer exposes the therapist, game and streaming services.

4 Pilot Evaluation and Results

Study Description. The study was conducted in two parts. In the former, older adults participated in a usability study to evaluate the application. In the latter, an expert therapist was interviewed for his opinions regarding the application and its collaborative support. In the usability study, participants were adults aged 60 or older, with gender and social status indistinct. The evaluation was carried out in a research laboratory of a local public university, equipped with two computers where the BalloonsRescuer game was installed. The evaluation procedure consisted of a welcome message, initial explanation, and a questionnaire about demographic data. Then, the Gesture Therapy virtual therapy platform was demonstrated along with its characteristic gripper, with which the participant freely played for about a minute. Later, the BalloonsRescuer game was demonstrated, explaining the participant the rules and how to play it collaboratively. Subsequently, the participant played a round of three minutes along with one of the researchers. To finalize, System Usability Scale (SUS) [10] and

Technology Acceptance Model (TAM) [11] questionnaires (7-point Likert scale) were applied. The expert interview consisted of an initial introduction and explanation about the application, a demonstration regarding the collaborative features of the application for the therapist, a demonstration of the use of the game, and a closing interview to gather his opinion about the proposed application.

Study Results Part I - Older Adults. Participants were 7 older adults, with an average age of 65.8 years (sd 4.92) – 4 women and 3 men. All participants declared to have daily contact with technology and all of them own a mobile device.

Regarding ease of use, the game was perceived as easy to use (median = 7), easy to operate (median = 6) and easy to learn (median = 7). Participants highlighted that the game mechanics were simple, with few options and few movements. In addition, they perceived that game actions seemed to be consistent with reality. They really appreciated their being able to conduct the therapy in pairs. Regarding usefulness, the game was perceived as useful for physical and cognitive rehabilitation (median = 6), and that it could help improve performance in activities of daily living (median = 7), especially in the motility of upper limbs (median = 7). Regarding intention of use, most participants declared that they would use it if they had it available at their home, as it is easy to interact with it and to operate it. Also, they considered that they would become proficient in using the game. However, three participants said that they would not use it that often, as they are not that much attracted to video games. Regarding the remote participation of the therapist, participants considered that it was very important to be accompanied at a distance by the therapist; and highlighted the aspect of adapting the configuration of the game according to their therapy session results.

Study Results Part II - Expert Therapist. The expert therapist was a 55-year-old male clinical psychologist, with 10+ years of experience in motor and cognitive rehabilitation, whom works at Ensenada's Integral Rehabilitation Center (CRIE). The interview was conducted at his work office, with three researchers conducting the interview and demos for about 1 h. Regarding ease of use, the therapist considered that the videogame was easy to use, and that the gripper is an adequate interface, as even patients with spasticity could manage it. He also considered that it was easy to configure a therapy session, consult the video streaming service and consult the results of the therapy session of the patients in a Web page. Regarding usefulness, he considered that the game adequately addressed motor rehabilitation aspects (e.g. repetitive movements, different types of movements) and cognitive stimulation aspects (e.g. recall instructions, recognize colors and patterns, spatial orientation). He also considered that the feature to let patients collaborate or compete while conducting their therapy was very useful as patient interaction and socialization are highly recommended [5]. Finally, regarding the features directed to the therapist, he considered them as the most useful aspects of our proposal, as these features would allow him to be virtually present during the remote therapy session. This virtual presence would generate a beneficial feeling of support and empathy to the patient. Further, this would allow him to continuously monitor the therapy to identify the patient's progress or limitations, and continuously reassess the patient's state and reconfigure the therapy for the next sessions, so that it could better adapt to the patients' abilities.

5 Conclusions and Future Work

Regarding this work in progress report, our main findings are that (i) the proposed collaborative application was well received by the target subjects, the elderly and therapist participants; (ii) elderly subjects found the videogame as being highly useful and easy to use, and reported having a high intention to use it if had it available at home; (iii) the therapist subject also found the videogame as being useful and easy to use, and highlighted the usefulness and ease of use of the collaborative features specially directed to therapists. In particular, both older adults and the therapist highlighted the possibility for the therapist to accompany older adults during their conducting their therapy exercise as the most useful feature, along with the feature of adapting the configuration of the next therapy session based on the elder's performance in the previous sessions.

These results provide promising evidence towards the feasibility of developing a videogame that would extend the virtual platform as a collaborative tool for the physical rehabilitation and cognitive stimulation of the elderly. However, it is necessary to further evaluate the proposed tool and collaborative features, with a higher number of participants of both kinds, for a longer time, and with the gripper control integrated to the videogame, so as to actually confirm the observed trends, and better establish the scope and impact of these results. Also, as a future work, we will add a feature to the Web application to allow the therapist grouping patients with similar conditions, aiming at avoiding potential patients' frustrations, due to possible different levels of physical impairment among them.

References

1. Levin, M.F.: Can virtual reality offer enriched environments for rehabilitation? Expert Rev. Neurother. **11**, 153–155 (2011)
2. Tárraga, L., Boada, M., Modinos, G., Espinosa, A., Diego, S., Morera, A., Guitart, M., Balcells, J., López, O.L., Becker, J.T.: A randomised pilot study to assess the efficacy of an interactive, multimedia tool of cognitive stimulation in Alzheimer's disease. J. Neurol. Neurosurg. Psychiatry. **77**, 1116–1121 (2006)
3. Gamberini, L., Alcaniz, M., Barresi, G., Fabregat, M., Ibanez, F., Prontu, L.: Cognition, technology and games for the elderly: an introduction to ELDERGAMES project. PsychNology J. **4**, 285–308 (2006)
4. Novak, D., Nagle, A., Keller, U., Riener, R.: Increasing motivation in robot-aided arm rehabilitation with competitive and cooperative gameplay. J. Neuroeng. Rehabil. **11**, 64 (2014)
5. Gerling, K.M., Mandryk, R.L.: Long-term use of motion-based video games in care home settings. In: CHI 2015, pp. 1573–1582, Seoul, Republic of Korea (2015)
6. Maier, M., Rubio Ballester, B., Duarte, E., Duff, A., Verschure, P.F.: Social integration of stroke patients through the multiplayer rehabilitation gaming system. In: Göbel, S., Wiemeyer, J. (eds.) GameDays 2014. LNCS, vol. 8395, pp. 100–114. Springer, Heidelberg (2014)

7. Morán, A.L., Orihuela-Espina, F., Meza-Kubo, V., Grimaldo, A.I., Ramírez-Fernández, C., García-Canseco, E., Oropeza-Salas, J.M., Sucar, L.E.: Borrowing a virtual rehabilitation tool for the physical activation and cognitive stimulation of elders. In: Collazos, C., Liborio, A., Rusu, C. (eds.) CLIHC 2013. LNCS, vol. 8278, pp. 95–102. Springer, Heidelberg (2013)
8. Morán, A.L., Meza, V., Ramírez-Fernández, C., Grimaldo, A.I., García-Canseco, E., Orihuela-Espina, F., Sucar, L.E.: Revisiting the user experience of a virtual rehabilitation tool for the physical activation and cognitive stimulation of elders. In: Pecchia, L., Chen, L.L., Nugent, C., Bravo, J. (eds.) IWAAL 2014. LNCS, vol. 8868, pp. 203–210. Springer, Heidelberg (2014)
9. Sucar, L.E., Orihuela-Espina, F., Velazquez, R.L., Reinkensmeyer, D.J., Leder, R., Hernández-Franco, J.: Gesture therapy: an upper limb virtual reality-based motor rehabilitation platform. IEEE Trans. Neural Syst. Rehabil. Eng. **22**, 634–643 (2014)
10. Brooke, J.: SUS-A quick and dirty usability scale. Usability Eval. Ind. **189**, 194 (1996)
11. Venkatesh, V., Davis, F.D., College, S.M.W.: Theoretical acceptance extension model: field four studies of the technology longitudinal. Manag. Sci. **46**, 186–204 (2000)

Supporting the Design of an Ambient Assisted Living System Using Virtual Reality Prototypes

José C. Campos[1]([✉]), Tiago Abade[1], José Luís Silva[2],
and Michael D. Harrison[1,3,4]

[1] HASLab/INESC TEC & Departamento de Informática,
Universidade do Minho, Braga, Portugal
`jose.campos@di.uminho.pt, pg20691@alunos.uminho.pt`
[2] Madeira-ITI, Universidade da Madeira, Funchal, Portugal
`jsilva@uma.pt`
[3] Newcastle University, Newcastle upon Tyne, UK
[4] Queen Mary University of London, London, UK
`michael.harrison@newcastle.ac.uk`

Abstract. APEX, a framework for prototyping ubiquitous environments, is used to design an Ambient Assisted Living (AAL) system to enhance a care home for older people. The environment allows participants in the design process to experience the proposed design and enables developers to explore the design by rapidly developing alternatives. APEX provided the means to explore alternative designs through a virtual environment. It provides a mediating representation (a boundary object) allowing users to be involved in the design process. A group of residents in a city-based care home were involved in the design. The paper describes the design process and lessons learnt for the design of AAL systems.

Keywords: APEX · Virtual environment · Smart space · OpenSimulator · Participatory design · Rapid prototyping

1 Introduction

Ambient Assisted Living (AAL) systems [1] can improve quality of life if designed appropriately. They can compensate for the potential cognitive and physical deficits of older people without being an obstacle to those who do not have these deficits. The design challenges for AAL systems (ubicomp environments in general, for that matter) are well documented and include: predicting user experience of the system; limiting the cost of deployment that arises through iterating design (an expensive process when building physical environments); minimizing the disruption caused when deploying potentially flawed prototypes simply for testing.

For AAL systems to be successful they must be designed with the participation of their users [2]. Users should be able to explore and experience the system before design and implementation is completed. However, exploring a

© Springer International Publishing Switzerland 2015
I. Cleland et al. (Eds.): IWAAL 2015, LNCS 9455, pp. 49–61, 2015.
DOI: 10.1007/978-3-319-26410-3_6

prototype design of any kind necessarily causes departure from the world that the environment is designed to create. As Weiser commented: "Calm technology engages both the center and the periphery of our attention, and in fact moves back and forth between the two" [3]. The designer should be able to explore system requirements with potential users in a world that does not intrude on these fundamental issues of attention. The problem is made more difficult [4] because older people are a very diverse group whose attention spans are commonly short often because of a lack of interest in the technology.

Rapid prototyping can help to explore a user's experience of a candidate design early in the development process. In principle this can be achieved at minimal cost while at the same time reducing disruption to the target environment. APEX is designed to produce early prototypes of whole environment behavior [5,6]. It provides a framework that combines modeling of the control logic of the devices in a proposed environment with a virtual reality (VR) simulation of the target environment. The platform has also been used as the basis for serious games development [7,8].

This paper describes how APEX was used as the medium of communication in a participative design process for a proposed AAL system in a care home for the elderly. By participative we mean a "concern for the user's point of view" [9]. We show how the prototype environment developed using APEX provided a low cost vehicle to support assessment of the proposed design by providing a vivid experience for participants. The paper offers two main contributions. It describes how: (1) the APEX framework enables rapid development of alternative designs, making design ideas more concrete for participants; (2) a mixed reality environment enables older participants to engage more effectively with the design concepts and to provide constructive feedback about design proposals.

The remainder of the paper is structured as follows: Sects. 2 and 3 introduce the APEX framework and the care home, respectively; Sect. 4 presents the prototype used; Sect. 5 discusses the participative process followed and Sect. 6 possible alternatives; Sect. 7 ends the paper with a discussion on lessons learnt.

2   APEX Prototyping

APEX (see [6] for a more detailed description) integrates an existing 3D Application Server (OpenSimulator[1]) with a modeling tool (CPN Tools[2]) and physical devices (e.g. smart phones). 3D application servers, such as OpenSimulator provide a fast means of developing virtual worlds. Because OpenSimulator is open source, it is possible to extend and better configure the tools.

APEX-based prototypes enable users to navigate and interact with a virtual world simulation (through an appropriate viewer) as well as with some of the physical devices of the envisaged ubiquitous environment. A design process is envisaged in which the environment can be gradually made more concrete by substituting actual physical devices for virtual devices. Through the prototypes,

---

[1] http://opensimulator.org (last accessed: 2 March 2015).
[2] http://cpntools.org/ (last accessed: 2 March 2015).

users can experience many of the features of the proposed design. The three distinctive features of APEX are that it allows rapid and multi-layered prototyping of ubicomp environments. It provides a 3D virtual environment as a basis for representing the evolving design in a way that can be explored by users through an immersive experience. It also enables the connection of actual devices, as intended for the envisaged ubicomp environment, further improving the immersive user experience and enabling a refinement process, reducing the level of virtuality by gradually populating the environment with physical components.

Several users can establish connections simultaneously, using different points of view in the OpenSimulator server. Users experience the proposed solution as avatars by navigating and interacting with the simulation and with each other (e.g. by chat, movement, etc.). The avatar can be controlled by mouse/keyboard, Wiimote or smartphone.

Several ubicomp prototypes, mostly based on existing physical spaces, have been developed as part of the framework's design and development. Examples include a smart library [10,11] and an AAL system aimed at children who are asthma sufferers [6]. The present paper describes the first time the framework has been used to support a design exercise with real users.

3   The Care Home

'Casa do Professor' is a private non-profit social-welfare association aimed at teachers. The organization, which initially provided cultural and leisure services to its members, has gradually extended its scope and today offers a range of services, including continuous professional development and a residential home for retired teachers. The care home is contained in an adapted city-center house in Braga, Portugal. Because it is contained in a historic building, and because the building is multi-purpose, the organization of the rooms and their connection via corridors is complex, making navigation difficult. The ground floor comprises a living room, a dining room and a bar as well as offices and a reception area. The basement comprises an auditorium and other rooms for meetings and workshops. There are also services for the residents in the basement, for example, hairdressing and some medical care. The residents' own rooms are found on the first and second floors.

The house currently accommodates more than twenty residents. A range of support, including medical care, is provided twenty-four hours a day. Many activities offered are provided specifically for residents. Residents may also participate in other activities that are aimed at all members of the association. The house mixes public and private spaces and public and private activities. This requires a degree of openness that can hinder activities designed to ensure the safety of residents. It is not practical, for example, to log those who enter or leave the building.

The aim of the project was to design an AAL system, which could be used to help manage the space and provide relevant services to its users. It aims to cater for the diverse needs of residents, their carers and management. The designed facilities should not be disruptive to the residents' everyday lives. The first stage in designing the environment involved meeting with the institutional stakeholders to obtain their views about what facilities would be useful in the house. These meetings provided the material for an initial design that was later further discussed and developed. The second stage involved a participative design session with a group of residents using the design as developed in the first stage, with its variants, as a basis for exploration. Ideally we would have liked to engage with residents earlier in the process, however management were concerned to keep disruption to the residents' daily routine to a minimum. Additionally we were asked to postpone engagement with residents until such time as a concrete design proposal was available to be discussed.

The four meetings with institutional stakeholders provided material for the basic requirements upon which the initial designs were based. These requirements were:

- knowing the whereabouts of care home residents;
- being aware of whether tenants are in their rooms or not;
- providing the means for tenants to call for assistance, ensuring a distinction between urgent and non-urgent situations.

A further meeting established *how* the required services should be delivered to carers and inhabitants. GPS was not possible inside the house and therefore wifi was proposed as a pragmatic though coarse solution. A light by each resident's door was proposed as a means of indicating whether the room was occupied. Buttons by the door were proposed as a means of enabling a resident to call for help. Two buttons were to distinguish between urgent and non-urgent calls. Their location, to be by the door, was agreed upon. These early discussions drove the design of the initial prototype. They prompted consideration of additional features that the AAL system could provide. The complete set of features is discussed in Sect. 5.

Fig. 1. A physical and corresponding virtual bedroom

4 The Prototype

A prototype was developed to encapsulate and explore the discussed design ideas. It was important that the prototype should support sufficient features of the proposed design and sufficient texture of the environment to enable the residents to experience the systems *as if they were there*.

The proposed AAL system as prototyped included a "virtual home" and an Android smart-phone application using the phone's motion sensor. A virtual world was created to represent one of the floors that is exclusively dedicated to residential use. The floor is composed of ten bedrooms connected by corridors. The rooms are organized around a central stairwell and elevator shaft. Two of the rooms are accessed through a bridge over the main stairs on one side of the building. Pictures of the home's interior and surroundings were used to help develop the prototype, used as memory aids, to guarantee the virtual world was as faithful as possible to the actual house. Figure 1 shows an actual room from the house with its virtual counterpart.

The development of the virtual environment consumed two person days of effort. This effort included the actual development, once the blueprint and photographs were available. In this first version of the prototype each simulated bedroom was equipped with two buttons placed by the door, and a presence light placed outside the room over the door. Adding these features to the model took between two and three hours. This effort included adding each object to the world and specifying its behavior. A mobile Android app was developed. It was designed for use by the staff in the house, so that it was possible to receive notifications from the system if, for example, a button in a room was pressed by a resident. The app indicates the location of an alarm on a house map. The mobile phone's motion sensor was used as a fall detector alerting the staff if its owner falls.

5 Participative Design

The prototype was the medium of communication for the design. It was demonstrated, discussed and explored with the house's director, and then with the residents. A focus group was convened that included eleven people associated closely with the care home: nine residents, a psychologist who met this group of residents weekly, and the head of the care home. Two members of the APEX team were involved in the design exploration. One was charged with presenting and potentially iterating the prototype, asking questions and promoting the discussion, while the other took notes, and also engaged in the discussions.

5.1 The Focus Group

The residents in the group were all in the 70+ age group. They claimed no knowledge or understanding of smart houses or ambient assisted living. It became clear during discussion that residents had no difficulty identifying the environment with the house. They were able to identify which rooms belonged to whom. For example one of the residents became anxious when the demonstrator used the avatar to enter *her* room. As the avatar walked towards the room, the resident first commented that the room belonged to her. When the demonstrator did not understand what was happening the psychologist suggested that he entered the next room instead. This situation was repeated at a later stage, and at that time the psychologist made a signal for the room not to be entered.

Five scenarios were used as illustration. The participants' views, in relation to each scenario as well as the role of the technology presented, were then recorded. Depending on the participants' reaction, questions or further alternatives were put forward. Initially the idea of adding guiding lights to the bathroom was illustrated using the prototype. The residents recognized that going to the bathroom in the dark was potentially difficult. They did not feel the need for lights however because each room had its own en-suite bathroom. Lighting switches were placed by each bed for convenience. A presence light outside each room, indicating whether residents were in or not (see Fig. 2), did not stimulate any interest. Our impression was that this feature would be of more interest to staff than to residents. The head of the care home had proposed the idea in an earlier meeting, and had identified as important the need to be aware of the movement and presence of people inside the house (for example, to satisfy health and safety regulations). The open nature of the house and the continual coming and going of people on the lower, more public, floors made this a particular issue.

Fig. 2. Presence lights by the doors

The two buttons used to call for help in emergency and normal conditions were illustrated using the prototype. The buttons were viewed negatively by participants. The proposed solution was seen as being too confusing. Some residents were concerned that they would press the wrong button and that rooms already had a calling button. The existing button was however not of the type (or in the position, being by the bed) presented in the prototype.

It was clear throughout the conversation that there was tension between the staff (in particular the head of the house) and residents. Staff wanted to be able to differentiate real distress calls from more trivial ones. This feature was not available in the current system as was identified as an issue during the earlier meetings. The residents on the other hand wanted a simple system that would not compromise their independence.

A further criticism of the button solution related to their position. It was felt that in an emergency the button, positioned by the door, would not be easy to reach. As commonly happens there were conflicting requirements: on the one hand independence was desired; on the other hand there were criticisms of location for a concept that would remove independence.

Presenting residents with AAL technologies using the adopted format risked appearing patronizing, thereby generating negative responses that did not fairly reflect the value of the technology. Our approach was not to present solutions to *their* problems, but rather to ask for their advice and opinion on the envisaged technologies. By empowering the group in this way the risk of offending or patronizing its members was diminished.

The position of the buttons in the room was adjusted to foster discussion of the button placement. Alternatives presented included moving buttons to the WC or closer to the bed (see Fig. 3). As the scenarios were presented, the prototype and its environment were modified interactively to demonstrate alternatives to the meeting. After some discussion about whether the button by the bed was enough, or whether it should be complemented by another, and where the other should be placed, it became evident that, although at first residents were reluctant to admit it explicitly, providing assistance in the bedrooms was indeed a relevant service from their perspective. While discussing the best positioning of the buttons, one resident explained in detail how she had fallen from the bed and had a very difficult time trying to climb back to reach for the calling button. Example scenarios elicited from the participants provided a rich source of discussion.

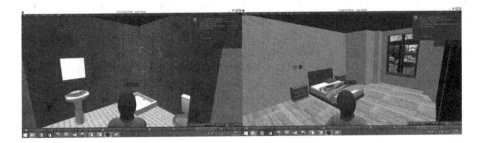

Fig. 3. Discussing the buttons' location

Following this productive discussion, the motion sensor aimed at detecting falls was then illustrated. This demonstration used a smart phone that was connected to the prototype. The prototype virtual environment provided in the desktop display was augmented by the smart phone application. The scenario illustrated both how a sensor would be able to detect sudden movements and how the system would then notify carers through the smart phone application. While recognizing this to be a very useful possibility, some residents expressed concerns about how the sensor device would be worn. The possibility of using a bracelet to contain the sensor was well received. Having a panic button on the device was also discussed after suggestion by one of the participants. The discussion generated positive, if not enthusiastic, feedback. However there were also concerns, mostly expressed by the psychologist, about false positives and the types of movements that would trigger the device.

Finally, the idea of the device serving as a localization device inside the house was also explored. Residents were shown how staff members would be able to see their location on a map. The general opinion was that the device would not be very useful in the common areas of the house where other people are present. Someone suggested, with general agreement, that this feature would be most useful outside the house. Residents felt that when they were out in the street they were most vulnerable. It was agreed that the location service should indicate where residents were, whether outside the house or in their room. While administrators were interested in being able to discover quickly where residents were, both to contact them when necessary, and to monitor their well being, the residents focused on their personal safety and of feeling uncomfortable when left alone.

5.2   Updated Requirements

The initial requirements were updated based on the focus group feedback. The new requirements combine the original requirements, as discussed with the house administrators, and the views of the house's residents as identified during the focus group. The fact that participants did not use the prototype themselves, but rather saw it being used, inevitably limited the sense of immersion. Discussion by participants revolved around what the house could become, and not about being in the new house. They found it difficult to identify with the possibility that they would live there. Even so, relevant insights were gained from the exercise.

The fact that participants did not (as required by house management) interact with the prototype in person might also raise questions as to whether this type of prototype would be effective when used directly by participants. Issues relating to type of engagement and how to collect data and feedback are important to understanding the value of this type of design. Previous experience, using the framework directly, has shown that engagement is easy to achieve [7, 11]. This experience ranges from prototyping existing or envisaged ubicomp systems (e.g. a library or a bar at a theatre), to a serious game aimed at primary school children. Deployment has been mostly desktop/laptop based, but the use of a CAVE environment was also tested successfully.

The environment can also be instrumented to collect information about the behavior of users [7] as they interact with it. In situations were the number of test subjects is high, making direct observation impractical, questionnaires designed to be used after participation have been used. Video recording has also been considered, but so far not used in the absence of appropriate ethical clearances.

A further point to consider is that only the managers and the psychologist were consulted and not other staff in the home. This will inevitably have biased the initial requirements. This omission resulted from the home's internal policy. It did not however hinder our goal of studying the applicability of the approach, and does not invalidate the conclusion that the approach was indeed useful. In future interactions, house staff can be integrated into the process if agreed by the administration.

6   Discussion of Alternative Approaches

Other examples of form or medium used to support participatory design have included:

Video. Video has been used as a prompt in participatory design [4], showing scenarios in which the envisaged technology can be used. Researchers have developed facilities for editing documentary film so that participants can understand and respond to possible design proposals [12,13].

One problem with this approach is a lack of flexibility to support quick reaction to the users' attitudes towards the prototype and input. Using video only it would not be possible to adjust movement in the house in response to specific resident's reactions, or experiment with different locations for the buttons.

Theater. Live theater has been used in participatory design [14]. Drama has been used to give texture to scenarios in which a proposed design is intended to be used. An interactive scenario method, including improvisation, and the engagement of participants as actors in scenarios [15], has also been used.

This is an interesting approach. In this particular case, while one of the demonstrators enacted some scenarios through the avatar, and by manipulating the mobile phone, no other participants were involved as actors. However, the combination of virtual reality prototypes with the enactment of specific scenarios by users raises an interesting prospect to be explored in the future.

Paper Prototyping. Paper prototyping has been used as a Rapid Participatory Design Technique [16] that enables speedy redrafting and change of design ideas. This approach is less immersive than the other approaches already mentioned. However it provides a mechanism for sketching alternatives rapidly.

Our main concern with paper prototyping was a result of the lack of computer literacy of the residents. Our impression is that paper prototyping is too low fidelity to allow stakeholders to imagine what it would be like to be in the ubicomp environment. However, this is something that requires further work.

Laboratory-Based High Fidelity Prototypes. High fidelity prototypes of part of the proposed environment (in this case an ambient kitchen) have been used to provide a physical context in which design ideas relating to the kitchen, and more broadly to other aspects of the environment under design, can be considered [17].

The Aware Home [18] at Georgia Institute of Technology (GaTech) contains two identical floors with nine rooms, each designed to explore emerging technologies and services in the home. The Aware Home team is also exploring the use of a suite in a senior living residence. Their concern is to overcome mobility limitations relating to older adults who might be unable to travel to do their usual tasks.

The issue here is the cost of these approaches, something we address through the use of virtual reality representations of the actual environments.

In situ High Fidelity Prototypes. Building and deploying an initial version of the system could in principle be a feasible option, using recent embedded technologies such as Arduino, but would be too disruptive to the house's operation, and to the residents' own daily routine. It would also mean that exploration of the prototyped system would imply moving about in the house. While this might at first seem to be a better approach, the logistics, and potential for disruption, of such an approach made it less attractive.

A Dolls' House. A dolls' house has been used as the physical context for considering design issues in an AAL [19,20]. While the house is a rigid design it provides a graphic reminder of the context as design discussion is conducted.

It is possible to think of the APEX developed prototype as a virtual reality based version of a dolls' house, with the advantage of being more dynamic (in the sense that elements in the house can exhibit behavior).

Virtual Reality. The advantage of participatory design with virtual environments is the flexibility that it affords. Video, theater and physical dolls' houses all provide barriers to flexibility. However a possible disadvantage of VR is the validity of the feedback obtained when compared with these other approaches. Work exploring the use of VR to assess user experience has indicated that VR is indeed a viable alternative that enables appropriate user experience, see Rebolo et al. [21] when framed by appropriate methodologies. Others have explored the use of virtual reality in participatory design. Davies [22] have developed a VR-based tool developed for participatory design. They argue that this tool can be seen as part of the toolset used by design experts.

Mixed Reality. Using mixed reality in participatory design has the advantage that it improves user immersion, enabling participants to interact both with physical and digital objects in real time, potentially enhancing attention span. Bruno et al. [23] use VR with physical devices to involve participants in product interface design rather than ubiquitous environment design. They have demonstrated the efficacy of focus groups in the analysis of virtual products and demonstrated how users can be co-designers using VR prototyping. These results accord with Reich et al. [24] who claim that ideal participation involves customers as co-designers. However, some limitations were identified: (i) observing users outside of their daily context may lead to a variation of the modes of interaction with the product; (ii) haptic devices cannot be used when interacting with a virtual environment.

The APEX framework makes it possible to change and to explore mixed reality environments, the behaviors of the (physical) smart elements that are part of the design, in the context of possible scenarios. All these elements can be changed and re-presented relatively quickly. We know of no other work, using such a multi-layered approach, that includes the combination of virtual and physical devices in participative design.

Designing AAL Services. Another perspective that also uses participatory design has been described by Menschner and others [25]. The interesting feature of their work, from the point of view of APEX, is to see the problem as concerned with service design. The APEX framework encourages a view of ubiquitous environments as delivering implicitly a set of services. These services can be characterized in APEX using CPN. The CPN provides a specification that an off-the-shelf service should satisfy or provides a precise characterization of how an existing service should be modified.

7   Conclusions and Lessons Learnt

This paper has described our experience of using APEX, a prototyping platform for ubiquitous computing systems, to design an AAL system. It was shown how the developed prototypes enabled the exploration of the system from the early phases of design. Speedy iteration of the AAL design was made possible by using APEX. While the different components of the design were relatively simple, the system was rich enough to illustrate conflicting requirements between stakeholders. When designing for groups such as older adults care should be taken to find adequate strategies to involve them in the design process. Our design process empowered the stakeholders, and older participants in particular, to engage with the design concepts and to provide constructive feedback about design proposals.

The virtual environment provided good support for evaluation, enabling potential users of the system to help shape it. This supports claims found elsewhere in the literature (e.g. [21]). When exploring the design, differences between the perceptions and opinions of the different stakeholders (director versus residents) were identified. These related to the utility and desirability of the features of the design as well as their interpretation. As a result of the exercise an updated set of requirements were produced to better reflect the interests of all involved. New devices and functionalities were added to the design, while others were removed. This again illustrates how the prototype empowered stakeholders to take an active role in the design of the system.

To conclude, it has been shown that APEX can be used as a prototyping platform for AAL systems, and that these prototypes, in the context of participative design, constitute a useful tool by enabling participants, as co-designers, to explore and contribute to a system's design (cf. [26]). As a result, a design solution will be produced that will enhance their experience of the system and avoid usability pitfalls.

Acknowledgments. We would like to express out gratitude to all at *Casa do Professor* that made the study reported upon in this paper possible. José C. Campos acknowledges support by the FCT – Fundação para a Ciência e a Tecnologia (Portuguese Foundation for Science and Technology) within project ID/EEA/50014/2013. José Luís Silva acknowledges support from project PEST-OE/EEI/LA0009/2015. Michael Harrison was also funded by EPSRC research grant EP/G059063/1: CHI+MED (Computer–Human Interaction for Medical Devices).

References

1. Wichert, R., Klausing, H. (eds.): Ambient Assisted Living. Advanced Technologies and Societal Change. Springer, Heidelberg (2014)
2. Brereton, M., Buur, J.: New challenges for design participation in the era of ubiquitous computing. CoDesign **4**(2), 101–113 (2008)
3. Weiser, M., Brown, J.: The coming age of calm technology. In: Denning, P., Metcalfe, R. (eds.) Beyond Calculation, pp. 75–86. Springer, New York (1996)
4. Lindsay, S., Jackson, D., Schofield, G., Olivier, P.: Engaging older people using participatory design. In: Proceedings of the SIGCHI Conference on Human Factors in Computing Systems, CHI 2012, pp. 1199–1208. ACM (2012)
5. Silva, J.L., Campos, J., Harrison, M.: Formal analysis of ubiquitous computing environments through the APEX framework. In: Proceedings of the 4th ACM SIGCHI Symposium on Engineering Interactive Computing Systems, EICS 2012, pp. 131–140. ACM (2012)
6. Silva, J.L., Campos, J.C., Harrison, M.D.: Prototyping and analysing ubiquitous computing environments using multiple layers. Int. J. Hum. Comput. Stud. **72**(5), 488–506 (2014)
7. Gomes, T., Abade, T., Campos, J., Harrison, M., Silva, J.: A virtual environment based serious game to support health education. EAI Endorsed Trans. Ambient Syst. **14**(3), e5 (2014)
8. Gomes, T., Abade, T., Campos, J., Harrison, M., Silva, J.: Rapid development of first person serious games using the APEX platform: the asthma game. In: Proceedings of the 30th Annual ACM Symposium on Applied Computing, pp. 169–174. ACM (2014)
9. Halskov, K., Hansen, N.B.: The diversity of participatory design research practice at PDC 2002–2012. Int. J. Hum. Comput. Stud. **74**, 81–92 (2015)
10. Abade, T., Campos, J.C., Moreira, R., Silva, C.C.L., Silva, J.L.: Immersiveness of ubiquitous computing environments prototypes: a case study. In: Streitz, N., Markopoulos, P. (eds.) DAPI 2015. LNCS, vol. 9189, pp. 237–248. Springer, Heidelberg (2015)
11. Abade, T., Gomes, T., Silva, J.L., Campos, J.C.: Design and evaluation of a smart library using the APEX framework. In: Streitz, N., Markopoulos, P. (eds.) DAPI 2014. LNCS, vol. 8530, pp. 307–318. Springer, Heidelberg (2014)

12. Hook, J., Green, D., McCarthy, J., Taylor, S., Wright, P., Olivier, P.: A VJ centered exploration of expressive interaction. In: Proceedings of the SIGCHI Conference on Human Factors in Computing Systems, CHI 2011, pp. 1265–1274. ACM (2011)

13. Raijmakers, B., Gaver, W.W., Bishay, J.: Design documentaries: inspiring design research through documentary film. In: Proceedings of the 6th Conference on Designing Interactive Systems, pp. 229–238. ACM (2006)

14. Newell, A.F., Carmichael, A., Morgan, M., Dickinson, A.: The use of theatre in requirements gathering and usability studies. Interact. Comput. 18(5), 996–1011 (2006)

15. Strömberg, H., Pirttilä, V., Ikonen, V.: Interactive scenarios - building ubiquitous computing concepts in the spirit of participatory design. Pers. Ubiquit. Comput. 8(3–4), 200–207 (2004)

16. Osman, A., Baharin, H., Ismail, M.H., Jusoff, K.: Paper prototyping as a rapid participatory design technique. Comput. Inf. Sci. 2(3), 53–57 (2009)

17. Olivier, P., Xu, G., Monk, A., Hoey, J.: Ambient kitchen: designing situated services using a high fidelity prototyping environment. In: Proceedings of the 2nd International Conference on PErvasive Technologies Related to Assistive Environments, PETRA 2009, pp. 47:1–47:7. ACM (2009)

18. Kientz, J.A., Patel, S.N., Jones, B., Price, E., Mynatt, E.D., Abowd, G.D.: The georgia tech aware home. In: CHI 2008 Extended Abstracts on Human Factors in Computing Systems, pp. 3675–3680. ACM (2008)

19. Urnes, T., Weltzien, A., Zanussi, A., Engbakk, S., Rafn, J.K.: Pivots and structured play: Stimulating creative user input in concept development. In: Proceedings of the Second Nordic Conference on Human-Computer Interaction, NordiCHI 2002, pp. 187–196. ACM (2002)

20. Kanis, M., Alizadeh, S., Groen, J., Khalili, M., Robben, S., Bakkes, S., Kröse, B.: Ambient monitoring from an elderly-centred design perspective: what, who and how. In: Keyson, D.V., et al. (eds.) AmI 2011. LNCS, vol. 7040, pp. 330–334. Springer, Heidelberg (2011)

21. Rebelo, F., Noriega, P., Duarte, E., Soares, M.: Using virtual reality to assess user experience. Hum. Factors 54(6), 964–982 (2012)

22. Davies, R.C.: Adapting virtual reality for the participatory design of workenvironments. Comput. Support. Coop. Work 13(1), 1–33 (2004)

23. Bruno, F., Muzzupappa, M.: Product interface design: a participatory approach based on virtual reality. Int. J. Hum. Comput. Stud. 68(5), 254–269 (2010)

24. Reich, Y., Konda, S.L., Monarch, I.A., Levy, S.N., Subrahmanian, E.: Varieties and issues of participation and design. Des. Stud. 17(2), 165–180 (1996)

25. Menschner, P., Prinz, A., Koene, P., Kbler, F., Altmann, M., Krcmar, H., Leimeister, J.: Reaching into patients homes - participatory designed AAL services. Electron. Markets 21(1), 63–76 (2011)

26. Carroll, J.M., Rosson, M.B.: Participatory design in community informatics. Des. Stud. 28(3), 243–261 (2007)

Ambient Assisted Living Environments

A Mechanism for Nominating Video Clips to Provide Assistance for Instrumental Activities of Daily Living

Joseph Rafferty[1(✉)], Chris Nugent[1], Jun Liu[1], and Liming Chen[2]

[1] School of Computing and Mathematics,
University of Ulster, Northern Ireland, UK
rafferty-j@email.ulster.ac.uk,
{cd.nugent,j.liu}@ulster.ac.uk
[2] School of Computer Science and Informatics,
De Montfort University, Leicester, UK
liming.chen@dmu.ac.uk

Abstract. Current assistive smart homes have adopted a relatively rigid approach to modeling activities. The use of these activity models have introduced factors which block adoption of smart home technology. To address this, goal driven smart homes have been proposed, these are based upon more flexible activity structures. However, this goal-driven approach does have a disadvantage where flexibility in this activity modeling can lead to difficulty providing illustrative guidance. To address this, a video analysis and nomination mechanism is required to provide suitable assistive clips for a given goal. This paper introduces a novel mechanism for nominating a suitable video clip given a pool of automatically generated metadata. This mechanism was then evaluated using a voice based assistant application and a tool emulating assistance requests by a goal-driven smart home. The initial evaluation produced promising results.

Keywords: Annotation · Automated speech recognition · Assistive living · Guidance · Parsing · Ontology · Semantic web · Smart environments · Video · Vocal interaction

1 Introduction

The composition of the worldwide population is changing, producing a never before recorded level of global aging. Projections show that by 2050 over 20 % of the population will be aged over 65 years old [1, 2]. Having such an aged population will increase the number of cases of age related illness [3]. Such increased cases of illness will subsequently increase burden on healthcare provision. This problem will be further compounded by the ever-decreasing global Potential Support Ratio (PSR). The PSR is the ratio of those who are the working age compared to those that are 65 or over. The PSR is trending towards a ratio of 4:1 by 2050, historically this has been 12:1 in 1950 and 9:1 in 2009 [1].

Ambient Assistive Living (AAL) is a technological approach which provides solutions to alleviate a portion of these aging related problems [4]. AAL provides these by

© Springer International Publishing Switzerland 2015
I. Cleland et al. (Eds.): IWAAL 2015, LNCS 9455, pp. 65–76, 2015.
DOI: 10.1007/978-3-319-26410-3_7

addressing the problems associated with aging and increase the independence of individuals. A core element within AAL focuses on providing solutions which assist individuals with completion of activities of daily living (ADL) and instrumental activities of
daily living (IADL). ADLs cover basic tasks such as bathing, dressing, feeding oneself,
hygiene and toileting [5]. IADLs cover more complex tasks which are essential for living
independently in a community, these include tasks such as financial management, meal
preparation, correctly self-administering prescribed medication and shopping [6].

AAL solutions for ADLs/IADLs may come in many forms but the majority of
solutions can broadly be classified as complex residential solutions, in the form of a
Smart Home (SH), and less complex solutions, such as prompting, guiding and
reminding systems.

The research presented within this paper introduces a novel mechanism of matching
video clips to a user goal, typically representing an ADL/IADL. This is achieved
through querying a semantic store that consists of automatically generated metadata
and user goals. Enabling dynamic matching of relevant, video-based, instruction for a
goal-driven SH and additionally enables a less complex solution based around using a
spoken query to a voice assistant mobile application.

The remainder of the paper is arranged as follows: Sect. 2 provides an overview of
related work; Sect. 3 details the approach used in this study; Sect. 4 provides an
evaluation of an implementation of the approach and Sect. 5 concludes the paper.

2 Related Work

SHs are residential environments that have been augmented with technology to promote independent living. Currently, SHs operate in a 'bottom-up' approach. In this
approach, an environment is furnished with a suite of sensors. These sensors generate
signals that in turn are processed with the objective of recognizing the inhabitant
activities. Following the results of this processing, support mechanisms, deployed
throughout the residential area, provide assistance as necessary [4, 7]. The assistance
that current SHs provide is typically in the form of prompting systems, monitoring of
behavioral trends and/or remote assessment of vital signs.

Prompting systems within SHs provide guidance for an inhabitant once specific
criteria are encountered, generally representing troubled progression with a task. Prompts
may consist of video, audio or text, or a combination of these media. Of these types of
prompts, video incorporating audio narration has shown to provide a promising method
of providing instruction as it provides informative and relatable guidance [4, 8, 9].

The bottom-up approach, whilst functional, has some issues stemming from its
sensor centric nature. SHs that employ this approach do not handle variation in activity
in a flexible manner [4, 7, 10–13]. To enable efficient operation, SHs require a large
number of sensors placed into an environment. Retrofitting a large number of homes
with such a sensor suite is realistically not feasible due to financial restrictions in
addition to high levels of disturbance that would be caused to an inhabitant. Finally,
reusability of some bottom-up SHs are severely limited due to reliance of a record of
events that occur within a specific environment [4, 7, 10–13]. These problems represent

a significant barrier to the adoption of SHs. To address these issues a goal-driven, top-down, approach to SHs has been proposed [14]. These goals are defined through domain knowledge using a web application. Further information on these Goals can be obtained from [14].

In a goal-driven approach, inhabitant activities are modelled as goals, which contain action plans. Actions plans contain a number of actions, such as "Boil Kettle", in order to detail how to achieve a goal.

A goal may inherit a number of sub goals, offering a flexible method of modelling inhabitant activity within a SH. An example of this flexibility is shown in Fig. 1, where 7 goals that have associated action plans are combined to produce a total of 16 inhabitant goals.

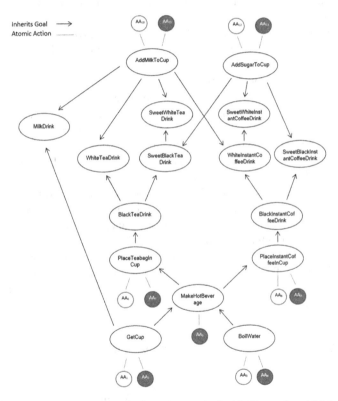

Fig. 1. The flexibility of modelling activities using goals. In this illustration, 16 inhabitant goals have been produced by combining 7 goals that have associated action plans and actions.

This flexible modelling introduces a situation where a large number of dynamically generated goal action plans would require relatable video-based guidance to exist and be associated with that particular combination. This represents a problem as to produce this would require a large amount of effort, in both recording the videos and linking to the potentially expanding pool of actions plans.

To address this a mechanism of matching dynamically generated action plans with automatically generated video clip meta-data would need to be produced. This is a focus of the novel video nomination mechanism introduced in this paper.

The use of SHs represents an overly complex solution for supporting end users that are mostly independent and suffering mild cognitive impairment (MCI). In cases of MCI, the use of less complex ADL/IADL assistive solutions offer a more cost effective and invasive route to providing assistance [9, 15–18].

In this research area, solutions have been produced which provide on demand video assistance, reminder based assistance and prompting based guidance for single tasks.

One approach, offered by the EU AAL Personal IADL Assistant (PIA) project [1], provided a promising avenue to helping with IADLs [9, 19].

In PIA, assistance was provided through a home by use of narrated video clips. The main user experience for this project was offered by an Android application that ran on tablets and smart phones.

These video clips were recorded by dedicated caregivers, which subsequently uploaded them to a cloud-based repository. Once uploaded to this repository, these clips could then be linked to NFC[2] tags. These tags were affixed to objects related to the IADL which assistance would be provided for.

When an inhabitant of an environment required assistance, they simply needed to request it by waking an android device from sleep, aligning it to an NFC tag and placing in sufficient proximity to the tag. When performed successfully, the application would read the tag then download and play the associated video.

Multiple focus groups provided a mostly favorable evaluation of the approach offered by PIA but voiced concerns with issues related to correctly aligning tags and the use of an overly complex user interface [9, 19]. To address these limitations a voice-based assistant was implemented which queried the video matching mechanism produced by this research. This application provided an avenue for partially evaluating the performance of this mechanism for providing assistance. The use of this voice-based assistance offers a more simplified, natural, user interface and circumvents the alignment issues introduced by use of NFC tags. The function and performance of this mechanism in providing assistance for goal driven SHs and within the PIA voice assistant is elaborated on within the following section.

3   Automatic Selection of Appropriate Video Guidance for User Goals

In this study, a mechanism capable of nominating suitable video clips to provide relevant assistance for SH inhabitant goals and IADLs has been produced. This method is intended to select appropriate instructional videos for dynamically constructed SH

---

[1] Personal IADL Assistant, PIA – EU AAL Funded Research Project (AAL-2012-5-033), available at: http://www.pia-project.org/.

[2] NFC, Near Field Communication – a short range wireless communication technology.

inhabitant goals and IADLs, as specified by a goal-driven SH or through use of the PIA voice assistant.

This method is designed to extend and integrate with previous research the authors have produced which automatically generates rich metadata for video clips by use of narration analysis. This previous research was implemented within an evaluation platform called ABSEIL (Audio BaSEd Instruction profiLer) [20]. The video matching research presented in this paper has also been implemented within the ABSEIL system to enable evaluation.

In the automatic metadata generation within ABSEIL, video clips are converted to audio clips. These audio clips are then sent to an Automated Speech Recognition (ASR) service, which produces a transcription. This transcription is then processed to detect if any actions from inhabitant goals, such as "Boil Kettle", are uttered. Additionally, ABSEIL would identify different classes of semantically compatible utterances to facilitate better matching of terms used in videos to those modelled in inhabitant goals. These utterances are present in four distinct search sets. These sets are direct, homophone substitution, synonym substitution and homophone/synonym substitution.

The direct set of terms are those goal actions that were present within the transcription. The homophone substitution set adds an element of correction for transcription errors where phonetically confused terms were possibly identified, for example the transcription may have misidentified the phrase "poor water" when in actuality the phrase "pour water" was uttered and is present in goal atomic actions. The synonym substitution set adds scope for semantically compatible terms being present in the transcription, for example, "take cup" is semantically compatible with the utterance "take mug". The final search set combines the approach of both of these previous search sets to enable a broader range of compatible terms to be detected. In this approach, synonym substitutions are generated by using a semantic lexicon and homophone substitutions are generated using a homophone dictionary. A graphical representation of this approach is shown in Fig. 2.

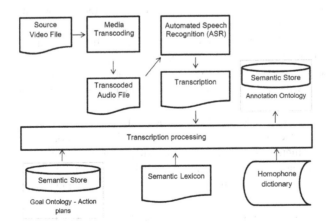

Fig. 2. An overview of the automatic metadata generation process employed by ABSEIL.

When matches in the search sets are discovered they are stored in a video annotation ontology [21]. This ontology stores the depicted action in addition to optional timestamp and duration and properties. This ontology has 4 sub-classes, representing each of the four search sets. Additionally, metadata is stored about the video including a unique SHA512 hash digest of the file, allowing identification of a video from an online repository, where the video is stored. The classes and object data properties of this ontology are shown in Fig. 3.

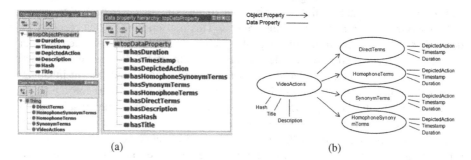

(a)   (b)

Fig. 3. The classes object properties and data properties of the video action annotation ontology, as shown in the protégé ontology-engineering tool (a) and as a hierarchy of concepts (b).

Through the use of ontologies, this metadata can be easily be shared and reasoned with by use of Semantic Web Markup Language (SWRL) rules and SPARQL queries [22]. The use of these semantic rules and queries facilitate reasoning across a number of ontologies, including the goal library of a goal-based SH system. This ability to reason across metadata and goal ontologies is central to the approach that is used by this video matching method. The goal ontology of this SH, which records the goal names and atomic actions required for nominating appropriate video clips, is show in Fig. 4.

This mechanism was integrated into the ABSEIL system and was made accessible through a REST based web service frontend. This allows consumer applications (in this case, the goal-driven SH and the voice assistant application) to issue a request to the query/transcription processing web service.

In the case of the SH system, it can issue a request in the form of a specific goal name, this name will be from a goal that is preset in the shared semantic store that ABSEIL has access to.

In the case of the voice assistant application, it issues a request containing a transcription of a user's voice query, as provided by the Google ASR API. These transcriptions are then processed against a list of goal names from the semantic store, using the Lucene-based technique detailed in [20], to determine if any were uttered. If any goal matches are identified, the goal name is used in the video nomination process used directly by the SH.

Once the nomination process has been completed, it will respond to the client applications. If a video is identified, its SHA512 hash is returned to the client. The client can then use that hash to obtain the video from a cloud-based repository. In the

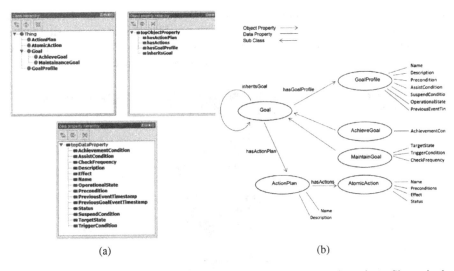

Fig. 4. The classes, object properties and data properties of the SH goal ontology. Shown in the protégé ontology-engineering tool (a) and as a hierarchy of concepts (b).

event that a suitable match is not nominated, a null value will be returned to the client to indicate this. An overview of this process is shown in Fig. 5, which specifically shows how the voice assistant app consumes the video nomination mechanism. The goal-driven SH system consumes the mechanism in a similar manner but does not use the ASR component required by the voice assistant application.

The function of this video nomination service is best illustrated though use of the voice assistant application. This application is shown responding to a voice query of

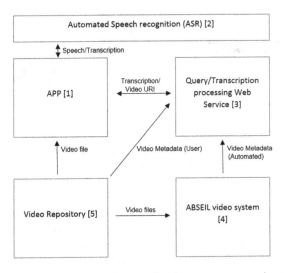

Fig. 5. An overview of how client applications request a nominated video

"show me how to set a timer" in Fig. 6. This was mapped to a "Set Timer" goal, which then was used to automatically nominate the most suitable video in the repository, this happened to be setting a timer on an iPad. If a more suitable video, with less identified actions was present in the repository it would have been nominated instead.

Fig. 6. An overview the voice assistant application consuming the video nomination mechanism. (a) Shows the application in standby, (b) shows the application obtaining a transcription from the google text to speech service, in (c) the transcription is being sent to the REST-based query service, (d) shows a successfully nominated video being played and (e) shows the result of no relevant video being nominated.

The video nomination process takes a goal name and then applies semantic reasoning to determine the most appropriate video from a number of candidates.

The reasoning behind this video nomination mechanism was implemented through a combination of SWRL, SPARQL and logic (where appropriate). This logic is shown formally in Table 1.

Table 1. The rules and queries that perform the reasoning in the nomination mechanism.

Rule/Query	Description
hasGoalProfile(?g, ?gp), hasGoalProfile(?ig, ?igp), inheritsGoal(?g, ?ig), Name(?gp, ?gn) -> hasGoalProfile(?g, ?igp)	This SWRL rule reasons about goal inheritance, facilitating querying actions, such as boil kettle, from inherited goals. This enables generation of action plans from dynamically created activity structures
SELECT ?acts WHERE {{?p ug:Name ?gn. ?goal ug: hasGoalProfile ?p. ?goal ug:hasGoalProfile ?pn. ? allGoals ug:hasGoalProfile ?pn.}.{?allGoals ug: hasActionPlan ?ap. ?ap ug:hasActions ?aa. ?aa ug:Name ?acts}}	This SPARQL query combines with the previous SWRL rule to extract a list of actions from a goal ontology. This will produce a list of actions for a given goal, as represented by $?gn$ in this query
$G = \{G,x; x = 1, \ldots, N\}$	A set of goals (G_x) a inhabitant may pursue
$G = <A>$	Goals have Actions (A) that need to be performed to complete the goal tasks
$MD = \{MDx; x = 1, \ldots, N\}$	A set of metadata generated by the ABSEIL system. These are DM, SM, HM and SHM, representing the direct, synonym, homophone and synonym/homophone sets
$MD = <A, H>$	Generated metadata sets have an associated a set of actions (A) and a hash record (H) used to identify videos
$CMD = \{x \in (A_{DM_x} \bigcap A_{SH_x} \bigcap A_{HM_x} \bigcap A_{SHM_x}); x \in A_{G_x}\}$	The DM, CSM, CHM, CSHM sets are transformed into to a candidate metadata set. This set only contains metadata entries that contain all the actions present in the nominated goal.
$NV = \{x \in CMD_x \Leftrightarrow x = \min\{A_{CMD_x}\}\}$	NV is the metadata record of the nominated video. The nominated video is the metadata record in the CMD set that has the lowest number of actions. The hash record of NV is returned to a client, allowing it to locate and play the video

4 Evaluation

In order to evaluate this video nomination mechanism it was implemented within the ABSEIL system and was accessible via a REST-based web service. Implementation as part of a REST-based service allowed testing of this mechanism from two different perspectives; that of the voice assistant application and a goal nomination tool emulating an assistance request from a goal-driven SH.

Prior to this evaluation process, the ABSEIL system had profiled and generated the metadata for 20 videos. This metadata was used as the basis for video nomination in this evaluation. Additionally, the goal ontology for the SH contained a range of goals covering IADLs, all but two of these were represented in at least one of the videos previously processed by ABSEIL.

During this evaluation, 60 total requests were sent to the nomination mechanism using both the voice application and goal nomination tool.

A set of 40 requests were expected to produce a positive result where a match was found. This match was compared to manual assessment to determine if it was the most suitable video for that goal. This set is referred to as set A. A set of 20 requests were expected to produce a negative result where a match should not be found. These request nominated goals that should have no matching video instruction. This is referred to as set B. A summarization of this evaluation is presented in Table 2.

Table 2. The accuracy of the video nomination process as determined by queries issued by a voice assistant application and a goal nomination tool. Set A are queries that are expected to produce a reply containing a video. Set B are queries that queries for goals with no associated video and so should produce a null reply.

		Goal nomination tool	Mobile application	Set Accuracy
Set A	*Request count*	20	20	72.50 %
	Correct response count	17	12	
	Accuracy	85.00 %	60.00 %	
Set B	*Request count*	10	10	100.00 %
	Correct response count	10	10	
	Accuracy	100.00 %	100.00 %	

In this evaluation a number of incorrect responses were received which were related to wrong nomination and incorrect production of transcriptions. Both the goal nomination tool and mobile application were susceptible to wrongly nominated videos when two specific goals were requested. This was due to nomination of a large, mostly unrelated, video, which held some utterances of goal activity as part of a lengthier instructional video. These actions were depicted within the video but were a small element of the instruction being shown. This wrongful nomination could lead to confusion if the person in need of assistance did not watch the entire video. A future revision of this nomination mechanism will make matching more conservative in order to factor out videos with too many unrelated actions.

Additionally, the voice assistant application was susceptible to transcription errors. During evaluation, the google-provided transcription was logged. Under examination, these logs were compared against what was expected. This revealed a number of cases where transcription errors which were the cause of the erroneous reply from the server.

5 Conclusion

The research presented in this paper presents a novel mechanism for nominating assistive videos from a pool of candidates that have automatically generated metadata.

The production of this mechanism facilitates provision of assistance in two different types of assistive systems; a voice assistant application to provide assistance with IADLs for those living with MCI and a goal-driven SH for those that have a more advanced cogitative impairment. The effectiveness of this system was evaluated from both the perspective of the voice assistant application and the goal-driven SH, in both cases this matching system has shown promising results. Future work will integrate this mechanism into a goal-driven SH system to allow it to assist inhabitants. This video nomination mechanism will then undergo a revision to address the issues highlighted during evaluation. The revised version will then be evaluated in a more thorough evaluation where this is an element of a complete SH system. In addition, the produced voice assistant is in need of a more thorough usability evaluation. Additional efforts may improve the voice processing that is present in the voice assistant by incorporation of a more advance natural language processing system.

Acknowledgments. This work has been conducted in the context of the EU AAL PIA project (AAL-2012-5-033).The authors gratefully acknowledge the contributions from all members of the PIA consortium.

References

1. United Nations: World Population Ageing 2009. Population Studies Series (2010)
2. United Nations: Concise Report on the World Population Situation in 2014 (2014)
3. De Luca, A.E., Bonacci, S., Giraldi, G.: Aging populations: the health and quality of life of the elderly. Clin. Ter. **162**, e13 (2011)
4. Acampora, G., Cook, D.J., Rashidi, P., Vasilakos, A.V.: A survey on ambient intelligence in health care. Proc. IEEE. Inst. Electr. Electron. Eng. **101**, 2470–2494 (2013)
5. Katz, S., Ford, A., Moskowitz, R.: Studies of illness in the aged: the index of ADL: a standardized measure of biological and psychosocial function. JAMA **185**, 914–919 (1963)
6. Lawton, M., Brody, E.: Instrumental Activities of Daily Living Scale (IADL) (1988)
7. Chen, L., Hoey, J., Nugent, C.D., Cook, D.J., Yu, Z.: Sensor-based activity recognition. IEEE Trans. Syst. Man, Cybern. Part C (Appl. Rev.) 1–19 (2012)
8. Lapointe, J., Bouchard, B., Bouchard, J.: Smart homes for people with Alzheimer's disease: adapting prompting strategies to the patient's cognitive profile. In: Proceedings of the 5th International Conference on PErvasive Technologies Related to Assistive Environments, vol. 3 (2012)

9. Rafferty, Joseph, Chris Nugent, L.C., Qi, J., Dutton, R., Zirk, A., Boye, L.T., Kohn, M., Hellman, R.: NFC based provisioning of instructional videos to assist with instrumental activities of daily living. In: Engineering in Medicine and Biology Society (2014)

10. Cook, D.J., Das, S.K.: How smart are our environments? An updated look at the state of the art. Pervasive Mob. Comput. **3**, 53–73 (2007)

11. Chan, M., Estève, D., Escriba, C., Campo, E.: A review of smart homes- present state and future challenges. Comput. Methods Programs Biomed. **91**, 55–81 (2008)

12. Poland, M.P., Nugent, C.D., Wang, H., Chen, L.: Smart home research: projects and issues. Int. J. Ambient Comput. Intell. **1**, 32–45 (2009)

13. Rashidi, P., Mihailidis, A.: A survey on ambient-assisted living tools for older adults. IEEE J. Biomed. Heal. Inf. **17**, 579–590 (2013)

14. Rafferty, J., Chen, L., Nugent, C., Liu, J.: Goal lifecycles and ontological models for intention based assistive living within smart environments. Comput. Syst. Sci. Eng. **30**, 7–18 (2015)

15. Kerssens, C., Kumar, R., Adams, A.E., Knott, C.C., Matalenas, L., Sanford, J.A., Rogers, W.A.: Personalized technology to support older adults with and without cognitive impairment living at home. Am. J. Alzheimers. Dis. Other Demen. **30**, 85–97 (2015)

16. Hoey, J., Poupart, P., Bertoldi, A.Von, Craig, T., Boutilier, C., Mihailidis, A.: Automated handwashing assistance for persons with dementia using video and a partially observable Markov decision process. Comput. Vis. Image Underst. **114**, 503–519 (2010)

17. Cleland, I., Nugent, C.D., McClean, S.I., Hartin, P.J., Sanders, C., Donnelly, M., Zhang, S., Scotney, B., Smith, K., Norton, M.C., Tschanz, J.T.: Predicting technology adoption in people with dementia; initial results from the TAUT project. In: Pecchia, L., Chen, L.L., Nugent, C., Bravo, J. (eds.) IWAAL 2014. LNCS, vol. 8868, pp. 266–274. Springer, Heidelberg (2014)

18. Meiland, F., Reinersmann, A., Bergvall-Kareborn, B., Craig, D., Moelaert, F., Mulvenna, M., Nugent, C.D., Scully, T., Bengtsson, J., Dröes, R.-M.: COGKNOW: Development of an ICT device to support people with dementia. J. Inf. Technol. Healthc. **5**, 324–334 (2007)

19. Burrows, M., Dutton, R., Schulze, E., Zirk, A.: PIA – Practical Support for Everyday Life Results of the User Tests. In: 2014 Conference on eChallenges e-2014, pp. 1–7 (2014)

20. Rafferty, J., Nugent, C.D., Liu, J., Chen, L.: Automatic summarization of activities depicted in instructional videos by use of speech analysis. In: Pecchia, L., Chen, L.L., Nugent, C., Bravo, J. (eds.) IWAAL 2014. LNCS, vol. 8868, pp. 123–130. Springer, Heidelberg (2014)

21. Chandrasekaran, B., Josephson, J.R., Benjamins, V.R.: What are ontologies, and why do we need them? IEEE Intell. Syst. **14**, 20–26 (1999)

22. Che, H.: A semantic web primer. J. Am. Soc. Inf. Sci. Technol. **57**, 1132 (2006)

Improving the Portability of Ambient Intelligence Systems

Gervasio Varela[✉], Alejandro Paz-Lopez, José A. Becerra,
and Richard J. Duro

Integrated Group for Engineering Research,
University of A Coruña, Ferrol, Spain
{gervasio.varela,alpaz,ronin,richard}@udc.es

Abstract. Ambient Intelligence and Ambient Assisted Living systems are
required to provide a natural user experience, where the interaction is resolved
by using devices and modalities adapted to the user abilities and preferences,
and even to the environment conditions. Because of the variety of devices and
technologies, and the diversity of scenarios, developing these interaction systems is a complicated task. This paper proposes an UI abstraction framework for
the development of AmI and AAL systems that effectively improves the
portability of those systems between different environments. It allows developers to design and implement a single UI capable of being deployed with
different devices and modalities regardless the physical location.

Keywords: User interfaces · Human-computer interaction · Distributed-ui ·
Ambient-intelligence · Ambient-assisted-living

1 Introduction

Ambient Intelligence (AmI) and Ambient Assisted Living (AAL) systems are about
people and their needs. These systems put the users at the center of the focus with the
main goal of improving their quality of life by assisting them in their daily life.

Therefore, in AmI and AAL systems the interaction with the user is a critical aspect
[1]. These systems are expected to provide a natural user experience, where the UI is
blended in the environment [2], with the interaction reduced to the minimal expression,
and using interaction devices and modalities adapted to the user needs and abilities. In
order to achieve this kind of user experience, AmI and AAL developers are usually
required to build the user interfaces (UIs) of their systems by relying on a combination
of different devices distributed in the physical environment [3, 4].

But not only do they have to use different types of devices, coming from different
manufacturers and technologies, in order to build a natural and adapted user interface,
they have to use different interaction modalities (voice, touch, tangible UIs, gestures,
etc.). This leads to a variety of devices, depending on the user abilities and preferences,
and even on the environment conditions [5, 6], due to the fact that the same user
interface will not be perceived as natural by different types of users, in different
environments. For example, a voice-based UI may be a good option for a blind user in

© Springer International Publishing Switzerland 2015
I. Cleland et al. (Eds.): IWAAL 2015, LNCS 9455, pp. 77–88, 2015.
DOI: 10.1007/978-3-319-26410-3_8

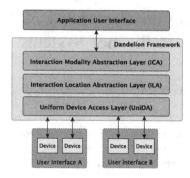

Fig. 1. Block diagram of the Dandelion UI abstraction framework for AmI and AAL systems.

their home, but is probably a poor choice for a deaf user, or even for the blind user in a noisy environment like a crowded street.

Developers, and their code, are exposed to handle all that heterogeneity, and in the end, in order to provide an adequate user experience in different physical environments and with different kinds of users, developers are required to design and implement different user interfaces for each combination of environment and user, thus considerably increasing the complexity, and therefore the costs, of developing AmI and AAL systems.

Looking at the related work, there are two prominent, but generally unrelated, sources of solutions for this problem. On the one hand we have the field of Physical User Interfaces, which has been producing solutions to facilitate the use of physical devices to interact with the user, like the iStuff [3] or EIToolKit [1] frameworks. But these frameworks lack high-level abstraction capabilities, and thus they require the modification of code to port an UI to a new environment where different devices and modalities are required. On the other hand we have UI focused solutions, like Egoki [5], the Multi-Access Service Platform [6] or the Personal Universal Controller [7], which generate tailored graphical user interfaces for the services or devices available in a smart environment. These frameworks are focused on graphical or voice-based UIs, and do not support the interaction with the user through a combination of multi-modal physical devices physically distributed in the environment.

In this paper we present a UI abstraction technology for the development of AmI and AAL systems that effectively improves the portability of those systems between different environments. It does so by elevating the level of decoupling between the developers, their code, and the final modalities and physical devices used to implement the UI for a particular combination of user and environment characteristics. The main idea behind this framework is that developers should be able to design and implement a single UI, and then deploy it with different devices and modalities in different physical locations.

This paper is organized as follows. Section 2 provides a brief overview of the complete abstraction framework. Next, Sects. 3, 4 and 5 describe the three different abstraction levels provided by the framework. In Sect. 6 we present an example of a

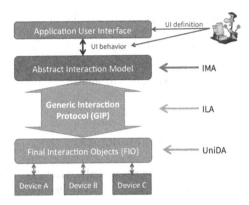

Fig. 2. Overview diagram of the Dandelion architecture.

real AAL user interface implemented with the proposed framework, and finally, in Sect. 7 we present some conclusions.

2 Ambient Intelligence UI Abstraction Framework

The Dandelion framework [9] has been designed as a UI development framework for AmI and AAL systems, with the idea of facilitating the design and implementation of distributed physical UIs, capable of being deployed with different devices in different environments in order to preserve the system's natural interaction constraints.

Figure 1 shows a block diagram of the proposed framework. As can be seen, the framework, establishes three abstraction layers between the application user interface and the different sets of devices that are going to be used for each combination of user and environment characteristics.

First, the Uniform Device Access framework or UniDA [10, 11], presented with more detail in Sect. 3, provides homogenous access to a network of heterogeneous devices. Second, the Interaction Modality Abstraction layer, presented in more detail in Sect. 4, allows developers to use a single API to access any kind of device, regardless of their modalities, functionalities and technologies. And third, the Interaction Location Abstraction Layer, ILA, allows developers to design and implement the UI without knowledge about the physical location of the devices, also enabling the easy connection, at deploy-time of distributed devices to the UI logic.

During deployment time, developers or installers must provide Dandelion with a mapping file that establishes associations between the generic operations of the IMA and the different devices that are going to implement each one of those generic interaction operations.

The combination of the three different abstraction layers constitutes an abstraction framework for AmI and AAL that allows developers to implement the UI at a high level of abstraction, and postpone until deploy-time, the selection of which devices and modalities to use in each use case.

In the next three sections we are going to describe in the detail each one of the Dandelion abstraction layers. First, in Sect. 3, we are going to describe the UniDA abstraction layer. Next, in Sect. 4 the Interaction Modality Abstraction layer, and in Sect. 5 the Interaction Location Abstraction Layer. Finally, in Sect. 6 we are going to present an example of how to use Dandelion to implement a portable UI for an AAL system.

3   Abstraction from Device Technologies

AmI and AAL developers usually rely on embedded devices, like sensors, actuators, or appliances, to build a technologically augmented environment to interact naturally with the user. The market for this kind of devices is very fragmented and very poorly standardized, thus making the provisioning of support for the wide diversity of devices than can be found in different scenarios very difficult.

In order to alleviate this problem, we have designed and implemented the UniDA framework (Uniform Device Access, UniDA), which provides a distributed abstraction layer to facilitate and reduce the costs of developing applications that require the use of multiple heterogeneous physical devices. UniDA homogenizes the APIs of different devices that provide the same functionality, thus reducing the number of technologies, APIs and protocols that the developer and application must know.

Figure 3 compares the vision of the hardware devices that an application has when it uses a set of heterogeneous physical devices with and without UniDA. The top half shows the vision of applications that use the devices directly, using their specific APIs and protocols. The bottom half shows the vision of applications that use UniDA to interact with physical devices.

In the first case, the applications see different islands of devices and they have to include particular logic to interact with each specific technology and device available in the network, thus complicating the development process and making the addition of new devices more difficult. In the second case, the applications see a homogeneous network

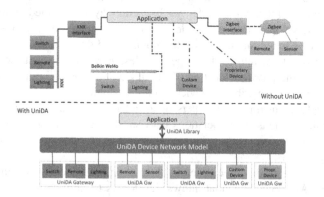

Fig. 3. UniDA changes the vision of the network of devices, from a set of isolated islands depending on the technology, to a homogeneous network where all the devices are accessible through the same medium.

of devices, where a common protocol and a small set of APIs allow access to the devices independently of their underlying technologies and APIs. This way, the applications do not require knowledge of specific technologies, and new devices can be easily added without requiring any, or at most minimal, modifications of the application logic.

Conceptually, the UniDA framework is composed of two main elements with many possible practical implementations. On the one hand, a common device network model for the description of an instrumentation network and its devices and functionalities. On the other hand, a distributed operation protocol for the communication between the different distributed elements of the system.

The device network model provides the homogeneous vision of the heterogeneous network of devices. It takes the similarities between the different existing technologies and builds a generic concept model representing the essential characteristics of every possible device. This concept model, inspired in the DogOnt ontology [12], in combination with a series of generic APIs, one for each type of device, are the only knowledge of the devices that developers need to have, allowing client applications to access the functionality of the available devices without using any specific APIs.

The distributed communication protocol allows the interaction between the client applications and the devices deployed throughout the environment, encapsulating the particular network protocols required by each device.

For illustration and demonstration purposes we have provided a reference implementation of UniDA using the J2SE platform. This implementation is composed of two main software components, complemented with some configuration tools:

- The UniDA Library. A software library that implements the device network model and provides a simplified façade to obtain information about the network of devices (devices available, their functionalities, device state information, etc.), and to remotely execute the different generic operations of each device-type API.
- The UniDA Gateways. Proxy-like components, one for each supported device technology, receive the UniDA generic operations (through the implementation of the distributed operation protocol) and are in charge of translating them into specific concepts and operations of a particular technology, using specific APIs and protocols for each device. These gateways are usually deployed on remotely accessible embedded hardware devices that are physically connected to the end devices or to other instrumentation network technologies.

As has been seen, UniDA reduces the number of concepts and APIs that an AmI and AAL developer must know and manage in their applications, thus effectively reducing the complexity and cost of building applications that use heterogeneous devices, and furthermore facilitating the use of devices from distinct technologies in different cases.

4 Abstraction from Interaction Modalities

The Abstract Interaction Model provides one unique API of generic interaction concepts/operations which, inspired in the Abstract UI Model of the UsiXML project [8], is composed of a very reduced set of just five different high-level interaction operations: input, output, action, request focus and selection. And, as can be seen in Fig. 2, by implementing the UI control logic on top of the Abstract Interaction Model API, developers and their code are isolated from the specific knowledge and particular characteristics of the different devices used to physically interact with the user.

In Dandelion developers are required to use the Abstract Interaction Model with two different purposes. On the one hand, developers must design and specify the abstract user interface, which consists in a specification of the user interaction requirements or necessities of an application. This is, how many inputs, outputs, selections, actions, etc., the UI needs to perform, and how all those elements are related together. This abstract UI can be described using the XML language.

On the other hand, they must implement the UI behavior, again by using an implementation of the Abstract Interaction Model API (we have provided one reference implementation using JAVA). This behavior logic indicates when to perform an input or output defined in the abstract UI, or what to do when a user performs an action or a selection.

For inputs, actions and selections, developers can specify callback objects associated to the elements of the abstract UI. Those callbacks will be automatically called by Dandelion when the user interacts with the devices that are associated to those abstract interaction operations.

With regards to outputs, focus request and showing selections, the logic code just issues those operations using the Abstract Interaction Model API and Dandelion will be in charge of executing the required specific operations in the final devices in order to perform the requested operation.

This way, developers are able to design and code the UI without any knowledge about the particular interaction modalities, technologies, and devices that are going to be used to implement each particular interaction operation. It will be at deployment time, as we will see in the next section, when the final implementation of the UI, using real physical devices, will be carried out, thus enabling developers to reuse the same UI code with different physical implementations of the UI.

5   Abstraction from Physical Distribution of Devices

The goal of the Interaction Location Abstraction layer is to isolate developers, and UI code, from the particular set of distributed devices that are going to be used in each deployment.

For that purpose, as displayed in Fig. 2, we have introduced the Generic Interaction Protocol (GIP) [13], which is in charge of connecting the generic interaction elements of the abstract UI with the end devices represented by a set of Final Interaction Objects. It does so by physically transporting the generic interaction operations, coming from the Abstract Interaction Model, to the end devices.

Once deployed, the operation of a Dandelion UI is as follows. The application interaction logic executes generic interaction operations using the Abstract Interaction Model façade, which translates those operations into their respective messages in the GIP. Next, it sends those messages over the network using the GIP, which will transport them to the devices that will perform the real interaction with the user, and vice-versa, when a user performs some particular interaction with a device, it will generate a new GIP message and sent it over the network to the application. The operations will be received by the Abstract Interaction Model, which will notify the application using the adequate callback object.

In order to transport the messages to the adequate devices the GIP needs to know which devices are going to realize each one of the interaction operations defined in the abstract UI. For that purpose, developers or installers have to provide, at deployment-time, a mapping file associating the different abstract interaction operations to particular end devices available in the environment.

This process of generating a new mapping file for a new deployment is, in reality, the process of implementing a new user interface for a particular combination of user characteristics and environment conditions. While, the UI definition and behavior logic remains untouched, the particular interaction modalities and devices can change dramatically from one use case to a another, just by providing a new mapping file.

The end devices that receive the GIP operations from the network, as previously introduced, are represented in by the Final Interaction Objects concept. The FIOs are software abstractions of physical devices. They are in charge of encapsulating the particular behavior, technologies and APIs of each device behind the generic interaction interface of the GIP. When a FIO receives an interaction operation, it must translate it to a particular set of operations in the specific APIs of its supported device. For example, if we execute an output operation and it is received by two different FIOs, one using a voice synthesizing system, and one using a display with a graphical UI, the first one will show the output message by synthesizing the text as voice, for example using the Festival API, while the other will show the message by using a graphical toolkit API.

In our reference implementation the GIP is implemented using a messaging protocol that supports the publisher/subscriber paradigm. Each component of the system, essentially the Abstract Interaction Model façade and the FIOs, act as a publisher or subscriber of GIP events, depending on the situation. Therefore, on the one hand, the FIOs will act as publishers of GIP events generated from actions of the user, while the Abstract Interaction Model will act as a subscriber of those events. On the other hand, the Abstract Interaction Model will act as a publisher of events generated from operations requested from the UI behavior logic and the FIOs as subscribers of those events.

The FIOs establish the final connection between the abstract side of the UI and the real and physical interaction with the user. Because of that, it is a key aspect for Dandelion to have available as many FIOs as possible, supporting many different devices and technologies. This way, building new UIs for a new use case will be very easy, just a matter of specifying a new mapping file without requiring any new coding. Dandelion uses UniDA to provide integrated support for many different technologies (KNX home automation, Philips HUE, and many others).

Nevertheless, in some cases, developers will be required to implement specific FIOs, for example when a custom graphical UI is required, a new technology needs to be used, or when a custom device is required for the UI. In order to facilitate the implementation of these new FIOs, our reference implementation of the GIP uses STOMP as messaging protocol and JSON for data coding, thus facilitating the implementation of FIOs in almost any programming language and software platform.

6   Use Case Example

In this section we are going to present an example of how Dandelion can be used in a real AAL system. Our research group has been participating in the development of a home-care assistant system for elderly people named OMNI Virtual Assistant. Its objective is to improve the self-sufficiency of elderly people in their daily life at home, and it uses Dandelion to support the variable interaction requirements of different users.

The system is designed to be embedded in the user's home and provide them with three core functionalities: tele-presence service through video-calls with family, friends or tele-care centers; remote health monitoring; and daily routine management.

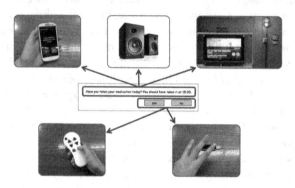

Fig. 4. The three generic operations of the Notification UI (output and two actions) can be implemented by using very different interaction modalities and devices.

```
<aui:AbstractUIModel>
    <aui:AbstractInteractionUnit id="NotificationDialog" ... >
        <aui:DataInputOutputFacet id="NotificationMessage" minCardinality="1"
            maxCardinality="1" dataFormat="string" inputSupport="false"        outputSupport="true" ... >
            <aui:dataType>text</aui:dataType>
        </aui:DataInputOutputFacet>
        <aui:TriggerFacet id="YesAction">
            <aui:triggerType>operation</aui:triggerType>
        </aui:TriggerFacet>
        <aui:TriggerFacet id="NoAction">
            <aui:triggerType>operation</aui:triggerType>
        </aui:TriggerFacet>
    </aui:AbstractInteractionUnit>
</aui:AbstractUIModel>
```

Fig. 5. XML code required for the definition the abstract UI of the OMNI Notification UI.

It is executed in a set-top-box shaped device connected to a TV screen, where the different functionalities are naturally integrated in the TV workflow as new channels. One channel dedicated to call each family member, friend or caregiver, and one channel per doctor or health monitoring application.

The interaction subsystem is kept deliberately simple to facilitate its use by elderly people with very different levels of knowledge and experience in information technology. The system operates in a proactive way, asking questions when it is necessary to perform actions. This way, users interact with the system exclusively by changing channels and by answering questions using a 'Yes' or a 'No' action.

The TV screen is the primary output device, and a remote controller, with only five buttons, is the primary input device. While this setup should be enough for many users, elderly people represent a quite heterogeneous group of people with very different abilities [14]. There may be people with visual disabilities for whom the TV screen will be a poor output channel. There may be people with motor or psychic disabilities and problems to use the remote controller, etc. In order to accommodate this large diversity of abilities, OMNI requires a multimodal user interface where each user is able to interact with the system using the combination of devices that better fits her requirements.

In order to reduce the costs, in time and effort, of building such multimodal and portable UI, the OMNI system relies on the Dandelion framework.

6.1   Building the OMNI Notification User Interface

Due to space limitations, in this paper we are going to focus on a particular functionality of OMNI, the Notification subsystem. It is in charge of notifying events to the users, like for example when to take some medication, when to visit the doctor, when a call is being received, or even when someone is ringing at the door.

As previously introduced in this paper, the first step when using Dandelion is to design the user interface at the abstract level, specifying the different interaction operations that the UI needs to perform.

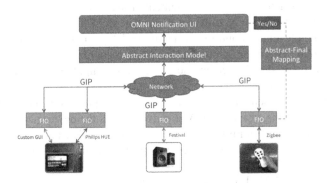

Fig. 6. The OMNI can be deployed with different FIOs (devices) for different use cases.

The OMNI Notification UI, as shown in Fig. 4, resembles a message dialog in graphical user interface. It must use an output operation to show a message to the user, and two different action operations, to receive the response of the user, 'Yes' or 'No'. But in the case of OMNI, these tree generic interaction operations must be implemented in very different ways, using different interaction modalities and devices, according the characteristics of the user and the environment in which the system is deployed. The definition of this UI is done using XML, as shown in Fig. 5, where as can be seen, there are three main elements definied. One DataInputOutputFacet for the output message, and two TriggerFacet for the two actions.

Once the abstract UI has been described, the next step is to implement the UI behaviour logic. In this case, it consists in the implementation of two callback objects to execute the actions associated to the 'Yes' and 'No' TriggerFacets, and the execution of the *showOutput(Object data)* method of the Abstract Interaction Model façade in when it is necessary to show a notification to the user.

At this point, the UI is designed and implemented, and we can already deploy it in different environments, as we will see in the next subsection.

6.2 Deploying the OMNI Notification UI in Different Scenarios

After the implementation of the UI behavior logic, the next step is to deploy it in different scenarios, with different combinations of user abilities and environments conditions. It will be at this point when we will have to select which particular devices we are going to use for each generic interaction operation, which in the case of the OMNI Notification UI, are the output message, and the two actions.

As previously introduced, this deployment is achieved by specifying a mapping file between the generic operations described in the abstract UI, and a set of FIOs that are available in the deployment environment.

Figure 6 shows various possible examples of deployments for the OMNI UI. As can be seen, the UI logic uses the Abstract Interaction Model, which relies on the GIP to transport the generic interaction operations to a set of different FIOs, that will be in charge of using specific devices to interact with the user. In this case we can see four different devices, which allow us to implement at least three different versions of the OMNI Notification UI for three different cases. The default usage scenario, using the TV as output and the remote controller as input. An UI for blind user, using the Festival voice synthesizing system for output, and a gesture recognizer for the input. And a UI for a deaf user, using the TV screen and some colored lights for the output, and the remote controller for input.

Ideally, the deployment of a Dandelion UI will require only the definition of a mapping file. That is the case if UniDA already supports the devices we need, or if we have already implemented a FIO for the devices, for example from a previous project. But sometimes, we have to use custom devices or custom graphical UIs, so we have to implement our own FIOs.

In the case of the OMNI, for a default user and a deaf user we are using a custom graphical UI as the output device, and a custom remote controller for input. Thus we have had to implement two different FIOs. If the FIOs are implemented in Java, Dandelion provides a small framework to facilitate their implementation, otherwise, developers must implement a STOMP subscriber/publisher application, and send/receive GIP messages encoded using JSON. These two technologies are widely supported by many different platforms and very easy to use, so it is quite simple to implement FIOs in other technologies than Java.

In our case, the display FIO is implemented, using Java, as a software-only interaction resource. It creates a semi-translucent window and superimposes it over the OMNI channel screens during a specified amount of time. It supports only one output interaction facet with string type data.

Regarding the remote controller FIO, we have used UniDA in order to make its implementation easier. Thus, a remote UniDA gateway implements the physical connection with the remote controller using Zigbee, and the FIO uses the UniDA library to interact with the gateway.

As previously introduced, for deaf users we are using an additional device to perform the output of the message redundantly. It is a Philips HUE colored light, it is already supported by UniDA, so we don't need to implement a new FIO, and it notifies the presence of a notification by outputting different colors depending on the type of the output messages. These lights could be deployed in different places of the home, so that a deaf user can know when there are new notifications without looking at the TV in the living room.

Finally, for a blind user, the OMNI notification UI uses a FIO implemented using the Festival Speech Synthesis System, and a gesture recognizer FIO, implemented using the Open Natural Interface (OpenNI) framework for cameras with depth sensors for the input. It receive events of hand and arm gestures detected through the depth sensor cameras, and then translates those gestures to GIP action events, to send them to the Abstract Interaction Model.

7   Conclusions

This paper has presented a distributed UI abstraction technology that uses a model-driven approach to support the development of AmI and AAL systems. Using this technology, developers are able to design and implement user interfaces by declaratively describing their interaction requirements using high-level interaction concepts and operations and using a single API to access any kind of interaction device, regardless of their functionalities and modalities. Furthermore, the UIs are designed without knowledge about the underlying heterogeneous technologies in charge of controlling the networks of physical devices. This characteristics allow UI developers to postpone until deploy-time the selection of which interaction devices and modalities to use in each scenario, thus applications can be more easily deployed on a variety of scenarios and migrated between them. Nevertheless, the framework could be improved with the addition of learning capabilities in order to produce more customized UIs, using inferred feedback information from the users.

Acknowledgment. This work has been partially funded by the Xunta de Galicia and European Regional Development Funds under grants GRC 2013-050 and redTEIC network (R2014/037).

References

1. Blythe, M.A., Monk, A.F., Doughty, K.: Socially dependable design: The challenge of ageing populations for HCI. Interact. Comput. **17**, 672–689 (2005)
2. Kranz, M., Holleis, P., Schmidt, A.: Embedded interaction: interacting with the internet of things. In: IEEE Internet Computing (2010)
3. Ballagas, R., Ringel, M., Stone, M., Borchers, J.: iStuff: a physical user interface toolkit for ubiquitous computing environments. In: Proceedings of the SIGCHI Conference on Human Factors in Computing Systems, pp. 537–544. ACM (2003)
4. Xie, L., Antle, A.N., Motamedi, N.: Are tangibles more fun? In: Proceedings of the 2nd International Conference on Tangible and Embedded Interaction - TEI 2008, pp. 191–198 (2008)
5. Miñón, R., Abascal, J.: Supportive adaptive user interfaces inside and outside the home. In: Ardissono, L., Kuflik, T. (eds.) UMAP Workshops 2011. LNCS, vol. 7138, pp. 320–334. Springer, Heidelberg (2012)
6. Blumendorf, M., Feuerstack, S., Albayrak, S.: Multimodal user interfaces for smart environments: the multi-access service platform. Computer 478–479 (2008)
7. Nichols, J., Myers, B.A., Rothrock, B., Nichols, J.: UNIFORM : automatically generating consistent remote control user interfaces. In: Proceedings of the SIGCHI Conference on Human Factors in Computing Systems (2006)
8. Vanderdonckt, J., Limbourg, Q., Michotte, B., Bouillon, L., Trevisan, D., Florins, M.: USIXML : a user interface description language for specifying multimodal user interfaces the reference framework used for multi-directional UI development. In: Proceedings of W3C Workshop on Multimodal Interaction WMI, pp. 19–20 (2004)
9. Dandelion framework. https://github.com/GII/dandelion
10. Varela, G., Paz-Lopez, A., Becerra, J.A., Vazquez-Rodriguez, S., Duro, R.J.: UniDA: uniform device access framework for human interaction environments. Sensors **11**(10), 9361–9392 (2011). MDPI
11. UniDA framework. http://www.gii.udc.es/unida
12. Bonino, D., Corno, F.: DogOnt - ontology modeling for intelligent domotic environments. In: Sheth, A.P., Staab, S., Dean, M., Paolucci, M., Maynard, D., Finin, T., Thirunarayan, K. (eds.) ISWC 2008. LNCS, vol. 5318, pp. 790–803. Springer, Heidelberg (2008)
13. Varela, G., Paz-Lopez, A., Becerra, J.A., Duro, R.J.: The generic interaction protocol: Increasing portability of distributed physical user interfaces. Rom. J. Hum. Comput. Interact. **6**(3), 249–268 (2013)
14. Brault, M.W.: Americans with disabilities. Technical report, US Census Bureau (2012)

Promoting Healthy Nutrition Behavior Using Mobile Devices and Ubiquitous Computing

Felipe Besoain[1,2,3](✉), Antoni Perez-Navarro[2,3], Felipe Ojeda[1],
and Jose Antonio Reyes-Suarez[1]

[1] Escuela de Ingeniería en Bioinformática, Universidad de Talca,
Avenida Lircay s/n, Talca, Chile
{fbesoain,fojeda,jareyes}@utalca.cl
[2] Estudis d'Informática, Multimedia i Telecomunicacio,
Universitat Oberta de Catalunya, Rambla del Poblenou 156, Barcelona, Spain
[3] Internet Interdisciplinary Institute (IN3), Universitat Oberta de Catalunya,
Av. Carl Friedrich Gauss, 5, Castelldefels, Barcelona, Spain
{fbesoain,aperezn}@uoc.edu

Abstract. Excessive weight and obesity are worldwide problems that are related to a variety of health issues. Several methods have been utilized recently to educate people and communities about topics related to nutrition behaviors. How can we develop educational mechanisms for healthy behaviors, focusing on a target group and their context? To reply to this question we developed a ubiquitous software called Ubinut, with the objective of sending messages through mobile devices. The software sends messages supervised by a nutritionist. These messages are related with specific contexts. To test the software we conducted a feasibility test with 40 random university students. During the trial period we received nearly 700 evaluations of the messages. With our first findings we developed a second version of the software including geofencing, called Geonut. The main contribution of this work is the launching of healthy messages when the users are more likely to make poor nutritional decisions.

Keywords: Ubiquitous computing · Geofencing · Mobile devices · Ehealth

1 Introduction

Excessive weight and obesity are worldwide problems associated with a variety of health issues. These problems are directly related to the current lifestyle of the population [1]. People have fast paced lives, constantly on the run, with little time to devote to buying and preparing healthy meals. In addition, they receive limited education or information about nutrition.

Chile is one of the countries where this problem of excessive weight and obesity has risen, mainly during the last 10 years. In 2005, 69 % of males 30–100 years of age had a Body Mass Index (BMI) over 25; in 2010, this rose to 74.1 % and in 2015, it reached 78.6 %. This is of great concern since a BMI over 25 indicates that a

© Springer International Publishing Switzerland 2015
I. Cleland et al. (Eds.): IWAAL 2015, LNCS 9455, pp. 89–100, 2015.
DOI: 10.1007/978-3-319-26410-3_9

person is overweight. Females showed the same tendency: in 2005 the average was 72.0 %, in 2010 it was 76.7 % and in 2015 it grew to 80.5 % [3].

A national health survey (conducted by the Chilean Health Secretary) confirmed this situation, showing that 67 % of the population in Chile is overweight. This problem has been accompanied by a steady rise in several diseases and health conditions in the Chilean population such as diabetes (9,4 %), high cholesterol (38,5 %), sedentary lifestyles (88,6 %), high blood pressure (26,9 %) and high risk of heart disease (17,7 %) [4].

Several methods have been utilized recently to educate people and communities about topics related to nutrition behaviors. Some noteworthy examples are: multimedia campaigns for health promotion and prevention [5], use of online forums, websites [6,7], social-media (Facebook, Tweeter) [10], and mobile phones, among others [8,9]. Furthermore, information and communication technologies, especially mobile devices, are currently deeply integrated into people's lives [20].

In the present paper, in contrast to the previously mentioned examples, we propose an approximation based upon the principles of ubiquitous computing in order to contextualize the educational measures in users' daily routines, using mobile devices and their potential communication technologies.

Our goal is to use these technologies to create a natural, non-invasive entry point for educating the target users and promoting healthy nutrition behaviors based on users' specific contexts [11,12]. With this in mind, we developed two applications for Android smartphones called Ubinut and Geonut.

Ubinut was developed in the first phase of the study. It delivers messages based on users' local contexts to promote healthy nutrition behavior. Messages are posted by a nutritionist who decides which messages to post and when they have to be delivered. To increase the effectiveness of messages, we applied concepts of ubiquitous computing [13], which means that the software is omnipresent, but imperceptible to users. Thus, users forget about the presence of the application, so that messages are received unexpectedly. In addition, we are very careful with the number of messages sent in one day, since previous experiences [8] show that users are more likely to ignore messages if they receive more than one per day, because they are overwhelmed by them.

Ubinut also incorporates the possibility for users to rate each of the received notifications, as well as send questions back to a nutritionist. With this functionality, the nutritionist gains real time perceptions from the users. To test the software, a study was carried out. It was conducted among 40 university students who volunteered to evaluate Ubinut.

Geonut was developed in the second phase of the study. It is a fork of Ubinut based on the feedback from the test. The main novelty is the incorporation of georeferenced points of interest (POIs) related to fast food restaurants, cafeterias and pubs, among others. The main objective of this feature is to send a healthy notification, automatically, when users are in risk zones where they are more likely to make poor nutritional decisions. This approach is based on geofencing: detecting and considering the user's presence in a defined area [21].

This document is structured as follows: Sect. 2 describes the motivation of the project as well as the Ubinut and Geonut applications; Sect. 3 presents our findings from the test carried out with a volunteer group; finally, the document closes with concluding remarks and an outlook towards further work.

2 Motivation of the Project

The main question to be addressed in this work is how to make people think about healthy nutrition while going about their daily routine. To answer this question, we propose to launch alerts and recommendations via users' smartphones, based on their context [12].

We define three main contexts:

- Time: Critical times during the day when users can make healthy, or unhealthy, nutritional decisions.[1]
- Weather: Conditions that affect opportunities for exercise or other healthy behaviors. For example, on a sunny day, users might receive a notification about the benefits of walking or the importance of staying hydrated, messages that would not be sent on a rainy day.
- Geographic location (geofencing): Risk zones where users are more likely to make poor nutritional decisions due to high exposure to publicity that promotes unhealthy food. Examples of these zones are food courts in malls, supermarkets, city streets with food carts or fast food windows.

The present project was divided into two phases. The first phase, Ubinut, takes into consideration the previously defined contexts of time and weather. The second phase, Geonut, adds the context of geographic location (geofencing).

We take into consideration the contexts described above, as well as the external variables of typical foods and cultural behavior. These contexts and variables create a unique set of circumstances for users in their daily routines that are reflected in the messages. For instance, we do not send messages with topics related to breakfast at lunch time, because they would be out of context. Furthermore, we do not promote, for example, playing an outdoor sport on a day when it was raining or the weather didn't allow it; instead we promoted a different healthy habit. It is important to note that, instead of focusing on prohibition or warning messages, we focus on giving a healthier option to users.

One clarifying example of the use of this context and timing is the placement of shocking images on cigarette boxes. These images reflect the risk of smoking, showing for example a photo of damaged lungs. Thus, when smokers reach for a cigarette, they receive a strong, visual preventive message. Our software intends to do the same, alerting users at a specific moments. Nevertheless, our software goes a step further and even collects the users' perceptions at that time.

---

[1] These times are culturally specific. For example, in Chile, lunch is most commonly eaten at 1:00 p.m., whereas in other countries it might be eaten either earlier or later. Also, lunch is the biggest meal in Chile, rather than dinner.

The omnipresence and imperceptibility of this notification service is a defining characteristic of ubiquitous computing [2]. The main advantage of this system is that users are not conscious of the fact that their smartphones are being used as health care devices. The key is then to determine how a smartphone could trigger the launch of a message based on these contexts. To understand how we address these questions, we present two general use cases.

2.1   Use Cases

To understand how the software behaves, we present two general use cases: the first corresponds to Ubinut and the second to Geonut. These use cases briefly explain each process and its interaction with the various solution components, which will also be outlined in this section. The first use case triggers a message when the application detects a new message in the database of the system; the second use case triggers a message when the user is in a risk zone (defined above).

Use case: General use of the system (Fig. 1)
Actor(s): Android Application, Information server.
Purpose: To detect a message stored in the information server and notify the user with it.
Summary: This use case begins when the nutritionist sends appropriate healthy messages through a Website. The *notification service* of the Android application detects a new message on the information server. The message is downloaded using a RestFul service. Then the message is communicated to the user, through the *notification manager*. The user receives the message and then has the opportunity to rank it using a system of one to five stars; furthermore, the user can send questions to the nutritionist, and the nutritionist can respond to these questions.
Preconditions: (1) The smartphone should be connected to the Internet; (2) a nutritionist should post a new message on the web system taking into consideration the previously defined contexts.

Use case: General detection of a risk zone
Actor(s): Application, Information server.
Purpose: To detect a risk zone at an appropriate time and notify the user with a message.
Summary: This use case begins when the notification service detects a POI near the user's current position. From a local database, a message is communicated to the user through the *notification manager*.
Preconditions: (1) The application has been downloaded and stored messages for the user from the information server; (2) the user has configured the smartphone's GPS, allowing the application to read data from it; (3) the application has downloaded and stored the risk zones from the information server.

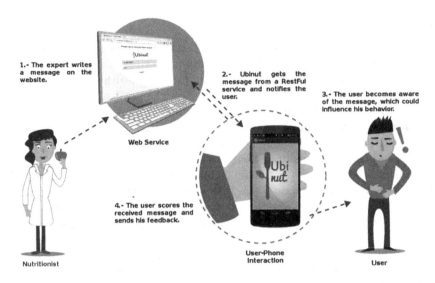

Fig. 1. Graphical representation of the solution for use case: "General use of the system".

Based on the general use cases, we take into consideration the following aspects:

- Creation and storage of the messages
- Development of a web service for multiple clients
- Creation and storage of the geodata sources (risk zones)

2.2 Software Description

The system was developed following the System Development methodology as a Design and Creation research strategy [16]. To implement a distributed system that is scalable and independent, we used principles of Representational State Transfer (REST) architectural style for distributed hypermedia systems. REST defines a set of architectural principles focusing on a system's resources. The various states of the resources are addressed and transferred using the Hypertext Transfer Protocol (HTTP/1.1) and Uniform Resource Identifiers (URI). The main advantage of this approximation is that it allows the system to interact with any client capable of implementing HTTP protocol. The architecture of the solution is available on [15], and it is divided into three main layers (Presentation, Business, Data layer).

In the following subsections, Ubinut and Geonut will be described with their respective components. It is important to note that Geonut uses Ubinut's architecture, but adds new features and modules using the same principles of RESTFul service of communication with the server.

2.3   Ubinut

As described in the general use case, users install the application, which then works in the background as a service that is imperceptible to the users. Through a website, the Ubinut nutritionist sends appropriate healthy messages taking into account the context in which they will have the greatest effect. The users receive the message and then have the opportunity to rank it using a system of one to five stars; furthermore, users can send questions back to the nutritionist and the nutritionist can respond to these questions. Both the ranking of the messages and the questions from users are saved on a web server.

The Ubinut system has three main components: the Ubinut Application, the web interface and the database. The first component, the Ubinut Application, works in the background as a service on Android smartphones. This means that users do not have to open the application to make it run, see it or get any information from it. Rather, it is running all the time. Thus, the application is able to receive ubiquitous messages from the web interface. We get new messages from the server on the smartphones at any time. Another feature of the application is that it allows users to send questions to the nutritionist in charge of the study; then, the nutritionist can review and answer the questions through the web interface, which is the second component.

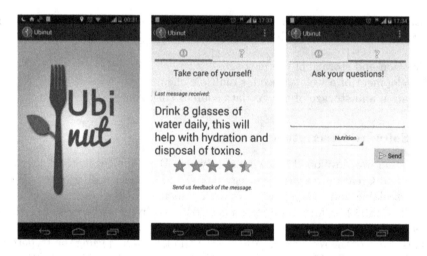

Fig. 2. Images of Ubinut. From left to right: the opening image of the application, an example of a received message and the user's evaluation, and the section in which users can ask the nutritionist questions.

The web interface is a website that allows the nutritionist to post a message in reply to the questions that users ask. This message is then stored in the database, which is the third component. More specifically, when the nutritionist posts a message on the website, all the smartphones will recognize the message as new, and will deliver it to the owner. Furthermore, the database stores users' perceptions of the received messages. This means, once users receive a notification, that the application prompts them to score the message on a scale from 1 to 5; and this information is then stored in the database. This allows the nutritionist to get perceptions in real time and analyze the data for future studies. Figure 2 shows a message on the mobile device and the web interface of the system.

2.4 Geonut

The Geonut system has been developed taking into consideration our findings from the Ubinut test with users. Details about the test are described in the results section. Geonut is a solution for the general use case: *General detection of a risk zone (geofencing)*. We use the same architecture as in Ubinut, but adds the functionality of launching messages automatically when the user is getting close to some kind of POI.

The risk zones come from two different sources: (1) Private source: the data layer on the server side, where we store private POI corresponding to places such as restaurants, cafeterias, and ice cream stores, among others (usually a small set of POIs); and (2) Public source: from a RESTFul service of OpenStreetMap [17], where we download all public POI related to food, pubs, cafeteria, etc. (usually a large set of POIs). In summary, the main difference between these two sources is that the first is private whereas the second is public, taking information from OpenStreetMap.[2]

Working with geolocation has two main drawbacks: (1) GPS must be active and it reduces battery duration; and (2) internet access must be available in order to download and update maps and a huge amount of information must be downloaded. With respect to the first drawback, two strategies were applied to save battery life. First, the user can configure how often the GPS sensor is polled, for example every 3, 5 or 12 h. Second, to maximize the efficiency of the GPS use, if when the GPS sensor is polled, no location can be established with high accuracy, then the GPS is put on standby for one hour (since it is assumed that the user is in an indoor area). To solve the second drawback, Geonut downloads the information related to the POIs nearby every user once the application is installed and the smartphone is connected to the internet. All this information is stored in a local database. Thus, future queries of the POIs do not need internet access. For both kinds of sources (public and private), the service downloads data from a defined perimeter around the user's position. The POIs are received through a RESTFul service on the client side, and every datum is saved in a local SQLlite Database.

Geonut adds a service to the Ubinut system that also runs in background. This new service obtains the geoposition of the user and compares it with the local database in order to detect if the user is inside a risk zone (a risk zone consists of a POI and a surrounding circle, with a defined radius).

If the user is within a risk zone, the user is notified through the *notification manager* with a previously stored message. The user will also have the chance to score the received message for future analysis.

---

[2] The users can set this source in the preferences section of the application.

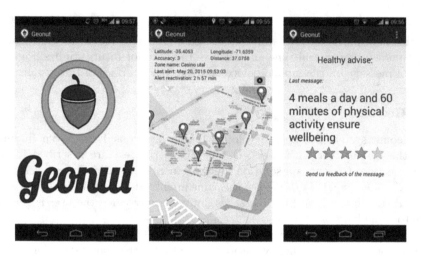

Fig. 3. Images of Geonut. From left to right: the opening image of the application, section in which users can see a map with the risk zones nearby them (we also show the latitude and longitude of the nearest POI and the date of the last message received), and an example of a received message and the user's evaluation.

In a general context, users will go about their normal routine and the Geonut application will automatically detect (through the detection service) when they are at risk of falling into temptation of eating unhealthy food by being inside of a risk zone. The timing of the notification is very important because users are in a moment in which they could make a poor nutrition decision. Moreover, users do not expect that the notification will arrive at that moment, since they are unaware of the application because it runs in background. Therefore, the information is presented ubiquitously based on that context.

Figure 3 shows a message on the mobile device, and a mapview with the POI or risk zones of the system.

3   Results

The next step of the present work is to test the effectiveness of promoting healthy nutrition habits through contextualized messages delivered via smartphone. The test has been carried out with the Ubinut application. The study was designed according to the recommendations suggested by several reports for medical or therapeutic like interventions as in [18, 19], specially focused on practicality issues of applying such a ubiquitous system.

Forty volunteer university students were enrolled to participate actively in the feasibility evaluation of the Ubinut system. Ninety-five percent of the participants declared that they utilized social networks through their smartphones frequently (at least twice a day). Their age was between 18 and 28 years. Seventy percent of them were women. The Body Mass Index (BMI) distribution among participants was 78 % between 18,5 and 24,9 and 22 % more than 25. Even though most of them had an under-risk BMI level, it is important to consider that the Ubinut system aims to have a preventive role more than a remedial one.

In the feasibility evaluation, one nutritionist participated, writing the messages and responding to student questions. The nutritionist responded to the questions within 24 h.

The study had a duration of 40 days; we delivered a total of 40 messages through the system (one per day) with different nutrition information tips. The messages were designed according to the specific context of the users, considering for instance the season of the year when the study was applied and public policy guidelines: (i) we took advantage of the occurrence of the national independence holidays in Chile, when people usually increase their food intake significantly and eat a great amount and variety of typical Chilean food, which includes the excessive consumption of fatty meat and alcoholic beverages. On these days special messages were designed and sent to users considering specific nutritional tips about this; and (ii), during the 40 day period we delivered a series of 11 messages closely related to a document prepared by the Chilean Government with healthy living tips, called the "Food Guide for the Population" [14].

During the trial period we received 699 evaluations from users, which rated the different messages on a 1-to-5 scale, obtaining an average of nearly 17 responses a day. The mean of the ratings received during the whole period was 3,89 indicating that the information sent to participants was highly rated in general. It is important to highlight those messages scored with the highest rating by the participants, considering only those with scores above average plus one standard deviation. These messages are described in Table 1. We noticed that messages delivered on national independence days (17th and 18th of September) were among the highly scored. This shows that users seem to appreciate messages with contextualized information with the time they are sent. Particularly, in this case the messages were associated with traditional foods and local traditions that take place during this period.

Regarding the sent messages related to the Chilean Government Food Guide, interestingly, we found that 7 from the 11 tips contained in this guide were among the highly rated messages. This finding allows us to assess the real impact that the public nutritional guidelines have on participants, which seems to provide a positive opinion about them. It is noteworthy that only 50 % of the participants declared to know about these guidelines previous to the feasibility study.

To assess the impact of using the Ubinut system, a survey was applied to all participants before and after the feasibility study was developed. This was done in order to identify potential changes in behavior, attitudes and knowledge about nutrition and healthy living. The results of the surveys suggest that participants seem in general to improve their knowledge about healthy food and healthy life habits. In most of the analyzed topics, among 15 % to 40 % more participants declared to have a certain level of knowledge after using the Ubinut system.

Based on the feedback from users, two points of interest were identified: (1) the time when messages were received, (2) the location where messages were received.

As we proposed earlier, timing is the key for a message to have a positive impact on the users. The Ubinut system delivers the messages through a

Table 1. Messages sent by the system scored with the highest rating by the participants. Messages sources: N = Ubinut nutritionist, G = Government guide.

Message sent "txt"	Average scoring
1 hour of aerobics burns between 270 and 350 calories (N)	4,6
To stay hydrated, drink six to eight glasses of water a day. Water is essential to maintain body temperature and fluid balance (N)	4,6
Take care of your heart avoiding fried and fatty food such as sausages and mayonnaise. Consumption of saturated fat is the main risk factor for cardiovascular disease (G)	4,5
Barbecues and sausages must be combined with salads and leafy green vegetables, not potatoes or bread (N)	4,5
Traditional dances are also considered as aerobic exercise. If you dance an hour, you are burning the equivalent to a *choripan* (type of fatty hot dog) hot dog or a glass of *mote* con *huesillos* (a high sugar beverage) (N)	4,4

RESTFul service, and therefore the smartphone needs to be connected to the internet in order to receive the message. If the smartphone is not connected at the time the message is sent, then the user will get the message as soon as it gets connected. However, the issue of being connected was minor since the target group was University students that spent most of their time on campus, which is fully covered with wireless internet connection. An important improvement that was noted is related to the places where users could receive a message. There is a special context in which users could make decisions about healthy eating. This context is when they are going to eat or pass places such as a cafeteria, supermarket, fast food windows, etc. In all these places, because of the publicity and advertisements, users could make unhealthy decisions. In the motivation section, we described this situation as the Geographic location context (geofencing).

Taking into consideration these issues and improvements, we developed Geonut. This includes the *geographic location context (geofencing)* as a key feature. Geonut delivers healthy messages when the application detects that the user is near a POI with the right timing and context. It also solves the need for connectivity with a local database of messages and POIs. Therefore, there is no need to be connected to the Internet in order to get a notification in a ubiquitous geographic location context.

4   Conclusion and Future Work

The aim of this research was to investigate how ubiquitous computing in general, and smartphones in particular, could be useful and contribute to improve nutrition behaviors. Smartphones are considered useful for this goal because they are very popular, have internet connection, and are constantly carried by users and used in multiple contexts by them. Therefore, two Android applications have been proposed to improve nutrition behaviors: Ubinut and Geonut. Both applications work in the background and users are unaware that they are running (ubiquitous context) on their mobile device. They send context aware messages to users.

Ubinut sends a healthy message considering two special contexts: time and weather. The messages are posted by a nutritionist, who decides which message to send and when. Moreover, users are able to rate each message once it is received and ask direct questions to the nutritionist. The target of the application is, therefore, people who are already conscious about the need to develop healthy habits and nutritionists who want to try a different method to hold the attention and to engage their patients. The focus of the messages is on making users aware of healthy habits in a special context, but it is important to note that the final decision is then up to the user.

From the test developed, it can be seen that users like their active participation, thanks to the rating of the messages. We have seen that messages must be related to users' contexts and daily routines to achieve our goals. In this way, users feel comfortable and receive the advice in a positive way. They also value positively the interaction with the nutritionist. Therefore, we think that it is important that, to be useful, this kind of application needs some active participation from the users: they like to be not only a passive receptor of messages, but also interact with them. However, the main drawback of Ubinut is that the nutritionist cannot send the message when the user is near a restaurant or a cafeteria, where it is important to be aware of healthy food. This geolocalization dimension is solved with Geonut.

Geonut adds new modules and functionalities to the Ubinut Android application which has a modular architecture. The principal focus of Geonut is to extend the possible context where the application can prevent a risk behavior in a defined geographical location (geofencing). Another difference between Geonut and Ubinut is that the sending of messages by Geonut when the user is near POIs is automatic, instead of sending messages mediated by a nutritionist.

Further work will address three directions: first, developing a new algorithm for Ubinut so that it can send messages automatically, taking into consideration variables from the defined context, for example real time connections with geolocated weather stations, and thus drawing on aspects of smart environments; second, implementing a more accurate ontology algorithm in order to improve the automatic system that sends messages in Geonut, making the selected messages closer to those that a nutritionist would choose; and third, measuring the impact of Geonut as a ubiquitous system for promoting healthy habits through an evaluation methodology, such as the four group test.

References

1. World Health Organization: Obesity and overweight. Who fact sheet N311, 27 abril 2015. http://www.who.int/mediacentre/factsheets/fs311/en/
2. Weiss, C.: Ubiquitous computing. Ind.-Organ. Psychol. **39**(4), 44–52 (2002)
3. World Health Organization: Indicators @ apps.who.int. https://apps.who.int/infobase/Indicators.aspx
4. de Salud, M.: Principales Resultados (2011). http://www.munitel.cl/eventos/seminarios/html/Documentos/2011/SEMINARIO
5. Evans, W.D., Necheles, J., Longjohn, M., Christoffel, K.K.: The 5-4-3-2-1 Go! intervention: social marketing strategies for nutrition. J. Nutr. Educ. Behav. **39**, S55–S59 (2007)
6. Burgess-Champoux, T.L.: Innovative use of technology in nutrition education research. J. Nutr. Educ. Behav. **45**(1), 1 (2013)
7. Cohen, N.L., Carbone, E.T., Beffa-Negrini, P.A.: The design, implementation, and evaluation of online credit nutrition courses: a systematic review. J. Nutr. Educ. Behav. **43**, 76–86 (2011)
8. Hingle, M., Nichter, M., Medeiros, M., Grace, S.: Texting for health: the use of participatory methods to develop healthy lifestyle messages for teens. J. Nutr. Educ. Behav. **45**, 12–19 (2013)
9. Lenhart, A., Ling, R., Campbell, S., Purcell, K.: Teens and mobile phones. Technical report (2010)
10. Lohse, B.: Facebook is an effective strategy to recruit low-income women to online nutrition education. J. Nutr. Educ. Behav. **45**(1), 69–76 (2013)
11. Kaplan, W.A.: Can the ubiquitous power of mobile phones be used to improve health outcomes in developing countries? Glob. Health. **2**, 9 (2006)
12. Salah, A.A., Lepri, B., Pianesi, F., Pentland, A.S.: Human behavior understanding for inducing behavioral change: application perspectives. In: Salah, A.A., Lepri, B. (eds.) HBU 2011. LNCS, vol. 7065, pp. 1–15. Springer, Heidelberg (2011)
13. Weiser, M.: The computer for the 21st century. Sci. Am. **265**(3), 94–104 (1991)
14. de Salud, M.: Norma General Tcnica No148 Sobre Guias Alimentarias para la Poblacin. http://www.inta.cl/doc_noticias/GUIAS_ALIMENTARIAS_2013.pdf
15. Ubinut Web site (2015). http://srvbioinf.utalca.cl/ubinut/#home. Accessed 21 April 2015
16. Oates, B.J.: Researching Information Systems and Computing, 1st edn. SAGE Publications Ltd, London (2005)
17. Open Street Map project. http://www.openstreetmap.org/
18. Bowen, D.J., Kreuter, M., Spring, B., Cofta-Woerpel, L., Linnan, L., Weiner, D., Bakken, S., Kaplan, C.P., Squiers, L., Fabrizio, C., Fernandez, M.: How we design feasibility studies. Am. J. Prev. Med. **36**(5), 452–457 (2009)
19. Leon, A.C., Davis, L.L., Kraemer, H.C.: The role and interpretation of pilot studies in clinical research. J. Psychiatr. Res. **45**, 626–629 (2011)
20. Restivo, K., Llamas, R.T., Shirer, M.: Worldwide Smartphone Market Expected to Grow 55% in 2011 and Approach Shipments of One Billion in 2015 (2011)
21. Cardone, G., Cirri, A., Corradi, A., Foschini, L., Ianniello, R., Montanari, R.: Crowdsensing in urban areas for city-scale mass gathering management: geofencing and activity recognition. IEEE Sens. J. **14**(12), 4185–4195 (2014)

Combining Technical and User Requirement Analysis to Support Wellbeing at the Workplace

Anna Wanka[1], Sophie Psihoda[1], Rainer Planinc[2(✉)], and Martin Kampel[2]

[1] Department of Sociology, University of Vienna, Vienna, Austria
anna.wanka@univie.ac.at
[2] Computer Vision Lab, TU Wien, Vienna, Austria
rainer.planinc@tuwien.ac.at

Abstract. The development of a technical system in order to support wellbeing of the workplace (This work is supported by the EU and national funding organizations of EU member states under grant AAL 2013-6-063.) demands for considering the requirements of the user, while developing state-of-the-art technology. Hence, in a first step, the requirements of the end user need to be analyzed as well as sensor technology of state-of-the-art sensors in order to match technology according to the user's needs. Within this paper different sensors technologies are compared and the requirements of end user at the workplace are analyzed. By matching both, technological as well as sociological aspects allows for the development of technical system, fitting to the demands of end user.

Keywords: User centered design · Requirement analysis · Sensor technology · AAL

1 Introduction

A significant amount of jobs require employees to sit for 8 h (or even longer) while performing their tasks [1]. During younger years, employees are not bothered with physical problems, but while getting older, more and more issues due to extensive sitting occur. In combination with not ergonomically designed working places, mal-nutrition (nutrition requirements change during our lifetime) and only little exercising, severe problems can arise, especially for people in the age of 50+ [2, 3]. Furthermore, the cognitive capability decreases, whereas (together with many other factors) the stress level increases. This leads to employees feeling not very well, which indicates a reduced quality of life due to physical (e.g., back) and psychological (e.g., stress) problems.

The introduction of a computer vision based system allows supporting employees at the workplace. The developed system monitors the user and provides feedback (e.g., in case of longer unhealthy postures) automatically so that the user can change the posture accordingly. However, since a system focusing on the wellbeing of older adults

© Springer International Publishing Switzerland 2015
I. Cleland et al. (Eds.): IWAAL 2015, LNCS 9455, pp. 101–112, 2015.
DOI: 10.1007/978-3-319-26410-3_10

does not only need to deal with technical, but also with social aspects, the integration of users is essential. Hence, the aim of this paper is to assess the user requirements for the development of a platform in order to prevent physical and psychological problems already at an early stage. Thus ensures a user-centered design, focusing on the needs of end-user while considering state-of-the-art technology.

The system consists of four different modules, which in combination lead to an enhanced quality of life of older adults in their working environment, but also to an increase of the overall wellbeing. The combination of these modules provides a training program for physical and psychological exercises and consists of the modules physical training, workplace ergonomics, nutritional balance and stress management optimized for the needs and wishes of older adults. Only by combining physical, ergonomic, nutritional and cognitive aspects, a holistic approach to enhance the wellbeing and quality of life of older adults can be developed. The proposed system is well-balanced and holistic in order to meet the end-user's needs and to offer benefits and an enhanced quality of life for older adults at the workplace. Hence, end-users need to be integrated already from the very beginning in order to develop a system according to their needs.

This paper describes the proposed platform, its modules and compares different sensor types to be used. Moreover, a user requirement analysis in order to identify the important aspects of the proposed modules is performed. The rest of this paper is structured as follows: Sect. 2 describes the overall system whereas the methodology for the user requirement analysis is described in Sect. 3. Section 4 describes the obtained results of both, the sensor evaluation as well as the user requirements to be considered during the system development. Finally, results are discussed in Sect. 5 and a conclusion is drawn.

2 System Overview

The wellbeing platform comprises of four modules: physical training, workplace ergonomics, nutritional balance as well as stress management. All modules, except the one for nutritional balance, are based on a correct pose estimation of the user. Pose estimation can be performed by first extracting features in the image which describes local changes between different poses. After collecting the images, the system needs to be trained and novel input poses need to be classified based on this training data. Determining the pose of a human is done in 3D space. To overcome the ill-posed problem of extracting 3D poses out of 2D images, the RGB images were replaced by depth images obtained from a 3D sensor. By using depth images, Fanelli et al. in [4] use regression in combination with a random forest for determining a human's head pose. Similar features are also used by Shotton et al. [5] where the first system for obtaining a human's pose is described. Each body part casts votes for a single class. The final pose is estimated by generating confidence-scored 3D proposals of how the body parts are connected. As a 3D sensor is able to overcome the ill-posed problem of extracting 3D information out of 2D images and is proven to be very robust against clutter and environmental changes, the input for the proposed system will also be based on this sensor for human pose estimation. Nevertheless, RGB images provide valuable information necessary to perform other tasks than 3D pose estimation (e.g., detection of a chair or a desk). As this information is also needed for the proposed framework, RGB images serve as an additional input source. Especially the stress management module will benefit from the additional RGB input images. Although the position of the shoulder and the body posture are already an indicator whether the person is stressed or relaxed, the facial expression is analyzed in order to detect stress symptoms. Due to the combination of different stress related proxies, the level of stress is detected.

In order to detect deviations during physical exercises, ergonomical issues at the workplace or the stress level, an appropriate sensor need to be used. Although cameras are widely used in the area of surveillance, the emerging of 3D sensors and its applications are of interest since more accurate results can be obtained. In order to choose an appropriate sensor, common sensor types are evaluated and compared with respect to their application at the workplace. The evaluation is based on a comparison of the sensor specifications, with a specific focus of its application at the workplace.

3   User Requirement Analysis

The wellbeing platform is being developed on the basis of a user-oriented requirement analysis. End-users, in this respect, were categorized into three groups: (a) employees at the age of 50 years and older, (b) managerial staff at the age of 50 years and older and (c) managerial staff responsible for employees 50 years and older, independent of their own age. The requirement analysis focuses on stresses and strains older employees are facing at the workplace, the available strategies and resources to cope with these burdens and thus targets the question where the wellbeing platform is most needed and how it can interface to the 'real' working lives of older employees. The standardized questionnaire covers 12 thematic areas: (1) images of ageing, (2) information about the workplace, (3) health behavior at the workplace, (4) strains at the workplace, (5) resources at the workplace, (6) work satisfaction, (7) cooperation with colleagues[1], (8) cooperation with the supervisor (see footnote 1) respectively cooperation with the employees[2], (9) retirement plans, (10) health, (11) acceptance of the wellbeing platform and (12) socio-demographic variables.

For the mode of data collection an online survey was chosen. Following Grooves et al. [6], this decision was informed by two considerations: First, the presence of an interviewer could have potentially affected the answers provided by respondents, in particular to sensitive questions about their health and workplace strains. Second, the online survey ensured that the privacy of the respondents was granted which was of particular concern for respondents in shared offices. A telephone survey would have allowed for the possibility that other people present while the survey was conducted would have known the respondents' answers and thus would have seriously impacted the privacy of the respondents.

Another concern that arises when conducting business surveys is the possibility of a sponsorship effect, in particular when the respondents are asked sensitive questions

---

[1] Managerial staff was not asked this set of questions.
[2] Only managerial staff was asked this set of questions.

about the treatment of older employees or about the cooperation with their supervisors and colleagues. If the company acts as the sponsor of the survey, clearly the proximity of the respondents to the sponsor would have had negative effects on the results. Admitting negative attitudes towards a target group (f.e. the supervisor) will be difficult if the sponsor is a member of that group, as is also indicated by Grooves et al. in [6]. While a sponsorship effect in business surveys on sensitive questions about the workplace can never be excluded, precaution was taken in two respects: First, the responses were stored on a server with restricted access to the university research team only and second, the invitations to participate in the survey were sent from a university mail address. Both made it possible to circumvent the company as a sponsor of the surveys and to reassure anonymity. Using a university as a sponsor with business populations has also been concluded as beneficial by Faria and Dickinson in [7].

The quantitative online survey is being carried out between October 2014 and June 2015 in selected enterprises and public institutions in the four partner countries Austria, Germany, Netherlands and Romania. As the survey has not been completed in the Netherlands, results from Austria, Germany and Romania are being presented. In order to avoid a possible bias resulting from one company and two organizations initially making up 70 % of the Austrian data, a sample of 600 people was drawn which allows for a more equal representation of the ten participating organizations in Austria. With regards to the sample constitution, 40 % of the participating organizations operate in the private sector, 60 % in the public sector and nearly all of them in the service sector. The sex-ratio accounts for 53.2 % women and 46.8 % men; the average age is 52.5 years. Similarly for the German data, also a sample of 120 people was drawn in order to allow for a better representation of the 18 participating organizations. The German sample is dominated by the public sector accounting for 85 % of the participating organizations. The sex-ratio accounts for 55 % women and 45 % men and the average age is 54.5 years. No adjustments were necessary for the Romanian sample of 104 people from two companies from the private sector, mainly involved in manufacturing. The sex-ratio accounts for 35.6 % women and 64.4 % men; the average age is 54.1 years.

4 Results

4.1 Evaluation of 3D Sensors

The following table compares different 3D sensors regarding features, being important for the use within a workplace. The sensors being compared are Microsoft Kinect and Microsoft Kinect 2, Asus Xtion pro live and the SoftKinetic sensor. These sensors are chosen since their performance is expected to be quite similar and thus, a detailed comparison is necessary in order to choose an appropriate sensor. Table 1 shows a comparison of different 3D sensor types depending on various features. Although the system requirements for the Kinect 2 are quite high (Windows 8, USB 3, powerful processor), data provided by the Kinect 2 is of high quality.

Table 1. Comparison of 3D sensors

	Kinect v1	Kinect 2	Asus Xtion Pro Live	SoftKinetic DepthSense DS 311
Technology	Structured light	Time of flight	Structured light	Time of flight
Depth range	0.4 m–4.5 m	0.5 m–4.5 m	0.8 m–3.5 m	0.15 m–1 m, 1.5 m–4 m
Color image resolution	640 × 480 (30 fps) 1280 × 960 (10 fps)	1920 × 1080 (15 – 30 fps)	1280 × 1024 (15 fps)	640 × 480 (60 fps)
Depth image resolution	320 × 240 (30 fps)	512 × 424 (30 fps)	320 × 240 (60 fps) 640 × 480 (30 fps)	160 × 120 (30 fps)
Field of view (H × V)	57° × 43°	70° × 60°	58° × 45°	57° × 42°
Data connection	USB 2.0	USB 3.0	Single USB 2.0	USB 2.0
Power connection	External	External		USB 2.0
Physical dimensions (w × h × d)	38.3 × 15.6 × 12.3 cm	24.9 × 6.6 × 6.7 cm	18 cm × 5 cm × 3.5 cm	24 cm × 4 cm × 5 cm
Insensitive to sunlight	No	Yes	No	No
SDKs available	Yes	Yes	No	Yes
Supplier situation	Not available	Good	Not available	Limited
Depth data quality	Ok	Good	Ok	Ok
Price	n/a	∼ 135€	∼ 140€	n/a
Supported OS	Windows (7, Embedded 7, 8)	Windows (8, 8.1, Embedded 8)	Windows (XP, Vista, 7, 8) Linux Ubuntu	Windows (7, 8), Linux and Android 4.1
Supported Programming Languages	C++, C#, Visual Basic, .NET	C++, C#, Visual Basic,.NET	C++, C#, Java	C, C++, C#, Plugins for Flash and Unity 3D
System requirements CPU RAM Graphic card	32 bit/64 bit, dual core 2.66 GHz 2 GB DirectX 9 support	64 bit, dual core 3.1 GHz 4 GB DirectX 11 support	No, depending on data processing	n.a

Especially in combination with the SDK provided by Microsoft, Kinect 2 offers high qualitative data together with high-resolution images. Moreover, skeleton tracking performed by the Microsoft SDK 2 is more robust in comparison to OpenNI and the first version of the SDK. On the other hand, the use of Microsoft Kinect requires the use of a Windows PC and thus does not allow running the system on cheap embedded devices. Despite this drawback, Kinect 2 is chosen to be used within the wellbeing system due to its performance (depth and skeleton tracking data) and availability.

4.2 User Requirements: Objective and Subjective Demand

Beyond technological requirements, user requirements are crucial if the system shall actually be used. Here we can differentiate between objective and subjective demands: An objective demand is assumed if a person faces burdensome work conditions in a field that the wellbeing system targets – physical training, workplace ergonomics, nutritional balance and stress management –, whereas a subjective demand is given if the persons themselves say they would like to use the wellbeing system.

Objective demand: Work strains

Workplace Ergonomics. In regard to workplace ergonomics, different characteristics of a workplace have to be considered, like the time spent sitting at work, time spent in front of a digital screen or the amount of screen breaks exerted. These workplace characteristics usually don't fall into the responsibility of the individual employee but are rooted in workplace conditions and working routines. Thus it is important that the ergonomic conditions of workplace are regularly inspected and favorable behavior, like exerting screen breaks, is monitored. Otherwise, negative physical conditions caused by unfavorable ergonomic working terms might impair – particularly older – employees' performance capabilities.

In Austria, respondents of the participating organizations work on average 40.3 h a week or 8.1 h a day (including overtime hours), of which 7.3 are spent sitting and 6.8 in front of a screen. In Germany, these figures amount to 40.1 h a week or 8 h a day, of which 6.2 h are spent sitting and 5.7 h are spent in front of a screen. In Romania, responding employees work on average 44.1 h a week or 8.8 h a day, of which 5.2 are spent sitting and 3.7 in front of a screen. Despite all employees' facing frequent daily screen work, less than one quarter (Austria: 12.4 %, Germany: 11.1 %, Romania: 24 %) exerts regular screen pauses as proposed by the European Display Screen Directive (Directive 90/270/EEC) [8].

The differences in the share of sitting and screen time point to the different structures given in the participating organizations: While employees of the Romanian companies are also involved in manual labor, Austrian and German organizations mainly belong to the service sector, involving mostly administrative and managerial work. In contrast to public opinion, this kind of work can also be burdensome to the physical condition of older employees: 38.7 % of German and 29.2 % of Austrian respondents report to be (very) strongly exposed to unfavorable ergonomic conditions, whereas this figure amounts to only 9.1 % in Romania. 86.3 % of Austrian, 83.3 % of German and 66.7 % of Romanian respondents state to have suffered some kind of pain during the past seven days. On average, German respondents mentioned 2.5, Austrian respondents 2.1 and Romanian respondents 0.9 physical conditions potentially caused by ergonomic work position as well as too much sitting and on-screen time[3].

In most participating organizations, however, monitoring of workplace ergonomics is not yet common: About half of the respondents in Germany and Romania (Germany: 44.2 %, Romania: 42.9 %) stated that they had not had their workplace ergonomics checked by an expert yet. In Austria, 84 % have had at least one inspection of the ergonomic conditions of their workplace.

Nutritional Balance and Physical Training. Apart from ergonomic conditions the individual health behavior of older employees and their managers is important for maintaining workplace wellbeing. Despite partly relying on individual motivation, the organizational context can also play a part in encouraging favorable health behavior – for example, by offering workplace health promotion, free fruits and water or just simply attractive stairways that turn the elevator into a less appealing option.

---

[3] Including: pain in the head, neck, shoulders, spine, arms/hands, knees, legs/hips, eyes.

Complementing individual and organizational factors, the regional or national cultures in regard to food and exercise also matter.

Thus, in the wellbeing sample, nutritional habits differ greatly between the three partner countries, with German and Austrian respondents eating slightly healthier: While 71.8 % of respondents of German organizations stated to eat fruits or vegetables at least once a day, this accounts for 54.7 % of Austrian and only 37.6 % of Romanian respondents. Similarly, 21.9 % of Romanian, but only 13.8 % of Austrian and 11.1 % of German respondents drink less than 1 liter a day.

Differences also appear in regard to where and how lunch is taken. In Germany and Romania, most respondents prepare their lunch at home and take it to work (Germany: 34.2 %, Romania: 47.6 %). Whereas this is the only commonly mentioned lunch option in Romania[4], many German respondents also have lunch at their workplace canteen (32.5 %) or buy a quick lunch at the supermarket (15 %). In Austria, lunch options are most diverse: 30.7 % buy their lunch at the supermarket, 24.2 % prepare it at home, 20 % eat at a restaurant and 17.7 % at the workplace canteen. About one in six respondents does not have lunch at a typical workday at all (Austria: 17.5 %, Germany: 13.3 %, Romania: 11.1 %).

The workplace, however, mostly seems to hinder favorable nutritional behavior: The majority of respondents declare that their nutritional habits are healthier during their leisure time than during work. This might partly be due to stressful working conditions, as a significant amount of respondents in Austria and Germany states to eat less healthy and less regularly when encountering work stress (Germany: 44.2 %, Austria: 37.2 %, Romania: 9 %).

Apart from nutritional behavior, physical activity is important in maintaining a healthy lifestyle. However, physical activity is improvable among the respondents: 39.8 % of Austrian, one third of German (32.7 %) and one quarter of Romanian (24 %) respondents say that they usually walk or ride a bike for less than 30 min a day. In line with lack of physical movement and unhealthy nutrition, the average BMI indicates slight average overweight in all participating organizations (Austria: 25.5, Germany and Romania: 26.1).

However, even if regular movement is seldom, the majority of Austrian and German respondents state to exercise on a regular basis (Austria: 83.2 %, Germany: 79.6 %, Romania: 40.8 %). Country resp. organizational differences can partly be traced back to health promotion activities offered by the company: Workplace activity programs exist in 70.8 % of participating German and 55 % of participating Austrian organizations and are, if available, utilized by 61.2 % resp. 42.1 %. In participating Romanian companies, however, no such programs exist.

Stress Management. There are different stressors and strains that employees are exposed to at work that can affect their health behavior and health condition. We can differentiate between social stressors (comprising violence or threat, discrimination, bullying, lack of respect and emotional burden) and time-related stressors (comprising

---

[4] Other options below 10 %.

work overload, interruptions and lack of breaks). Among the wellbeing sample, time-related stressors are the most common type of work strains: About one third of Austrian (28.7 %) and German (34.2 %) respondents state to be (very) strongly exposed to social stressors and more than half (Austria: 51,5 %, Germany: 55.8 %) to be (very) strongly exposed to time-related stressors. In Romania, 5.8 % of respondents stated to be (very) strongly exposed to social stressors and 13.5 % to be (very) strongly exposed to time-related stressors. Accordingly to the differences in stress exposure, 34.5 % of Austrian and 36.7 % of German respondents, but only 17.4 % of Romanian respondents experienced negative stress effects on their psychological wellbeing throughout the past working week, like feeling tense, irritated, rushed, worried or depressed.

Despite differing levels of exposure to stress, emotional burden is the most commonly mentioned social stressor and work interruptions the most commonly mentioned time-related stressor in all three countries.

Subjective demand: System acceptance

Despite existing objective demand, as portrayed in the previous section, subjective demand might differ. In the wellbeing survey, employees 50 years and older were asked which module they would most likely be willing to use, whereas supervisors were asked which module they would most likely make available to their older employees.

Overall there seems to be a high acceptance of a system like the wellbeing platform among employees 50 years and older in Austria, Germany and Romania. Acceptance is lowest in German organizations, however, country-differences are not significant and low. So are differences in acceptance between the four modules. Whereas among older Austrian and German respondents the workplace ergonomics module is most popular, stress management was slightly more popular in Romania (Figs. 1 and 2).

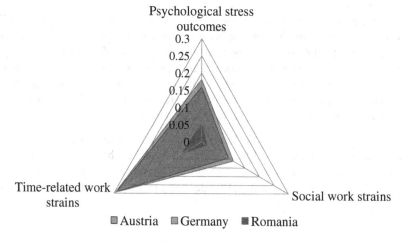

Fig. 1. Work strains and stress outcomes; indices weighed by number of items

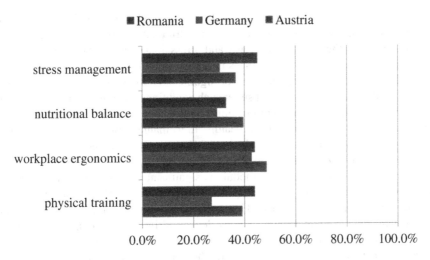

Fig. 2. Percentage of those who would definitely use the module; employees 50+

Willingness to make the software available to older employees is higher among managers in all countries than is the willingness to use the modules on the side of the older employees themselves. Again, workplace ergonomics and stress management are the most popular modules among managers of older employees (Fig. 3).

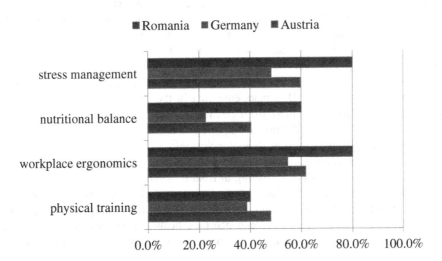

Fig. 3. Percentage of those who would definitely use the module; supervisors

Which factors influence subjective demand, or, more specifically, in how far does objective demand influence subjective acceptance of older employees? Data shows that subjective and objective demands do not always match. Moreover, the (mis-)match differs in regard to the different modules and by country. While in Austria and Germany the subjective demand for the ergonomic and nutritional modules are not driven by objective demand, the physical exercise and stress management modules are. This means that, for example, older employees in Austria and Germany who are exposed to unfavorable ergonomic conditions are not significantly more accepting of the ergonomics module than those who don't suffer such conditions – neither are those suffering more physical conditions, working more hours, sitting more or sitting more in front of a screen, the older or those who feel less healthy. In Romania, however, older employees who report more pain symptoms and a higher BMI are significantly more likely to accept the ergonomic and nutritional modules.

Contrarily, the physical activity module is significantly more accepted by persons who report more pain symptoms in all partner countries ($p<0.05$) and longer working hours in front of a screen (Austria, Germany) resp. sitting (Romania; $p<0.05$). The stress management module, finally, is most demand-driven: Older employees that are more exposed to social and time-related stressors[5], who experience more negative psychological stress outcomes ($p<0.01$) and who suffer more pain symptoms ($p<0.05$) are significantly more likely to use the stress management module.

5 Discussion

The aim of this paper was to assess the user requirements and sensor technologies for the development of a platform in order to prevent physical and psychological problems caused by unfavorable working conditions of employees 50 years and older. From a technical point of view, the use of the Kinect version 2 is recommended since it offers accurate tracking results of body parts. However, in contrast to other sensors, the hardware to be used in combination with the Kinect is highly restricted, since only Windows based systems can be used. In order to develop a platform not being dependent on a single sensor type, at the beginning the Kinect provided by Microsoft will be used, whereas new 3D sensors emerging in the future will be evaluated and integrated into the wellbeing platform if possible.

Portraying the results of the user requirement analysis conducted in the course of the wellbeing-project we can draw three conclusions:

First, user requirement analyses clearly detect problematic situations that a technological solution can tackle (e.g., sitting in front of a screen takes up the majority of working time at white-collar workplaces). And these workplaces are often not reviewed in regard to their ergonomic conditions. Hence, a system monitoring ergonomic conditions allows to support workers to enhance their health. Especially the use of a 3D sensor allows analyzing the posture of the body and thus preventing unhealthy ergonomic conditions.

---

[5] This only accounts for Austria; in Germany, only time-related stressors are significantly correlated to subjective demand. In Romania, social or time-related stressors have no significant influence.

In addition to physically burdensome working conditions, psychological stress is increasingly becoming the cause for early retirement in Europe. In the white-collar wellbeing sample, half of respondents are (very) strongly exposed to time-related stressors and one third to social stressors. Stress, in particular, reinforces unhealthy lifestyles among older employees. Due to use of several stress related proxies, stress can be detected and countermeasures can be provided in order to reduce the stress level.

Working under unhealthy conditions entails significant negative long-term health effects, and these effects already show in the wellbeing simple of older employees: One third of white-collar respondents in Austria and Germany reported physical pain symptoms potentially caused by unfavorable ergonomic conditions, ranging from pain in the head, neck, shoulders, spine, arms, hands, knees, legs, hips and eyes, as well as psychological stress outcomes, like feeling tense, irritated, rushed, worried or even depressed. The average BMI indicated overweight in all countries.

Although the use of a technical system does not guarantee employees to stay healthy, regular use of the wellbeing system can reduce physical pain and improve stress management. Future work will evaluate the influence of the wellbeing system on the health status of employees over the course of several months.

Second, user requirement analyses are important to detect context-specific differences in work strains and requirements. Work strains and thus demands for a technological solution differ by individual, by workplace, by organization, by sector and not least by the regional and national context. The wellbeing survey shows that strains and demands differ greatly between white- and blue-collar workplaces, but also between Eastern and Western European countries. For example, awareness for and exercising of healthy lifestyles was more pronounced in the Austrian and German sample, but workplace stressors seemed to be lower in the Romanian corporations. For technological solutions that aim to facilitate healthy working conditions, this emphasizes the importance of adaptability to ensure maximum appropriateness for different contexts and (national as well as organizational) cultures. Hence, one focus of the wellbeing system is the personalization in order to adapt to personal requirements and consider personal needs.

Third, and finally, user requirement analyses help to identify the borders at which technological solutions must blend into organizational health promotion activities. Healthy behavior must be facilitated by and in line with work processes and routines and companies must make an attempt in offering older employees specific support to keep them healthy, capable and prevent early retirement. Small things can be done to enhance the physical wellbeing of older employees, from offering workplace activity programs to attractive stairways, free fruits, monitoring regular screen pauses or inspecting the ergonomic working conditions – things that are not yet common sense. It might be more complicated, yet equally rewarding, to change harmful work processes that cause psychological stress, ranging from unnecessary interruptions, lack of breaks or work overload to emotional burden, mobbing and discrimination. In regard to these common work stressors, technological solutions can only be effective when combined with changes of organizational culture and the support of all hierarchical levels.

References

1. McCrady, S., Levine, J.: Sedentariness at work; how much do we really sit? Obesity **17**(11), 2103–2105 (2010)
2. Castanharo, R., Duarte, M., McGill, S.: Corrective sitting strategies: an examination of muscle activity and spine loading. J. Electromyogr. Kinesiol. **24**(1), 114–119 (2014)
3. Caneiro, J.P., OSullivan, P., Burnett, A., Barach, A., ONeil, D., Tveit, D., Olafsdottir, K.: The influence of different sitting postures on head/neck posture and muscle activity. Manual Ther. **15**(1), 54–60 (2010)
4. Fanelli, G., Gall, J., Van Gool, L.: Real time head pose estimation with random regression forests. In: Conference on Computer Vision and Pattern Recognition, pp. 617–624 (2011)
5. Shotton, J., Fitzgibbon, A., Cook, M., Sharp, T., Finocchio, M., Moore, R., Kipman, A., Blake, A.: Real-time human pose recognition in parts from single depth images. In: Conference on Computer Vision and Pattern Recognition, pp. 1297–1304 (2011)
6. Grooves, R.M., Fowler Jr., F.J., Couper, M.P., Lepkowski, J.M., Singer, E., Tourangeau, R.: Survey Methodology, 2nd edn. Wiley, New Jersey (2009)
7. Faria, A.J., Dickinson, R.: The effect of reassured anonymity and sponsor on mail survey response and speed with business population. J. Bus. Ind. Mark. **11**, 66–76 (1996)
8. Council Directive 90/270/EEC of 29 May 1990 on the minimum safety and health requirements for work with display screen equipment (fifth individual Directive within the meaning of Article 16 (1) of Directive 89/391/EEC). http://eur-lex.europa.eu/legal-content/EN/TXT/HTML/?uri=CELEX:31990L0270&from=EN. Accessed 14 June 1990

Towards Resilient Services in the Home

A Home Service Platform with Support for Conflict Resolution

Marios Sioutis[✉], Kiyofumi Tanaka, Yuuto Lim, and Yasuo Tan

Japan Advanced Institute of Science and Technology, Asahidai 1-1,
Nomi, Ishikawa, Japan
{smarios,kiyofumi,ylim,ytan}@jaist.ac.jp

Abstract. Commercially available automation systems for the home are enjoying rising popularity in recent years, promising the dream of a smart home environment. However they leave a lot to be desired in terms of device and network protocol interoperability as well as the sophistication of the services that they provide. As an avenue to realize the dream of a truly smart home, many research efforts have suggested middleware platforms which offer device access to software applications that incorporate intelligent decision making. In this paper, a home platform with support for run-time conflict resolution among smart services is introduced. The conflict resolution features of this platform include device access rights, service priorities, condition sets and notification events. The effectiveness of the above features is demonstrated in several scenarios in which services adapt to context changes. We conclude that such conflict resolution mechanisms are a necessity for every middleware platform that aims to have multiple services concurrently operating in the home environment.

1 Introduction

The rapid advance in consumer electronics has led to an increasing number of network-enabled devices in the home environment. Home automation systems such as [2] that control lights, windows, air condition units and locks among other things are now commercially available and targeted towards the technology enthusiast consumer.

As is the case with any emerging technology, several shortcomings of these automation systems have been identified. Firstly, these automation systems usually rely heavily on some specific network communication protocol, failing to take advantage of devices that do not support it. Secondly, the services offered by such systems are limited in scope, usually encompassing only simple automation tasks. Finally, such systems are rarely open for development to third party application developers, thus missing out on a great opportunity for more diverse automation applications and the revenue that could be generated from them.

In response to these limitations, the research community has come up with platforms such as [6,10] that address some of the challenges outlined above. Two platforms that stand out due to their commercial backing are HomeKit [1]

© Springer International Publishing Switzerland 2015
I. Cleland et al. (Eds.): IWAAL 2015, LNCS 9455, pp. 113–124, 2015.
DOI: 10.1007/978-3-319-26410-3_11

from Apple and HomeOS [3,4] from the research division of Microsoft. A common theme among these platforms is the need to model home devices in terms of their functionality regardless of the underlying network communication protocol. By doing so, device interoperability is considered to be a mostly solved problem. All that is necessary for a new device to be integrated and become usable by a platform is a software component, commonly known as a "driver" or a "bridge" that can map semantic operations to concrete commands of the underlying communication protocol. With a broad support for devices and the interoperability issues solved, richer and more complex services can now be developed.

The next step is to introduce third party service developers to the platform. As the number of services goes up, unwanted interactions among services will eventually occur. Due to the large number of unique home configurations, available devices and concurrent execution of services, guaranteeing the correct operation of a service becomes a difficult task. Conflict detection among services has been discussed in [5,7,9]. A formal verification approach will be of limited use. It is our conviction that the most realistic approach is to have the responsibility for the correct operation of a service shared by the home automation platform and the services themselves.

To ensure resilient services in the face of concurrent execution, the home platform must provide adequate primitives that can capture the semantics of a conflict and help the smart service take corrective actions. At the same time, it is also of significant importance that the developer can utilize these primitives with ease during the development of a service.

The remaining paper is structured as follows. In the next section the overall platform architecture is introduced and compared to competing platforms like HomeKit and HomeOS. In Sect. 3, the overall approach for device modeling is introduced. In Sect. 4, the primitives that aid in the concurrent operation of services are introduced. In Sect. 5, generic guidelines for developing resilient services that react to context changes for the proposed platform are laid out. In Sect. 6, conflict scenarios that demonstrate the effectiveness of the proposed home platform are presented. When conflicts or changes in the context arise, services may try to take corrective actions or choose to suspend their operation until further changes occur. In the final section we outline the biggest benefits of using the suggested platform. Furthermore, we discuss future work that is currently underway.

2   Platform Architecture and Comparisons

2.1   Proposed Platform

The proposed platform architecture can be seen in Fig. 1. As is the case with any middleware, the home platform mediates the access to the resources of the home in a centralized manner. Software services can search and access resources through a well defined Home Platform API.

The communication with the actual devices is delegated to software bridges. Each bridge is capable of understanding the semantic operation of a device and is responsible to translate this operation to a format supported by the underlying network communication protocol of that device. Bridges are protocol specific and can manage multiple devices at once. Depending on the bridge implementation and the underlying network communication protocol, device discovery may be possible. Any device reported by a bridge can then be used as a resource by the services running on the proposed platform.

The use of bridges solves the problem of interoperability; as long as a bridge is available for a given network communication protocol, devices that support that protocol become available as resources in the home platform.

The proposed platform is supposed to reside inside the house, with any external connectivity being strictly optional. The platform was implemented using Java, and in future revisions it will be redistributable as an OSGi bundle.

2.2 HomeOS

In comparison, Microsoft's HomeOS is comprised of four layers: the application layer, the management layer, the device functionality layer and the device connectivity layer.

The application layer is the layer where applications run. Applications are packaged as modules, with each module being isolated as to not affect the operation of the rest of the system. The management layer takes care of the security considerations of the platform. A system of access rules controls access to devices. This management layer addresses security considerations such as controlling unconstrained access to devices by applications.

The last two layers correspond closely to the bridges and the virtual devices of our system. The device connectivity layer is responsible for communicating with devices using network communication protocols such as Z-Wave and DLNA. It is also responsible for device discovery. After a device has been successfully identified, it is passed on to the device functionality layer where its functionality is mapped to protocol agnostic APIs, ready to be used by the developers.

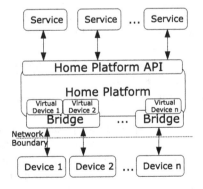

Fig. 1. Platform architecture

2.3   HomeKit

Apple has released a developer's guide for its HomeKit platform. In this documentation, a HomeKit database is featured prominently as the sole provider of information to applications. This database contains all the necessary information for devices and their states, allowing applications to receive updates as these states change.

Upon launch, HomeKit is said to support a multitude of devices that use various network communication protocols, modeled according to their functionality. However, the starkest difference between HomeKit and the proposed platform as well as HomeOS is the scope of HomeKit's applications; they only focus on simple automation tasks, with the end user responsible for their correct operation. No features regarding conflict resolution are available.

3   Device Modeling

The proposed home platform, HomeOS and HomeKit have followed a similar approach towards modeling devices and their functionality. Each platform has its own way of defining semantic primitives that map to specific operations of a device.

3.1   Proposed Platform

In the proposed platform, a base `Operation` class exist. More concrete implementations of this class have specific semantic meaning associated to device functionality. Operations provide appropriate accessor methods for setting the arguments for the operation as well as retrieving the result of the operation after its invocation finishes. A preliminary set of operations has already been defined, but it will be extended and/or revised when the need to support more diverse devices arises.

By offering concrete operations as typed classes, modeling devices becomes easier. A base device implementation must support a `doOperation` method and a `getSupportedOperations` method. The first method is the entry point for invoking an operation on a device. Internally, the device can register a handler for a given type of operation and delegate its processing to that handler. Furthermore, the second method exposes the operations a device supports, information used when a service is searching for appropriate devices.

Invoking an operation on a device using the `doOperation()` method may raise exceptions. There are four types of exceptions currently supported by the proposed platform. An "operation not supported" exception will be thrown if the device does not support a given operation. An "insufficient access rights" exception will be thrown when the service that requests the operation does not have sufficient access rights for the specified device. Network errors will cause "network communication" exceptions to be raised and, finally, if the operation is not fulfilled in a timely manner a "timeout" exception will be raised.

For a service developer, programming directly with operations and devices can be complicated. To solve this problem, a special set of "device adapter" classes have been provided. These adapter classes provide user friendly methods such as `TurnOn()`, `setTemperature(int degrees)` which, internally, generate the appropriate operation instances and invoke them on the underlying device. Device adapters also have configurable behavior regarding their handling of exceptions. Certain types of exceptions can be silenced, letting through only the exceptions that the service is interested in handling. Also, the result of the last invoked operation is always stored, and can be queried later without having to resort to `try/catch` blocks in the code.

3.2 HomeOS and HomeKit

In HomeOS, it is the responsibility of the Device Functionality layer to provide APIs that are easy to use. The modules of this layer provide device functionality to applications using programming interfaces known as *roles*. Each device may support multiple roles and a device can be queried for the roles it supports. However, because roles and operation names are represented as strings, it is difficult to enforce type safety.

In HomeKit, devices are referred to as "accessories". These accessories offer "services" which in turn are associated with "characteristics". Ignoring the disparity in nomenclature, services can be seen as the equivalent of roles in HomeOS. Each characteristic of a service represents a unique functionality of the underlying device, such as for example, if a light is turned on or off. The definitions of services and their characteristics are controlled by Apple.

4 Primitives for Conflict Resolution

In the current development stage of the platform, there are four main primitives used for conflict detection and resolution: device access rights, priorities for services and users, condition sets and finally event notification mechanisms.

4.1 Device Access Rights

There are three types of access rights currently implemented in the proposed system: no access, read-only access and read-write access. A service that is interested in using a device will hold one of the above mentioned rights.

When a service has a "no access" access right for a device, it can only query general information regarding the device, such as its supported operations, its location and its name.

A service that holds a read-only access right for a device is able to invoke a limited set of operations on that device. More specifically, the read-only access right is designed for gathering information related to the current state of the device. For example, read-only operations on an air condition unit would be getting the current temperature setting, its current operation mode (heating, cooling, etc.), its current power consumption etc. A read-only access right would also be an appropriate fit for sensors.

A service with a read-write access for a device can invoke all operations offered by that device. Whereas read-only operations are associated with data gathering, write operations are associated with actuation. For an air condition unit, operations such as setting the desired temperature and operation mode would be considered write operations, since they embody some sort of actuation that affects the home environment.

Using this model of access rights, many services may have concurrent access to a device for information gathering purposes, since such access poses no threat to the concurrent operation of services. In contrast, read-write access rights for a device may be held only by a single service at any given time. If multiple services could hold write access for the same device, the danger of conflicting operations arises, negatively impacting the user's experience.

4.2   Service and User Priorities

Each service of the proposed platform is associated with a priority. In the current form, priorities are numerical values ranging from 1 to 10, with 1 being the lowest priority and 10 being the highest priority. The users in the home environment are also associated with priority levels and can adjust the priority level of services they own. Services come with a suggested priority, a priority setting that the developer of the service deems appropriate for it. As a general rule of thumb, services that interact with a multitude of devices should hold lower priorities. In contrast, services that have a well defined goal (for example, a home theater service) can be assigned higher priority.

The reasoning for the above rule of thumb is simple. Services that access many different types of devices have a higher risk of interfering with other services compared to services that use only a few devices. Furthermore, services with a clear goal that use only a few select devices either tend to be interactive services that the user is currently paying attention to, or their importance may be high, thus a higher priority level can be justified.

4.3   Condition Sets

The proposed platform offers primitives used to encapsulate the notion of a condition set. Such a condition set maintains two distinct sets of conditions: context conditions and device access conditions.

Context conditions can be used to represent the necessary conditions (such as location, time, etc.) that have to be fulfilled in order for the home service to execute its task. Device access conditions encode information regarding the devices that will be used during the operation of the service.

Condition sets can be used as a synchronization mechanism. The main thread of a service can wait on such a condition set until all the conditions in the condition set are met. As soon as this happens, the main thread continues on with its main task.

Condition sets also offer the reverse functionality: as soon as one of the conditions can no longer be met, the main thread of a service will be notified. The service then takes on any appropriate clean up or corrective actions and then wait on the modified condition set once again. Any device associated with a device access condition in this set will be automatically released.

The main logic behind the condition sets can be seen in Fig. 2.

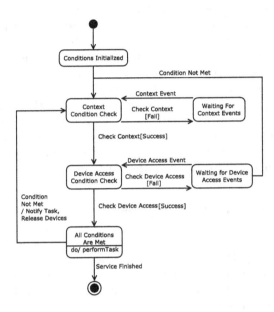

Fig. 2. Behaviour of condition sets

4.4   Events

During its operation, a service may receive events associated with its execution context. The most prominent event type is that of a change in the access rights of a device it is currently using or it wants to use.

A service that requests read-write privileges for a device will be granted read-write access to that device if and only if there are no other services with equal or higher priority currently interested in using that device. This also means that a service may lose its read-write access rights for a device to a service with a higher priority at any time.

Another type of event supported by the proposed platform is a user motion event. A service may request to be notified for any changes regarding the position of a user. A common theme is to respond to the user entering or leaving a specific room. It is expected that non-intrusive and affordable indoor location systems will materialize within the next few years, thus we designed the proposed platform with such an indoor location subsystem already in mind.

4.5   Comparison to HomeOS

Access control policies in HomeOS are expressed as Datalog rules. The datalog rules dictate whether a resource is available for use. A resource in this context usually refers to a device. If there is no rule that grants access to that resource, access will by default be denied.

Access to a resource is associated with a group of users, a HomeOS module, start and end time, a day of the week, a priority and finally an access mode. The module parameter usually refers to a home service, which is bundled as a HomeOS module. These rules have to be set up by the user beforehand and they address legitimate concerns over the unconstrained access to resources by services. The current state of access control is discussed in [8].

Although datalog rules provide fine-grained control over resources, run-time considerations such as concurrent access for information gathering, losing control of a device to a service with higher priority and explicit locking mechanisms are not adequately addressed. In case of resource conflicts, services with lower priority may be terminated, without any chance for a graceful recovery, severely limiting the concurrency of services on the platform.

5   Developing Resilient Services

A typical smart service for the proposed platform transitions through various states during its life cycle. During an initialization phase, a service will attempt to gather any necessary information for its operation. Based on this information, a set of conditions can be formulated. When the set of these conditions is fulfilled, it can proceed to its main operation state, the state in which the actual service logic is implemented.

A representative state diagram for a simple service, the conditions of which do not change through its life cycle is depicted in Fig. 3. Such a service reacts to various event notifications emitted by the home platform.

When an event notification arrives during the main operation state, the service should examine the event and decide whether the necessary conditions for its operation still hold true. Should this not be the case, the service should revert back to the "waiting for events" state and wait for further events. Using this approach, the service voluntarily suspends its execution, until its operating conditions are fulfilled sometime in the future.

In contrast to the simple service model, more resilient services that can react in the face of context changes are now possible. The state diagram for such services is depicted in Fig. 4. The biggest difference compared to simple services is the extra "Corrective Measures" state during which possible alternative actions are considered. In both models, the task of checking conditions can be accomplished with the use of condition sets.

When a service is facing a context change, it can take one of the following two actions: either decide that the context change will not affect its normal operation or, as a response to the context change, alter the necessary conditions

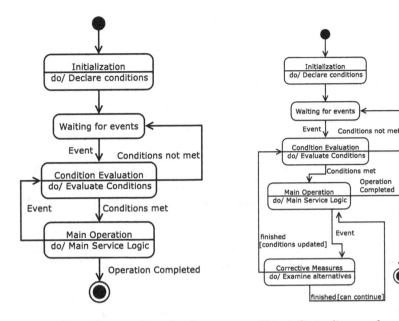

Fig. 3. State diagram for a simple service

Fig. 4. State diagram for a service with corrective actions

for its execution. In the first case, the service decided that the context change is not significant enough to warrant any reaction and reverts back to its main operation state. In the second case, due to the context change, a service may decide to use a different set of devices than before to fulfill its tasks, thus altering its execution conditions which must be reevaluated.

6 Demonstration

For evaluation purposes, various test services were deployed on the proposed platform. The proposed platform currently operates with a set of virtual devices, as well as a virtual location subsystem which can report the location of the users.

In our test scenario, four services were concurrently executing: a smart listening service that follows the user around the house, an energy saving service that would turn off any unused devices, a home theater service and finally a scheduled task service that performs tasks as scheduled by the user. The details regarding these services can be seen in Table 1.

With these services concurrently executing, several interactions were witnessed. The first interesting interaction was between the smart listening service and the energy saving service. As the user of the smart listening service moves inside the house, the service receives motion event notifications. When the user enters a room, the service tries to find an available speaker device in that room.

Table 1. Service details

Service	User	Priority	Devices used
Smart listening service	Mom	5	Speakers
Energy saving service	Dad	1	Any device
Home theater service	Kid 2	7	Speaker and screen
User-scheduled task service	Mom	9	Speaker

If such a speaker device exists, it releases any previously held speakers. The energy saving service requests read-write access to all the devices in the house, turning off any device for which the access was granted. Furthermore, should more devices be released in the future, it will be notified of their availability and also turn them off.

The interaction occurs when the user steps into a room with a speaker available: the smart listening service gains control of the device from the energy saving service. In turn, by releasing the previously held speaker, the energy saving service gets notified, and turns that speaker off. Due to the higher service priority of the listening service, it is always able to access the most appropriate speaker for the situation. Due to the notification mechanism regarding access rights, the energy saving service is able to achieve its task and turn off all devices not currently in use. The raw output can be seen in Fig. 5.

```
Smart Listening Service: User moved into room: Sleeping1
Smart Listening Service: Releasing previous speaker with name: Speaker3
Smart Listening Service: New speaker device: Speaker4
Smart Listening Service: Turning speaker on..
Smart Listening Service: speaker with name Speaker4 is playing back stream with description: Random Podcast
EnergySavingService: access changed event
EnergySavingService: Device: Speaker4, new access rights: READONLY
EnergySavingService: access changed event
EnergySavingService: Device: Speaker3, new access rights: READWRITE
EnergySavingService: turned off device: Speaker3
```

Fig. 5. Interaction between energy saving service and smart listening service

Another interaction involves the energy saving service, the home theater service and the user scheduled task service. The scenario develops as follows: first, the home theater service gets control of a speaker and screen device in the main living room (the energy saving service loses control of these two devices). While the user (which is a child of the family) watches the movie, a prerecorded message from the mother of the family starts playing back, requiring the speaker currently used by the home theater service. The home theater service temporarily loses access to the speaker and voluntarily suspends itself, using a condition set. After the loss of the speaker, access rights to the screen are also released. Since the screen is now an unused device, the energy saving service gets control of it and turns it off. The corresponding raw output can be seen in Fig. 6.

After a minute, the playback of the prerecorded message is complete, and the speaker is released by the high priority scheduled task. Now, the home theater

```
Condition set for service: Home Theater Service with Conditions became unsatisfiable.
HTS suspending self!
EnergySavingService: access changed event
EnergySavingService: Device: TV1, new access rights: READWRITE
Condition Set for service Scheduled Actions with Conditions became Active!
EnergySavingService: turned off device: TV1
HTS was interrupted!
Service: Scheduled Actions with Conditions, wakeup! perform task...
Service: Home Theater Service with Conditions, waiting on condition..
Speaker Task: playing back stream!
Speaker Task: Stream Description: kids don't stay up late!
```

Fig. 6. First half of interaction among home theater service, energy saving service and user scheduled task

service is notified through its condition set that all the conditions are met and it can resume playback. Upon doing so, the home theater service gains control of the speaker and the screen, while the energy saving service due to its low priority loses control of the screen. This interaction can be seen in Fig. 7.

```
Speaker Task: task finished!
Speaker Task: release the speaker!
ConditionSet: task with description: Speaker Task: reminding the kids to not stay up late finished!
Task: Speaker Task: reminding the kids to not stay up late finished!
Condition Set for service Home Theater Service with Conditions became Active!
Condition set for service: Scheduled Actions with Conditions became unsatisfiable.
EnergySavingService: access changed event
EnergySavingService: Device: TV1, new access rights: READONLY
Service: Home Theater Service with Conditions, wakeup! perform task...
HTS: turning Screen ON
HTS: playing video stream: Test video stream
HTS: playing audio stream: Test audio stream
```

Fig. 7. Second half of interaction among home theater service, energy saving service and user scheduled task

The above services and their interactions are *representative of the interactions that can happen among smart services in a home platform.* All of the above mentioned services could successfully adapt to the loss (or gain) of device access rights, as well as adapt to the change of context. With the use of primitives for conflict resolution, it is now possible to design and implement resilient and more reactive services than before.

7   Conclusion and Future Work

In conclusion, the proposed platform provides a compelling set of primitives for conflict resolution among services. Using these primitives, smart home services that can adapt and react in the face of conflicts are now possible. The conflict resolution features introduced in this paper are generic enough to capture the essence of conflicts regarding device usage in the home environment and should be part of any future platform that aspires to more than simple automation.

As future work, environmental conflicts will be addressed. Operating devices that have conflicting effects on the environment can have a negative impact on the user's experience. To solve this, physical aspects of the environment such as temperature, humidity, illumination, sound and noise levels should be treated as resources themselves, with the home platform having the role of controlling them. Smart services should be able to make requests regarding these properties such as for example "set the temperature of this room to 25°C", and allow the platform to decide the best way to fulfill such requests.

References

1. Apple HomeKit. https://developer.apple.com/homekit/. Accessed 28 May 2015
2. INSTEON. http://www.insteon.com/. Accessed 28 May 2015
3. Dixon, C., Mahajan, R., Agarwal, S., Brush, A., Lee, B., Saroiu, S., Bahl, P.: The home needs an operating system (and an app store). In: HotNets IX. ACM, October 2010
4. Dixon, C., Mahajan, R., Agarwal, S., Brush, A., Lee, B., Saroiu, S., Bahl, P.: An operating system for the home. In: NSDI. USENIX, April 2012
5. Hu, H., Yang, D., Fu, C., Fang, W.: Towards a semantic web based approach for feature interaction detection. In: 2010 2nd International Conference on Software Technology and Engineering (ICSTE), vol. 2, pp. V2-330–V2-334, October 2010
6. Papadopoulos, N., Meliones, A., Economou, D., Karras, I., Liverezas, I.: A connected home platform and development framework for smart home control applications. In: 2009 7th IEEE International Conference on Industrial Informatics, INDIN 2009, pp. 402–409, June 2009
7. Rathnayaka, A., Potdar, V., Kuruppu, S.: Evaluation of wireless home automation technologies. In: 2011 Proceedings of the 5th IEEE International Conference on Digital Ecosystems and Technologies Conference (DEST), pp. 76–81, May 2011
8. Ur, B., Jung, J., Schechter, S.: The current state of access control for smart devices in homes. In: Workshop on Home Usable Privacy and Security (HUPS), HUPS 2014, July 2013
9. Wilson, M., Magill, E., Kolberg, M.: An online approach for the service interaction problem in home automation. In: 2005 Second IEEE Consumer Communications and Networking Conference, CCNC 2005, pp. 251–256, January 2005
10. Wu, C.L., Liao, C.F., Fu, L.C.: Service-oriented smart-home architecture based on OSGi and mobile-agent technology. IEEE Trans. Syst. Man Cybern. Part C Appl. Rev. **37**(2), 193–205 (2007)

Introducing Ambient Assisted Living Technology at the Home of the Elderly: Challenges and Lessons Learned

Diego Muñoz, Francisco J. Gutierrez$^{(\boxtimes)}$, and Sergio F. Ochoa

Computer Science Department, University of Chile,
Beauchef 851, 3rd Floor, Santiago, Chile
{dimunoz, frgutier, sochoa}@dcc.uchile.cl

Abstract. The promise of pervasive computing applications is to surround people with affordable, transparent and unobtrusive technology. However, several barriers including usability concerns, a lack of perceived usefulness, and low technology self-efficacy may jeopardize the successful adoption of ambient assisted living (AAL) systems, particularly by the elderly. Following the development of the SocialConnector system, which mediates and coordinates the communication effort of family members with their elders, this paper describes the iterative design process conducted to help improve the acceptance of the system by end-users. This process considered the implicit and explicit concerns and expectations of the intended target users, and it involved three improvement cycles along an action research approach. Through this process, we obtained a set of lessons learned that aim to describe how to unobtrusively introduce sensing and monitoring technology at the home of the elderly. Keeping simple yet meaningful interaction metaphors helps increase the learnability and perceived usefulness of AAL technology by the elderly.If older adults perceive the value of having such kinds of tools installed in their homes, then they are prone to assume them as part of their lives. Likewise, situational and activity awareness mechanisms, such as visual notification badges and audio-enhanced user interfaces, can be used to persuade the elderly to approach the system and eventually use it. Finally, the design of AAL solutions also requires active consideration of the needs and attitudes of other family members, particularly those who assume an active role in the caring process of their elders.

Keywords: Elderly · Technology acceptance · Appropriation · Design implications · Ambient assisted living

1 Introduction

Over the last few years we have seen the instrumentation of people and environments with several purposes; for instance, to improve the service provision to passersby, monitor the health condition of people, or detect particular situations (e.g., fires, robbery, or falls) in a certain area. Most services require the placement of some kind of sensor, either on a person or in the environment, to get the required information to effectively provide such a service. Following this idea, pervasive computing systems

© Springer International Publishing Switzerland 2015
I. Cleland et al. (Eds.): IWAAL 2015, LNCS 9455, pp. 125–136, 2015.
DOI: 10.1007/978-3-319-26410-3_12

try to embed these sensors in the environment as much as possible, in an unobtrusive manner for its end-users.

Most people do not have problems with such an instrumentation process, particularly those who use and actively recognize the benefits of mobile and ubiquitous technology. However, digital illiterate people (e.g., most older adults) usually do not feel comfortable wearing sensors or seeing their homes instrumented with obtrusive sensors. Therefore, embedding these devices in the immediate surroundings of the elderly, or making the latter wear these sensors, represents a challenge for designers of these types of solutions.

Particularly, older adults have been under the spotlight over recent years, due to the large variety of opportunities that technology provides, not only for their own monitoring but also to assist and improve their quality of life. Nevertheless, the question of how to deploy sensors where they are required, without stressing and disrupting the elderly, still remains open. Even if some approaches grounded in the efforts of the pervasive computing and HCI communities may provide several interacting alternatives to deal with the described situation (e.g., a smart TV equipped with a Kinect camera, or monitoring systems relying on the lectures provided by hidden RFID tags), a general solution still depends on the type of sensor that needs to be deployed, and on the main interaction paradigm preferred and assumed as natural by the target users.

Some years ago, the authors developed the SocialConnector system [18], which runs in a tablet mounted on a wall at the home of the elderly. It allows them to interact with other family members despite their apparent lack of a technology background. Given that the system runs over a tablet, it is also used as a sensor, which helps evaluate and monitor the mood of the elderly in real time, thus keeping informed family members and caregivers accordingly. This monitoring service runs in the backend of the application, so it is not visible for older adults. Therefore, the elderly are not fully aware of the potential benefits that this sensor is able to provide them and also to their families. By considering this lack of value perceived by older adults and the fact that these devices consume electricity, the elderly frequently decide to turn off the device.

In order to understand how to make the elderly aware of the benefits of having ambient assisted living (AAL) technology installed at their homes, we followed a formal process to get lessons learned that can help other researchers and developers to deal with this challenge. In particular, we aim to reflect on the best alternatives in terms of design that would entice the elderly to keep the SocialConnector system turned on in a real-life scenario. In fact, although a preliminary system evaluation indicated that the elderly consider SocialConnector as a valuable tool [17, 18], several usability and usefulness limitations were also identified. This paper presents the redesign process of SocialConnector, in terms of improving both the usability of its user interface and the perceived usefulness of the services provided to older adults. The redesign process followed an action research approach [20], involving three improvement cycles with an active participation of end-users. Then, the main contribution of this article is to present a set of lessons learned that would help AAL technology designers to increase the perceived value, usability and appropriation of their solutions, particularly when they are targeted to the elderly.

The following section discusses the related work. We then describe the redesign process of the SocialConnector system and highlight the main design implications derived from the evaluation of each improvement cycle. Next, we discuss the lessons learned from the whole process, and their relevance when envisioning improving AAL technology acceptance by the elderly. Finally, we present the conclusions and provide further perspectives on future work.

2 Related Work

There is a consensus that technology can help older adults improve their quality of life [1, 9]. However, deploying assisted living technologies into the older adults' homes and enticing the elderly to actively use them can represent a major challenge. Literature reports several reasons that explain this situation, including unfamiliarity with current technology, computer anxiety, and low perceived usefulness [4, 27].

Chen and Chan [2] present a review of empirical research on technology acceptance by older adults, based on 19 published studies. These studies considered the use of TAM2 (Technology Acceptance Model) [25] for diagnosing the technology acceptance level of the elderly (Fig. 1). Particularly, the perceived usefulness of the system and the perceived effort required to use it, are the most influential variables for the technology acceptance in older adults.

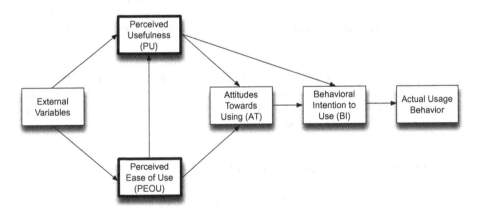

Fig. 1. Simplified version of TAM2 [25]

According to Chen and Chan [2], the strategies adopted to increase the usability and perceived usefulness of these systems usually depend on cultural aspects of the users. Indeed, the authors state that while European and American elders show a positive attitude toward the inclusion of technology in their homes, it is not clear what happens in Asian and Latin American countries, given that few studies have been conducted in those socio-cultural contexts.

Concerning the particular case of AAL technologies, the probability of adoption of these systems by older adults is still uncertain [10, 13]. Several barriers including usability problems [5, 7], a lack of perceived usefulness [10, 15, 22] and technology self-efficacy [10, 16] are the main issues that can jeopardize the successful adoption of these technologies [12].

Considering these previous works, there seems to be a consensus that perceived usefulness and perceived ease of use, i.e., the key variables identified by TAM2 [25], are also the most influencing aspects that determine the technology adoption of older adults, including AAL technologies [2, 13]. However, there is not a common recipe for addressing the usability and usefulness of AAL systems, since they depend on socio-cultural aspects of the end-users and also the type of device deployed at the home of the elderly [6].

Following this line of reasoning, researchers have been trying to increase the perceived usability of Websites by improving their accessibility following the Web Content Accessibility Guidelines, issued by the World Wide Web Consortium [26]. In order to improve the usability of computer-based systems for the elderly [14, 19, 28], the literature reports that effort should be devoted to provide clearly visible elements all throughout the user interface, with the content presented in an understandable manner and focused on the object of the provided service without presenting unnecessary information.

Similarly, in an attempt to improve the perceived usefulness of services provided by domestic technology to mediate intra-family communication, such services should introduce affordances for interaction without opening an obligation to the involved participants [23]. For instance, effective approaches already covered in the literature include family calendars [8] and photo displays retrieving information from social media streams [3].

In summary, the reviewed literature indicates that the best way to increase the feasibility to deploy the SocialConnector system into the homes of elderly people is improving its usability and perceived usefulness. In order to achieve this goal, we performed three action research cycles [20] to improve these aspects of the system. The next section describes this reengineering process.

3   Redesigning the SocialConnector System

SocialConnector is a ubiquitous application that was initially conceived to increase the social inclusion of older adults through the use of technology [18]. The system runs in a tablet installed on a wall at the home of the elderly (Fig. 2), and it allows them to interact with other family members using gestures and speech.

Older adults can exchange messages (emails) and hold videoconferences with other members. However, the elderly are not actually aware of the all the provided services, because the system interface hides the complexity of these processes. The first version of the SocialConnector also included a Web application that allows other family members (typically, adult children and grandchildren) to interact with the elderly.

The system was acceptable for the end-users, but several improvement opportunities were also identified [17, 18]. This motivated the authors to conduct three action research cycles that are explained in the next sections, which allowed us to get some lessons learned.

Fig. 2. Older adult using the system

3.1 First Improvement Cycle

In this stage we installed the system at the living room of a house where three elderly people live (Fig. 2). The people were a man (76 years old) and two women (74 and 70 years old). The use of the system was monitored during three consecutive days. The elderly used the tool to interact with other family members; particularly with four adult children (aged 54, 47, 46 and 39 years old) and four grandchildren (aged 22, 21, 16 and 13 years old).

The elderly also counted with the assistance of an adult child that supported and monitored the usage of the system during the three days. The main goal of this experience was to identify what services, provided by the system (i.e., exchange of private and public messages, and videoconference), were valuable for the older adults, and also if the way to access these services was appropriate for them. After that period, we conducted a focus group with the elderly, one with the adults and one with the young people. Detailed results of this study can be found in [18].

The findings from this improvement cycle indicate that the elderly were able to use the system services and felt comfortable doing it. However, we verified that after such a period, they used the system only when someone else was supporting them. According to TAM2, this situation would indicate that the value of the system perceived by the elderly is not enough for taking the initiative to use it. Moreover, the elderly mentioned that they do not want to follow a login process for using the system.

The focus groups with adult children and grandchildren indicated that all of them do not want to use a Web application to interact with their elders. Instead, they prefer to use regular communication applications (e.g., email client applications or videoconference tools) to interact with the elderly. Moreover, and similarly to the older adults, they do not want to follow a login process to use the system services. In summary, the concepts represented by the envisaged Web application were neither particularly valuable nor useful for adult children and grandchildren. This feedback was considered for the next improvement cycle of the system.

3.2 Second Improvement Cycle

The new version of the application for older adults included a digital portrait service – Tlatoque [3] – that displays photos, which are automatically retrieved from the

Facebook accounts of the family members. This helped increase the perceived value of the system by the elderly [18]. In addition, we implemented an automatic login process for improving the system usability. Regarding the role of supporting family members, we discarded the Web application for interacting with the elderly. Instead, we developed message exchange services that allow family members to use their preferred communication media (e.g., Gmail, Skype, Facebook) to interact with their elders.

This improved version of the system was evaluated through a proof of concept during three days. The participants were the same as those who took part in the first improvement cycle, aiming to assess the pertinence and added perceived value of the redesigned and new services. Besides, we conducted a user study with a different group of nine elders, in order to verify if the new version of the system could be considered as useful and usable for them.

Proof of Concept with the Elderly. The elderly that used the new system implementation found it usable and particularly more useful than the original one. Both the automatic login service and the new photo display were considered as highly valuable. In contrast, they found the public message service as non-useful, because they did not understand its purpose. Indeed, the users felt that this service did not fit their mental model on how social interactions are conducted. For instance, they assimilated private messages as the process of writing and sending a letter; videoconferences were related to phone calls, and the photo display was related to a family photo album. The lack of understanding about the meaning of the public messages also appeared in the previous evaluation, but it was not identified as such. In terms of usability, the elderly found the system usable, but they realized that the main menu (Fig. 3a) is not visible when a service turns active (e.g., in Fig. 3b and c), which disoriented them. The representation of the temporal order of messages was also perceived as unclear. For instance, in Fig. 3b, if users tap on the arrow at the right, it was not clear if the message shown would be the next or the previous, in temporal order. This proof of concept also allowed us to identify several other minor usability limitations.

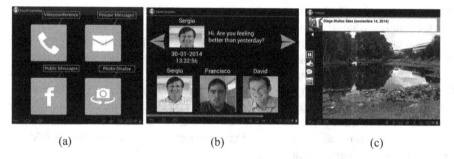

(a)   (b)   (c)

Fig. 3. User interface of the second improvement cycle of SocialConnector: (a) main menu, (b) private message service, (c) photo display

User Study. Nine elderly aged between 61 and 89 years old participated in a user study. In this evaluation process, we used paper prototyping [21] and the thinking aloud protocol [24]. The users followed a protocol for evaluating the system services and were asked to indicate why they chose one or another option of the user interface. Although the participants were able to successfully accomplish the proposed tasks, several limitations were identified. For instance, some of them did not understand the meaning of some icons in the user interface; others were not able to go back to the main menu after using a service. All of them perceived the public messages as not having enough value for them, and many made mistakes when trying to find a specific private message, particularly when following the temporal order of the displayed information. These results are consistent with those obtained in the proof of concept, so they were used as input for the next improvement cycle.

Evaluation with Adults and Older People. In order to determine if the new interaction paradigm was appropriate for the rest of the family (i.e., those using their preferred communication media for interacting with the elderly), we asked the participants of the first evaluation to complete a set of tasks with their elders. We conducted semi-structured interviews with the participants once they have completed the proposed tasks. The supporting family members felt comfortable with the proposed interaction paradigm, mainly because they considered that it provided them flexibility and allowed them to interact with their elders almost effortlessly. Detailed results of this study can be found in [17].

Summary of the Evaluation. The obtained results indicate that the proposed interaction paradigm was appropriate for adult children and grandchildren, and no further requirements were identified for these users. Concerning the perception of the older adults, we identified three main design aspects to improve: (1) the elderly need to have the main menu visible at all times, to be aware that they have several options available for interacting with others or for interacting with family information; (2) every element in the user interface must be explicit about the function it performs (a single icon is not enough); (3) the concept of public messages was not intuitive for the elderly; and (4) the navigation plan used in every service must remain the same.

3.3   Third Improvement Cycle

The third action research cycle was focused on addressing these aspects of the system and evaluating some new ones. We therefore designed a new version of the user interface, where the public messages service was removed. Moreover, we explicitly introduced redundancies in the form of text labels to improve the understanding of icons (Fig. 4). In addition, we added a notification service that periodically features the weather forecast to the elderly, and also offers a family member birthday reminder. Finally, badges were introduced to provide activity awareness about new messages and photos.

Seven older adults, aged 61 to 74 years old, evaluated the usability and usefulness of the system. The number of participants evaluating the system in this opportunity adheres to existing recommendations in usability engineering [11]. The evaluators were asked to use a high-fidelity interactive prototype to complete a set of representative tasks, using the services provided by the system, similarly to the previous experiences.

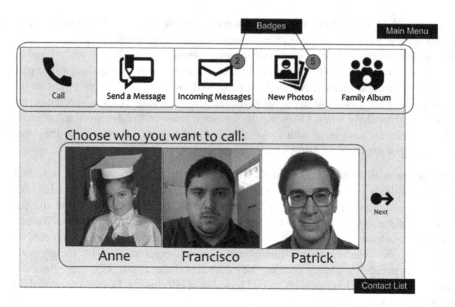

Fig. 4. New user interface of the system

User Interface Usability. The older adults (OA) found the user interface usable. As they were performing the tasks, the amount of mistakes and the average time decreased, probably because of a learning effect. Some of the participants stated they would actually use the system if they were taught how to do it, or that they would learn how to use it if they had enough practice.

OA1: *"Although it was complicated at the beginning [to use the system], now it is not that much. If you practice about three times, you start getting how it is done"*

Most of the elderly understood the meaning of the main menu buttons; in the other cases, they did it after a brief explanation. The other elements of the user interface (e.g., badges, other icons, and buttons) were also mostly understood, and even considered as useful by the elderly.

OA2: *"I think it is quite useful that the system reminds you when you have new messages or photos. I can easily note when there are new things to see!"*

Services Usefulness. The elderly considered that videoconferences, new photos, and the family album are the most useful services provided by the current implementation of SocialConnector. This could be due to their preference to have face-to-face communication and because they need assistance to see photos in social networking services (SNS), such as Facebook or Flickr.

OA3: *"I like these [services] very much. My granddaughters and my daughter always show me photos, but I always depend on someone to do it"*

Finally, most of the elderly praised the value provided by the notification service for reminding birthdays and special events of supporting family members. Among the reasons given by the elderly is that they find here an opportunity to plan in advance how to greet them, and the chance to facilitate a physical encounter, such as a family reunion.

4 Lessons Learned During the Redesign Process

This redesign process allowed us to identify several aspects that can help other researchers realize the opportunities and limitations of technology in the homes of the elderly. By considering the typical and expected reluctance of many older adults to use technology, the system should be not only *pervasive*, but also *usable* and *valuable* for them. Otherwise, the solution will be perceived as an unnecessary intervention to their home, as well as a disruption to their daily lives, which makes them feel uncomfortable. Next, we present the lessons learned about pervasiveness, usability and usefulness of AAL supporting social systems.

Pervasiveness. In this sense, the pervasiveness of the SocialConnector system was addressed through several mechanisms; for instance, an automatic login service, as well as automatically turning the system screen on and off. Indeed, depending on the time of day, the screen of the system is turned off when the elderly are sleeping, and it is turned on when they wake up. In addition, the system automatically retrieves information from the supporting family members' SNS accounts, aiming to provide situational awareness to the elderly about the doings and whereabouts of their relatives. Finally, family members can use their preferred communication media to interact with the elderly, which increases the pervasiveness of the system for all users.

Perceived Usability. The system usability was also addressed through several mechanisms; for instance, the design of the user interface is simple and keeps the same interaction paradigm in all services. The new design of the main menu allows the users to keep a visual reference about both, the service they are currently using and a shortcut to any other service. Every service included in the system represents a concept that is well known for the elderly. The system uses badges to provide visual awareness about new photos and messages, and visual notifications as birthday reminders and special events. Much of this information is automatically provided by the system, without any explicit action being required by the elderly. This design decision not only provides a benefit to the end-users, but also allows them to assimilate the system services at their own pace.

Perceived Usefulness. Visual information is highly valuable for older adults. This is evidenced in their appreciation toward the provided photo albums, videoconferences and birthday reminders. If the users perceive the value of having an artifact such as SocialConnector installed in their home, and the system does not unnecessarily disrupt them, then they assume the system as a part of their life. In our case, given that we aim to sense the mood of the elderly, as part of a broader health monitoring and sustainable care model, having the system actively being used by the participants is mandatory for achieving such a goal.

Similarly, the family members involved in the supporting network of the elderly must also consider the system as being useful. Any AAL solution should ease family members' to accomplish with their routines without unnecessarily disrupting them. Otherwise, there is a high probability that they will stop using the system.

5   Conclusions and Future Work

Embedding technology at the home of the elderly is mandatory to support most AAL systems; however, it represents a challenge not only for designers, but also for older adults who could feel that technology invades their spaces and reduces their privacy. To deal with this challenge, this article reports the redesign process of the SocialConnector system, which was not initially perceived as useful by older adults.

Following the TAM2 guidelines and an action research process, the usability and perceived usefulness of the system were improved, as well as its pervasiveness. Three improvement cycles were performed with the support of the end-users, and a set of lessons learned was gathered from this process.

Keeping simple yet meaningful interaction metaphors, like emulating the usage of the tablet as a digital portrait, helped increase the learnability and perceived usefulness of the system. The idea of facilitating public messages was not particularly useful for the elderly, probably because it did not align with their mental model. However, the elderly praised the interaction possibilities offered by the videoconferences and private messages, as they consider them a way to maintain the contact with their family members. Similarly, notification badges for providing activity awareness, birthday reminders and special events, and audio-enhanced interaction with the user interface also proved useful when trying to persuade the elderly to approach the system and trigger its usage. These design implications are general enough to help other researchers deal with this challenge when they have to deploy a technological solution at the home of an elderly person.

Achieving the goal of making the elderly accept and use the provided technology is a first, but key step to performing more complex and interesting activities. In our case, the SocialConnector system currently allows us to monitor in the field other aspects of the older adults, such as their mood, health status and movements. This has the potential to help us implement sustainable health care models for the elderly, where both family members and caregivers can act as facilitators, actively engaging in the process.

Acknowledgements. This work has been partially supported by the Fondecyt Project (Chile), grant: 1150252. The work of Francisco J. Gutierrez has been supported by the Ph.D. Scholarship Program of Conicyt Chile (CONICYT-PCHA/Doctorado Nacional/2013-21130075).

References

1. Bouma, H., Fozard, J.L., Bouwhuis, D.G., Taipale, V.: Gerontechnology in perspective. Gerontechnology 6(4), 190–216 (2007)
2. Chen, K., Chan, A.H.S.: A review of technology acceptance by older adults. Gerontechnology 10(1), 1–12 (2011)
3. Cornejo, R., Tentori, M., Favela, J.: Ambient awareness to strengthen the family social network of older adults. Comput. Support. Coop. Work 22, 309–344 (2013)

4. Czaja, S., Charness, N., Fisk, D., Hertzog, C., Nair, A.N., Rogers, W.A., Sharit, J.: Factors predicting the user of technology: findings from the Center for Research and Education on Aging and Technology. Psychol. Aging **21**(2), 333–352 (2006)
5. Demiris, G., Rantz, M.J., Aud, M.A., Marek, K.D., Tyrer, H.W., Skubic, M., Hussam, A.A.: Older adults' attitudes towards and perceptions of 'smart home' technologies: a pilot study. Inform. Health Soc. Care **29**(2), 87–94 (2004)
6. Doyle, J., Bailey, C., Ni, C., van den Berg, F.: Lessons learned in deploying independent living technologies to older adults' homes. Univ. Access Inf. Soc. **13**(2), 191–204 (2014)
7. Fisk, A.D., Rogers, W.A., Charness, N., Czaja, S.J., Sharit, J.: Designing for Older Adults: Principles and Creative Human Factors Approaches. CRC Press, Boca Raton (2012)
8. Forghani, A., Neustaedter, C.: The routines and needs of grandparents and parents for grandparent- grandchild conversations over distance. In: Proceedings of CHI 2014, pp. 4177–4186. ACM Press, Toronto ON, Canada (2014)
9. Fozard, J.L.: Impacts of technology on health and self-esteem. Gerontechnology **4**(2), 63–76 (2005)
10. Heart, T., Kalderon, E.: Older adults: are they ready to adopt health-related ICT? Int. J. Med. Informatics **82**(11), e209–e231 (2011)
11. Holzinger, A.: Usability engineering methods for software developers. Commun. ACM **48** (1), 71–74 (2005)
12. Jaschinski, C., Ben Allouch, S.: Ambient assisted living: benefits and barriers from a user-centered perspective. In: Proceedings of AMBIENT 2014, Rome, Italy (2014)
13. Jaschinski, C.: Ambient assisted living: towards a model of technology adoption and use among elderly users. In: Proceedings of UbiComp 2014 Adjunct Publication, pp. 319–324. ACM Press Seattle WA, USA (2014)
14. Kurniawan, S., Zaphiris, P.: Research-derived web design guidelines for older people. In: Proceedings of ASSETS 2005, pp. 129–135. ACM Press, Baltimore MD, USA (2005)
15. Melenhorst, A.S., Rogers, W.A., Caylor, E.C.: The use of communication technologies by older adults: exploring the benefits from the user's perspective. In: Proceedings of the HFES Annual Meeting 2001, vol. 45, no. 3, pp. 221–225 (2001)
16. Morris, A., Goodman, J., Brading, H.: Internet use and non-use: views of older users. Univ. Access Inf. Soc. **6**(1), 43–57 (2007)
17. Muñoz, D., Cornejo, R., Gutierrez, F.J., Favela, J., Ochoa, S.F., Tentori, M.: A social cloud-based tool to deal with time and media mismatch of intergenerational family communication. Future Gener. Comput. Syst. (2014, in press)
18. Muñoz, D., Gutierrez, F.J., Ochoa, S.F., Baloian, N.: SocialConnector: a ubiquitous system to ease the social interaction among family community members. Comput. Syst. Sci. Eng. **30** (1), 57–68 (2015)
19. Patsoule, E., Koutsabasis, P.: Redesigning web sites for older adults. In: Proceedings of PETRA 2012, Heraklion, Crete, Greece (2012)
20. Reason, P., Bradbury, H.: Handbook of Action Research, 2nd edn. Sage, London (2007)
21. Sefelin, R., Tscheligi, M., Giller, V.: Paper prototyping - what is it good for?: a comparison of paper and computer-based low-fidelity prototyping. In: Proceedings of CHI 2003 Extended Abstracts, pp. 778–779. ACM Press, Ft. Lauderdale FL, USA (2003)
22. Steele, R., Lo, A., Secombe, C., Wong, Y.K.: Elderly persons' perception and acceptance of using wireless sensor networks to assist healthcare. Int. J. Med. Informatics **78**(12), 788–801 (2009)
23. Tee, K., Brush, A.J.B., Inkpen, K.M.: Exploring communication and sharing between extended families. Int. J. Hum Comput Stud. **67**, 128–138 (2009)
24. van Someren, M.W., Barnard, Y.F., Sandberg, J.A.: The Think Aloud Method: A Practical Guide to Modelling Cognitive Processes. Academic Press, London (1994)

25. Venkatesh, V., Davis, F.: A theoretical extension of the technology acceptance model: four longitudinal field studies. Manage. Sci. **46**(2), 186–204 (2000)
26. Web Content Accessibility Guidelines (WCAG) 2.0. http://www.w3.org/TR/WCAG20. Accessed 16 Jun 2015
27. Yao, D.F., Qiu, Y.F., Du, Z.X., Ma, J.Q., Huang, H.: A survey of technology accessibility problems faced by older users in China. In: Proceedings of W4A 2009, pp. 16–25. ACM Press, New York NY, USA (2009)
28. Zaphiris, P., Pfeil, U., Xhixho, D.: User evaluation of age-centred web design guidelines. In: Stephanidis, C. (ed.) Universal Access in HCI, Part I, HCII 2009. LNCS, vol. 5614, pp. 677–686. Springer, Heidelberg (2009)

Behaviour Analysis and Activity Recognition

An Approach for Agitation Detection and Intervention in Sufferers of Autism Spectrum Disorder

Joseph Rafferty$^{(\boxtimes)}$, Jonathan Synnott, and Chris Nugent

School of Computing and Mathematics,
University of Ulster, Coleraine, Northern Ireland, UK
{j.rafferty,j.synnott,cd.nugent}@ulster.ac.uk

Abstract. Autism spectrum disorder (ASD) is a condition that is being diagnosed in a growing portion of the population. ASD represents a range of complex disorders with a number of symptoms including social difficulties and behavioral issues. Some individuals suffering from ASD are prone to incidents of agitation that can lead to escalation and meltdowns. Such incidents represent a risk to the individuals with ASD and others who share their environment. This paper introduces a novel approach to monitor triggers for these incidents with an aim to detect and predict an incident happening. Non-invasive sensors monitor factors within an environment that may indicate such an incident. Combined with an NFC and smart phone based mechanism to report incidents in a relatively friction free manner. These reports will be combined with sensor records to train a prediction system based on supervised machine learning. Future work will identify the best performing machine-learning technique and will evaluate the approach.

Keywords: Autism · ASD · Agitation · Assistive technologies · Computer vision · Machine learning · NFC · Sensors

1 Introduction

Autism spectrum disorder (ASD) is a condition being diagnosed in a growing portion of the population [1]. Recent studies have shown that globally around 1 % of the population is affected [1, 2] with growing incidence among children. ASD represents a range of complex behavioral disorders. These disorders arise from issues in early brain development, before 3 years of age [3]. The symptoms of these disorders include difficulties with social interaction, social imagination, communication through both verbal and non-verbal means, impulse control, self-awareness and monitoring, restrictive behavior, anxiety, sleeping and/or a tendency towards repetitive behavior [3]. There is no known cure for this condition but treatments, support mechanisms and medications exists to help alleviate symptoms [3].

Treatments include behavioral change control therapy. Support mechanisms include assignment of caregivers and the use of assistive technologies. These are typically resource intensive, requiring long periods to show results. The efficiency and effect of medications vary by each case. Support mechanisms show promise in

© Springer International Publishing Switzerland 2015
I. Cleland et al. (Eds.): IWAAL 2015, LNCS 9455, pp. 139–145, 2015.
DOI: 10.1007/978-3-319-26410-3_13

alleviating the symptoms and increasing the quality of life of suffers but the use of caregivers represents a large resource investment. Assistive technologies have shown promising results in a number of domains [4, 5] and can be applied to supporting ASD sufferers [6], reducing the resources required to support individuals.

Those affected by ASD are susceptible to agitation, leading to escalation and meltdowns. Escalation and meltdowns may manifest as aggressive outbursts, physically aggressive behavior, tantrums and self-harming. Agitation has a number of triggers, classified in four ways [3, 7–9]; the individual does not get what they want, the individual is not doing what they want to do, the individual is not able to regulate internal stimuli and an individual is not able to cope with changes in environmental stimuli. To provide support for these individuals, these triggers can be monitored relative to a profile for an individual or a setting. On detection of agitation factors related to a profile, provision of proactive care can reduce likelihood of an escalation or meltdown. Traditional monitoring of triggers are provided through use of caregivers, introducing a financial and logistical constraint, to the detriment of the overall care quality. Current technological approaches to this monitoring have some deficiencies that are addressed by this study.

The remaining sections of this paper summarize related work, detail the approach devised, reflect on future work and provide a conclusion to this paper.

2 Related Work

A number of works exist with the goal of supporting individuals with ASD through use of technology [6, 10]. These approaches focus on either monitoring and/or promoting performance of specific tasks. Typically, this monitoring is used to help inform an assessment or in some cases provide data to trigger an intervention.

One project [6], intends to bring the assessment of children with ASD into their home environment in order to allow intervention in a manner which requires minimal human involvement. The system detects agitation through analysis of signals from a wearable electroencephalogram (EEG) device[1]. On detection of agitation, camera based systems identify eye movement and capture pictures of the environment. An eye-tracking device was then used to identify stimuli that is may be causing this agitation. This represents a promising but invasive solution due to the technology used.

The majority of current works focus on performance of specific tasks, typically with the goal of training an individual with ASD to exert more neuro-typical behaviors. Works that do monitor an individual with ASD to provide intervention employ a range of technologies which introduce a risk of intrusion or privacy concerns [6, 10]. Additionally, some of these approaches require the use of wearable devices or observation mechanisms that may invade an individual's privacy. The use of wearable devices, in particular, may cause discomfort for the individual, in addition to introducing an element where they lack control, and so may trigger agitation.

---

[1] Electroencephalography - recording electrical brain activity through electrodes on the scalp.

In order to address these shortcomings, the authors have devised a novel approach to monitoring an individual with ASD, detecting agitation and alerting caregiving staff who can then intervene appropriately. In this approach, individuals' environment is monitored in a way that is non-invasive and respects privacy.

3   A Non-invasive Approach to Monitoring Individuals with ASD to Detect Agitation and Provide Intervention

The devised approach, presented in this section, focuses on monitoring documented triggers for agitation that stem from external stimuli and behavior that may indicate agitation (such as repetitive movements) [3, 7–9]. The factors monitored are noise levels, temperature levels, number of occupants, inter-occupant proximity, occupant movement, emissive temperature of occupants and repetitive movements. These factors are observed through a combination of three sensors. The sensors employed are a microphone, thermal vision sensor and optional wireless fitness bracelets wearable.

These sensors record data in a manner that respects the privacy of occupants. The microphone monitor sound levels. Sampled audio is never recorded or stored. The thermal vision sensor observes the environment using a low-resolution grid monitoring emissive heat; as such, it cannot discern any identifiable features or activity requiring high-resolution perception. The use of fitness bracelets provides accelerometer data and individual tracking via triangulation [11], as the presence of wearable technology may spur agitation this will be optional. Data from these sensors are relayed to a backend server, which stores these records in both a relational database and a big data store.

In the event that an individual becomes agitated or experiences an escalation or a meltdown, a mechanism is provided to allow caregivers to annotate this. This mechanism uses smart devices (phones/tablets). These annotations in combination with the records stored will then be used to build a predicative model through machine learning.

Once a model has been produced, it will be used to observe a window of live records from these sensors. If an upcoming incident is predicted, an alert is issued to caregivers through smart devices. Machine learning in this approach allows detection be tailored to specific individuals/occupants of an area, facilitating the differences between triggering factors among individuals. A graphical representation of this approach is shown in Fig. 1. This approach is discussed in detail in the remainder of this section.

The thermal vision sensor used in this approach provides monitoring of the majority of the factors that may trigger agitation, except audio level and on-body movement. This sensor perceives through a 16×16 grid of temperature readings.

Raw data from this sensor is sent to a server, once received a daemon processes it to extract all desired features. The daemon uses computer vision based Gaussian blob detection to detect individuals and non-environmental heat sources [12]. The results of this blob detection are then used in conjunction with the raw sensor data to demine a number of features, which are; occupant emissive temperature, environmental temperature, inter-occupant proximity, occupant count, location and movement. Figure 2(a) shows the sensor Fig. 2(b) shows the results of the computer vision processing.

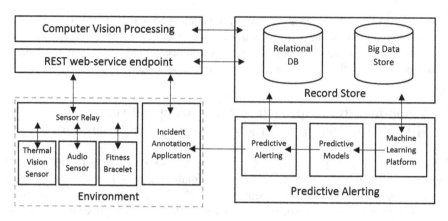

Fig. 1. The architecture of the developed agitation monitoring and intervention platform

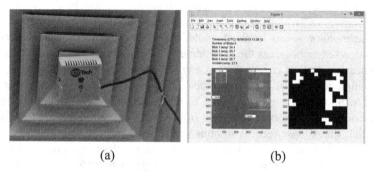

(a)   (b)

Fig. 2. The thermal vision sensor used in this approach (a). The processing of this thermal vision sensor using Gaussian blob detection to identify and track occupants (b).

Additionally, a microphone is used to sample noise levels in the environment. Noise is an important factor to monitor in agitation detection as environmental noise can have cause triggers and the noise an individual emits may indicate an impending incident. Sound is recorded from this microphone at a rate of 6 Hz with the Root Mean Square (RMS) value, accurately representing audio volume [13], being calculated and stored.

Signals are transmitted by fitness bracelets relaying accelerometer data, a unique ID and the calculated received signal strength value, which can be used in positional tracking. Currently no fitness bracelet has been selected for use in this platform, as an evaluation of suitable units needs to occur.

These sensor records need context to provide a way to analyze which changes of the monitored factors caused agitation. To provide this context, a mechanism must be provided that allows caregivers to annotate sensor records indicating when an event occurred. A low-friction solution is implemented through NFC tags affixed to walls in an environment. NFC tags are passively powered, stickers that have wirelessly accessible, reprogrammable memory. These tags can then be enrolled onto the system with a record containing the ID of the sensor monitoring the tags environment. This programming is performed by an application that runs on android-based smart devices.

If an individual suffers agitation, escalation or a meltdown, a caregiver equipped with a smart device taps it to the NFC tag; an installed application then reports the incident. This process does not need the application explicitly opened to function. These reports/annotations can then be edited, classified (agitation, escalation or meltdown) and reviewed via a web app, if desired. This approach allows sensor records to be swiftly annotated little complexity. Having such a low complexity approach will maximize the number of annotations that may be recorded.

Machine learning will be used in conjunction with these annotations to produce predictive models. These models will be integrated into the deployed server infrastructure and will be used to identify potential incidents and inform caregivers by analysis of live data. The use of machine learning allows automatic personalization of agitation detection for specific individuals, adapting to their specific triggers. Additionally, if, through manual analysis of annotations and sensor data, a common trend for agitation is found this prediction system may incorporate logical rules in conjunction with machine learning to provide an assured response approach. This assured response approach would provide prediction without a need to train the model beforehand. This predictive mechanism is elaborated more in the future work section.

4   Future Work

The core of this approach has been implemented with future work focusing on implementing and evaluating the predictive alerting platform. To implement this, an evaluation of machine learning approaches would be undertaken to determine the best one for this application. These approaches learn from features in a data set, presented over a window of time. The selected features correlate to factors for agitation, specifically, the following:

(a) Individual occupant temperature; average, minimum and peak values
(b) Ambient temperature within monitored locale; average, minimum and peak values
(c) Number of occupants within monitored locale; average, minimum and peak values
(d) Number of events where occupants experienced extreme proximity
(e) Duration of occupant extreme proximity
(f) Audio level within monitored locale; average, minimum, peak and RMS values
(g) Amount of occupant movement; time in motion and distance
(h) Individual occupant loitering; duration, number of instances and location
(i) Accelerometer data representing movement; peak acceleration values and number/frequency of instances of rest followed by movement

A number of supervised machine learning techniques will be evaluated to determine those that are most suited to the variety of factors that will be considered. To achieve this, this system will first be placed in an environment occupied by individuals with ASD. Collected data will be used to evaluate which technique provides the greatest predictive accuracy. Once the prediction mechanism has been fully implemented, the performance of the overall approach will be evaluated in a small-scale trail.

5 Conclusion

This paper presents a novel approach to monitoring individuals with ASD with a goal of detecting and predicting incidents of agitation, escalation and meltdowns. The devised approach is non-invasive and respects the privacy of the individuals by monitoring in a manner that does not store any identifiable images or sounds. The approach incorporates a low-friction annotation mechanism to allow caregivers to report incidents. These annotations are used to provide insight into the events that lead to an incident and will be used to produce a predictive model using supervised machine learning technique.

An optional but more invasive monitoring element, in the form of a fitness bracelet, can be used to provide additional insight into factors that may indicate agitation. The use of such a bracelet would be determined on a per-individual bracelet due to the additional stress that wearing such a device may cause those suffering from ASD.

Future work will collect data from an environment using this approach and this data will be used to evaluate a number of supervised machine learning techniques. Once a technique, or combination of techniques, has been selected, the approach will be deployed in a small-scale trial to evaluate its overall efficacy.

Acknowledgments. The authors gratefully acknowledge the contributions of Dr. Jonathan Synnott for his exemplary work on the thermal vision processing core used in this approach. This work received support from Invest NI under the Competence Centre Programme Grant RD0513853.

References

1. Kim, Y.S., Leventhal, B.L., Koh, Y.-J., Fombonne, E., Laska, E., Lim, E.-C., Cheon, K.-A., Kim, S.-J., Kim, Y.-K., Lee, H., Song, D.-H., Grinker, R.R.: Prevalence of autism spectrum disorders in a total population sample. Am. J. Psychiatry **168**, 904–912 (2011)
2. Baron-Cohen, S., Scott, F.J., Allison, C., Williams, J., Bolton, P., Matthews, F.E., Brayne, C.: Prevalence of autism-spectrum conditions: UK school-based population study. Br. J. Psychiatry **194**, 500–509 (2009)
3. Levy, S.E., Mandell, D.S., Schultz, R.T.: Autism. Lancet. **374**, 1627–1638 (2009)
4. Rafferty, J., Nugent, C., Chen, L., Qi, J., Dutton, R., Zirk, A., Boye, L.T., Kohn, M., Hellman, R.: NFC based provisioning of instructional videos to assist with instrumental activities of daily living. Engineering in Medicine and Biology Society (2014)
5. Acampora, G., Cook, D.J., Rashidi, P., Vasilakos, A.V.: A survey on ambient intelligence in health care. Proc. IEEE. Inst. Electr. Electron. Eng. **101**, 2470–2494 (2013)
6. Bonfiglio, S., Chetouani, M., Giuliano, A., Maharatna, K., Muratori, F., Donnelly, M., Paggetti, C., Pioggia, G.: MICHELANGELO, an European research project exploring new, ICT-supported approaches in the assessment and treatment of autistic children. Neuropsychiatr. Enfance. Adolesc. **60**, S210 (2012)

7. Miles, J.H., McCathren, R.B.: Autism Overview. GeneReviews at GeneTests: Medical Genetics Information Resource, pp. 1–29 (2005)
8. Newschaffer, C.J., Croen, L.A., Daniels, J., Giarelli, E., Grether, J.K., Levy, S.E., Mandell, D.S., Miller, L.A., Pinto-Martin, J., Reaven, J., Reynolds, A.M., Rice, C.E., Schendel, D., Windham, G.C.: The epidemiology of autism spectrum disorders*. Annu. Rev. Public Health **28**, 235–258 (2007)
9. Brown, S.: Autism Spectrum Disorder and De-escalation Strategies (2015)
10. Odom, S., Thompson, J., Hedges, S., Boyd, B., Dykstra, J., Duda, M., Szidon, K., Smith, L., Bord, A.: Technology-aided interventions and instruction for adolescents with autism spectrum disorder. J. Autism Dev. Disord. **25**, 1–15 (2014)
11. Wang, Y., Yang, X., Zhao, Y., Liu, Y., Cuthbert, L.: Bluetooth positioning using RSSI and triangulation methods (2013)
12. Synnott, J., Nugent, C., Jeffers, P.: A thermal data simulation tool for the testing of novel approaches to activity recognition. In: Pecchia, L., Chen, L.L., Nugent, C., Bravo, J. (eds.) IWAAL 2014. LNCS, vol. 8868, pp. 10–13. Springer, Heidelberg (2014)
13. Wold, E., Blum, T., Keislar, D., Wheaten, J.: Content-based classification, search, and retrieval of audio. IEEE Multimedia **3**, 27–36 (1996)

Influence of Seasons on Human Behavior in Smart Environments

Fabien Barthelot[1,2]([⊠]), Marc Le Goc[1], and Eric Pascual[2]

[1] Aix Marseille Université, CNRS, ENSAM, LSIS UMR 7296, 13397 Marseille, France
[2] Centre Scientifique et Technique du Bâtiment,
290, Route des Lucioles, BP209, 06904 Sophia-Antipolis, France
fabien.barthelot@cstb.fr

Abstract. The aim of the presented work is to give an operational solution to model and to monitor the behavior of peoples in smart buildings together with the power consumption optimization of the environment resources. The proposed solution is based on the discovery, the modeling and the validation of behavioral knowledge with an unsupervised learning process included in a whole Knowledge Discovery in Database process. The particularity of the proposed approach is that the learning process has been design to work on the timed data directly provided by a smart environment. This paper describes the approach and its application to a real world building of offices. The application puts on the light one of the most difficult problem in this kind of approach, the seasonality of human behavior, that changes the behavior models over time, making the usual approaches difficultly practicable.

Keywords: Inductive learning · Machine learning · Knowledge discovery · Data mining · Behavior modeling · Smart environments

1 Introduction

Silver Economy, Smart Grids, Smart Environments, Open Data, etc., are terms generally used to evoke new important scientific fields and societal issues where human peoples are at the core of an informational environment allowing assistance to operate on the environment resources, and simultaneously, optimized control of the resources consumption. Such informational environments lead to the development of digital services, including software developments and Data Sciences, to increase the autonomy of people (very young children, elderly, workers, etc.) when interacting with their environment and other peoples, physically or not, to achieve some quotidian tasks. So a lot of new propositions appears to this aim. But most of them fail on an important problem: the stochastic properties of human behavior. To model human behavior in their living environment, the technologies must be able to adapt their functioning to the habits, the life desires, and the aims of the people. This constitutes one the key to define adequate technologies and services, new scientific approaches must be defined.

© Springer International Publishing Switzerland 2015
I. Cleland et al. (Eds.): IWAAL 2015, LNCS 9455, pp. 146–151, 2015.
DOI: 10.1007/978-3-319-26410-3_14

But the stochastic properties of human behavior make difficult to model it and so to adapt the services to the needs for people. This paper aims to illustrate this problem with a real application of a recent mathematical theory, the Timed Observation Theory (TOT, [3]), specifically designed to model humans' interactions on its environment directly from the informational tracks which these interactions leave. This theory established a new machine learning and knowledge modeling approach that is applied on a real world problem to put on light one of the property of the stochastic properties of human behavior: the seasonality. The next section is then dedicated to describes the works related with the presented approach. Section 3 is then dedicated to the description of a real world application and the phenomenon this application put on the light: the seasonality of human behavior. Section 4 ends this paper with the presentation of the future works this application allowed to define.

2   Related Works

Two main approaches have been studied. In the first type of approaches, the behavior monitoring is based on expert's models that a recognition task uses to analyze the flow of data provided by sensors. The CASAS project of the Washington State University that is currently considered as the project reference in matter of smart homes [5], but there exists numerous similar project over the world. One of the main difficulties with such approaches is the mismatch between *a priori* models and data provided by sensors. This problem can be approached by the improvement of the convergence between models and data with the adaptation of models with available *a priori* data sets [6].

The second type of approaches is less common because it is more recent. They are based on a learning and modeling process of human behavior directly from the available data. The learning process is typically designed as a Knowledge Discovery in Database process (KDD) where Data Mining algorithms like decision trees, neural networks, Naive Bayes Classifier or Genetic Algorithms, play a central role [7,8]. Such an approach defines the KDD process as a supervised machine learning functionality that use *a priori* knowledge to build the sets right and wrong behavior examples(cf. ([9] for a complete state of the art). The problem of the data set representativity (and to a lesser extent, its completeness) arises so that the KDD process earths up on a major problem: the stochastic properties of human behavior strongly increases the difficulty to produce adequate data sets and then adequate models. One of the reasons for that is the role that time play in the constitution of data sets. Most of the proposed Data Mining algorithms having been designed for non timed data, their extensions to timed data, like AprioriAll [10], SPAM ([11]), SPADE ([12]) or Winepi/Winepi [13,14] algorithms present two main drawbacks: (i) the number of discovered models increases in a non-linear way with the *a priori* setting of the values of the algorithm parameters [15], and (ii) the threshold values of the decision criteria ([16]), even if only a very small fraction of these models are interesting. To solve these two problems, the Timed Observations Theory (TOT, [3]) allowed the definition of a new KDD approach, specifically designed to learn directly from timed data without any parameters.

A Java tool called TOM4K (Timed Observations Management of Knowledge) implements the main concepts of the TOT to combine human and machine learning abilities to produce adequate models of dynamic process from timed data. The crucial advantage, and the originality of the TOM4K learning and modeling process is the unique knowledge representation formalism that is shared between human experts (TOM4D models [17]) and machines (TOM4L models [1]): the comparison and the combination is then very simple and natural, notably thanks to the abstraction method TOM4A [17].

3   The EcOffice Application

The application of the described approach is made on the data of EcOffice project at the Centre Scientifique et Technique du Bâtiment (CSTB) of Sophia Antipolis, located in the Provence-Alpes-Côte d'Azur (PACA) region of France (southeast), during the year 2011. The aim of the EcOffice project was to invite the office users of the building of the CSTB to detect bad consumption habit through adopting new behaviors.

The A1 building is made with 16 offices and a reading room. Each office is dedicated to one or two users. An office is made one or two windows. To the aim of the EcOffice project, two types of sensors have been implemented in the offices of the A1 building: power monitoring and ambient sensors. In this study, only the ambient sensors are under consideration: opened/closed doors and windows, ceiling lamp, heater, air conditioning and ambient temperature. The studied period of the EcOffice database is 12 months long, from Marsh 2011 to February 2012 (i.e. 904 996 timed observations). The conceptual office defines the terms used to described the equipments of the offices. This conceptual office allowed to define the EcOffice ontology defined to analyze the sensors' data contained in the 2011 database. The advantage with the use of a generic ontology is that the behavioral models are provided with a unique language, whatever are the specificities of the concerned temporal period, the observed building, the analyzed office and its instrumentation, and the number of the office users. As a consequence, the behavioral models can be compared together, and the data can be merges to build more generic models. The EcOffice ontology contains 285 terms It has been developed with the TOM4T tool (Timed Observation Modeling for Talking), a tool similar to Protégé, and implemented in a ontology manager called TOM4DM, an application developed by our partner in this study, the TOM4 company. TOM4DM normalizes and corrects multiples databases, produced by various sources, thanks to the vocabulary contained in different ontologies, to produce a unique database containing the corrected and normalized data so that statistics can be computed.

The aim of our study is to demonstrates that it is possible to model human behavior from timed data despite of its strong stochastic properties. Our claim is that when using timed data, behavioral regularities emerges from the random behavior of human. To this aim, we produces the behavior models of the offices number 7 and 16, for each month of the year 2011. The office number 7 is dedicated to only one person and is made with two windows. The office number 16 is dedicated to two persons and is made with one windows. As a consequence, we consider that these two offices are very representative of the global behaviors of the users of the offices of the A1 building. Figure 1 shows the behavioral models for the months of March, April, May, October, November and December of 2011, for the office number 7 (the same observations are made for all other office) computed by TOM4BN algorithm [2, 4]. The first evidence is the multiples differences of the behavioral models over months: there is no months where the models are the same. This shows the first part of our claim: human behavior is so random that it is impossible to define *a priori* models to recognize or to simulate human behavior. Nevertheless, it can be seen that the models are all made with two independent sub-models: the *T-Model* concerning the temperatures (i.e. concerning the radiator and the air conditioning), and the *W-Model* concerning the use of the windows and the ceiling lamp. When analyzing precisely these two models, 2 temporal periods can be clearly distinguished. The first period covers December to April. During this period, the *T-Model* always contains the *ART* path (Air conditioning-Radiator-Temperature), showing the way the user of the A7 office controls the office temperature with the radiator. The second period covers May-November. During this period, the *W-Model* always contains the *W2fW1fW2tW1t* path (Windows2.false -Windows1.false -Windows2.true - Windows1.true).

The interpretation of these observations is the following: monthly observed, the human behaviors leads to define two seasons, a cold seasons from December to April where the office temperature is controlled by the radiator (the use of the windows is random), and a warm seasons where the temperature is mainly controlled with the windows (the radiator is no more used during the warm season). When considering the PACA region of France (i.e. southeast), this result is obvious. It is then very satisfactory that our algorithm allows to produce such evidences. This result confirms the second part of our claim: regularities emerges from the stochastic properties of human behavior. It is also very clear that the energy consumption is directly linked with the seasons and this example demonstrates that the seasons can be discovered when modeling human behavior through the interaction between a human and its environment (here the office instrumentation).

Finally, this example shows that it is possible to automatically model human behavior directly from raw timed data, but these models requires an abstraction step to be correctly interpreted. This is the aim of the TOM4A abstraction method.

4   Conclusion

This paper describes an operational approach to model human behavior in the context of smart buildings where the optimization of the usage of the environment resources is crucial, notably the power consumption.

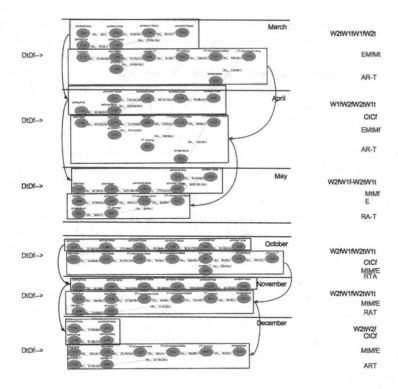

Fig. 1. Example of seasonal behavior.

The proposed approach is based on a recent mathematical framework, the Timed Observation Theory (TOT, [3]), designed to model dynamic processes from timed data. The TOT is the basis of a Knowledge Engineering methodology called TOM4D (Timed Observation Modeling for Diagnosis, [17]) and a knowledge discovery process called TOM4L (Timed Observation Mining for Learning, [1]). The main concepts of the TOT have been implement in a Java tool called TOM4K (Timed Observations Management of Knowledge) to combine human and machine learning abilities to produce adequate models of dynamic process from timed data. The approach is applied on a real world application, in the southeast of France. The models demonstrates that regularities emerges from the stochastic properties of human behavior. In particular, this example demonstrates an evidence: human behavior, and so energy consumption, strongly depends of the seasons.

The observations made with this application will be refined in the next future with a decomposition of a year in 52 weeks and the analysis of all the models made for each offices of the studied building. A real time learning and continuously modeling version of the algorithm described is this paper is currently under development to be implemented, during summer 2015, in the CSTBox (http://cstbox.cstb.fr)that collects the data and sends alarms when required.

References

1. Benayadi, N.: Contribution à la découverte de connaissances à partir de données datées (phdthesis) Univertité Paul Cezanne Aix-Marseille III (2010)
2. Benayadi, M., Le Goc, M.: Discovering N-ary timed relations from sequences. In: Proceedings of the 3rd International Conference an Agents and Artificial Intelligence, ICAART 2010, 22–24 January 2010, Valencia, Spain, pp. 428–433 (2010)
3. Le Goc, M.: Notion d'observation pour le diagnostic des processus dynamiques: Application a Sachem et a la découverte de connaissances temporelles Faculté des Sciences et Techniques de Saint Jérôme (2006)
4. Le Goc, M., Ahdab, A.: Learning Bayesian Networks From Timed Observations. Academic Publishing, Saarbrücken (2012)
5. Cook, D.J., Crandall, A.S., Thomas, B.L., Krishnan, N.C.: CASAS: a smart home in a box. Computer **46**, 62–69 (2012)
6. Cook, D.J., Krishnan, N.C., Rashidi, P.: Activity discovery and activity recognition: a new partnership. IEEE Trans. Syst. Man Cybern. Part B (TSMCB) 43(3), 820–828 (2013)
7. Colak, I., Sagiroglu, S., Yesilbudak, M.: Data mining and wind power prediction: a literature review. Renewable Energy **46**, 241–247 (2012)
8. Arends, M., Hendriks, P.H.J.: Smart grids, smart network companies. Utilities Policy **28**, 1–11 (2014)
9. Roddick, F.J., Spiliopoulou, M.: A survey of temporal knowledge discovery paradigms and methods. IEEE Trans. Knowl. Data Eng. **14**, 750–767 (2002)
10. Agrawal, R., Srikant, R.: Mining sequential patterns. In: Proceedings of the 11th International Conference on Data Engineering (ICDE 1995) (1995)
11. Ayres, J., Flannick, J., Gehrke, J., Yiu, T.: Sequential PAttern mining using a bitmap representation. In: Proceedings of the Eighth ACM SIGKDD International Conference on Knowledge Discovery and Data Mining, KDD 2002 (2002)
12. Zaki, M.J.: SPADE: an efficient algorithm for mining frequent sequences. Mach. Learn. **42**, 31–60 (2001)
13. Mannila, H., Toivonen, H., Verkamo, A.I.: Discovering Frequent Episode in Sequence. In: Fayyad, U.M., Uthurusamy, R. (eds.) Proceedings of the First International Conference on Knowledge Discovery and Data Mining (1995)
14. Mannila, H., Toivonen, H., Verkamo, A.I.: Discovery of frequent episodes in event sequences. Data Min. Knowl. Discov. **1**, 259–289 (1997)
15. Mannila, Heikki: Local and Global Methods in Data Mining: Basic Techniques and Open Problems. In: Widmayer, Peter, Triguero, Francisco, Morales, R., Hennessy, Matthew, Eidenbenz, Stephan, Conejo, Ricardo (eds.) ICALP 2002. LNCS, vol. 2380, p. 57. Springer, Heidelberg (2002)
16. Han, J., Kamber, M.: Data Mining: Concepts and Techniques. Morgan Kaufmann, San Francisco (2006)
17. Pomponio, L., Le Goc, M.: Reducing the gap between experts' knowledge and data: the TOM4D methodology. Data Knowl. Eng. **94**, 1–37 (2014)

The HELICOPTER Project:
A Heterogeneous Sensor Network
Suitable for Behavioral Monitoring

Claudio Guerra, Valentina Bianchi, Ferdinando Grossi, Niccolò Mora,
Agostino Losardo, Guido Matrella, Ilaria De Munari,
and Paolo Ciampolini[✉]

Dipartimento di Ingegneria dell'Informazione, Università degli Studi di Parma,
Viale delle Scienze 181/a, 43124 Parma, Italy
paolo.ciampolini@unipr.it

Abstract. In this paper, the infrastructure supporting the HELICOPTER
AAL-JP project is described. The project aims at introducing behavioral analysis
features for early detection of age-related diseases: to this purpose, a heterogeneous sensor network has been designed and implemented, encompassing in
the same vision environmental, wearable and clinical sensors. In order to make
environmental sensors suitable for behavioral inference, the issue of activity
tagging (i.e., attribution to a given user of the action detected by the sensors)
needs to be tackled. Within the HELICOPTER scenario, cooperation between
environmental and wearable sensors is exploited to this aim. Preliminary results
offer encouraging perspectives: piloting phase, which will validate the approach
on a larger scale, is close to start.

Keywords: Ambient assisted living · Wireless sensor network · Behavioral
analysis

1 Introduction

Ambient Assisted Living technologies are being developed, supporting independent
life of elderly people. According to such a vision, the living environment itself becomes
an active component of the elderly empowerment strategy, by increasing the comfort,
safety and self-reliance in dealing with daily living activities [1, 2]. Among disparate
technologies contributing to the AAL, predecessors can be found in home automation
technologies, as well as in telemedicine ones. In this paper, an approach which aims at
effectively merging such technologies in an integrated, holistic vision is presented.
The HELICOPTER (*Healthy lifestyle support through comprehensive tracking of
individual and environmental behaviors* [3]), carried out in the framework of the
European AAL Joint Programme, aims at implementing strategies for prevention and
early discovery of age-related disease by means of effective interaction among

On behalf of the HELICOPTER project partnership.

© Springer International Publishing Switzerland 2015
I. Cleland et al. (Eds.): IWAAL 2015, LNCS 9455, pp. 152–163, 2015.
DOI: 10.1007/978-3-319-26410-3_15

environmental and clinical sensing technologies. The overall project rationale and goals are described in Sect. 2 below, whereas the devised physical infrastructure is introduced in Sect. 3. Section 4, instead, deals with a specific, conceptual aspects underpinning the system implementation; in order to exploit "environmental" sensors for inferring behavioral information, the need arises (in a multiple user environment) for discriminating the actual user interacting with a given sensor, i.e., to "tag" environmental sensor outcome with user information. A simple solution, based on cooperation among wireless sensors, has been investigated and tested. A few conclusions are eventually drawn in Sect. 5.

2 The HELICOPTER Project

A number of chronic diseases, which are actually endemic among elderly population, could be more effectively treated (or even prevented) by accounting for frequent monitoring of suitable indicators: clinical sensors have been developed, suitable for home use, which can be used to this purpose. Connecting such sensors to a communication network enables telemedicine services, providing a link toward caregivers and the healthcare system: however, the end-user is left the whole burden of frequently checking relevant physiological parameters; i.e., the monitoring quality fully relies on end-user scrupulousness in complying with the given schedule. This is, of course, adequate when a specific medical condition occurs, whereas, in a prevention-oriented daily routine, may be often perceived as a boring, intrusive task, possibly jeopardized by mild cognitive or memory issues and thus scarcely sustainable. On the other hand, besides objective measurement of clinical parameters, many of the target diseases may reveal themselves through a variety of behavioral "symptoms", which can be assessed by means of indirect indicators, easily detected by means of simple, environmental sensing devices. Such indirect signs, for instance, include changes in the feeding or sleeping patterns, in the toilet frequency, in physical activity, etc. Of course, such indirect hints are not reliable enough for actual clinical diagnosis, but may provide a first-level detection of anomalies, addressing the user, or the caregivers, toward more accurate assessment, based on clinical evaluation [4].

Starting from such consideration, the HELICOPTER combines in a single, interoperable system different kinds of detectors, ranging from passive, environmental sensors to home clinical instruments, with the aim of implementing a hierarchical procedure for assessing "diagnostic suspicions" for a set of specific age related diseases. Such approach is regarded as a form of "automatic triage", in the sense that the system is capable of recognizing conditions which are compatible with actual occurring of such diseases and thus to drive the end-user through a sequence of increasingly accurate assessment procedures, possibly culminating in addressing to professional care.

Thus, the HELICOPTER approach aims at implementing continuous, unobtrusive monitoring of user's habits, which are possibly meaningful to health assessment. This, in turn, may reflect on relieving the user from too demanding self-checking routines (avoiding boredom, discomfort and illness stigma), at the same time providing the caregivers with a new evaluation dimension, based on "low-intensity", long-term behavioral analysis.

The system concept is illustrated by the sketch in Fig. 1: end user(s) interact with the system through a heterogeneous layer of sensors. Environmental sensors are distributed into the living environment, whereas wearable sensors may provide a more detailed insight about user motion and position; finally, a set of networked clinical sensors are exploited to provide measurement of specific physiological parameters.

Through wireless connections, all sensors feed the system database, providing a detailed, multi-faceted picture of the user's habits and status. Based on such an information set, an artificial reasoning engine looks for behavioral anomalies, i.e. relative changes in the behavioral patterns (either sudden, abrupt changes or slow drifts). Based on information fusion, the likelihood of some specific medical conditions is evaluated, and suitable feedbacks are addressed to the end-users themselves and to their caregiving network.

In order to illustrate the system aim, we refer here to a simple example, related to the **heart failure** diagnostic suspicion. Congestive heart failure (CHF) is among the primary causes of hospitalization in elderly population, and regular lifestyle monitoring is recommended to control it and minimize its impact on quality of life.

CHF shows up with a set of symptoms which lend themselves to illustrate the HELICOPTER approach quite easily; in fact, people suffering from CHF tend to develop one or more among the following behavioral indicators:

- Increased urinary frequency and/or nocturia
- Sudden changes of body weight
- Decrease of physical activity, due to tiredness and fatigue
- Discomfort in sleeping lying in bed, due to edema

which can be somehow detected be means of "non clinical" sensors:

- Toilet sensor
- Bodyweight scale
- Wearable motion sensor
- Bed and chair occupancy sensors

Besides that, main diagnostic instruments, suitable for home use, include the measurement of blood oxygen concentration (oxymeter) and of the blood pressure. Thus, the HELICOPTER system foresees a hierarchical approach to infer a CHF diagnostic suspicion: the user's behavior is constantly monitored to infer early symptoms of a CHF crisis. To this purpose, a model (currently based on Bayesian Belief Networks, a detailed description of which goes beyond the scope of this paper) combines outcomes of different home sensors and evaluates the likeliness of the heart failure condition: should the evaluation score exceed a given threshold, the user is (automatically) addressed to the appropriate clinical parameter checks. Data coming from the oxymeter are acquired by the HELICOPTER system: should data coming from the portable, networked oxymeter confirm the suspicion, the system alerts the user and his caregiving networks, addressing him to appropriate medical control.

Similarly to the example above, a set of relevant diseases has been selected in the current HELICOPTER development stage, developing related behavioral models. The model list includes:

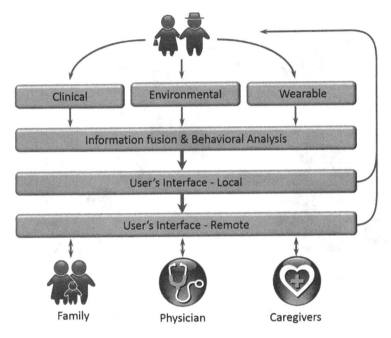

Fig. 1. HELICOPTER system conceptual view

- Hypoglycaemia
- Hyperglycaemia
- Cystitis
- Heart failure
- Depression
- Reduced physical autonomy
- Prostatic hypertrophy
- Bladder prolapse

Although each model may actually involve a different set of sensors, the overall hierarchy is similar, exploiting the environmental and wearable sensors for inferring potentially troublesome situations, to be confirmed by involving clinical devices into the evaluation. Although conceptually straightforward, the actual system implementation implies several challenging issues, which are discussed in sections below.

3   HELICOPTER Heterogeneous Sensor Network

Based on the above description, the conceptual scheme in Fig. 1 maps over the heterogeneous network depicted in Fig. 2. Home sensors pertain to different classes:

- **clinical** sensors provide the system with accurate data about physiological parameters; their management implies user awareness and action;

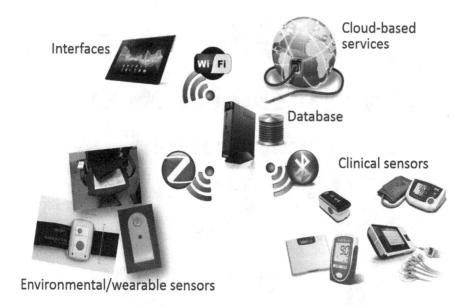

Interfaces

Cloud-based
services

Database

Clinical sensors

Environmental/wearable sensors

Fig. 2. HELICOPTER physical network

- **environmental** sensors provide data related to the user interaction with the home environment, possibly linked to behavioural meaningful patterns; no user awareness or activation is required; if multiple users are sharing the same environment, criteria for identification of the actual interacting user are needed;
- **wearable** devices provide information about individual activity, also inherently carrying identification information.

Sensors exploit different wireless protocols: namely, clinical sensors are present in a limited number and do not need to be scattered over the whole home area, and thus do not need to cover large transmission paths; we therefore follow the mainstream, commercial approach by using standard BlueTooth communication technology. Environmental and wearable sensors, instead, poses more severe constraints in terms of network transmission range and topology, so we adopt the ZigBee communication protocol to this purpose.

All wireless sensors communicate with a home gateway device, consisting of a tiny PC, equipped with suitable radio transceivers [5]. The PC runs a supervision process, which takes care of several functions, besides managing the actual sensor communication. Data coming from the periphery are suitably abstracted, making them independent of actual physical feature of the given sensor, and stored in a system database. The HELICOPTER database enables communication among different system modules: in particular, behavioural analysis and anomaly detection is carried out by dedicated modules which acts as "virtual sensors" producing "events" (e.g., anomaly alerts or diagnostic suspicions) which are stored back to the database, in the very same fashion data coming from physical sensors are managed. Similarly, a variety of interfaces can be implemented (aimed at end-users or caregivers) which query the database for system status. I.e., the database is at the crossroads among different subsystems (sensing, processing, interfaces) and thus supports system modularity; a suitable data structure has been devised and implemented, exploiting a MySQL open-source architecture.

Clinical Sensors. Clinical sensors are exploited for the (self) assessment of physiological parameters: all involved sensors need to be easy to use, suitable for being used by the user himself (or by untrained relatives). The HELICOPTER system will provide the user with help and guidance in handling clinical sensors and will automatically manage data logging and transmission over the system infrastructure. I.e., no additional burden (with respect to customary device use) is placed on the user for dealing with system communication.

The list of currently considered sensors, includes:

- Body Weight scale (A&D Medical UC-321PBT)
- Blood Pressure Monitor (A&D Medical UA-767PBT)
- Pulsoxymeter (SAT 300 BT fingertip device, Contec Medical Devices Co. Ltd)
- Glucometer (FORA G31b, Fora Care Inc.)
- Portable ECG (TD-2202B, TaiDoc Technology Corporation)

It is worth stressing that commercial, off-the-shelf devices have been selected and that the overall system design is making no specific assumption on the specific kind or brand of sensors adopted. I.e., the system is open to communicate with a much wider variety of sensors than that actually planned and will perspectively be able to deal with sensor subsequently made available to the market by third parties, at the expense of properly introducing suitable descriptors in the database structure described mentioned above.

Environmental Sensors. The use of sensors of many different kinds and functions is planned, in order to feed the behavioural model; in this case too, we rely either on commercial, off-the-shelf devices or (whenever a more specific function is needed) on purposely designed devices. In both cases, we adopt the IEEE 802.15.4/ZigBee wireless transmission protocol, which allows for ample choice of commercial devices and lends itself to efficient power management. Sensors have been selected based also on user-related features, i.e., the need of actual user awareness in sensor management; installation requirements and intrusivity were evaluated.

Environmental sensors available for exploitation in the HELICOPTER framework include:

- **Room presence sensor, based on** Passive InfraRed (PIR) technology
- **Door/drawer sensor, exploiting** magnetic contact (Reed switches), useful for detecting behavioural patterns related to diagnostic suspicion models mentioned above (e.g., opening the food cabinet, indirectly relating to the food intake frequency and time).
- **Fridge sensor,** providing information about fridge opening and internal temperature and humidity. It provides information related to feeding habits as well, besides allowing for simple warnings (door left open, temperature too high, ...)

- **Hob sensor,** consisting of a differential temperature sensor (one sensor is located close to the hob, the other far from heating components, to provide ambient temperature reference). It works as a retrofit option for any kind of kitchen hob (gas, electric, induction) and provides information about cooking/feeding habits, besides safety warning (forgotten burning stove).
- **Bed/chair occupancy sensors,** based on sensitive pads of different shapes and size, coupled to a wireless transceiver. Provides information about sleep patterns and other daily living habits.
- **Toilet sensor,** based on proximity sensors, monitoring the toilet usage frequency and time distribution.
- **Electrical Power meter,** monitoring power consumption of electrical devices relevant to daily living habits assessment (e.g., television set).

Network configuration is carried out automatically, with each sensor registering to the ZigBee network when first turned on, and automatically entering the home ontological description.

Wearable Sensors. Wearable sensors are a key component in the HELICOPTER scenario and exploit the wireless sensor platform MuSA [6], specifically designed with assistive purposes and shown in Fig. 3. Internal MuSA architecture features a CC2531 SoC [7], which fully manages wireless communication (compliant with ZigBee 2007 PRO protocol, and with the ZigBee "Home automation" standard profile) and local computing: signal acquisition and processing is carried out by MuSA on-board circuitry. Radio communication is hence kept at a bare minimum (alarm messages and network management), saving battery energy.

MuSA embeds a Inertial Measurement Unit (IMU, ST device LSM9DS0-iNEMO [8]), featuring a 3D digital linear acceleration sensor, a 3D digital angular rate sensor and a 3D digital magnetic sensor within the same chip. The IMU is exploited to evaluate human body position and orientation information, primarily aimed at fall detection purposes. Within the HELICOPTER project, fall detection features (although

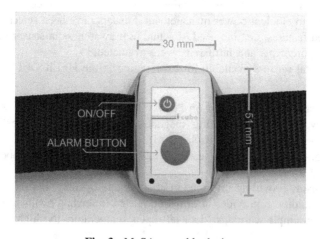

Fig. 3. MuSA wearable device

still available) are not in the main focus, and MuSA is involved with two basic aims: (*i*) providing behavioural information and (*ii*) supporting user identification and localization. More specifically, MuSA will contribute to the overall behavioural picture with information about user motion. Both quantitative indicators (walking speed, for instance) and qualitative ones (concerning gait balance, for instance) will be made available to behavioural models implemented at higher hierarchical levels. Also, MuSA will be exploited for user "tagging" and for approximate user localization within the home environment, as explained in Sect. 3 below.

4 Activity Tagging

Each sensor in the above list provides information contributing to the behavioral picture onto which the automatic triage HELICOPTER concept is based. However, if we assume that more than one single person is living in the monitored environment, each elementary information in such a framework needs some attributes to be uniquely defined: the actual performed action, the performing user and his position.

Depending on the sensor class, we may lack part of such information: environmental devices are placed at a fixed, known location and provide explicit information about the action (e.g., opening the fridge door), but have no knowledge about the performing user. On the other hand, wearable sensors inherently carry identification information, but their position in the home space is to be determined, as well as the actual performed action, by means of artificial reasoning. Clinical sensors, although portable, can be considered similarly to environmental devices: their position is not actually relevant, whereas knowing the actual user interacting with them is, of course, mandatory. I.e., in a multi-user environment, we need to attribute data coming from environmental and clinical sensors to a specific user (possibly without asking the user to deal with explicit identification procedures). Localization features can be exploited to this purpose: in general, however, indoor location is a complex and multi-faceted issue. A large number of systems have been proposed, based on various methods or technologies, ranging from RSSI [9] or time of flight [10] to geo-magnetic field [11] and Mutually Coupled Resonating Circuits [12]. It is worth underlining, however, that HELICOPTER aimed application poses quite different constraints (in terms of required accuracy, system intrusiveness and affordable costs) with respect to the main fields such localization technologies have been developed for. In particular, we do not need precise, geographic localization and we may content ourselves with a topological association instead. Looking for an inexpensive and scarcely intrusive solution, we therefore developed a low-cost gateway system named CARDEAGate, capable of detecting a person crossing a door or any given gateway, and, if he is wearing a MuSA device, to identify him.

CARDEAGate operating principle, illustrated by Fig. 4 exploits the absorption of a radio signal power caused by the body of the person crossing the radio link propagation path [13] and is based on the consequent modulation of the Received Signal Strength Index (RSSI, [14]). CARDEAgate consists of a couple of ZigBee transceiver (G_a and G_b) each having the size of a standard USB flash drive. They can be mounted, for instance, on opposite jambs of a door, the line between G_a and G_b being the monitored region. Unlike optical-based sensors, CARDEAGate does not need line-of-sight visibility, so it can easily be embedded into doorframes, home furniture or stand behind curtains and thin (non-metallic) walls. This makes the system also less intrusive, and allows for smooth integration into most home environments. Detection exploits the perturbation in EM waves propagating between the two transceivers caused by the crossing user's body.

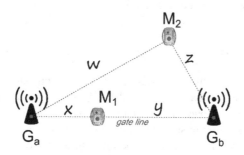

Fig. 4. CARDEAGate system

To this purpose, G_a and G_b exchange a message every 200 ms and monitor the RSSI: if a sudden loss is observed (i.e., the user's "shadow"), a person crossing the gateway is inferred. Then, if the crossing person actually wears a MuSA device, the identification procedure proceeds: G_a and G_b transmit an identification request to the MuSA devices in the network and send the RSSI of received replies to the ZigBee network coordinator. At the supervision level (managed by the HELICOPTER home gateway) a decision strategy is implemented, which finds out which MuSA most likely crossed the gateway. Elementary geometrical reasoning is exploited to this purpose: starting from the simple consideration that the device crossing the gateway is the one which features the lowest sum of distances from either gate transceiver: in Fig. 4, for instance, M_1 is the device crossing the gate line, whereas M_2 lies nearby. Thus:

$$x + y < w + z$$

where x, y, w and z are the distance between mobile and fixed nodes, as indicated in figure. Following, for instance, [14], RSSI can be correlated to the distance $d_{i,j}$ between a given transceiver couple (i, j):

$$d_{i,j} = k * 10^{-RSSI_{i,j}}$$

where k is a constant involving signal propagation features, related to the actual signal path. Such a constant, in principle, is not necessarily uniform along different triangulation legs. Nevertheless, for the sake of simplicity, we can assume a constant value as a worst case scenario: by supposing that propagation along the gate line is better of propagation along longer path (which does not hold rigorously true in general, but makes sense for a sensible gate placement) considering a uniform propagation constant

k may result in relative underestimation of "outer" device distances, thus not harming the selection criteria below. We define the distance sum:

$$S_j = d_{j,A} + d_{j,B} = k(10^{-RSSI_{1,A}} + 10^{-RSSI_{1,B}})$$

so that, with reference to Fig. 4, if the inequality $S_1 < S_2$ holds true, the crossing of M_1 is assessed, and M_2 otherwise. Such a test is straightforwardly generalizable to a larger number of involved users.

The approach has been validated on different test conditions, evaluating both detection (i.e., the ability of recognizing a person's passage) and identification performance. A simple test is summarized in Fig. 5, referring to a two-user scenario, in which a person wearing a MuSA (M1) walked through the gateway (installed on an actual door) and another person, with a second MuSA (M2), was wandering around. 40 tries were carried out and the results were evaluated, illustrated by the scatter plot in figure, where every point refer to the S_1, S_2 estimation for a given condition. As shown, all conditions where correctly interpreted, with the clearance from the diagonal line providing a confidence indicator for the inferred information.

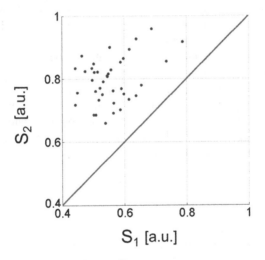

Fig. 5. CARDEAGate: distance sums scatter plot

The strategy introduced so far allows to identify a user at specific locations within the home environment (where gates have been placed). CARDEAGate can be exploited to monitor the access to zones of interest (a room or even the fridge, an armchair, etc.). It is not to be considered as a full "localization" system, but provide useful hints in "attributing" actions detected by environmental sensor to actual home guests, based on low-level fusion of data coming from environmental and wearable sensors. The approach can be generalized to other sensors, different from the gate-line: each sensor, in fact, already inherently include a ZigBee transceiver which can be exploited for the very same purpose. I.e., in principle, the gate function can be extended to other sensors, having different primary functions, with no need of additional hardware devices. In this case, whenever a sensor detects an action, it carries out user identification as well, thus allowing for tagging the activity with user information.

Such a strategy, involving a couple of ZigBee devices to provide location reference, can be further simplified, just relying on the interaction between a single ZigBee beacon and the mobile MuSA devices. In this case, when an action is detected, absolute estimation of the distance $d_{i,j}$ is carried out, attributing the activity to the user featuring the lower distance (i.e., the highest RSSI). This allows for embedding identification capabilities into any ZigBee sensor node; similarly, identification for other sensors not exploiting ZigBee protocol can be obtained just by adding a simple and inexpensive companion ZigBee device to them. Most notably, in the HELICOPTER environment, clinical sensors are coupled to a ZigBee identification node, allowing for automatically tagging clinical data with user information.

Accuracy in the order of 90 % was evaluated by testing the single-node identification feature over a wide range of situations, in a multi-user, multiple sensors lab environment emulating a living environment. Due to uneven propagation features, the single-node approach is, of course, less accurate than the triangulation-based one; nevertheless, identification feature does not trigger any "mission-critical" activity and simply supports building of behavioural profiles, on a statistical basis. Hence, some errors occurring in tricky situations can be tolerated, just resulting in statistical noise and not jeopardizing the whole picture.

Finally, at a higher hierarchical level, raw data can be combined, accounting for some combinational and sequential logic: artificial reasoning may help in solving possible ambiguities and in validating identification data. E.g., by matching sequence of gate crossings and PIR responses, the system may "follow" users along their home walk, and thus have some preliminary information about distribution of users in different rooms; this, in turn can be used to rule out some user-sensor combinations and to simplify the identification/attribution task.

5   Conclusions

In this document, the complete home infrastructure supporting HELICOPTER services is described. More specifically, clinical, wearable and environmental sensors have been selected and implemented. Both commercial and custom devices have been considered. Since behavioural modelling requires individual data discrimination, attributing information coming from environmental sensors to a given user (within the family members set, for instance) is of paramount importance. Hence, specific identification features have been studied, with the aim of finding general solution and of trading off among performance, cost and system intrusivity.

The approach described above is being currently implemented within the project activities: a fully functional prototype has been already demonstrated in a lab environment, and pilot studies, involving over 50 elderly homes, are due to start in Summer 2015.

Acknowledgement. This work has been supported by the Ambient Assisted Living Joint Program (HELICOPTER project, AAL-2012-5-150).

References

1. Grossi, F., Bianchi, V., Matrella, G., De Munari, I., Ciampolini, P.: Internet-based home monitoring and control. Assistive Technol. Res. Ser. **25**, 309–313 (2009)
2. Matrella, G., Grossi, F., Bianchi, V., De Munari, I., Ciampolini, P.: An environmental control hw/sw framework for daily living of elderly and disabled people. In: Proceedings of the 4th IASTED International Conference on Telehealth and Assistive Technologies, Telehealth/AT 2008, pp. 87–92 (2008)
3. http://www.helicopter-aal.eu/
4. Losardo, A., Grossi, F., Matrella, G., De Munari, I., Ciampolini, P.: Exploiting AAL environment for behavioral analysis. Assistive Technol. Res. Ser. **33**, 1121–1125 (2013)
5. Grossi, F., Bianchi, V., Losardo, A., Matrella, G., De Munari, I., Ciampolini, P.: A flexible framework for ambient assisted living applications. In: Proceedings of the IASTED International Conference on Assistive Technologies, AT 2012, pp. 817–824 (2012)
6. Bianchi, V., Grossi, F., De Munari, I., Ciampolini, P.: Multi sensor assistant: a multisensor wearable device for ambient assisted living. J. Med. Imaging Health Inform. **2**(1), 70–75 (2012)
7. http://www.ti.com/product/cc2531
8. http://www.st.com/web/en/catalog/sense_power/FM89/SC1448/PF258556
9. Tian, Y., Denby, B., Ahriz, I., Roussel, P.: Practical indoor localization using ambient RF. In: 2013 IEEE Instrumentation and Measurement Technology Conference (I2MTC), pp. 1125–1129 (2013)
10. Santinelli, G., Giglietti, R., Moschitta, A.: Self-calibrating indoor positioning system based on ZigBee devices. In: 2009 IEEE Instrumentation and Measurement Technology Conference (I2MTC), pp. 1205–1210 (2009)
11. Saxena, A., Zawodniok, M.: Indoor positioning system using geo-magnetic field. In: 2014 IEEE Instrumentation and Measurement Technology Conference (I2MTC), pp. 572–577 (2014)
12. De Angelis, G., De Angelis, A., Dionigi, M., Mongiardo, M., Moschitta, A., Carbone, P.: An accurate indoor positioning-measurement system using mutually coupled resonating circuits. In: 2014 IEEE Instrumentation and Measurement Technology Conference (I2MTC), pp. 844–849 (2014)
13. Wilson, J., Patwari, N.: Radio tomographic imaging with wireless networks. IEEE Trans. Mob. Comput. **9**(10), 621–632 (2010)
14. Parker, S.J., Hal, J., Kim, W.: Adaptive filtering for indoor localization using ZIGBEE RSSI and LQI measurement. Adapt. Filtering Appl. **14**, 305–324 (2007)

High-Level Context Inference for Human Behavior Identification

Claudia Villalonga[1,2]([✉]), Oresti Banos[1], Wajahat Ali Khan[1], Taqdir Ali[1],
Muhammad Asif Razzaq[1], Sungyoung Lee[1], Hector Pomares[2],
and Ignacio Rojas[2]

[1] Department of Computer Engineering, Kyung Hee University, Yongin, Korea
{cvillalonga,oresti,wajahat.alikhan,taqdir.ali,
asif.razzaq,sylee}@oslab.khu.ac.kr
[2] Research Center for Information and Communications Technologies
of the University of Granada, Granada, Spain
{hector,irojas}@ugr.es, cvillalonga@correo.ugr.es

Abstract. This work presents the Mining Minds Context Ontology, an ontology for the identification of human behavior. This ontology comprehensively models high-level context based on low-level information, including the user activities, locations, and emotions. The Mining Minds Context Ontology is the means to infer high-level context from the low-level information. High-level contexts can be inferred from unclassified contexts by reasoning on the Mining Minds Context Ontology. The Mining Minds Context Ontology is shown to be flexible enough to operate in real life scenarios in which emotion recognition systems may not always be available. Furthermore, it is demonstrated that the activity and the location might not be enough to detect some of the high-level contexts, and that the emotion enables a more accurate high-level context identification. This work paves the path for the future implementation of the high-level context recognition system in the Mining Minds project.

Keywords: Context recognition · Context inference · Ontology · Ontological reasoning · Human behavior identification

1 Introduction

The automatic identification of human behavior has evoked an enormous interest in the last years. Diverse technologies have been investigated to perform human behavior identification. For example, some works employ the use of geolocalization systems to track the user position and derive behavioral patterns [12,13]. Other studies build on video, audio or a combination of both modalities to recognize some primitive emotional states [10]. Video systems [17] and on-body sensors [7,14] have predominantly been considered for the recognition of people physical activity. With the boom of the wearable and mobile technology, several commercial solutions are increasingly available at the reach of most consumers.

© Springer International Publishing Switzerland 2015
I. Cleland et al. (Eds.): IWAAL 2015, LNCS 9455, pp. 164–175, 2015.
DOI: 10.1007/978-3-319-26410-3_16

Misfit Shine [2] or Jawbone Up [1] are examples of these systems, which primarily focus on the analysis of the user body motion to keep track of their physical activities.

Human behavior identification is a complex problem that requires the analysis of multiple factors. Likewise, it requires to approach the person observation from various perspectives, including physical, mental and social aspects. Accordingly, current domain-specific solutions are seen to be certainly insufficient to deal with the magnitude of this problem. Instead, more complete platforms combining diverse technologies to infer people lifestyle and provide more personalized services are required. In this direction, Mining Minds [5,6], a novel digital framework for personalized health and wellness support, provides technologies to infer low-level and high-level person-centric information, mainly the user context and behavior, and their physical, mental and social state. This paper focuses on the Mining Minds Context Ontology, used in Mining Minds to help describing the human behavior and to infer high-level context from low-level information.

Prior work supports the use of ontologies in Mining Minds. Ontology-based modeling overcomes the limitations of other models in terms of flexibility, extensibility, generality, expressiveness, and automatic code generation [19]. Moreover, ontology-based models can benefit from ontology reasoning and are one of the most promising models that fulfill the requirements for modeling context information [3]. Thus, ontology-based models are nowadays one of the main approaches to model context. Many ontologies have been created in the last years in order to model the user's context; however, none of them covers all the aspects required in Mining Minds. The CoBrA-Ont ontology [8] extends the SOUPA (Standard Ontologies for Ubiquitous and Pervasive Applications) [9] and defines people, places, and activities. The CoDAMos ontology [16], defines the user, among other entities, and defines for the users their mood, their absolute or relative location and some environmental variables. The CONON (CONtext ONtology) [20] is an upper ontology which defines general concepts like location, activity, and person. The Pervasive Information Visualization Ontology (PiVOn) [11] defines in the user ontology, their location, identity, activity, and time. The mIO! ontology [15] defines, among others, an ontology for the user, and for the location. Finally, the human activity recognition ontology [18] models individuals and social activities: personal, physical, professional activities and postures.

The rest of the paper is organized as follows. Section 2 introduces the architecture for High Level Context Awareness in Mining Minds. Section 3 describes the Mining Minds Context Ontology, which models context in a comprehensive manner. Some examples of the context classes illustrate the different modeling principles. Section 4 presents the inference method for the identification the user's context based on the Mining Minds Context Ontology. Several examples of context instances illustrate the modeling principles and inference logic. Finally, main conclusions and future steps are presented in Sect. 5.

2   Mining Minds High Level Context Awareness

In Mining Minds, the core technologies devised for the inference and modeling of the user's context constitute the Information Curation Layer [4]. Low Level

Context Awareness (LLCA) and High Level Context Awareness (HLCA) are the main components of this layer. LLCA converts into categories, such as physical activities, emotional states, locations and social patterns, the wide-spectrum of data obtained from the user interaction with the real and cyber-world. HLCA models and infers more abstract context representations based on the categories identified by LLCA. HLCA builds on the Mining Minds Context Ontology (Sect. 3) and applies ontological inference to identify the user's context (Sect. 4). HLCA (Fig. 1) consists of four main components: High-Level Context Builder, High-Level Context Reasoner, High-Level Context Notifier, and Context Ontology Manager. The High-Level Context Builder receives the low-level information - activities, emotions, and locations - identified by LLCA and generates the ontological concepts representing an unclassified context. The Low-level Context Mapper interprets the received low-level information and transforms it into the corresponding ontological concepts. The Low-level Context Synchronizer searches for concurrent low-level information. The Context Instantiator creates a new instance of an unclassified high-level context which links to the comprising low-level information. The unclassified context is served to the High-Level Context Reasoner for its verification and classification. The Context Verifier checks the semantic and syntactic consistency of the unclassified context. The Context Classifier classifies the unclassified context into one of the different high-level contexts by applying ontological inference. Once a new context has been identified, the High-Level Context Notifier makes it available to the other Mining Minds layers for the creation of personalized health and wellness services and recommendations. The Context Ontology Manager provides persistence of the Mining Minds Context Ontology and supports the easy access and storage of context information.

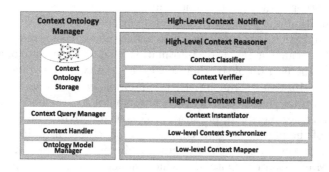

Fig. 1. Mining Minds high level context awareness architecture.

3   Mining Minds Context Ontology

The Mining Minds Context Ontology models high-level context in a comprehensive manner using the OWL2 ontology language. The ontology is available at http://www.miningminds.re.kr/lifelog/context/context-v1.owl. The main concept of this ontology is the `Context` class (Fig. 2), which defines the different high-level contexts. These contexts build on low-level information, including the recognized activities, detected locations, and recognized emotions. The `Activity`, the `Location`, and the `Emotion` classes have been described to model the different low-level information (Fig. 2(a)). These primitive classes are related to the `Context` class via the object properties `hasActivity`, `hasLocation` and `hasEmotion`. The `hasActivity` property has as domain the `Context` class and as range the `Activity` class. The `hasLocation` property has as domain the `Context` class and as range the `Location` class. The `hasEmotion` property has as domain the `Context` class and as range the `Emotion` class. The different recognized activities are modeled as 16 disjoint subclasses of the `Activity` class: `LyingDown`, `Sitting`, `Standing`, `Walking`, `Jogging`, `Running`, `Cycling`, `Hiking`, `Dancing`, `Stretching`, `Eating`, `Sweeping`, `ClimbingStairs`, `DescendingStairs`, `RidingElevator`, and `RidingEscalator`. The `Location` class has 8 disjoint subclasses used to model the detected locations: `Home`, `Office`, `Restaurant`, `Gym`, `Mall`, `Transport`, `Yard`, and `Outdoors`. The recognized emotions are modeled through the 8 disjoined subclasses of the `Emotion` class: `Happiness`, `Sadness`, `Anger`, `Disgust`, `Fear`, `Boredom`, `Surprise`, and `Neutral`.

The `Context` class has 9 disjoint subclasses to define the different high-level contexts: `OfficeWork`, `Commuting`, `HouseWork`, `Gardening`, `HavingMeal`, `Amusement`, `Exercising`, `Sleeping`, and `Inactivity` (Fig. 2(b)). Each `Context` subclass is defined through complement classes and through existential and universal axioms that define the necessary and sufficient conditions of the equivalent anonymous class. How the equivalent anonymous classes for the nine `Context` subclasses have been described in Protégé is shown in Fig. 3. Three examples are discussed in the following to illustrate the different modeling principles.

The `OfficeWork` class (Fig. 3(a)) is defined as being equivalent to the anonymous class: `Context and (hasActivity some Sitting) and (hasLocation some Office) and (hasActivity only Sitting) and (hasEmotion only (Anger or Boredom or Disgust or Happiness or Neutral)) and (hasLocation only Office)`. This means that to be a member of the defined class `OfficeWork`, an instance of the `Context` class must have a property of type `hasActivity` which relates to an instance of the `Sitting` class, and this property can only take as value an instance of the `Sitting` class. Moreover the instance of the `Context` class must also have a property of type `hasLocation` which relates to an instance of the `Office` class and only to an instance of the `Office` class. Finally, and in case the instance of the `Context` class has a property of type `hasEmotion`, this property must relate to an instance of the `Anger` class, the `Boredom` class, the `Disgust` class, the `Happiness` class, or the `Neutral` class. This universal restriction does not specify that the relationship through the `hasEmotion` property must exist, but that if it exists, it must be to the specified class members. Thus, if an instance of the `Context` class, fulfills the two existential and universal restrictions on the properties `hasActivity` and

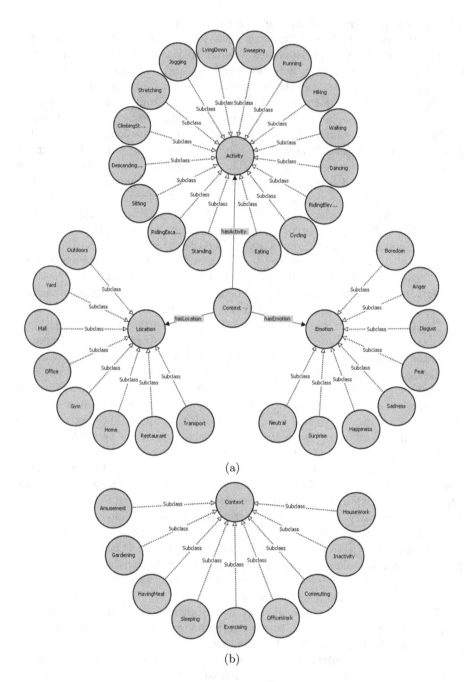

Fig. 2. Mining Minds Context Ontology: (a) `Context` class, `Activity`, `Location` and `Emotion` classes and subclasses, and `hasActivity`, `hasLocation` and `hasEmotion` properties; and (b) `Context` class and subclasses.

● **Context**
    and (**hasActivity** some **Sitting**)
    and (**hasLocation** some **Office**)
    and (**hasActivity** only **Sitting**)
    and (**hasEmotion** only
      (**Anger** or **Boredom** or **Disgust** or **Happiness** or **Neutral**))
    and (**hasLocation** only **Office**)

(a) OfficeWork

● **Context**
    and (**hasActivity** some
      (**Sitting** or **Standing**))
    and (**hasLocation** some **Transport**)
    and (**hasActivity** only
      (**Sitting** or **Standing**))
    and (**hasLocation** only **Transport**)

(b) Commuting

● **Context**
    and (**hasActivity** some
      (**Standing** or **Sweeping** or **Walking**))
    and (**hasLocation** some **Home**)
    and (**hasActivity** only
      (**Standing** or **Sweeping** or **Walking**))
    and (**hasEmotion** only
      (**Anger** or **Boredom** or **Disgust** or **Happiness** or **Neutral**))
    and (**hasLocation** only **Home**)

(c) HouseWork

● **Context**
    and (**hasActivity** some
      (**Standing** or **Sweeping** or **Walking**))
    and (**hasLocation** some **Yard**)
    and (**hasActivity** only
      (**Standing** or **Sweeping** or **Walking**))
    and (**hasEmotion** only
      (**Happiness** or **Neutral**))
    and (**hasLocation** only **Yard**)

(d) Gardening

● **Context**
    and (((**hasActivity** some **Eating**)
    and (**hasLocation** some
      (**Home** or **Restaurant**))
    and (**hasActivity** only **Eating**)
    and (**hasLocation** only
      (**Home** or **Restaurant**))) or ((**hasActivity** some **Sitting**)
    and (**hasLocation** some **Restaurant**)
    and (**hasActivity** only **Sitting**)
    and (**hasLocation** only **Restaurant**)))
    and (**hasEmotion** only
      (**Disgust** or **Happiness** or **Neutral** or **Surprise**))

(e) HavingMeal

● **Context**
    and (**hasActivity** some
      (**Dancing** or **Sitting** or **Standing** or **Walking**))
    and (**hasEmotion** some **Happiness**)
    and (**hasLocation** some **Mall**)
    and (**hasActivity** only
      (**Dancing** or **Sitting** or **Standing** or **Walking**))
    and (**hasEmotion** only **Happiness**)
    and (**hasLocation** only **Mall**)

(f) Amusement

● **Context**
    and (((**hasActivity** some **Hiking**)
    and (**hasLocation** some **Outdoors**)
    and (**hasActivity** only **Hiking**)
    and (**hasLocation** only **Outdoors**)) or ((**hasActivity** some **Stretching**)
    and (**hasLocation** some
      (**Gym** or **Home** or **Office** or **Outdoors**))
    and (**hasActivity** only **Stretching**)
    and (**hasLocation** only
      (**Gym** or **Home** or **Office** or **Outdoors**))) or ((**hasActivity** some
      (**ClimbingStairs** or **DescendingStairs**))
    and (**hasLocation** some
      (**Gym** or **Home** or **Office**))
    and (**hasActivity** only
      (**ClimbingStairs** or **DescendingStairs**))
    and (**hasLocation** only
      (**Gym** or **Home** or **Office**))) or ((**hasActivity** some
      (**Cycling** or **Jogging** or **Running**))
    and (**hasLocation** some
      (**Gym** or **Outdoors**))
    and (**hasActivity** only
      (**Cycling** or **Jogging** or **Running**))
    and (**hasLocation** only
      (**Gym** or **Outdoors**))))
    and (**hasEmotion** only
      (**Happiness** or **Neutral**))

(g) Exercising

● **Context**
    and (**hasActivity** some **LyingDown**)
    and (**hasLocation** some **Home**)
    and (**hasActivity** only **LyingDown**)
    and (**hasEmotion** only **Neutral**)
    and (**hasLocation** only **Home**)

(h) Sleeping

● **Context**
    and (not (**Amusement** or **Commuting** or **Exercising** or **Gardening** or **HavingMeal** or **HouseWork** or **OfficeWork** or **Sleeping**))
    and (**hasActivity** some
      (**LyingDown** or **RidingElevator** or **RidingEscalator** or **Sitting** or **Standing**))
    and (**hasActivity** only
      (**LyingDown** or **RidingElevator** or **RidingEscalator** or **Sitting** or **Standing**))

(i) Inactivity

Fig. 3. Mining Minds Context Ontology: Definition of the nine **Context** subclasses.

hasLocation, but does not asses a property of type hasEmotion, the instance will be inferred as being a member of the OfficeWork class.

The Amusement class (Fig. 3(f)) is defined as being equivalent to the anonymous class: Context and (hasActivity some (Dancing or Sitting or Standing or Walking)) and (hasEmotion some Happiness) and (hasLocation some Mall) and (hasActivity only (Dancing or Sitting or Standing or Walking)) and (hasEmotion only Happiness) and (hasLocation only Mall). This means that to be a member of the defined class Amusement, an instance of the Context class must have a property of type hasActivity which relates to an instance of the Dancing class, the Sitting class, the Standing class, or the Walking class, and this property can only take as value an instance of one of these four classes: Dancing, Sitting, Standing or Walking. Moreover the instance of the Context class must also have a property of type hasLocation which relates to an instance of the Mall class and only to an instance of the Mall class. Finally, the instance of the Context class must also have a property of type hasEmotion which relates to an instance of the Happiness class and only to an instance of the Happiness class. Summarizing, an instance of the Context class has to fulfill the described existential and universal restrictions on the properties hasActivity, hasLocation and hasEmotion in order to be inferred as a member of the Amusement class. Hence, the assertion of an instance of the Happiness class for the hasEmotion property is mandatory to infer the Amusement class. The type of the restrictions on the hasEmotion property is the main modeling difference between the Amusement class and the previously presented OfficeWork class. In the definition of Amusement class the hasEmotion property is mandatory due to existential and universal restrictions on this property, whereas in the definition of the OfficeWork class the hasEmotion property is optional since the restriction on this property is universal but not existential.

The Inactivity class (Fig. 3(i)) is defined as being equivalent to the anonymous class: Context and (not(Amusement or Commuting or Exercising or Gardening or HavingMeal or HouseWork or OfficeWork or Sleeping)) and (hasActivity some (LyingDown or RidingElevator or RidingEscalator or Sitting or Standing)) and (hasActivity only (LyingDown or RidingEle vator or RidingEscalator or Sitting or Standing)). This means that to be a member of the defined class Inactivity, an instance of the Context class must not be an instance of any of the other subclasses of Context, i.e., it must not be an instance of the Amusement class, the Commuting class, the Exercising class, the Gardening class, the HavingMeal class, the HouseWork class, the OfficeWork class, or the Sleeping class. Moreover the instance of the Context class must also have a property of type hasActivity which relates to an instance of the LyingDown class, the RidingElevator class, the RidingEscalator class, the Sitting class, or the Standing class, and this property can only take as value an instance of one of these five classes: LyingDown, RidingElevator, RidingEscalator, Sitting, or Standing. In the modeling of the Inactivity class, not only existential and universal restrictions are used, but also the concept of complement class.

4   Context Inference in Mining Minds

The Mining Minds Context Ontology is the means to infer high-level context from low-level information. Using a reasoner, an instance of the Context class, i.e., an unclassified high-level context, can be determined to be a member of one of the nine Context subclasses: OfficeWork, Commuting, HouseWork, Gardening, HavingMeal, Amusement, Exercising, Sleeping and Inactivity. The instances of unclassified context are defined as individuals of the Context class for which their properties and types are asserted. The instances of the Activity class are asserted through the hasActivity property. The instances of the Location class are asserted through the hasLocation property. The instances of the Emotion class are asserted through the hasEmotion property. Reasoning in OWL is based on the Open World Assumption (OWA), which means that it cannot be assumed that something does not exist until it is explicitly stated that it does not exist. Therefore, type assertions are used as closure axioms to indicate that an individual does not exist for a property of the unclassified context individual. Figure 4 shows several examples of instances of the Context class representing unclassified contexts and their inferred membership class computed using the HermiT reasoner in Protégé. In the following the examples are discussed in order to illustrate the modeling principles and the inference logic.

Figure 4(a) shows an instance of the Context class for which the hasActivity property has been asserted to take the value act_sitting, and the hasLocation property has been asserted to take the value loc_office; where act_sitting is an instance of the Sitting class and loc_office is an instance of the Office class. Due to the OWA, the instance of the Context class has been asserted the type hasActivity only ({act_sitting}) and the type hasLocation only ({loc_office}). These type assertions state that for this individual the hasActivity property only takes as value the instance act_sitting, and the hasLocation property only takes as value the instance loc_office. Furthermore, the Context instance has also been asserted the type not (hasEmotion some Emotion) in order to state that the individual does not have any property of type hasEmotion which takes any individual of the class Emotion. The reasoner is used to automatically classify this instance of the Context class. The instance complies with the OfficeWork class definition; therefore, it is classified as being a member of the OfficeWork class. Concretely, the Context instance fulfills the two existential and universal restrictions which state that the hasActivity relates to an instance of the Sitting class and only to an instance of the Sitting class, and hasLocation relates to an instance of the Office class and only to an instance of the Office class. Moreover, the universal restriction on the hasEmotion property does not state that the property must exist, as is the case in this instance; thus, the instance can be inferred as being a member of the OfficeWork class.

A similar Context instance is presented in Fig. 4(b); in addition to the property assertion for hasActivity and hasLocation, the hasEmotion property is asserted to take the value emo_boredom, which is an instance of the Boredom class. Furthermore, and in order to comply with the OWA, the corresponding

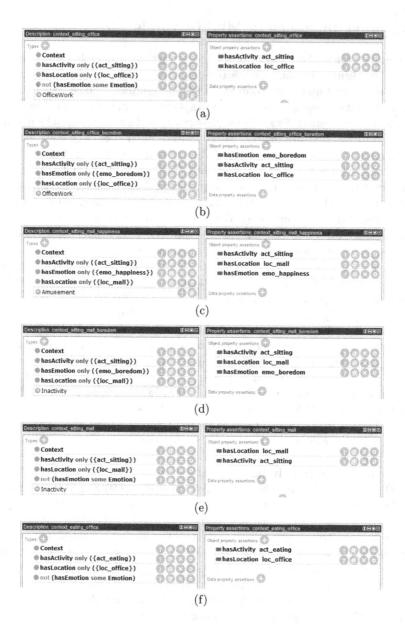

Fig. 4. Instances of the `Context` class which are classified as being members of the defined `Context` subclasses using the HermiT reasoner in Protégé. The inferred classes are highlighted in yellow: (a) `OfficeWork`, (b) `OfficeWork`, (c) `Amusement`, (d) `Inactivity`, (e) `Inactivity`, and (f) no class is inferred. `act_sitting` is an instance of the `Sitting` class, `act_eating` is an instance of the `Eating` class, `loc_office` is an instance of the `Office` class, `loc_mall` is an instance of the `Mall` class, `emo_boredom` is an instance of the `Boredom` class, and `emo_happiness` is an instance of the `Happiness` class.

type hasEmotion only ({emo_boredom}) is asserted for this Context instance. Not only does this instance comply with the existential and universal restrictions on the hasActivity property and the hasLocation property defined in the OfficeWork class definition, but also with the universal restriction on the hasEmotion property since the hasEmotion property exists and relates to an instance of the Boredom class. Thus, this Context instance is also classified by the reasoner as being a member of the OfficeWork class. The classification as members of the OfficeWork class of the two Context instances, one with an assertion on the hasEmotion property (Fig. 4(b)) and another one without it (Fig. 4(a)), proves the flexibility of the Mining Minds Context Ontology which enables the identification of high-level context even if one of the pieces of low-level information is missing. This is very helpful in real life scenarios where the emotion recognition systems are not always available and may produce detection events in a less regular basis than the activity recognizers or the location detectors.

Conversely, sometimes it is not possible to identify the high-level context if one of the low-level information is missing. Classifying Context instances which do not have asserted a hasEmotion property might be possible for some of the contexts like OfficeWork; however, this is not possible when the hasEmotion property is mandatory due to existential and universal restrictions defined on the Context subclass. This is the case of the Amusement class for which the assertion of an instance of the Happiness class for the hasEmotion property is required. The relevance of the hasEmotion property assertion can be observed for the Context instances presented in Figs. 4(c), (d) and (e). In these examples, only the Context instance in Fig. 4(c) is classified as being a member of the Amusement class since it is the only one for which the hasEmotion property is asserted to take as value an instance of the Happiness class, namely emo_happiness. The Context instance in Fig. 4(d) has asserted the hasEmotion property but this one takes as value emo_boredom which is an instance of the Boredom class and not an instance of the Happiness class; whereas the Context instance presented in Fig. 4(e) does not have a property of type hasEmotion. Therefore neither the Context instance in Fig. 4(d) nor the Context instance in Fig. 4(e) can be inferred as being members of the Amusement class. Even if a priori one could have expected the three Context instances being classified as the Amusement class, because for all three the hasActivity property has been asserted to take the value act_sitting, and the hasLocation property has been asserted to take the value loc_mall which is an instance of the Mall class, the different assertions of the hasEmotion property have proved the assumption to be wrong. This fact shows the relevance and influence on the high-level context of all low-level information types: activity, location and emotion. Moreover, this demonstrates that the activity and the location might not be enough to detect high-level context, and that the emotion enables a more accurate high-level context identification.

One should realize that the Context instance in Fig. 4(d) and the Context instance in Fig. 4(e) fulfill all the conditions to be inferred as being members of the `Inactivity` class, since they do not belong to any of the other subclasses of `Context` and they meet the restriction on the `hasActivity` property. Finally, some combinations of low-level information might not constitute a known high-level context. As an example, Fig. 4(f) shows a context instance which is not detected as any of the nine subclasses of `Context`.

5 Conclusions and Future Work

This study has introduced the Mining Minds Context Ontology, an ontology for the comprehensive and holistic identification of human behavior. The described ontology models high-level context based on low-level information, namely, activities, locations, and emotions. Conversely to other existing context ontologies for behavior recognition, the proposed model has demonstrated that activity and location information might not be enough to detect some of the high-level contexts, and that the emotion enables a more accurate high-level context identification. Moreover, the Mining Minds Context Ontology has been proved to be flexible enough to operate in real life scenarios in which emotion recognition systems may not always be available. Finally, it has also been shown that high-level contexts of diverse complexity can certainly be determined from the low-level information by reasoning on the Mining Minds Context Ontology. Next steps include the implementation of the proposed ontology and reasoning method to support online inference of unclassified context instances based on detected low-level information.

Acknowledgments. This work was supported by the Industrial Core Technology Development Program, funded by the Korean Ministry of Trade, Industry and Energy (MOTIE), under grant number #10049079.This work was also supported by the Junta de Andalucia Project P12-TIC-2082 and the grant "Movilidad Internacional de Jóvenes Investigadores de Programas de Doctorado Universidad de Granada y CEI BioTic".

References

1. Jawbone Up (2015). https://jawbone.com/up. (Accessed 14 September 2015)
2. Misfit Shine (2015). http://misfit.com/products/shine. (Accessed 14 September 2015)
3. Baldauf, M., Dustdar, S., Rosenberg, F.: A survey on context-aware systems. Int. J. Ad Hoc Ubiquitous Comput. **2**(4), 263–277 (2007)
4. Banos, O., Bang, J.H., Hur, T.H., Siddiqui, M., Huynh-The, T., Vui, L.-B., Ali-Khan, W., Ali, T., Villalonga, C., Lee, S.: Mining human behavior for health promotion. In: Proceedings of the 37th Annual International Conference of the IEEE Engineering in Medicine and Biology Society (EMBC 2015) (2015)
5. Banos, O., Amin, M.B., Khan, W.A., Afzel, M., Ahmad, M., Ali, M., Ali, T., Ali, R., Bilal, M., Han, M., Hussain, J., Hussain, M., Hussain, S., Hur, T.H., Bang, J.H., Huynh-The, T., Idris, M., Kang, D.W., Park, S.B., Siddiqui, H., Vui, L.-B., Fahim, M., Khattak, A.M., Kang, B.H., Lee, S.: An innovative platform for person-centric health and wellness support. In: Ortuño, F., Rojas, I. (eds.) IWBBIO 2015, Part II. LNCS, vol. 9044, pp. 131–140. Springer, Heidelberg (2015)

6. Banos, O., Bilal-Amin, M., Ali-Khan, W., Afzel, M., Ali, T., Kang, B.-H., Lee, S.: The mining minds platform: a novel person-centered digital health and wellness framework. In: Proceedings of the 9th International Conference on Pervasive Computing Technologies for Healthcare (2015)
7. Banos, O., Damas, M., Pomares, H., Prieto, A., Rojas, I.: Daily living activity recognition based on statistical feature quality group selection. Expert Syst. Appl. **39**(9), 8013–8021 (2012)
8. Chen, H., Finin, T., Joshi, A.: An ontology for context-aware pervasive computing environments. Knowl. Eng. Rev. **18**(03), 197–207 (2003)
9. Chen, H., Finin, T., Joshi, A.: The soupa ontology for pervasive computing. In: Tamma, V., Cranefield, S., Finin, T.W., Willmott, S. (eds.) Ontologies for Agents: Theory and Experiences, pp. 233–258. Birkhäuser, Basel (2005)
10. Datcu, D., Rothkrantz, L.: Semantic audio-visual data fusion for automatic emotion recognition. Emotion Recognition: A Pattern Analysis Approach, pp. 411–435 (2014)
11. Hervás, R., Bravo, J., Fontecha, J.: A context model based on ontological languages: a proposal for information visualization. J. UCS **16**(12), 1539–1555 (2010)
12. Liao, L., Fox, D., Kautz, H.: Extracting places and activities from GPS traces using hierarchical conditional random fields. Int. J. Robot. Res. **26**(1), 119–134 (2007)
13. Lin, Q., Zhang, D., Huang, X., Ni, H., Zhou, X.: Detecting wandering behavior based on GPS traces for elders with dementia. In: 12th International Conference on Control Automation Robotics & Vision, pp. 672–677. IEEE (2012)
14. Mannini, A., Intille, S.S., Rosenberger, M., Sabatini, A.M., Haskell, W.: Activity recognition using a single accelerometer placed at the wrist or ankle. Med. Sci. Sports Exerc. **45**(11), 2193–2203 (2013)
15. Poveda Villalon, M., Suárez-Figueroa, M.C., García-Castro, R., Gómez-Pérez, A.: A context ontology for mobile environments. In: Proceedings of Workshop on Context, Information and Ontologies, CEUR-WS (2010)
16. Preuveneers, D., et al.: Towards an extensible context ontology for ambient intelligence. In: Markopoulos, P., Eggen, B., Aarts, E., Crowley, J.L. (eds.) EUSAI 2004. LNCS, vol. 3295, pp. 148–159. Springer, Heidelberg (2004)
17. Ribeiro, P., Santos-Victor, J.: Human activity recognition from video: modeling, feature selection and classification architecture. In: Proceedings of International Workshop on Human Activity Recognition and Modelling, pp. 61–78. Citeseer (2005)
18. Riboni, D., Bettini, C.: COSAR: hybrid reasoning for context-aware activity recognition. Pers. Ubiquit. Comput. **15**(3), 271–289 (2011)
19. Mohsin Saleemi, M., Díaz Rodríguez, N., Lilius, J., Porres, I.: A framework for context-aware applications for smart spaces. In: Balandin, S., Koucheryavy, Y., Hu, H. (eds.) NEW2AN 2011 and ruSMART 2011. LNCS, vol. 6869, pp. 14–25. Springer, Heidelberg (2011)
20. Wang, X.H., Zhang, D.Q., Gu, T., Pung, H.K.: Ontology based context modeling and reasoning using owl. In: Proceedings of the Second IEEE Annual Conference on Pervasive Computing and Communications Workshops, pp. 18–22. IEEE (2004)

On the Development of a Real-Time Multi-sensor Activity Recognition System

Oresti Banos[1], Miguel Damas[2], Alberto Guillen[2], Luis-Javier Herrera[2],
Hector Pomares[2], Ignacio Rojas[2], Claudia Villalonga[2],
and Sungyoung Lee[1]([✉])

[1] Ubiquitous Computing Lab, Kyung Hee University, Yongin-si, Korea
{oresti,sylee}@oslab.khu.ac.kr
[2] Department of Computer Architecture and Computer Technology,
University of Granada, Granada, Spain
{mdamas,aguillen,jherrera,hector,irojas,cvillalonga}@ugr.es

Abstract. There exist multiple activity recognition solutions offering good results under controlled conditions. However, little attention has been given to the development of functional systems operating in realistic settings. In that vein, this work aims at presenting the complete process for the design, implementation and evaluation of a real-time activity recognition system. The proposed recognition system consists of three wearable inertial sensors used to register the user body motion, and a mobile application to collect and process the sensory data for the recognition of the user activity. The system not only shows good recognition capabilities after offline evaluation but also after analysis at runtime. In view of the obtained results, this system may serve for the recognition of some of the most frequent daily physical activities.

Keywords: Activity recognition · Wearable sensors · mHealth

1 Introduction

The identification of human activities has attracted very much attention lately. Typically, wearable sensors are used to register body motion signals that are analyzed by following a set of signal processing and machine learning steps to recognize the activity performed by the user [1]. Most of the existing works in this area contribute with diverse models that normally yield very high recognition capabilities [2,7]. However, a major part of these solutions have only been validated in controlled environments and through offline evaluations. More importantly, there is a lack of papers covering the whole design process for the development of a system that can actually recognize human activity in realistic settings. This paper aims to help filling this gap by contributing with a detailed description of the steps required to develop a fully functional activity recognition system for the real-world.

© Springer International Publishing Switzerland 2015
I. Cleland et al. (Eds.): IWAAL 2015, LNCS 9455, pp. 176–182, 2015.
DOI: 10.1007/978-3-319-26410-3_17

2   Sensing Infrastructure and Processing Hub

The use of single-sensor recognition systems has predominantly been fostered in the past [2,4]. However, multi-sensor configurations have recently been shown to be required when dealing with real-world technological and practical issues [8,11,12]. Likewise, dedicated systems have been used to gather and process the data coming from multiple sensors to estimate the user activity. Nevertheless, this trend has lately shifted towards the use of mobile devices since they offer higher computational power and memory capacity among other features. Accordingly, the system proposed here consists of three wearable inertial sensors (Fig. 1(a)), which are used for registering the user body motion, and a mobile application (Fig. 1(b)), devoted to collecting and processing the sensory data for the recognition and visualization of the user activity. Shimmer2 wearable sensors are used given the high reliability yielded by these commercial devices. The sensors are respectively placed on the subject's chest, right wrist and left ankle and attached through elastic straps. These placements cover most body movements assuming that the activities involve a symmetrical execution. The sensors measure the acceleration, rate of turn and magnetic field orientation of the body parts they are fastened to. The sampling rate used for all sensing modalities is of 50 Hz, enough for capturing human activity. The sensors are Bluetooth interfaced with the mobile device, which hosts an application built for the aggregation and processing of the data based on a given activity recognition model.

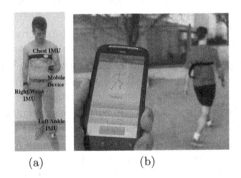

(a)   (b)

Fig. 1. (a) Study setup and sensor deployment. (b) Running application.

3   Activity Recognition Model Design

The process of designing an activity recognition model involves three steps: (1) collection of a dataset; (2) definition of candidate models; and (3) evaluation and selection of the most reliable model. The dataset used here comprises body motion recordings for ten volunteers wearing the inertial sensors as depicted in

Table 1. Activity set.

L1: Standing still (1 min)	L7: Frontal elevation of arms (20×)
L2: Sitting and relaxing (1 min)	L8: Knees bending (crouching) (20×)
L3: Lying down (1 min)	L9: Cycling (1 min)
L4: Walking (1 min)	L10: Jogging (1 min)
L5: Climbing/descending stairs (1 min)	L11: Running (1 min)
L6: Waist bends forward (20×)	L12: Jump front and back (20×)

Fig. 1(a), while executing a set of regular activities (Table 1) in an out-of-lab environment. A detailed description of the dataset can be found in [10].

Standard recognition models are built then for evaluation. All models use triaxial acceleration data since it is the most prevalent sensor modality in wearable activity recognition [5]. The signals are segmented through a 2-s non-overlapping sliding window approach, which proves a good trade-off between recognition speed and accuracy for the activities of interest [9]. Three incremental feature sets are considered for their discrimination potential and easy interpretation in the acceleration domain [4]: FS1 = "mean and standard deviation", FS2 = FS1 + "maximum, minimum and mean crossing rate" and FS3 = FS2 + "mode, median and kurtosis". Likewise, four of the most common machine learning techniques are used for classification: decision trees (DT), k-nearest neighbors (KNN), naive Bayes (NB) and nearest centroid classifier (NCC). The k-value for the KNN model is empirically set to three.

The resulting models are evaluated through a 10-fold cross validation process, which is repeated 100 times to ensure statistical robustness [3]. The F_1-*score* is used to measure the performance of each candidate model. The results obtained after evaluation are shown in Fig. 2. Those models utilizing DT for the classification process are clearly the most accurate among considered for all feature sets. Moreover, the feature set that leads to the best results is FS2. Thus, the model considered for implementation builds on the triaxial acceleration collected from the three wearable sensors; partitions these signals into data windows of two seconds; extracts the "mean, standard deviation, maximum, minimum and mean crossing rate" from every data window; and inputs these features to a DT classifier trained on all the dataset.

4   Activity Recognition Application Development

The activity recognition process is performed on a mobile device. Concretely, an intuitive app is developed to continously gather the data from the wearable sensors and process it according to the model described before. During the very first configuration of the app, the sensors must be Bluetooth paired with the mobile device (Fig. 3(a)). Each sensor is labeled to correctly match each data stream to the corresponding input of the recognition model (Fig. 3(b)). Thereafter, the

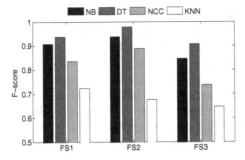

Fig. 2. Results from the offline evaluation of standard activity recognition models.

user can start the activity recognition process by clicking on the corresponding start button (Fig. 3(c)), which also triggers the streaming of the wearable sensors to the mobile device. From then on, the app shows the recognized activity based on the analysis of the movements performed by the user (Fig. 3(d)).

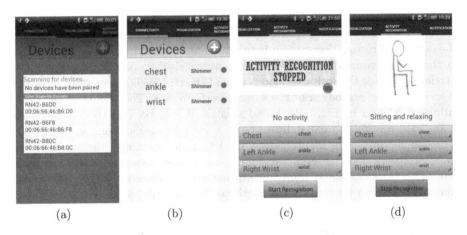

Fig. 3. Snapshots from the activity recognition application: (a) scan process for discovering the sensors; (b) wearable sensors are paired and further labeled according to their placement; (c) sensors are matched to the corresponding inputs of the recognition model; (d) the application recognizes the activity performed by the user.

The application has been implemented using the mHealthDroid framework [10]. This open source framework is devised to support the agile and easy development of mHealth applications on Android. The communication functionality relies on the mHealthDroid Communication Manager, which abstracts the underlying mobile and wearable devices, makes the communication transparent to the application and provides a unified and interpretable data format. Concretely, the mHealthDroid Adapters for Shimmer2 wearable devices are used for these devices to communicate with the mobile phone and to map their data to the proprietary format. In this manner, the registered triaxial acceleration samples are made available to the diverse components of the application.

A major interest in using mHealthDroid comes from the functionalities it provides for implementing a full recognition model. The Segmentation, Feature Extraction and Classification functionalities of the mHealthDroid Data Processing Manager are used here, some of which build on a stripped version of the popular WEKA Data Mining Software [6]. Thus, to realize the designed recognition model, a 2-s windowing process is generated, the required statistical features are instantiated and the trained DT model is implemented.

The sensory data collected during the execution of the system can also be stored on a local database. Although this is not required for the recognition of the user activity, it is considered here for a potential inspection and review of the collected data at the point of need. The mDurance storage functionality builds on top of the mHealthDroid Storage Manager, which provides a high level of abstraction from the underlying storage technology and enables data persistence, both locally and remotely. In the current implementation, the app stores data locally on a SQLite database deployed on the mobile phone SD card.

5   Real-Time Evaluation

The developed recognition system is validated at runtime in realistic conditions. To that end, five independent volunteers were asked to perform the complete activity set (Table 1). Both user's activity and smartphone's screen were recorded on video for the evaluation of the system performance. The results of the evaluation are shown in Fig. 4. In broad strokes, it can be said that the system shows good recognition capabilities. Only a few misclassifications are observed. For example, during the identification of "sitting and relaxing", the model sometimes interprets that the users are bending their waist forward or elevating their arms. This is explained by some abrupt movements observed during the execution of this activity for some of the participants. Similarly, some errors are found

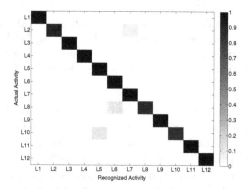

Fig. 4. Confusion matrix obtained from the online evaluation of the activity recognition model. Activities are identified through the labels used in Table 1.

for the detection of "knees bending or crouching", which is confused here again with "waist bend forwards". This is a consequence of some difficulties encountered by part of the users while performing this exercise, which translated into a moderate sway back and forth. Finally, a few misclassifications are observed among "walking", "jogging" and "running", which are basically originated from the varying cadence with which these activities were executed by the subjects.

6   Conclusions

This work has summarized the complete process for the realization of a multi-sensor activity recognition system for real-time applications. The system employs various wearable inertial sensors attached to different body parts to register a wide-spectrum of regular movements. The recorded data is transmitted to a mobile application that processes the information for the recognition of the user activity. This application develops on a recent mHealth framework that provides several functionalities significantly reducing the implementation time. Future extension of this work includes the incorporation of healthy physical lifestyles recommendations based on the analysis of the user activity patterns.

Acknowledgments. Work supported by the ICTD Program (10049079, Development of mining core technology exploiting personal big data) funded by the Ministry of Trade, Industry and Energy (MOTIE, Korea). This work was also supported by the Junta de Andalucia Project P12-TIC-2082.

References

1. Bulling, A., et al.: A tutorial on human activity recognition using body-worn inertial sensors. ACM Comput. Surv. **46**(3), 1–33 (2014)
2. Mannini, A., et al.: Activity recognition using a single accelerometer placed at the wrist or ankle. Med. Sci. Sports Exercise **45**(11), 2193–2203 (2013)
3. Arlot, S., Celisse, A.: A survey of cross-validation procedures for model selection. Stat. Surv. **4**, 40–79 (2010)
4. Kwapisz, J.R., et al.: Activity recognition using cell phone accelerometers. ACM SigKDD Explor. Newsl. **12**(2), 74–82 (2011)
5. Lara, O., Labrador, M.: A survey on human activity recognition using wearable sensors. IEEE Commun. Surv. Tutorials **PP**(99), 1–18 (2012)
6. Hall, M., et al.: The weka data mining software: an update. SIGKDD Explor. Newsl. **11**(1), 10–18 (2009)
7. Banos, O., et al.: Daily living activity recognition based on statistical feature quality group selection. Expert Syst. Appl. **39**(9), 8013–8021 (2012)
8. Banos, O., et al.: Dealing with the effects of sensor displacement in wearable activity recognition. Sens. **14**(6), 9995–10023 (2014)
9. Banos, O., et al.: Window size impact in human activity recognition. Sens. **14**(4), 6474–6499 (2014)
10. Banos, O., et al.: Design, implementation and validation of a novel open framework for agile development of mobile health applications. Biomed. Eng. Online **14**(S2:S6), 1–20 (2015)

11. Banos, O., et al.: Multi-sensor fusion based on asymmetric decision weighting for robust activity recognition. Neural Process. Lett. **42**(1), 5–26 (2015)
12. Zappi, P., et al.: Network-level power-performance trade-off in wearable activity recognition: a dynamic sensor selection approach. ACM Trans. Embed. Comput. Syst. **11**(3), 68:1–68:30 (2012)

Sensing for Health and Wellbeing

Fall Risk Assessment and Prevention Using Wearables

Asbjørn Danielsen[⊠], Bernt Arild Bremdal, and Hans Olofsen

Narvik University College, Narvik, Norway
{Asbjorn.Danielsen,Hans.Olofsen,
BerntArild.Bremdal}@hin.no

Abstract. Each year about 1/3 of elderly aged 65 or older experience a fall. Many of these falls may have been avoided if fall risk assessment and prevention tools where available in a daily living situation. We identify what kind of information is relevant to do fall risk assessment using wearable sensors in a daily living environment by investigating current research. Based on our findings we propose a fall risk awareness protocol as a fall prevention tool.

Keywords: Daily living · Fall risk assessment · Fall prevention · Fall risk awareness protocol · Fall prevention tool · Wearable sensors

1 Introduction

Fall risk assessment is a process in which the probability of a future fall is estimated. Fall risk prevention, on the other hand, address a most important question; how should one prevent falls from happening in the first place. We investigate fall risk assessment and prevention, separating each into prospective and context-aware while focusing on how wearable technology may contribute.

Most fall risk assessment approaches attempt to quantify the risk of falling based on interviews, clinical tests in a controlled environment guided by qualified health personnel, short term data collection studies, or nurses who recognize whether a patient suffer from a prominent risk of falling simply by watching them move about and reviewing their medical history [24]. All of these approaches, except for the experience-based evaluations done by nurses, are individual assessments attempting to predict the probability of a future fall, usually within the next 6-12 months.

In a clinical setting fall risk assessments are executed using functional tests and questionnaires. Functional tests, like Time-Up and Go (TUG) [11], the Berg Balance Scale [9], Performance-Oriented Mobility Assessment (POMA) [28] etc. are objective and used in clinical settings in terms of prospective fall risk analysis. They do not however take into account the responsiveness and discriminative ability of a relatively healthy population. Neither of these approaches is sufficient in terms of accuracy of fall risk assessment [12, 18]. Further on, the clinical fall risk assessment tools do not take into account hazards found in the normal daily living environment of the elderly such as carpets, pets, doorsteps etc., which may explain why the clinical tests fail to

© Springer International Publishing Switzerland 2015
I. Cleland et al. (Eds.): IWAAL 2015, LNCS 9455, pp. 185–195, 2015.
DOI: 10.1007/978-3-319-26410-3_18

distinguish fallers from non-fallers with a satisfying recognition percentage [13]. Finally, the Hawthorne effect may influence data collected in a clinical setting, further invalidating the findings.

In a systematic review by Oliver et al. [29] the predictive validity of STRATIFY for identifying hospital patients who will fall was evaluated. They concluded that even the best tools cannot identify high-risk individuals for fall prevention with a sufficient certainty. Gates et al. [12] reviewed 29 different functional screening tests for prediction of fall risk, and concluded that most tools discriminate poorly between fallers and non-fallers, and that the evidence is not sufficient in terms of screening instrument for predicting falls.

Prospective fall risk assessments has a number of shortcomings [12, 13, 18, 29], but many of the problems may be solved by close monitoring and counseling by health personnel. Such counseling is both expensive and time-consuming, and considering challenges most countries face in term of the elderly wave, other solutions should be explored. Collecting data related to activities in the daily living environment of the elderly makes it possible to evaluate the performance of activities, how the performance evolves over time, and how gait characteristics and other health status related properties evolve and correlate with the activities. This approach makes it possible to do fall risk assessment as an integrated and non-intrusive part of daily living.

Falls happen at specific times and in specific contexts. In order to prevent falls from happening, the current context such as time of day, current health status, and other relevant information of the current context need to be included in the analysis. Consequently, fall prevention should be separated into prospective fall prevention and context-aware fall prevention.

In this survey we look at fall risk assessment and fall prevention separating them into prospective and context-aware. We specifically investigate wearable approaches identifying information relevant to perform fall risk assessment and fall prevention in a daily living environment using wearables. Preventing falls from happening is in many respects the ultimate goal, both individually and in a social economic context. Fall prevention tool using wearable technology, for unstructured and unsupervised use, while being context aware are however difficult to find. Based on this observation we propose an approach on fall prevention and how it may be implemented using a fall risk awareness protocol.

2 Related Work

Reviews and surveys related to usage of wearable sensors and fall risk assessment is limited due to impracticalities like the size and wearability of sensors, battery lifetime, etc. Howcroft et al. [13] reviewed 40 studies using inertial sensors focusing on geriatric fall risk. The study differentiated on sensor placement, which variables where assessed in the studies, and which models of risk assessment was applied. In the study the use of inertial sensors was found promising in terms of fall risk assessment. Additionally they concluded that "future studies should identify fallers using prospective techniques and focus on determining the most promising sensor sites, in conjunction with determination of optimally predictive variables". Shany et al. [27] reviewed challenges associated with the use of wearable sensors for quantification of fall risk in older people. They focused primarily on how wearable sensors may be used in a clinical situation as an objective supplement to fall risk assessment, but recognized the value of unsupervised and unstructured sensory measurements. They further concluded that such measurements may become good indicators of fall risk if larger studies and high-quality trails are performed.

To the best of our knowledge, no reviews or surveys on fall prevention related to wearable sensor technology exist. Most studies focus on fall risk assessment rather than fall prevention. Majumder et al. [39] recognized abnormal gait using a smartphones accelerometer and gyroscope combined with a sensor shoe insole. They used abnormal gait as a fall risk indicator and used an alert message as feedback. Horta et al. [30] demonstrated that ElectroCardioGram (ECG), ElectroMyoGraphy (EMG), Galvanic Skin Response (GSR) or Electro Dermal Activity (EDA), respiration along with other signals could be used to identify patterns that increased the risk of an imminent fall. Feedback to the user was given by alert messages.

3   Fall Risk Assessment

Unstructured and unsupervised data collection using wearables in the daily living environment offers a unique insight into how different activities are performed and how these activities relate to fall risk. The number of studies investigating this approach is however very limited. As far as we have been able to determine, only 2 studies since 2012 have focused on fall risk assessment using wearable sensors, recording daily life activities from elderly (age > 65) and with reasonably size (participants > 50). In [20] van Schooten et al. investigated how quality of daily gait-characteristics influenced fall risk assessment using a 1-week data recording, and concluded that daily life accelerometry contributed substantially to identification of individuals at risk for falls. They also found that they were able to predict a future fall within 6 months with good accuracy. Weiss et al. [17] did a similar study based on 3-days recording rather than 1 week, concluding that accelerometer-derived analysis is useful in the context of predicting falls.

The potential causes why older adults fall are multidimensional and include predictive factors associated with the natural aging process, various disease processes, and polypharmacy [19, 21, 32] along with elements related to the current situation such as the individuals current health status, context and activity being performed. The prospective elements are valuable in terms of a long-term fall risk assessments, but do not take the actual situation at hand into context.

3.1   Prospective Fall Risk Assessment

Research shows that someone that has fallen is likely to fall again due to the 'post fall syndrome' [26]. In this context, the personal fall history and recognition of prior fall indicators is most important since they significantly influence the probability of a future fall. A number of studies have focused on this, and Table 1 summarizes the most important findings and gait parameters distinguishing fallers from non-fallers.

Table 1. Gait parameters separating fallers from non-fallers

Gait parameter	Finding
Gait speed	Non-fallers have significantly higher gait speed than fallers [13, 17, 20, 22]
Step duration	Step duration is significantly longer in fallers than in non-fallers [17]
Gait variability	Mediolateral variability is significantly lower with fallers while vertical variability is significantly higher for fallers as opposed to non-fallers [3, 13, 17, 20, 23]
Activity level	Heesch et al. [31] showed that at least daily moderate to vigorous-intensity physical activity is required for the primary prevention of falls to the ground. [20] found that fallers have significantly lower total locomotion than non-fallers
MultiScale entropy (MSE)	Riva et al. [1] show that fallers have significantly higher MSE (as an indicator of complexity in gait kinematics) than non-fallers
Local dynamic stability (Gait Stability)	Local Dynamic Stability is significantly lower for fallers than non-fallers [3, 14]
Harmonic ratio (HR)	Harmonic Ratio of the upper and lower trunk were consistently lower in fallers than non-fallers [1, 13, 15]

The prospective fall risk is further dependent on a number of other parameters. References [13, 20] found short stride length to be a significant indicator for prospective falls. Further on, stride time variability have been recognized as a significant factor in respect to differentiate prospective fallers from non-fallers; the larger variation, the more likely it is that a fall will happen within a year [13, 25].

Brown et al. [16] did a statistical study that concluded that instrumental activity of daily living (IADL) limitation stages can be used as a fall assessment tool: elderly with IADL limitation II or III are significantly more likely to fall compared to those with limitation 0. Weiss et al. [4] found that individuals without mobility disability but with IADL disability had difficulties with turns, had lower yaw amplitude during turns, were slower and had less consistent gait. Even though the findings in [4] are not significant, the findings could be used as indicators in a fall risk assessment due to the correlation with IADL limitation stages.

In addition to the parameters that may be recorded using wearable sensors, we know that the probability of falls increase by age [37], elderly with cognitive impairment has a higher probability for falls [38], living alone increase the risk of falling [36], and that falls are related to diseases and clinical health status in general.

3.2   Context-Aware Fall Risk Assessment

The long-term fall risk assessment is what most approaches have been investigating, though some work have been done in the area of context aware fall risk assessment, e.g. [34, 35]. Recognizing the context, both in terms of activity as well as the individuals' current health status hold great value. It is evident that factors like sleep quality and excessive daytime sleeping [6], dizziness [7], vertigo, and balance disorders [8] influence fall risk. Such risks may be identified using questionnaires in a prospective fall risk assessment, but may also be recognized using wearable sensors in the context aware analysis. We have not been able to find any studies focusing on these factors using wearable sensors.

It is further evident that some activities lead to a higher risk of falling than others. Robinovitch et al. [10] found that more than 60 % of all falls by elderly were related to incorrect weight shifting. Consequently, all activities involving weight changes, especially major weight changes like rising up from chair, sitting down, turning, etc. should be considered as inducing a higher risk of falling in a context-aware fall risk assessment.

Near falls are related to fall risks, but are more frequent than falls, and may precede falls [42]. Near falls or missteps are initiated by an initial or sudden loss of balance, but do not escalate to a fall due to the individual's ability to regain balance. If the ability to regain balance declines, the risk of an imminent fall rises. Consequently, recognizing near falls are valuable both in prospective and context-aware fall risk assessments.

Biofeedback monitoring may further increase the accuracy as shown by Horta et al. [30]. Tinetti et al. [37] found changes in gait characteristics as a significant indicator of imminent falls. Recognizing such changes are thus important, and experiments like [5] show how data from a low-cost insole using 12 force-sensitive resistors, calculating ground reaction force and ankle moment, has a very high correlation with clinical data. Such sensory systems are considered to be an accurate method to identify and analyze various step phases [2], making it possible to recognize characteristics that influence fall risk possible.

The context of a person may be associated with activities like sitting, sleeping, walking, climbing stairs, etc., and recognized using Artificial Intelligence algorithms as exemplified by Ernes et al. [33]. Recognizing more complex activities, like cleaning the house, preparing meal, eating, doing the dishes, etc. require sensory information that involve ambient sensing.

Context-aware fall risk assessment need not only consider the current situation. It also need to evaluate how performance of activities evolve in a long-term perspective, identifying trends and support for prospective fall risk assessment as well.

3.3   Sensor Placement and Sensor Properties

Inertial sensors constitute the most applicable sensor type to collect relevant data associated with gait characteristics. Accelerometers and gyroscopes are used in this context in a number of studies, but placement differs. Table 2 gives an overview of placement and analysis focus using inertial sensors.

The lower back is used in most studies due to the general acceptance by the individual wearing the sensor along with a notion that the closer the sensor is to the center of mass location, the more relevant data is collected.

Table 2. Sensor location and focus

Location	Gait study focus
Lower back	[1]: HR, index of harmonicity (IH), MSE, recurrence quantification analysis [4]: balance shifting in turns, yaw amplitude during turns, gait speed, and gait consistency [15]: HR [17]: Gait speed, step duration, gait variability [20]: Gait speed, activity level [23]: Gait variability [43]: Kinetic energy, gait speed, step duration, gait variability
Upper back	[3]: Local dynamic stability, gait variability [15]: HR
Insole	[5]: Ground reaction force, ankle moment, balance [25]: Gait variability [39]: Abnormal gait pattern
SmartPhone	[39]: Abnormal gait pattern
Hip	[14]: Local dynamic stability

4 Fall Prevention

Preventing falls from happening include fall risk assessment, calculating the risk, and acting correspondingly to the risk. Like fall risk assessment, the prevention strategy is dependent on the prospective risk and the risk associated with the current context.

4.1 Prospective Fall Prevention

In the prospective fall risk assessment, environmental hazards are evaluated along with health history and clinical tests to determine a long-term fall risk assessment. In this context wearables can be used as a tool to gather objective information related to different tests that provides health personnel a better foundation for fall risk assessment. In terms of actions avoiding falls from happening, this is normally supervised by qualified health personnel and includes exercise programs focusing on balance and strength, interventions to improve home safety, etc. [40]. Self-administered clinical tests may to some extent help to update prospective fall risk assessments, and in this context contribute to prospective fall prevention [41].

4.2 Context-Aware Fall Prevention

Context-aware fall prevention using wearables is based on both prospective and context-aware fall risk assessments as a continuous, real-time, context-aware process which main purpose is to provide feedback about the risk of falling. The feedback should be directed to everyone with formal or informal responsibilities in respect to care of the person being monitored, dependent on context.

Caporusso et al. [44] presented a pervasive fall prevention solution, incorporating both prospective and context-aware fall risk assessment. They used an individually adjusted threshold-based approach towards risk analysis, and non-invasive multimodal feedback. Sensors and feedback was implemented in a wristband that included a tri-axial accelerometer, an RGB LED, a transducer and bi-directional communication capabilities. Visual feedback was given to a user in form of RGB LED "traffic-light" and tactile feedback in the form of vibration. One main purpose of the wristband was to increase the individuals' awareness of their risk of falling, thereby preventing situations that may lead to falls. Experiments showed a very high acceptance to using a wristband (95 %), but did not conclude whether awareness of fall risk decreased the actual number of falls. Previous studies do however show correlation between awareness of falls and the actual number of falls [45].

5 Fall Risk Awareness

Collecting data related to activities in a daily living environment makes it possible to evaluate the execution of activities, how execution evolves over time, and how gait characteristics, balance, and other health status related properties evolve and correlate. This approach makes it possible to do context aware fall risk assessment while providing valuable information for objective long-term fall risk assessments. It further provides a basis to implement context-aware fall risk awareness protocol.

Dykes et al. [45] showed a positive correlation between awareness of fall risk and the actual number of falls. The awareness of fall risk is not only an individual process, but moreover a process involving everyone with formal or informal responsibilities in respect to care of the person being monitored. In [35] Backere et al. presented an approach towards context-aware fall prevention using ambient sensors. It was a social and context-aware platform for fall risk assessment with feedback using an ontology-based approach with multiple ambient sensors to determine context and risk. The approach included an alarm central, and distinguished between formal and informal caregivers. Feedback was implemented using smartphones, tablets, email and wristband.

We have identified a number of properties that significantly influence fall risk, and separated fall risk assessment and fall prevention into prospective and context aware. The positive correlation between awareness of fall risk and the actual number of falls seem to be very clear as well. We propose a new fall risk awareness protocol based on context aware fall risk analysis.

5.1 Fall Risk Awareness Protocol

The need to coordinate feedback in respect to fall risk awareness to all actors is a primary requirement. Still, feedback has to be easy to understand in order to be accepted by the elderly being monitored. We therefore propose a simplistic feedback system to the elderly as the basis for our fall awareness protocol. The feedback part of the system used by the elderly is integrated into a single device combining an alarm button, a vibration sensor for tactile feedback, an RGB LED emitter for visual feedback, sound capabilities for audible feedback, and two-way low energy consuming communication capabilities. It visually signals the elderly using a combination of blinking (the higher frequency the higher fall risk) and color traffic-light system (morphing from green to yellow to red dependent on risk assessment). If fall risk assessment indicates a low to medium fall risk, color and blinking are the only indicators the elderly is subjected to. However, if fall risk is from medium to high the messaging will be reinforced using vibrations after similar rules as used for blinking. When risk of an imminent fall is high, alarm sound or pre-recorded voice messages will be issued.

The contextual data in Fig. 1 refers to data, both inertial, ambient, and other data that is relevant to perform context aware fall risk assessment.

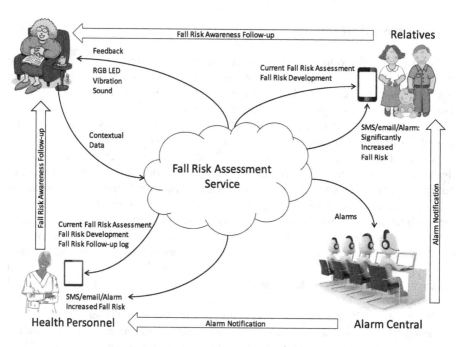

Fig. 1. Fall risk awareness protocol overview

Relatives and other informal caregivers need information related to fall risk as well. Similar, but more demanding requirements exist for health personnel. We propose to develop a service which is continuously updated with current fall risk, and which is able to communicate to other systems using standard protocols enabling messaging by email, SMS, and application specific protocols for immediate messaging and alarms.

The service should present fall risk assessment developments in respect to actual contexts as well as indicate expected future trends. The level of feedback is dependent on actor, risk-level, and whether the fall risk is decreasing or increasing. Figure 1 gives an overview of the proposed fall risk awareness protocol and illustrates how contextual data may be integrated into a fall risk assessment service making it possible to increase fall risk awareness.

6 Conclusions and Future Work

We have in this article focused on wearable approaches for fall risk assessment and fall prevention, and identified information relevant to implement fall risk assessment and fall prevention by investigating current research. Fall risk assessment and fall prevention have been separated into prospective and context-aware elements. Further, we have proposed a fall risk awareness protocol describing how awareness can be altered for the elderly being monitored using wearable sensors.

The fall risk awareness protocol presented here will be implemented in the NIAAR-project (Non-Intrusive Anomalous Activity Recognition) project funded by the Norwegian Research Council.

References

1. Riva, F., Toebes, M.J.P., Pijnappels, M., Stagni, R., van Dieën, J.H.: Estimating fall risk with inertial sensors using gait stability measures that do not require step detection. Gait Posture **38**, 170–174 (2013)
2. Razak, A.H.A., Zayegh, A., Begg, R.K., Wahab, Y.: Foot plantar pressure measurement system: a review. Sensors (Basel) **12**, 9884–9912 (2012)
3. Toebes, M.J.P., Hoozemans, M.J.M., Furrer, R., Dekker, J., van Dieën, J.H.: Local dynamic stability and variability of gait are associated with fall history in elderly subjects. Gait Posture **36**, 527–531 (2012)
4. Weiss, A., Mirelman, A., Buchman, A.S., Bennett, D.A., Hausdorff, J.M.: Using a body-fixed sensor to identify subclinical gait difficulties in older adults with IADL disability: maximizing the output of the timed up and go. PLoS ONE **8**, e68885 (2013)
5. Howell, A.M., Kobayashi, T., Hayes, H.A., Foreman, K.B., Bamberg, S.J.M.: Kinetic gait analysis using a low-cost insole. IEEE Trans. Biomed. Eng. **60**, 3284–3290 (2014)
6. Stone, K.L., Blackwell, T.L., Ancoli-Israel, S., Cauley, J.A., Redline, S., Marshall, L.M., Ensrud, K.E.: Sleep disturbances and risk of falls in older community-dwelling men: the outcomes of sleep disorders in older men (MrOS sleep) study. J. Am. Geriatr. Soc. **62**, 299–305 (2014)
7. Olsson, M., Midlöv, P., Kristensson, J., Ekdahl, C., Berglund, J., Jakobsson, U.: Prevalence and predictors of falls and dizziness in people younger and older than 80 years of age–a longitudinal cohort study. Arch. Gerontol. Geriatr. **56**, 160–168 (2013)
8. Graafmans, W.C., Ooms, M.E., Hofstee, M.A., Bezemer, P.D., Bouter, L.M., Lips, P.: Falls in the elderly: a prospective study of risk factors and risk profiles. Am. J. Epidemiol. **143**, 1129–1135 (1996)
9. Thorbahn, L.D., Newton, R.A.: Use of the berg balance test to predict falls in elderly persons. Phys. Ther. **76**, 576–583 (1996)
10. Robinovitch, S.N., Feldman, F., Yang, Y., Schonnop, R., Leung, P.M., Sarraf, T., Sims-Gould, J., Loughin, M.: Video capture of the circumstances of falls in elderly people residing in long-term care: an observational study. Lancet **381**, 47–54 (2013)
11. Podsiadlo, D., Richardson, S.: The timed "up and go" a test of basic functional mobility for frail elderly persons. J. Am. Geriatr. Soc. **39**, 142–148 (1991)

12. Gates, S., Smith, L.A., Fisher, J.D., Lamb, S.E.: Systematic review of accuracy of screening instruments for predicting fall risk among independently living older adults. J. Rehabil. Res. Dev. **45**, 1105–1116 (2008)

13. Howcroft, J., Kofman, J., Lemaire, E.D.: Review of fall risk assessment in geriatric populations using inertial sensors. J. Neuroeng. Rehabil. **10**, 91 (2013)

14. Lockhart, T.E., Liu, J.: Differentiating fall-prone and healthy adults using local dynamic stability. Ergonomics **51**, 1860–1872 (2008)

15. Doi, T., Hirata, S., Ono, R., Tsutsumimoto, K., Misu, S., Ando, H.: The harmonic ratio of trunk acceleration predicts falling among older people: results of a 1-year prospective study. J. Neuroeng. Rehabil. **10**, 7 (2013)

16. Brown, J., Kurichi, J.E., Xie, D., Pan, Q., Stineman, M.G.: Instrumental activities of daily living staging as a possible clinical tool for falls risk assessment in physical medicine and rehabilitation. PM R **6**, 316–323 (2014)

17. Weiss, A., Brozgol, M., Dorfman, M., Herman, T., Shema, S., Giladi, N., Hausdorff, J.M.: Does the evaluation of gait quality during daily life provide insight into fall risk? A novel approach using 3-day accelerometer recordings. Neurorehabil. Neural Repair **27**, 742–752 (2013)

18. Lee, J., Geller, A.I., Strasser, D.C.: Analytical review: focus on fall screening assessments. PM R **5**, 609–621 (2013)

19. Quandt, S.A., Stafford, J.M., Bell, R.A., Smith, S.L., Snively, B.M., Arcury, T.A.: Predictors of falls in a multiethnic population of rural adults with diabetes. J. Gerontol. A Biol. Sci. Med. Sci. **61**, 394–398 (2006)

20. van Schooten, K.S., Pijnappels, M., Rispens, S.M., Elders, P.J.M., Lips, P., van Dieën, J.H.: Ambulatory fall-risk assessment: amount and quality of daily-life gait predict falls in older adults. J. Gerontol. A Biol. Sci. Med. Sci. **70**, 608–615 (2015)

21. Fuller, G.F.: Falls in the elderly. Am. Fam. Physician **61**(2159–2168), 2173–2174 (2000)

22. Studenski, S., Perera, S., Patel, K., Rosano, C., Faulkner, K., Inzitari, M., Brach, J., Chandler, J., Cawthon, P., Connor, E.B., Nevitt, M., Visser, M., Kritchevsky, S., Badinelli, S., Harris, T., Newman, A.B., Cauley, J., Ferrucci, L., Guralnik, J.: Gait speed and survival in older adults. JAMA **305**, 50–58 (2011)

23. Moe-Nilssen, R., Helbostad, J.: Interstride trunk acceleration variability but not step width variability can differentiate between fit and frail older adults. Gait Posture **21**, 164–170 (2005)

24. Oliver, D., Healy, F.: Fall risk prediction tools for hospital inpatients: do they work? Nurs. Times **105**, 18–21 (2009)

25. Hausdorff, J.M., Rios, D.A., Edelberg, H.K.: Gait variability and fall risk in community-living older adults: a 1-year prospective study. Arch. Phys. Med. Rehabil. **82**, 1050–1056 (2001)

26. Tinetti, M.E., De Leon, C.F.M., Doucette, J.T., Baker, D.I.: Fear of falling and fall-related efficacy in relationship to functioning among community-living elders. J Gerontol. **49**, M140–M147 (1994)

27. Shany, T., Redmond, S.J., Marschollek, M., Lovell, N.H.: Assessing fall risk using wearable sensors: a practical discussion. Z. Gerontol. Geriatr. **45**, 694–706 (2012)

28. Tinetti, M.E.: Performance-oriented assessment of mobility problems in elderly patients. J. Am. Geriatr. Soc. **34**, 119–126 (1986)

29. Oliver, D., Papaioannou, A., Giangregorio, L., Thabane, L., Reizgys, K., Foster, G.: A systematic review and meta-analysis of studies using the STRATIFY tool for prediction of falls in hospital patients: how well does it work. Age Ageing **37**, 621–627 (2008)

30. Horta, E.T., Lopes, I.C., Rodrigues, J.J.P.C., Misra, S.: Real time falls prevention and detection with biofeedback monitoring solution for mobile environments. In: Proceedings of

the 2013 IEEE 15th International Conference on e-Health Networking, Applications and Services, pp. 594–600. IEEE, New York (2013)

31. Heesch, K.C., Byles, J.E., Brown, W.J.: Prospective association between physical activity and falls in community-dwelling older women. J. Epidemiol. Community Health **62**, 421–426 (2008)

32. Chu, L.W., Chi, I., Chiu, A.Y.Y.: Incidence and predictors of falls in the Chinese elderly. Ann. Acad. Med. Singapore **34**, 60–72 (2005)

33. Ermes, M., Pärkka, J., Mantyjarvi, J., Korhonen, I.: Detection of daily activities and sports with wearable sensors in controlled and uncontrolled conditions. IEEE Trans. Inf Technol. Biomed. **12**, 20–26 (2008)

34. Koshmak, G., Linden, M., Loutfi, A.: Dynamic bayesian networks for context-aware fall risk assessment. Sensors (Basel) **14**, 9330–9348 (2014)

35. de Backere, F., Ongenae, F., van den Abeele, F., Nelis, J., Bonte, P., Clement, E., Philpott, M., Hoebeke, J., Verstichel, S., Ackaert, A., de Turck, F.: Towards a social and context-aware multi-sensor fall detection and risk assessment platform. Comput. Biol. Med. (2014). doi:10.1016/j.compbiomed.2014.12.002

36. Kharicha, K., Iliffe, S., Harari, D., Swift, C., Gillmann, G., Stuck, A.E.: Health risk appraisal in older people 1: are older people living alone an "at-risk" group? Br. J. Gen. Pract. **57**, 271–276 (2007)

37. Tinetti, M.E., Speechley, M., Ginter, S.F.: Risk factors for falls among elderly persons living in the community. N. Engl. J. Med. **319**, 1701–1707 (1988)

38. Elliott, S., Painter, J., Hudson, S.: Living alone and fall risk factors in community-dwelling middle age and older adults. J. Community Health **34**, 301–310 (2009)

39. Majumder, A.J.A., Zerin, I., Ahamed, S.I., Smith, R.O.: A multi-sensor approach for fall risk prediction and prevention in the elderly. SIGAPP Appl. Comput. Rev. **14**, 41–52 (2014)

40. Gillespie, L.D., Robertson, M.C., Gillespie, W.J., Sherrington, C., Gates, S., Clemson, L.M., Lamb, S.E.: Interventions for preventing falls in older people living in the community. Cochrane Lib. **9** (2012)

41. Mellone, S., Tacconi, C., Schwickert, L., Klenk, J., Becker, C., Chiari, L.: Smartphone-based solutions for fall detection and prevention: the FARSEEING approach. Z. Gerontol. Geriatr. **45**, 722–727 (2012)

42. Srygley, J.M., Herman, T., Giladi, N., Hausdorff, J.M.: Self-report of missteps in older adults: a valid proxy for falls risk? Arch. Phys. Med. Rehabil. **90**, 786–792 (2009)

43. Marschollek, M., Rehwald, A., Wolf, K.-H., Gietzelt, M., Nemitz, G., Meyer Zu Schwabedissen, H., Haux, R.: Sensor-based fall risk assessment-an expert 'to go'. Methods Inf. Med. **50**, 420–426 (2011)

44. Caporusso, N., Lasorsa, I., Rinaldi, O., La Pietra, L.: A pervasive solution for risk awareness in the context of fall prevention. In: Proceedings of the 3rd International Conference on Pervasive Computing Technologies for Healthcare, pp. 1–8. IEEE, New York, (2009)

45. Dykes, P.C., Carroll, D.L., Hurley, A., Lipsitz, S., Benoit, A., Chang, F., Meltzerm, S., Tsurikova, R., Zuyov, L., Middleton, B.: Fall prevention in acute care hospitals: a randomized trial. JAMA **304**, 1912–1918 (2010)

Big Data Processing Using Wearable Devices for Wellbeing and Healthy Activities Promotion

Diego Gachet Páez[(⊠)], Manuel de Buenaga Rodríguez,
Enrique Puertas Sánz, María Teresa Villalba, and Rafael Muñoz Gil

Universidad Europea de Madrid, 28670 Villaviciosa de Odón, Spain
{gachet, buenaga, enrique.puertas, maite.villalba,
rafael.munoz}@uem.es

Abstract. The aging population and economic crisis specially in developed countries have as a consequence the reduction in funds dedicated to healthcare, is then desirable to optimize the costs of public and private healthcare systems reducing the affluence of chronic and dependent people to care centers; promoting healthy lifestyle and activities can allow people to avoid chronic diseases as for example hypertension. In this paper we describe a system for promoting an active and healthy lifestyle for people and to recommend with guidelines and valuable information about their habits. The proposed system is being developed around the Big Data parading using bio-signals sensors and machine learning algorithms for recommendations.

Keywords: Internet of things · Cloud computing · Elderly · Sensors, big data

1 Introduction

The aging population and the increase of people with chronic diseases is a common scenario in developed countries. According to World Health Organization, chronic diseases are the leading cause of death worldwide, as they cause more deaths than all other causes together, and affect more people of low and middle income. While these diseases have reached epidemic proportions, it could be reduced significantly by combating the risk factors and applying early detection, the indoor and outdoor monitoring joined with prevention measures and a more healthy life style can help so that millions of lives would be saved and avoid untold suffering.

For both chronic and pre-chronic people several dangerous clinical situations could be avoided or better monitored and managed with the participation of the patient, their caregivers and medical personnel.

This requires research and information gathering about socio-economic and environmental factors, dietary impact and life habits using sensors and devices, including software applications for monitoring personal activities and health signs. At the other hand, the use of recommender systems to promote a healthy lifestyle and wellbeing improves interaction with healthcare professional for a better disease management.

© Springer International Publishing Switzerland 2015
I. Cleland et al. (Eds.): IWAAL 2015, LNCS 9455, pp. 196–205, 2015.
DOI: 10.1007/978-3-319-26410-3_19

The rapidly growing popularity of health care and activity monitoring applications for smart mobile devices like smart phones and tablets provide new ways to collect information about people health status, both manually and automatically. Also, there are appearing new COTS (*Commercial Off-The-Shelf*) wearable medical sensors that can easily connect with the smart phones or tablets via Bluetooth and transfer the sensing measures directly to a public or private cloud infrastructure. This has provided a more efficient and convenient way to collect personal health information like blood pressure, oxygen saturation, blood glucose level, pulse, electrocardiogram (ECG), etc., that can be analyzed for generating alarms or furthermore, it would also be possible to track the patient's behaviors on a real-time basis and over long periods, providing a potential alert for signs of physical and/or cognitive deterioration [1].

It is beyond doubt that an active lifestyle can improve health conditions [2], a person with a poor physical health condition has a high risk of developing a chronic disease, such as diabetes or cardiovascular disease, nowadays, advances in information and communication technologies (ICT) as for example mobile communications, wearable computing, cloud and Big data infrastructures make more easy to develop integrated and cost-effective solutions for providing people feedback about their general health status and avoid reach a chronic disease.

2 Related Work

Empower citizens to manage their own health and diseases can contribute to have a more effective utilization of health services, reducing costs, and offering improvements in the quality of life in general. Continuous health monitoring may offer benefits to people with diseases (for example, with chronic diseases like Cardio Vascular Disease (CVD) or Chronic Obstructive Pulmonary Disease (COPD), and in need of some monitoring in their treatment), and also for healthy people, which can maintain their good state of health, preventing diseases thanks to the modification of their behavior and adoption of new healthy habits.

Some recent solutions focuses on the use of sensors and bio signals, such as devices for the measurement of blood pressure, heart rate, pulsioximeters, physical movements and distance walked, that are calculated using accelerometers or other mechanisms. These new systems are aimed mainly at users with chronic diseases, which need a deeper monitoring in some cases. Other systems are more oriented to healthy people who use them to improve their health status, or as prevention by incorporating healthy habits, favored with this kind of technology. There are also systems that offer a broad spectrum of functionalities and services, and may be suitable for both types of users.

The research effort in this direction has increased over the past years, and in the current European R&D Programme Horizon 2020, for example, the thematic priorities in "Health Demographic Change and Wellbeing", play an important role in the framework of the program of Social Challenges [3]. The latest projects with similar orientation, and previous in the framework of FP7, have a significant focus on the development of this type of solutions based on ICT to promote self-management of health and disease. In some cases the projects focus on remote monitoring and self-management of diseases such as CVD and COPD, offering solutions to patients that allow them to avoid the need to travel to the hospital for a revision, among other benefits [4]. Other projects put the focus in promoting healthy behaviors in individuals, without health problems, with a more preventive character [5]. Companies like Corventis, MicroStrain, Lord or AT4Wireless are focused on the development of services and/or biomedical devices related to telemedicine and monitoring of chronic patients based on the use of data retrieved from biosensors. Other products and services are more oriented towards the monitoring of healthy activities and prevention (e.g. hours of sleep and daily walk distances to prevent pre-hypertension), and are offered by companies like Fitbit, Jawbone or Garmin. Finally, other manufacturers like Tactio or iHealth offer products that are suitable for both types of users.

3 Proposed Architecture

The proposed architecture for collecting data in order to promoting wellbeing and physical activity is based on the need for a scalable data storage and high-performance computing infrastructure for efficiently storing, processing and sharing of health and activity sensor data. With this situation in mind we propose a simple, coherent, activity monitoring solution that take into account several factors like using noninvasive sensors, allowing the processing of high volumes of data coming from them including information from other sources as for example clinical texts; search and retrieval of medical related information from forums and designing appropriate visualization interfaces for each user type (patients, healthcare professionals, caregivers, relatives, etc.) among the implementation of security and ethical mechanism concerning the treatment of medical information.

According to the above features, our general architecture for activity monitoring as well as its associated services is presented in Fig. 1. The components shown are being developed under the project ipHealth [6], the architecture allows monitoring of both chronic or non-chronic patients as well healthy people that need to be monitored by different circumstances in both, home and external environment, and moreover it allow interaction with their family, the emergency systems and the Hospitals through the application of Cloud computing, Big Data and Internet of things approaches. From the technological point of view, the architecture consists of the following main elements:

- A smart mobile phone being used by user and which in turn accepts the data from wearable vital signs or activity sensors, and sends this information to Internet via the mobile network 3G/HDSPA or Wi-Fi connection using sensor's proprietary applications running in the mobile device. Sensors establish communication with the mobile device trough a Bluetooth connection.
- A cloud based (public as Amazon Web Service or private) infrastructure for data store and analytic module for activation of alarms to be sent to the patient and/or patient's caregivers, nursing or medical personnel. In fact this is the core of the system in order to produce alarms or early diagnose and new e-health services based on analysis of historical data using Big Data approach [7].

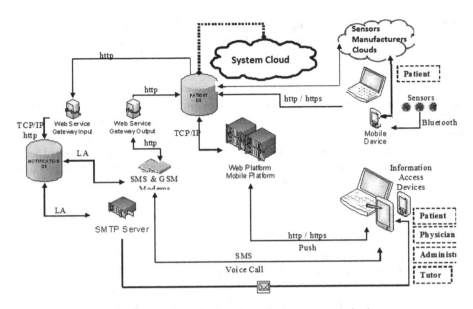

Fig. 1. Proposed architecture for patients remote monitoring

- Interoperability and messaging platform for delivery of information to all involved actors in the system, using the latest technological advances in communication (SMS, mail, voice automated systems and PUSH technology).
- A website platform that allows both, medical personnel and family caregivers, consult the associated patient information from desktop computer as well as from mobile devices.

For our system, health and activity data are taken mainly from sensor's manufacturers clouds using open APIs that allows developers to establish a connection between applications and health data generated by users with their products, it means we have to deal with those different APIs, which ends in a great heterogeneity of formats and services, a task that is difficult to manage from a more abstract and global point of view. In order to solve this problem, we also use "The Human API" [8] initiative, which aims to integrate, in a simple and convenient way for researchers, health data from many sensors and devices that are available in the market. Human API is a platform for working with health data that allows developers to retrieve information from different data sources (devices, wearables, APPs, services web, and others) and allows users to share these data with other applications of their choice.

Human API can also handle synchronizations with data from third-party sources, handles the administration of users to manage all their identities across all devices, integrated services and processes, and standardizes all data in through an API Rest that follows HIPAA regulations (for privacy and security of health data).

On the cloud side and due the large amount of data to be processed, we have decided not to use the classical SQL relational databases and file systems, instead we decided to use NoSQL databases and a Hadoop ecosystem [9], it enable us to implement machine learning algorithms in both batch and stream processing. This ensures the possibility of implementing different types of analysis algorithms keeping a horizontal scalability. Recently, there have been reported experiences of using similar architectures on hospital environments of equivalent sizing [10].

From the medical point of view, the architecture will allows the development of applications suitable for different scenarios as for example monitoring a pre-hypertensive patient who has just been diagnosed and for whom it is necessary to start a new set of healthy habits in conjunction with beta blockers that are usual drugs used as first option in these cases, and the treatment has unfavorable effects that need determine the patient heart rate. Controlling treatment adherence and drugs effects using wireless blood pressure monitor suppose a significant benefit for patients and doctors.

3.1 Wearable Devices

About the wearable devices used in our architecture, despite there are an increasing number of applications using mobile devices and sensors for healthcare, such systems have a major disadvantage, in general not offer a general architecture for data processing and analysis and also that approach does not consider major aspects like scalability and data security. Until recently, continuous monitoring of physiological parameters was possible only in the hospital setting, but today, with developments in the field of wearable technology, the possibility of accurate, continuous, real-time monitoring of physiological signals is a reality.

Table 1 summarizes the sensors that we are considering for using in our research about physical activity and cardio-vascular conditions.

At present time we are conducting tests for monitoring physical activity and cardio-vascular status using Bluetooth enabled blood pressure sensor and a Fitbit flex wristband. The iHealth BP7 wireless blood pressure (BP) self-monitor [11], is an oscillometric device that can test, keep a history of measurements, and share BP data and pulse rate with iOS (version 5.0 or higher) or Android mobile devices (version 3.0 or higher). Last firmware version is 1.3.5. The method of measure is through automatic inflation.

Regarding the validity and reliability of this monitor, has received CE medical certification (Europe), as well as, FDA approval (USA), and ESH Certification (European Society of Hypertension). The accuracy for pressure is ± 3 mmHg, and for pulse rate of ± 5 %. iHealth Labs provides an open API that allows developers to interact with cloud iHealth's data. This API uses OAuth (Open Authorization) 2.0 protocol for authentication and authorization, as same as Facebook, Google or Twitter among others.

FitBix Flex [12] is a wrist monitor and has as principal components an Ultra-Low Power ARM Cortex M3 Microcontroller, a Bluetooth Low Energy Connectivity IC, and a 3-axis smart accelerometer IC. An app for Android, iOS, and desktop platforms is available to perform synchronization. During synchronization, the Fitbit application forwards the user's buffered activity data to Fitbit-operated servers over the Internet, where the activity data is warehoused. The activity data is not persisted on the smartphone or personal computer, user data is fetched from the Fitbit cloud service during each synchronization.

Table 1. Considered sensors and applications

Devices	Indoor/outdoor application	Constant	Rank-alarm
Blood pressure sensor	Monitoring in cardiovascular disease (Angor, AMI. Insufficiency heart, congenital heart disease, ...) Monitor response to initial treatment or for comparing treatments	Blood pressure diastolic (TAD) and systolic (TAS). Heart rate	TAD < 50 MM HG or > 100 SBP < 100 or > 150 MM HG It depends if routine screening registration or acute complications
Wristband	Activity monitoring	Steps Calories burned Sleep periods	10000 steps per day 8 sleep hours

Its reliability has been tested in several studies [13], probing to be a valid device to measure energy consume during physical activity. Fitbit provides an API to integrate third-party applications getting and modifying user's data form Fitbit.com. The process begins with the registration of the new application which is given an API consumer key and secret. Applications must be authenticated using OAuth as same as iHealth. But Fitbit uses OAuth 1.0.

4 Scenarios and Use Cases

In our project we have worked on defining a set of scenarios and use cases applications of the proposed architecture. The scenarios include as primary users, the patients (or person improving healthy habits), health professionals who can keep track of their, and we have also considered medical students in their training process.

The platform services presented here aim at enable an integrated and intelligent access to related information for extracting useful knowledge in the context of the personalized medicine access. The scenarios considered for now are the Prehypertension and the Hypertension for young pregnant.

Prehypertension is the situation in which the patient has blood pressure values below hypertension, but it is advisable to introduce changes in his lifestyle preventively, such as weight reduction, smoking cessation, diet low in fat and sodium, physical activity and moderation in alcohol consumption, avoid stressful situations and monitor the adequacy of sleep. This type of data can be obtained from sensors in our architecture and self-monitoring and its tracing facilitate the introduction of changes in lifestyle.

On the other hand, Hypertension (HT) is the most common and important risk factor during pregnancy. There are experiences that have already proven useful in monitoring blood pressure at home as well as accurate. For example, in [14] the device used for this purpose automatically sends the data to be processed in order to alert the obstetrics when severe HT is produced. Moreover, that study showed that blood pressure was higher in clinical visit that when tension was recorded automatically.

Therefore, the use of sensors that automatically register the pressure levels in pregnant women proved be useful since may avoid unnecessary treatments for HT. In this scenery the parameter being studied right now to be self-monitored is the blood pressure. Other measures such as glucose in blood could be very interesting too, since the implications to the mother and the baby that could have in the future.

5 Preliminary Results

Data obtained from wearable sensors need to be processed, health data mining approaches are often used for tasks like prediction, detection of outliers (anomaly detection), clustering, and decision making [15]. Depending on the kind of task, supervised or unsupervised learning methods are applied. Supervised learning is mainly used for prediction or decision making. The models obtained through learning algorithms are predictive "classifiers," that is, sets of rules or other types of models in which other attributes are used to predict the class of new examples with unknown classes. Unsupervised learning can be used for tasks like clustering or finding association rules among data attributes. Therefore, the use of sensors that automatically register the pressure levels in pregnant women proved be useful since may avoid unnecessary treatments for HT.

Figure 2 shows results about the physical activity and BP of a monitored patient, from above to below and left to right we can see current values about heart rate and BP among other personal data, the graphics show the amount of steps made in a 30 day period, the steps in a day each 15 min, the percent of BP range in a one month period, the sleep hours in a month and the measures of BP and hearth rate in one month.

This is a valuable information for having an idea about the habits and daily patterns of a person and permits us to apply machine learning algorithms to implement recommender systems and detect tendencies about their general health status.

According to that values the recommender system for physical activity need take into account parameters and factors such as weight, age and sex. The recommendation is based on the change in blood pressure, physical exercise and weight values of the person. Recommendations can also include:

- Dietary-hygienic measures: relaxation therapies depending on high BP, avoid canned food, avoid salt, reduce stress, avoid smoking
- Food: suggestions on the best dietary changes that will improve health based on information collected in this regard.
- Recommendations on harmful substances: avoid smoking and smoky environments, alcohol.
- Recommendations for relaxation: high values of heart rate during day may vary to normal levels during sleep, which may indicate stress. In this case the recommendations include relaxing therapies like yoga. Otherwise, in case of high levels, medical assistance is recommended.
- Sending information to healthcare or medical assistance:
- Alerting a physician if any parameter too high.

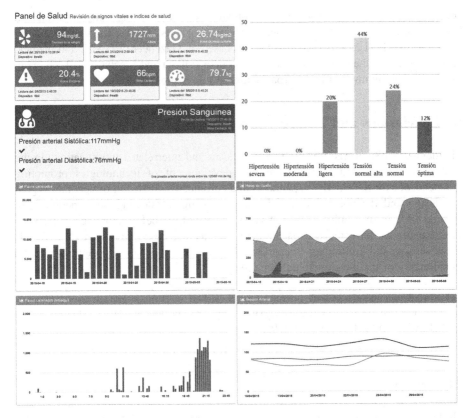

Fig. 2. System user interface showing information about activity and blood pressure

- Request for consultation on the basis of combination of parameters indicating a medical supervision needed.

Also in our system we consider as very important the user-generated content, like the information present in specialized forums with people with similar problems. From the point of view of the functionality in the scenarios that we have presented before, it is particularly suitable its use, allowing patients to share their concerns about certain health problems, progress associated with activities, methods to achieve goals and many other related issues with their situation of health. From the forums, users can provide indications to other relevant sources and it also allows users with professional profile to provide authorized information and monitor further comments. For the analysis of these information sources, current systems use advanced text analysis and NLP techniques.

The algorithms of analysis incorporate, increasingly, the use of semantic resources, including ontologies and domain specific databases, such as UMLS or SNOMED [16], providing a greater capacity of semantic interpretation, demanding growing computing capacity and data storage. From the point of view of automatic text analysis, our system is focused on the calculation of the similarity of consultations, giving the user direct access to the more similar that have been previously raised, finding sometimes satisfied his need or his problems resolved with previous contents. To do this, we use a similarity function [17] in a text analysis system based on Gazetteer of GATE and medical terms covered by the Open Biomedical Annotator (OBA) and Freebase [18], allowing to address synonymy and more broader lexical issues present in this domain.

6 Conclusions and Future Work

The demographic change will lead to significant and interrelated modifications in the health care sector and in the increasing development of technologies promoting independence for the elderly, dependents and chronic. The iPHealth project has as goal the design and developing of a technological platform allowing both, people with chronic diseases or healthy, to increase their quality of life before more acute episodes. In this paper we have focused on the main architecture description with some details about sensors and preliminary scenarios to be considered in order to demonstrate the functionality of the developed architecture.

Acknowledgements. This work is still being developed with funds granted by the Spanish Ministry of Economy and Competitiveness under project iPHealth (TIN-2013-47153-C3-1) and by ASISA Innovation Chair (CAT001206D).

References

1. Fundación Vodafone: Innovación TIC para las personas mayores. Situación, requerimientos y soluciones en la atención intgral de la cronicidad y la dependencia (2011). http://www.vodafone.es/static/fichero/pro_ucm_mgmt_015568.pdf
2. Centers for Disease Control and Prevention. Physical activity and health. http://www.cdc.gov/physicalactivity/everyone/health/index.html. Accessed 30 May 2015
3. European Commission: Health, demographic change and wellbeing. http://ec.europa.eu/programmes/horizon2020/en/h2020-section/health-demographic-change-and-wellbeing. Accessed 1 April 2015
4. Canale, S.: The bravehealth software architecture for the monitoring of patients affected by CVD. In: 5th Telemed, Nice, France, pp. 29–34 (2013)
5. Youm, S., Park, S.H.: How the awareness of u-healthcare service and health conditions affect healthy lifestyle: an empirical analysis based on a u-healthcare service experience. Telemed. J. E Health 21(4), 286–295 (2015)
6. ipHealth web site. http://www.esp.uem.es/gsi/ipHealth/
7. Páez, D.G., Aparicio, F., de Buenaga, M., Ascanio, J.R.: Big data and IoT for chronic patients monitoring. In: Hervás, R., Lee, S., Nugent, C., Bravo, J. (eds.) UCAmI 2014. LNCS, vol. 8867, pp. 416–423. Springer, Heidelberg (2014)
8. Human API web site. https://humanapi.co/
9. Prajapati, V.: Big Data Analytics with R and Hadoop. Packt Books, Birmingham (2013)
10. Sahoo, S.S., Jayapandian, C., Garg, G., Kaffashi, F., Chung, S., Bozorgi, A., et al.: Heart beats in the cloud: distributed analysis of electrophysiological big data using cloud computing for epilepsy clinical research. J. Am. Med. Inform. Assoc. 21(2), 263–271 (2014)

11. i. Labs, wireless blood pressure wrist monitor. http://www.ihealthlabs.com/blood-pressure-monitors/wireless-blood-pressure-wrist-monitor/
12. FitBit, FitBit Flex. http://www.fitbit.com/es/flex
13. Diaz, K.M., Krupka, D.J., Chang, M.J., Ma, Y., Goldsmith, J., Schwartz, J.E., Davidson, K. W.: Fitbit®: an accurate and reliable device for wireless physical activity tracking. Int. J. Cardiol. **185**, 138–140 (2015)
14. Denolle, T., Weber, J.-L., Calvez, C., Getin, Y., Daniel, J.-C., Lurton, O., Cheve, M.-T., Marechaud, M., Bessec, P., Carbonne, B.: Diagnosis of white coat hypertension in pregnant women with teletransmitted home blood pressure. Hypertens. Pregnancy **27**(3), 305–313 (2008)
15. Bellazzi, R., Zupan, B.: Predictive data mining in clinical medicine: current issues and guidelines. Int. J. Med. Inform. **77**, 81–97 (2008)
16. Elhadad, N., Pradhan, S., Gorman, S.L., Manandhar, S., Chapman, W., Savova, G.: SemEval-2015 task 14: analysis of clinical text. Semeval Notes **298**(133), 100 (2015)
17. Li, Y., McLean, D., Bandar, Z., O'shea, J.D., Crockett, K.: Sentence similarity based on semantic nets and corpus statistics. IEEE Trans. Knowl. Data Eng. **18**(8), 1138–1150 (2006)
18. Gachet Páez, D., Aparicio, F., de Buenaga, M., Padrón, V.: Personalized health care system with virtual reality rehabilitation and appropriate information for seniors. Sensors **12**(5), 5502–5516 (2012)
19. Chandola, V., Banerjee, A., Kumar, V.: Anomaly detection: a survey. ACM Comput. Surv. **41**, 15:1–15:58 (2009)
20. Al-Hajji, A.A.: Rule-based expert system for diagnosis and symptom of neurological disorders neurologist expert system (NES). In: Proceedings of the 1st Taibah University International Conference on Computing and Information Technology, Al-Madinah Al-Munawwarah, Saudi Arabia, pp. 67–72, 12–14 March 2012
21. Frantzidis, C.A., Bratsas, C., Klados, M.A., Konstantinidis, E., Lithari, C.D., Vivas, A.B., Papadelis, C.L., Kaldoudi, E., Pappas, C., Bamidis, P.D.: On the classification of emotional biosignals evoked while viewing affective pictures: an integrated data-mining-based approach for healthcare applications. Trans. Inf. Tech. Biomed. **14**, 309–318 (2010)

A Dual Approach for Quantitative Gait Analysis Based on Vision and Wearable Pressure Systems

Iván González[1]([✉]), Mario Nieto-Hidalgo[2], Jerónimo Mora[2],
Juan Manuel García-Chamizo[2], and José Bravo[1]

[1] MAmI Research Lab, University of Castilla-La Mancha,
Paseo de la Universidad, Ciudad Real, Spain
ivan.gdiaz@uclm.es
[2] Department of Computing Technology, University of Alicante, Alicante, Spain

Abstract. This paper proposes two approaches to characterize gait taking into account only quantitative measurements of dynamic nature. A pair of wireless sensorized insoles are used to obtain gait phases based on the involved forces, and a computer vision system externally estimates measurements through movement analysis. The wearable approach is composed of a pair of insoles, consisting of an assembly of FSRs and an inertial measurement unit. A micro-controller provides the captured data to a Bluetooth module that transmits it to be processed. The vision system obtains gait features using a single RGB camera. We have developed an algorithm to extract the silhouette using background subtraction, and locating heel and toe of each foot using the shape of the silhouettes. Detection of Heel-strike and Toe-off is based on gradient. Gait phases and other spatio-temporal parameters are derived from them.

Keywords: Gait analysis · Wearable pressure insoles · Gait phases · Gait event detection · Computer vision

1 Introduction

Quantitative Gait analysis (QGA) is the systematic study of human walking, in terms of kinematics, kinetic, energy expenditure and spatio-temporal parameters useful for the characterization of human gait.

Beyond the utilization of gait analysis to assess gait pathologies or to identify gait abnormalities [1,2], there are other uses, under the scope of QGA, which requires a controlled long-term gait monitoring to provide a reliable characterization of the gait changes over time. In this regard, an unobtrusive long-term gait monitoring system can be a powerful tool as a functional marker for diagnosing the clinical course of specific diseases. For example, the *inherent gait variability* [3,4] over time is a crucial aspect in the diagnosis of frailty syndrome and neurodegenerative diseases (such as Parkinson and some types of dementia).

The work presented here is part of a project focused on the early detection of frailty and dementia on elderly people through QGA and the assessment of

© Springer International Publishing Switzerland 2015
I. Cleland et al. (Eds.): IWAAL 2015, LNCS 9455, pp. 206–218, 2015.
DOI: 10.1007/978-3-319-26410-3_20

long-term gait pattern variations. At this stage of development, low cost systems for objective gait characterization are required. In this context, we propose two approaches for QGA based on vision and wearable pressure systems. Both solutions are focused on the spatio-temporal dimension of the human gait.

The wearable solution provides a gait phase detection system, based on fuzzy logic. It consists of an ambulatory system composed of a pair of wireless sensorized insoles. On the other hand, the vision system uses a single RGB camera located in a corridor to estimate gait events.

The insole approach allows the perception of the phenomenon from inside the kinematic system, analysing dynamic forces exerted on the foot insoles during walking. On the other hand, visual inspection also provides data of gait characteristics, although in this case the phenomenon is perceived from outside the kinematic system and it is linked exclusively with the involved temporal and spatial dimensions (ignoring dynamics).

The proposed insoles are well suited for gait phase demarcation, due to the accurate achieved in foot pressure patterns identification. In contrast, the visual inspection allows the robust detection of *Heel-strike* (HS) and *Toe-off* (TO) events, however is less appropriate for the segmentation of the internal stance's subphases due to occlusions. Additionally, the vision system can provide spatial parameters such as stride and step length by direct measurement of distances from the video when HS and TO occurs. These spatial parameters could only be estimated by the wearable system through a double integration of the acceleration signals provided by the inertial measurement unit in each insole. However, the obtained displacement would be only an estimation and not a direct measure.

The rest of this paper is organized as follows. Section 2 provides the related work of existing solutions for both, QGA using pressure-sensorized insoles (Sect. 2.1) and QGA through computer vision (Sect. 2.2). Then, Sect. 3 describes the details and the algorithms involved in each approach: the gait phase detection algorithm using the pressure-sensorized insoles (Sect. 3.1) and the artificial vision algorithm based on gradient analysis for gait event identification (Sect. 3.2). In Sect. 4, we present the evaluation results obtained for the two systems. Finally, Sect. 5 exposes the discussion and points future work.

2 Related Work

There are several approaches of QGA using pressure-sensorized insoles or computer vision. Relevant works are presented in the following subsections.

2.1 Quantitative Gait Analysis Through Wearable Systems. Pressure-Sensorized Insoles

In [5], Lopez-Meyer et al. are focused on QGA by means of pressure-sensorized insoles. They rely on the sum of five pressure sensors (FSRs, Force Sensitive Resistors) located in a shoe-based wearable to estimate HS and TO events.

More temporal parameters are obtained beyond HS and TO: gait cycle time, step time, stance, swing, single and double support.

Other remarkable work is proposed by Bamberg et al. [6]. This is a highly elaborated sensorized shoe composed of three orthogonal accelerometers and gyroscopes, four FSRs, two piezoelectric pressure sensors, two bend sensors and electric field height sensors to measure foot clearance. The device is able to collect data in any environment and over long periods. Bamberg et al. uses it for QGA in healthy and Parkinsonian subjects. The sum of FSR sensors is utilized to obtain HS and TO. Furthermore, foot orientation, velocity and stride length are estimated.

Crea et al. [7] take advantage of the accurate estimation of the ground reaction force and the center of pressure in their insole-based device, through the use of 64 opto-electric cells, which nearly cover the whole surface of the foot. They use these two biomechanical variables to implement a gait phase detection system, based on a single threshold.

The approach of Pappas et al. [8] offers a real-time gait phase detection system with support for continuous gait monitoring. However, they provide a gait phase detection by means of a rule-based approach as a finite state machine. In contrast, the pressure system presented here relies on a fuzzy-rule based approach. The main reason is that fuzzy logic can provide better accuracy in gait pattern detection [9], compared with threshold or fixed state rules, specially in the cases where subjects have extremely light pressure patterns, which results in low sensor signals.

2.2   Quantitative Gait Analysis Through Computer Vision Methods

In [10], the person silhouette during a gait sequence is used to define a set of key poses, each one is a "Pose Energy Image" that allows to capture fine grain temporal variations.

Use of the shadow projected by a person is proposed in [11] to improve gait recognition by means of aerial cameras. The combination of shadow and silhouette is also proposed to improve recognition using oblique cameras where there is a good view of both.

In [12], several feature extraction procedures from human silhouettes have been used for gait recognition. This study combine different techniques over two-dimensional contours to compute dissimilarity scores with respect to a set of reference human gait phase silhouettes, such as Fourier descriptor extraction, histogram matching, and dynamic time warping (DTW), among others.

A parkinsonian gait recognition system is proposed in [13]. From the silhouette, the bounding box is obtained to fit a human model. The skeleton is estimated by calculating the mean points of each body segment. Then, legs movement and posture inclination are obtained and compared with a normal gait model to calculate the similarity.

In [14,15] the silhouette bounding box is used to determine the gait cycle and the stride length.

The suitability of Kinect sensor to measure gait parameters during a treadmill walking with frontal view is examined in [16]. The study shows that detection of HS has less error than TO, because it is produced closer to the camera.

3 Case of Use

Our insole-based and computer vision-based systems for QGA are detailed in the following subsections.

3.1 Pressure-Sensorized Insole-Based Approach

The wearable system is composed of a pair of insoles, each of them consisting of an assembly of four FSRs and one inertial measurement unit (IMU). In order to manage data acquisition, one microcontroller is programmed to provide the data from the sensors to a Bluetooth module, and, in turn, this latter establishes the communication between the insole and an application, where data is processed.

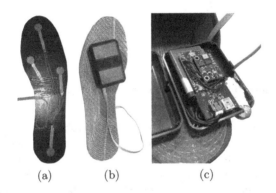

(a)   (b)   (c)

Fig. 1. *(a)* Arrangement of FSR sensors; *(b)* Prototype; *(c)* Arduino Fio + 9DOF IMU + 3.7V LiPO batt. + Bluetooth module WLS125E1P.

Figure 1 details the hardware setup. The arrangement of FSRs is illustrated in Fig. 1(a), four 0.5" diameter FSR sensors are placed on each insole, one at the hallux, two more at the forefoot and the last one at the heel. In the Fig. 1(b) the prototype can be observed, the hardware components are enclosed in a black plastic box which will be attached to the back posterior part of the tibia. In the Fig. 1(c), the components are shown in detail, the IMU, is the small board on top of the microcontroller. It is not being used for the gait phase demarcation, however, data derived from the ADXL345 accelerometer embedded on it and from the FSR sensors has been used together in [17] to classify foot movement patterns in real-time. Before the gait phase demarcation, the raw data from each insole are packaged, low pass filtered and sent to the gait monitoring application at 50 Hz.

Based on the gait phases proposed by Perry [1], our wearable system is able to demarcate the four subphases inside the stance phase (*loading response* (LR), *mid stance* (MSt), *terminal stance* (TSt) and *pre swing* (PSw)) and the entire *swing phase* (Sw), examining only the foot pressure patterns from the FSR sensors, by means of a gait phase detection algorithm, which is based on fuzzy logic.

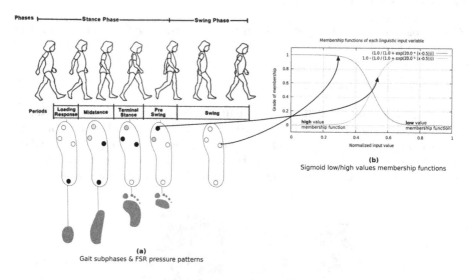

Fig. 2. Gait subphases and Sigmoid membership functions (Color figure online).

Figure 2(a) represents the stance subphases (LR, MSt, TSt, PSw) and the swing phase (Sw) the algorithm is able to recognize. The drawn insole below each subphase indicates how much force must be exerted on the FSR sensors (represented as circles) to identify the beginning of the related subphase. A black circle means that a high pressure must be exerted; On the other hand, if the circle is filled in white a low force or no force is expected. Finally, a gray circle means that the signal of that FSR is not relevant to describe the gait phase, by means of the foot pressure pattern. Below the insole representations in Fig. 2(a), the pressure patterns are approximately drawn as they are expected in each stance subphase.

To characterize the stance subphases and swing phase, each FSR is modelled as a linguistic variable (FSR_x), composed of two fuzzy sets (to indicate the grade of membership to the "*low pressure*" and "*high pressure*" state). In this way, the subphases can be expressed as a human-readable fuzzy rules. For example, The TSt subphase is modelled with the following fuzzy rule:

If FSR_{heel} is *low* AND FSR_{5th} is *high* AND FSR_{1st} is *high* $\Longrightarrow$ TSt   (1)

where FSR_{heel}, FSR_{5th}, FSR_{1st} represents the linguistic variables for the FSR sensors on the heel and on fifth and first metatarsals (forefoot), respectively.

To ensure a smooth transition between low and high pressures in each linguistic variable (FSR_x), the two fuzzy sets are represented by two normalized symmetric sigmoid functions (Fig. 2(b)). The red line represents the membership function to the *"low pressure"* state; similarly, the green line represents the membership function to the *"high pressure"* state.

Table 1 shows a schematic view of the composed fuzzy rule set. The output membership of each gait subphase is determined by means of an inference operator. In this case, each AND intersection between linguistic variables is interpreted as a Minimum T-norm.

Table 1. Fuzy rules set.

FSR_{heel}	FSR_{5th}	FSR_{1st}	FSR_{toe}	Gait phase (membership value)
high	low	low	low	LR$\longrightarrow$1
high	high	-	-	MSt$\longrightarrow$1
low	high	high	-	TSt$\longrightarrow$1
low	low	-	high	PSw$\longrightarrow$1
low	low	low	low	Sw$\longrightarrow$1

Using these defined rules, a non-pathological gait cycle will activate each subphase consecutively, one after another, in the expected order (LR, MSt, TSt, PSw, Sw, LR,...), and demarcated one at a time with a membership near 1. In this sense, a healthy gait will rarely have mis-detection of the gait subphases, their order altered or two activated rules at the same time (except a short time during transitions). The results provided in Sect. 4.1 helps to verify this assumption and to test the accuracy of the insole system.

3.2 Vision-Based Approach

The vision system is focused on extracting gait features through a single RGB camera. The reason behind this decision is that the designed algorithms could be easily ported to a mobile device minimizing the architecture and making the system more accessible. The proposed algorithm can detect both HS and TO temporal events using a side view of a person walking. The input of the algorithm are image sequences that are processed following Fig. 3 flow chart.

The first step is to obtain the subject's silhouette using a background subtractor and get the bounding box. The next step is to locate toe and heel of each foot.

Our algorithm does not use any marker attached to the body. Without such markers, we do not have information that allow us to segment through colour. However, it is possible to get the shape of the silhouette and we know that feet are located in the lower part, so we keep around 20 % of the lower part of the silhouette where the feet are located. External toe is obtained by using the $\text{argmax}_{x,y}(\forall_{x,y} \in silhouete : x)$ and the external heel by using the $\text{argmin}_{x,y}(\forall_{x,y} \in silhouete : x)$.

Then, we can also separate each foot estimating the foot width. Foot width is approximated analysing the bounding box width when feet are adjacent. Once it

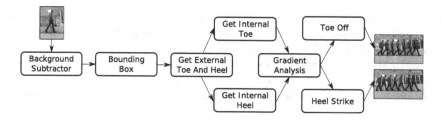

Fig. 3. Flow chart of the vision algorithm.

is estimated, we cut the silhouette in two using the previously calculated points plus or minus foot width respectively. Then, internal heel is the lower right pixel and internal toe the lower left pixel as shown in Fig. 4.

Fig. 4. Silhouette cut in two using foot width and internal toe and heel located.

Fig. 5. *(a)* (HS) Heel strike events; *(b)* (TO) Toe off events.

Once toe and heel are located for each frame, we perform a gradient analysis on the internal heel to detect HS event and on the internal toe to detect TO event. HS is detected when the heel stops moving (gradient goes from greater than zero to zero) and TO is detected when the toe starts moving (gradient goes from zero to greater than zero). Figure 5 shows the HS (Fig. 5(a)) and TO (Fig. 5(b)) events detected in a sequence.

Combining the detected gait events from both feet our vision approach can also estimate the same gait subphases from Perry's cycle as our insole-based approach. Each gait subphase's duration is computed through the use of two adequate gait events in the following set: heel strike (HS), opposite toe off (OTO), heel rise (HR), opposite heel strike (OHS) and toe off (TO).

The duration of the different phases are obtained as follows [1]:

$$LR = OTO \text{ - } HS; \quad MSt = HR \text{ - } OTO; \quad TSt = OHS \text{ - } HR; \quad PSw = HR \text{ - } TO; \quad Sw = HS \text{ - } TO;$$

For example, midstance's duration is estimated as the time difference between the timestamp of the heel rise event (HR) in the same foot minus the timestamp of the opposite toe off event (OTO).

HR event upon which MSt and TSt depend is estimated assuming that it is performed when feet are together in the closest position with each other, which corresponds to the minimum bounding box in the feet's silhouette.

4   Evaluation

The evaluation was focused on verifying the validity of both approaches for gait phase demarcation. Systems were separately compared with a reference system.

Test Subjects. The two approaches were separately tested on three male subjects. All candidates were adults (20–35 years) who presented healthy gait. Each subject performed three gait trials with each system.

Reference System. The detected gait phases in each trial, from both approaches, were compared with regard to a theoretical model of human gait [1], which is generally accepted by the experts and it is used as a ground truth. The theoretical model of human gait proposed by Perry was chosen, rather than an empirical reference system based on a specific lab setting or a commercial solution such as Vicon systems (Vicon Motion Systems Ltd., Oxford, UK) or the GAITRite electronic walkway (CIR Systems Inc., PA, USA). The theoretical model provides an approximation of the accuracy of both systems during the gait phase detection, avoiding inaccuracies from the laboratory instrumentation.

For each gait trial, the average time of each gait phase was computed and compared with the expected time for this particular phase in the reference system. According to the human gait cycle proposed by Perry, the loading response (LR) occupies 10 % of the total length of the cycle, mid stance (MSt) 20 %, terminal stance (TSt) 20 %, pre-swing (PSw) 10 %; and finally, swing (Sw) the remaining 40 % of the cycle time. For ease of comparison, the percentages of Perry's gait phases must be transformed into time units via the Eq. 2:

$$GPhaseTime = \frac{GPhase\%}{100} \times GCycleTime \tag{2}$$

where $GPhaseTime$ is the duration of the gait phase in the reference system, taking into account the defined percentage for this phase ($GPhase\%$) and the duration of the actual gait cycle ($GCycleTime$) that is being measured.

The adopted procedures for gait data recording in each approach are presented together with the evaluation results in Sects. 4.1 and 4.2, respectively.

4.1   Results of the Pressure-Sensorized Insole-Based Approach

Prior to the gait data capture, the subjects were asked to perform some walking tests with the wearable device attached as in Fig. 6(a).

Procedure. For each subject, three separated trials were stored during a walking forward sequence, each of them consisting of 10 gait cycles. The first and the last gait cycles in the trials were discarded, until enhancing stability (in the case of the beginning of the trial), and to avoid gait deceleration (at the end of the walking sequence).

For each valid cycle in all the trials, the five gait subphases (LR, MSt, TSt, PSw, Sw) were properly identified in the expected order (consecutively one phase after another and demarcated with the maximum membership ~1).

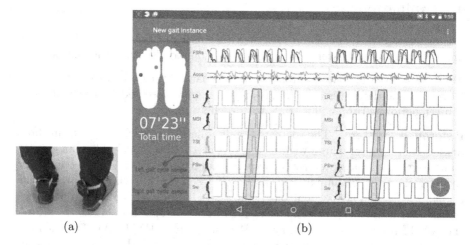

(a)   (b)

Fig. 6. *(a)* Wireless Sensorized insoles set-up; *(b)New gait instance* user interface (Color figure online).

In Fig. 6(b), there is a screenshot showing the user interface of the *New gait instance* dialog, which displays the segmented gait phases in real time during an explicit gait capture action. The drawn feet in the left column reflect the pressures registered by the FSR sensors using colored circles (darker when more pressure is exerted). The main frame on the right displays the FSR signal magnitudes and triaxial accelerations in each insole *(top)*, and the membership outputs to each gait phase (bottom). The screen capture in Fig. 6(b) reflects the beginning of a gait trial, with 7 cycles/strides collected. The highlighted areas in red enclose an example of gait cycle for the left foot and for the right foot, respectively.

Results. Table 2 exhibits the relative differences (in milliseconds) between the average duration of each gait phase estimated by the insole-based approach and the expected duration from the reference system. The values are computed for

Table 2. Accuracy comparison between the average duration of each estimated gait phase by the insole approach *vs.* Perry's reference system.

Subject	Trials	Left gait phases					Right gait phases				
		LR (ms)	MSt (ms)	TSt (ms)	PSw (ms)	Sw (ms)	LR (ms)	MSt (ms)	TSt (ms)	PSw (ms)	Sw (ms)
A	trial 1	10	115	13	-98	5	-32	134	9	-85	-14
	trial 2	-40	140	5	-86	-21	-5	121	14	-94	-1
	trial 3	-71	148	8	-97	20	-47	139	2	-75	6
B	trial 1	34	38	15	-42	-44	18	17	21	-64	-30
	trial 2	12	39	-3	-61	-40	43	42	26	-40	-41
	trial 3	59	29	5	-45	-46	48	29	17	-40	-38
C	trial 1	-14	101	-20	-50	8	-30	97	15	-65	11
	trial 2	-35	99	20	-75	5	-26	102	18	-51	8
	trial 3	-29	99	-11	-52	0	-23	104	7	-56	10
Avg		-8	90	4	-67	-13	-6	87	14	-63	-10
(±Std)		(±38)	(±42)	(±12)	(±21)	(±24)	(±33)	(±43)	(±7)	(±18)	(±20)

all the trials. A negative average duration denotes a shorter detected gait phase relative to the reference gait phase. Conversely, a positive average value denotes a longer detected gait phase relative to the reference gait phase. The last row contains the total average duration of each gait phase (Avg) and the standard deviation (Std).

As can be seen, the larger differences from the reference system are in the MSt phases (overestimated around 90 ± 40 ms) and in the PSw phases (underestimated around -65 ± 20 ms). In terms of accuracy, the relative differences are very similar for the left and right gait cycles.

4.2 Results of the Vision-Based Approach

Before the evaluation of the gait phase detection feature in the vision system an experiment to test the accuracy of the detected events was conducted.

Procedure. The performed procedure for gait data recording consisted of a RGB camera from a Kinect 2 device ((Microsoft Corporation, WA, USA) placed at ground level, 4 meters away from the gait path providing a side view. The RGB sensor was able to record images at 30 frames per second with a resolution of 1920×1080 pixels. The field of view of the RGB sensor at this position enabled the capture of six/seven steps of normal gait for each trial. "Start"and "stop" lines were placed 70 cm in front of and past the gait path to ensure the subjects reached the recording area at a comfortable pace and they did not decelerate before the end.

Results. To test the accuracy of the HS and TO detection, A set of 17 different gait trials was used. After manual marking of the HS and TO events as ground truth. We assumed an error of ±1 frame in the manual marking and ±1 frame in our algorithm. That means the error margin was ±2 frames. Comparing the ground truth with our algorithm output we observed a standard deviation of 1.49 frames for HS and 1.73 frames for TO. Both were below our error margin of ±2 frames. Table 3 shows the results obtained.

Table 3. Results of the vision algorithm for event recognition. Those with more than 2 frames between the ground truth and the algorithm output were marked as wrong.

Event	Total	False positives	Not detected	Wrong	Std
Heel Strike	97	2(2.06 %)	1(1.03 %)	6(6.19 %)	1.49 frames (49.17 ms)
Toe Off	92	0(0 %)	0(0 %)	8(8.7 %)	1.73 frames (57.09 ms)

After performing the accuracy test for gait event recognition, the same procedure for data recording was used to verify the validity of the vision approach for gait phase demarcation. Table 4 exhibits the relative differences (in milliseconds) between the average duration of each gait phase estimated by the vision approach and the expected duration from the Perry's reference system. The relative differences are acceptable in terms of accuracy, with smaller relative differences in comparison with the insole approach, although with larger dispersion.

Table 4. Accuracy comparison between the average duration of each estimated gait phase by the vision approach *vs.* Perry's reference system.

Subject	Trials	Left gait phases					Right gait phases				
		LR (ms)	MSt (ms)	TSt (ms)	PSw (ms)	Sw (ms)	LR (ms)	MSt (ms)	TSt (ms)	PSw (ms)	Sw (ms)
A	trial 1	-110	80	24	-66	71	-70	38	16	-70	87
	trial 2	-113	51	-4	-47	113	-37	93	60	-59	103
	trial 3	-69	-4	18	-24	80	-17	78	33	-23	23
B	trial 1	36	-84	-7	3	-20	22	10	43	22	-97
	trial 2	11	-22	-11	-22	-17	-12	-17	0	17	-33
	trial 3	36	-40	-7	3	-3	3	-10	7	37	-37
C	trial 1	-22	-33	11	-11	56	-9	38	27	2	20
	trial 2	-56	78	33	-11	40	-16	36	23	-38	113
	trial 3	-29	-13	42	-40	40	-39	33	11	-28	57
Avg		-35	1	11	-24	40	-19	33	24	-16	26
(±Std)		(±53)	(±53)	(±18)	(±22)	(±43)	(±25)	(±34)	(±18)	(±35)	(±67)

5   Discussion and Future Work

In the vision system the properly segmentation of HS and TO allows the extraction of spatial parameters as stride length and step length using reference distances from the video. Estimation of these parameters in the insole system, through the double integration of the acceleration signals, would be less accurate. On the other hand, the gait phase demarcation through the vision system is a complex task due to possible occlusions caused by one leg over the other, specially in mid stance and terminal stance phases. Due to the fact of using combined information from both feet to demarcate these gait phases and because the estimation of the HR event as the moment when the silhouette's bounding box is minimal, the vision approach will be more affected if the stride length is drastically reduced or a gait pathology is present. Therefore, in these cases, the analysis focused on the dynamic forces will provide better results.

Additionally, the insoles can identify gait phases in real time. Although it is not a requirement for this project, it is a powerful functionality to detect errors during execution or the lack of some of the phases, which is common in some gait pathologies (*e.g.*, heel walking, heel pain). A system to provide feedback to the subject in real time such as functional electrical stimulation (FES) can be developed as an independent future work. However, the mainly part of our future development must be focused on the integration of the two approaches, do joint assessments under controlled conditions and also in real-life scenarios and merge the results of both systems to reinforce each other. As outcome of this fusion, the estimated gait parameters will be used as a functional marker to determine whether a subject shows signs of dementia or frailty, in the second stage of the FRASE project (see Acknowledment). There will be also a new prototype of the insole system more compact and equipped with Bluetooth Low Energy (BLE).

Acknowledgment. This work is conducted in the context of the FRASE MINECO project (TIN2013-47152-C3-1-R). Also, we appreciate the support of UBIHEALTH project under International Research Staff Exchange Schema (MC-IRSES 316337).

References

1. Perry, J.: Gait analysis systems. In: Gait Analysis: Normal and Pathological Function, ch. 19–24. SLACK Incorporated: Thorofare, New Jersey (1992)
2. Theologis, T., Stebbins, J.: The use of gait analysis in the treatment of pediatric foot and ankle disorders. Foot Ankle Clin. **15**(2), 365–382 (2010)
3. Brach, J.S., Perera, S., Studenski, S., Newman, A.B.: The reliability and validity of measures of gait variability in community-dwelling older adults. Arch. Phys. Med. Rehabil. **89**, 2293–2296 (2008)
4. Hausdorff, J.M.: Gait variability: methods, modeling and meaning. J. NeuroEngineering Rehabil. **2**, 19 (2005)
5. Lopez-Meyer, P., Fulk, G.D., Sazonov, E.: Automatic detection of temporal gait parameters in poststroke individuals. IEEE Trans. Inf. Technol. Biomed. **15**(4), 594–601 (2011)

6. Bamberg, S.J.M., Benbasat, A.Y., Scarborough, D.M., Krebs, D.E., Paradiso, J.A.: Gait analysis using a shoe-integrated wireless sensor system. IEEE Trans. Inf. Technol. Biomed. **12**(4), 413–423 (2008)

7. Crea, S., Donati, M., De Rossi, S.M.M., Oddo, C.M., Vitiello, N.: A wireless flexible sensorized insole for gait analysis. Sens. **14**, 1073–1093 (2014)

8. Pappas, I.P.I., Popovic, M.R., Kelly, T., Dietz, V., Morari, M.: A reliable gait phase detection system. IEEE Trans. Neural Syst. Rehabil. Eng. **9**(2), 113–125 (2001)

9. Senanayake, C., Senanayake, S.M.N.A.: A computational method for reliable gait event detection and abnormality detection for feedback in rehabilitation. Comput. Methods Biomech. Biomed. Eng. **14**(10), 863–874 (2011)

10. Roy, A., Sural, S., Mukherjee, J.: A hierarchical method combining gait and phase of motion with spatiotemporal model for person re-identification. Pattern Recogn. Lett. **33**(14), 1891–1901 (2012)

11. Iwashita, Y., Stoica, A., Kurazume, R.: Gait identification using shadow biometrics. Pattern Recogn. Lett. **33**(16), 2148–2155 (2012)

12. Choudhury, S.D., Tjahjadi, T.: Gait recognition based on shape and motion analysis of silhoutte contours. Comput. Vis. Image Underst. **117**(12), 1770–1785 (2013)

13. Khan, T., Westin, J., Dougherty, M.: Motion cue analysis for Parkinsonian gait recognition. Open Biomed. Eng. J. **7**, 1–8 (2013)

14. Choudhury, S.D., Tjahjadi, T.: Silhoutte-based gait recognition using Procrustes shape analysis and elliptic Fourier descriptors. Pattern Recogn. **45**(9), 3414–3426 (2012)

15. Zeng, W., Wang, C., Yang, F.: Silhouette-based gait recognition via deterministic learning. Pattern Recogn. **47**(11), 3568–3584 (2014)

16. Xu, X., McGorry, R.W., Chou, L., Lin, J., Chang, C.: Accuracy of the Microsoft Kinect for measuring gait parameters during treadmill walking. Gait & Posture **42**(2), 145–151 (2015)

17. González, I., Fontecha, J., Hervás, R., Bravo, J.: An ambulatory system for gait monitoring based on wireless sensorized insoles. Sens. **15**(7), 16589–16613 (2015)

Mobile Monitoring Review: Comparative with MoMo Framework Solution

Vladimir Villarreal[1(✉)], Ramón Hervás[2], and Jose Bravo[2]

[1] GITCE Research Lab, Technological University of Panama, Chiriquí, Panamá
vladimir.villarreal@utp.ac.pa
[2] MAmI Research Lab, University of Castilla-La Mancha, Ciudad Real, Spain
{ramon.hervas,jose.bravo}@uclm.es

Abstract. The systematic review allows us to identify, assess, and interpret all possible relevant work associated with a question in particular or subject of an area. In this paper we will use the Kitchenham protocol, which allow for the proper selection of primary and secondary research related to mobile monitoring solution. The main objective of this review is to identify work, research and publications made in the field of mobile monitoring of patients through a framework or application generators. Next, we compare the different solutions with our solution: MoMo Framework. Our systematic review is based on the methodology B. Kitchenham. She proposes specific guidelines to carry out the systematic review in software engineering.

Keywords: Mobile monitoring · Systematic review · Ubiquitous computing · M-health

1 Introduction

The systematic review allows us to identify, assess, and interpret all possible relevant work associated with a question in particular or subject of an area. For them we will use some techniques or protocols [1] that you allow us the proper selection of primary and secondary research related to mobile monitoring solution. The main objective of this review is to identify work, research and publications made in the field of mobile monitoring of patients through a framework or application generators. She proposes specific guidelines to carry out the systematic review in software engineering.

The proposal is based on similar guidelines for researchers with the objective to re-use the knowledge and experience of a known and consolidated area of research. The main intention with the guidelines is introduce the concept of a rigorous review of current empirical evidence to the software engineering community. There are several characteristics that differentiate a systematic review of a conventional literature review:

- **Definition of the review Protocol:** It is in this section, which specifies the question of research that deals with and the methods that will be used to carry out the review.
- **Definition of the strategy of search:** the search strategy aims to detect much of the relevant literature as possible.
- **Search for documented:** by what readers to assess the rigor and integrity.

© Springer International Publishing Switzerland 2015
I. Cleland et al. (Eds.): IWAAL 2015, LNCS 9455, pp. 219–230, 2015.
DOI: 10.1007/978-3-319-26410-3_21

- **Explicit inclusion and exclusion criteria:** for each primary study to assess (a systematic review is a secondary study based on primary studies).
- **Systematic reviews:** Specifies the information that will be obtained from each of the primary studies, including quality criteria to evaluate each primary study. A systematic review is a prerequisite for the meta-analysis quantitative.

2   Definition of the Review Protocol

A review protocol defines the methods to be used in order to undertake a specific systematic review. A predefined protocol is necessary to reduce the bias of the researcher [1]. The following points are indicated in the guidelines for the development of a review Protocol:

- **The research question:** is the intent of the systematic review to answer a question that identifies areas of future research activities. The question of research of this systematic review is as follows: ¿*The development of a framework that allows the generation of parameterized applications that facilitate monitoring through communication between mobile and biometric devices for the medical monitoring of patients is possible?*
- **Definition of the search strategy:** our search strategy is based on two aspects evaluated, concerning mobile patient monitoring and the development of applications for mobile devices.
- **Search and data extraction:** the steps to follow for search and data extraction were based on the following steps: the topic selection, search for articles with titles relating to this topic, reading of summaries (abstracts) and keywords, selection of primary studies and comparative analysis of primary studies.

2.1   Criteria of Evaluation

For the analysis and evaluation of each of the related work, we have defined a set of criteria that will enable us to assess and locate aspects of design, adaptability, communication, security and costs in each research. The evaluation criteria for each evaluated work are:

- **Design**
  - *Cohesion*: This sub-criteria the following abbreviations and weights have been used for: High (AT) = 3, Medium (MD) = 2 and Low (BJ) = 1
  - *Mesh:* This sub-criteria the following abbreviations and weights have been used for: High (AT) = 3, Medium (MD) = 2 and Low (BJ) = 1
  - *Usability:* This sub-criteria the following abbreviations and weights have been used for: High (AT) = 3, Medium (MD) 2 and Low (BJ) = 1
- **Adaptability**
  - *Change and adaptive capacity:* This sub-criteria the following abbreviations and weights have been used for: High (AT) = 3, Medium (MD) = 2 and Low (BJ) = 1

- *Migration of the domain application:* This sub-criteria the following abbreviations and weights have been used for: High (AT) = 3, Medium (MD) = 2 and Low (BJ) = 1
- *Technological Migration:* This sub-criteria the following abbreviations and weights have been used for: High (AT) = 3, Medium (MD) = 2 and Low (BJ) = 1
- **Communication**
  - *External communication or data transmission:* This sub-criteria the following abbreviations and weights have been used for: High (AT) = 3, Medium (MD) = 2 and Low (BJ) = 1
- **Security**
  - *In data treatment:* This sub-criteria the following abbreviations and weights have been used for: High (AT) = 3, Medium (MD) = 2 and Low (BJ) = 1
  - *In data transfer:* This sub-criteria the following abbreviations and weights have been used for: High (AT) = 3, Medium (MD) = 2 y Low (BJ) = 1
- **Costs**
  - *Implementation:* This sub-criteria the following abbreviations and weights have been used for: High (AT) = 1, Medium (MD) = 2 y Low (BJ) = 3
  - *Maintenance:* This sub-criteria the following abbreviations and weights have been used for: High (AT) = 1, Medium (MD) = 2 and Low (BJ) = 3

3 Patient Mobile Monitoring Review

These research have brought with it the creation of different technological platforms that have offered a timely solution to problems of health care, within which we can find:

Health Buddy System [2] it is a system that provides health monitoring of patients by reducing the chances of hospitalization. Figure 1, the application communicate the patient at home to care provides. Everyday, patients respond a number of questions about their health and well being using the simple Health Buddy appliance. The data is sent over a telephone line or an Ethernet connection to a secure data center, data are available for review on the website of the Health Buddy.

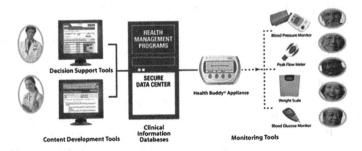

Fig. 1. Health buddy system functionality

MoMo Framework: looking for minimal interaction with the mobile device, all processing make from initial capture of vital signs. It is minimize that interaction, to help you use the patient providing you with replies and messages automatically.

AirStrip Patient Monitoring it is a software platform with a vision of critical patient information secure sending directly from the monitoring systems of the hospital bedside devices and health mobile clinical records [3]. AppPoint was also designed to solve the key challenges in the development of software for mobile phones, such as the development of native applications that provide a rich user experience requirements, while at the same time be able to scale and adapt to an ever-changing world of operating systems and mobile devices. This application has been developed for devices such as iPhone, iPod and iPad. As shown in a Fig. 2, stored information related to values obtained electrocardiograms, vital signs, medication, and laboratory results, allergies, among other lists.

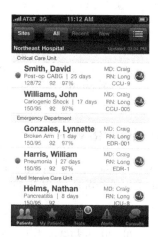

Fig. 2. AirStrip patient monitoring functionality

MoMo Framework: it avoids relying on a platform in particular, and includes like this application, additional information of the patient as a results of tests and examinations in general. Initially we developed software for platform architecture in particular, the most widespread, allowing you to adapt it to another making the minimum changes.

WellDoc it is an application designed to be a service of monitoring for diabetics [4], integrated with Ford Sync, designed for iOS, which allows you to monitor the current condition of a patient through the manual entry of food and glucose. Thanks to its integration with Sync, it will synchronize with this service via Bluetooth, which will detect if not we have introduced no record recently, and through a set of questions (Yes or No), make sure see if our blood levels are correct. It will suggest the next recommended action to take, or in extreme cases, will send a SMS to the contact that we have previously selected as of emergencies, with the option of sending another message to get home, confirming that we are sure (show Fig. 3).

MoMo Framework: this implemented regardless of the disease to control, has been developed to interact with a wide range of diseases that can be monitored through vital signs. We will implement case studies specific to meet your functionality.

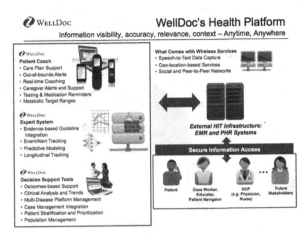

Fig. 3. High-level of WellDoc architecture overview

METABO [5] it is a system of monitoring and management of diabetes that aims at the recording and interpretation of the context of the patient, as well as to support decisions for the patient and the physician. METABO system consists of (a) a mobile device of the patient (PMD), (b) the different types of discrete biosensors, (c) a central subsystem (CS) located remotely in the hospital and (d) the control panel (CP) from which doctors can give their patient monitoring and also access to the CS. METABO provides a surveillance system that facilitates effective and systematic recording of diet, physical activity, medication and medical information (continuous and discontinuous glucose measurements).

MoMo Framework: still contemplating the appearance of monitoring that develops an architecture software that enables the monitoring and control of patients independent of the type of disease being treated, respecting each of the elements of the software architecture developed functional requirements initially raised.

Ambulation in [6] is an important tool to assess the health of patients suffering from chronic diseases that affect mobility such as multiple sclerosis (MS), the Parkinson's and muscular dystrophy through the assessment when they walk. **Ambulation** Android and Nokia N95 is a monitoring system of mobility that uses mobile phones to automatically detect the mobility of the user mode. The interaction required by the user with the phone is turn it on and keep it with him throughout the day, with the intention that could be used as your everyday mobile phone for voice, data and other applications, while Ambulation is running in the background. The phone loads the information gathered from the mobility and location on a server. Then display data through an intuitive, and secure Web-based service being available to the user, any family, friends or caregivers.

MoMo Framework: the patient monitoring application to run without interfering with everyday use given to the mobile device. This makes transparent functionality for the user and minimizing the interaction.

SenSAVE [7] with the project senSave developed a system for mobile monitoring of the parameters of vital signs. It takes the measures of blood pressure and the pulse of people related to cardiovascular problems in real time. In summary this system, studied the way that presents information, dialogue windows and alarm function, proving the usability of mobile devices (show Fig. 4).

MoMo Framework: it proposes communication between multiple mobile, and biometric devices based on a specific patient profile and the disease being treated. These vital signals control information is generated for patients.

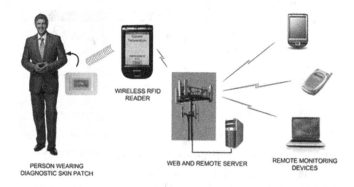

Fig. 4. Functional diagram of SenSAVE

U-Health in [8] has designed and developed a mobile system of health care with capacity of measurement of several physiological signs in real time. This system performs an analysis of data from the vital signs via the mobile phone and transmits these data through a network of wireless sensors. Mobile phone performs some simple data analysis first, and then immediately transmits these signals to a server for the diagnosis of doctor's hospital. The application of wireless technology in diagnostic system allows that the patient can be monitored anywhere, at any time and could not be hampered by physical constraints imposed by the cables.

MoMo Framework: it facilitates continuous monitoring of the patient; it offers control whenever the values of the measurements of vital signs are obtained. You can generate recommendations associated with this measurement, by offering an environment of continuous monitoring.

Healthwear in [9] addresses research that allows the monitoring of health conditions through electrocardiograms, heart rate, and saturation of oxygen, impedance pneumography and activity patterns. A new design was made to increase the patient's comfort during daily activities. The fabric is connected to a portable electronic unit of the patient (PPU) that acquires and develops the signals from the sensors. The PPU transmits the signal to a central site for processing through the use of GPRS wireless technology. This service applies to three different clinical settings: rehabilitation of cardiac patients, after an acute event, the program of early discharge in patients of chronic breathing and the promotion of physical activity cardio-respiratory stable outpatients.

MoMo Framework: avoid the use of equipment in the body, only it is necessary to have a biometric device to obtain vital signs. The use of equipment in the body is very intrusive. We want to minimize the alteration in the daily live of the patient, minimizing the intrusion.

MobiHealth [10] proposed the development of a framework that represents the vital signs of patients, show Fig. 5. This framework facilitates the storage of existing different notations to represent vital signs (FDA, CEN, HL7, DICOM). For this purpose they propose a XML schema to define the framework of representation of vital signs, by specifying a large number of these representations.

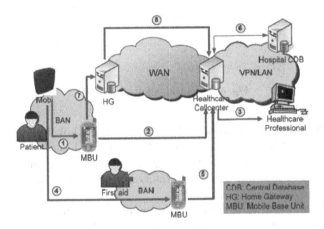

Fig. 5. Transmission of vital signs, MobiHealth system

MoMo Framework: this system proposes only a representation of the vital signals received by mobile devices creating data files of the representations of vital signs resulting from the mobility of users (patients) in heterogeneous environments. Our proposal is not based on a representation of vital signs, but in the control and interpretation of these.

eDiab. Fernández-Luque [11] developed a system for monitoring, assistance and education of people with diabetes, called eDiab. A central node (PDA or cellphone) provide health information, health tips, alarms and reminders. Glucose sensor is connected to a central node via wireless (Bluetooth/ZigBee) and the communication between the central node and the server is established with GPRS/GSM connection. Finally a subsystem for health education sends medical information and advice such as reminders of treatments. As shown in Fig. 6 the eDiab project is being designed with a multidisciplinary view: assistive technology, telemedicine and diabetes education. It is divided into two subsystems, one for the monitoring and control of diabetes and one for health education.

MoMo Framework: It includes aspects of control of patients, with the difference, that our proposal is based on the definition of the profile of the patient. This patient profile associated with measurements obtained from an illness, governs the behavior of the final application.

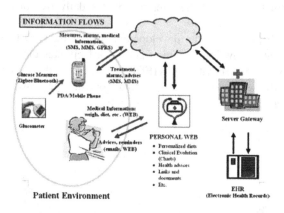

Fig. 6. Information flow in eDiab

LATIS Pervasive *Framework* (LAPERF). Tadj [12] with LATIS Pervasive Framework (LAPERF) provides a framework of base and automatic tools for the development and implementation of applications of pervasive computing. Its main application has been shown in the use of health care applications. We sought with this better integrity in pervasive systems.

MoMo Framework: is based on a description of activities associated with the location of the patient; communication is established between the patient and the medical specialist. The structure of the LATIS Pervasive framework are in level lower the Access Device Manager where all devices are located to access the framework (Smartphone, PDA, computers desktop, etc.). Security and Privacy Manager, is responsible for the unauthorized access by defining the system security policies.

MAHI. Mamykina [13] developed MAHI (Mobile Access to Health Information), an application that monitors to patients diagnosed with diabetes where acquired skills of reflective thinking by social interaction with diabetes educators. MAHI is a distributed mobile application that includes a conventional meter (LifeScan – OneTouch Ultra), Java (Nokia N80)-enabled mobile phone and a Bluetooth adapter that connects to the phone and the glucometer. Through this they recorded their levels of glucose in the blood and the changes related to diabetes, such as questions, problems and activities of interest, using the capture of images and sounds with the mobile.

MoMo Framework: does not intend to create a website, but that information will be contained in the mobile device of the patient, transmitting data to and from a remote server. This information is generated according to the activities developed by the patient and the measures obtained from biometric devices. The mobile device can be used in two roles: the patient role, specifically for the control and use of each patient and the medical role, where doctors will have access to the information of all patients assigned to it.

4 Analysis of Evaluated Applications Based in the Criteria

For the analysis of the studied applications, we will rely on the description and weight of the criteria and sub-criteria defined previously. These criteria allow us to analyze this block of related works, which have been classified as applications developed by companies or private developers.

- **Design:** in Fig. 7, this criteria has been tested according to the functions specified in the documentation presented in each application developed. Evaluated applications possess a mid-grade according to design criteria. The link sub-criteria have long been valued as the lowest criteria in the design, giving more importance to usability. MoMo offers design results in accordance with the criteria of cohesion, coupling, and usability. It's found a generalized definition of software architecture minimizing coupling but maximizing cohesion. With regard to usability, our software architecture is easily usable, as it has tried to minimize the unnecessary interactions by the user.

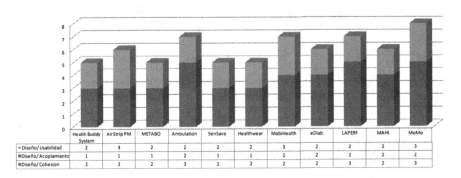

Fig. 7. Level design of the analyzed applications.

- **Adaptability:** the degree of the adaptability criteria and their sub-criteria, Fig. 8 shows the evaluation of each application analyzed in this article. The adaptability of the analyzed applications, go hand in hand with design criteria, it may be noted that it values with a mid-grade to this criteria. Much of the applications can be adapted to cover other existing technological aspects and other application domains. MAHI has been the application with lower degree of found adaptability, while Health Buddy System that has greater adaptability. MoMo offers a high level of adaptability both hardware and software technologies.
- **Communication** In Fig. 9, we evaluated applications using any communication technology. These include those offered by the networks of mobile telephony, Ethernet, WiFi and others. SenSave has been the application that most low degree of communication (data transmission) presents; they don't use existing communication

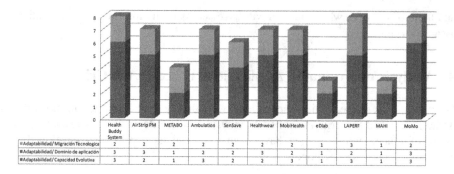

Fig. 8. Adaptability of the analyzed applications level

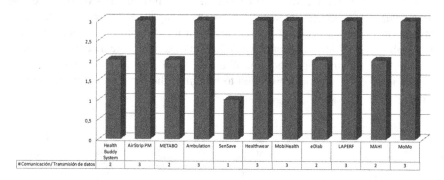

Fig. 9. Level of communication of the analyzed applications.

technology at the time of the analysis. MoMo still offers a high level of communication and data transmission.

- **Security:** other aspects discussed in found applications, is that of security, in Fig. 10. Just two of the total of applications, define the treatment of patient data. It specifies any protocol or guidelines to maintain the privacy of this data. On the other hand, the safety in data transfer has been an aspect moderately referred to, since some applications, leave this aspect to communication technology, if you use them and others do not consider it necessary. MoMo offers greater safety compared with other proposals.

- **Costs:** deploying the applications mostly presents an average both maintenance and implementation cost, show in Fig. 11. Because, they are very dependent on the technologies for which they were developed. It is difficult to decouple from this criteria since most applications are developed for specific platforms and technologies. A mid-grade weighting more minimizes the costs of changes that you want to perform in the future.

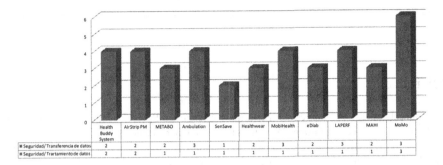

Fig. 10. Security level of the analyzed applications.

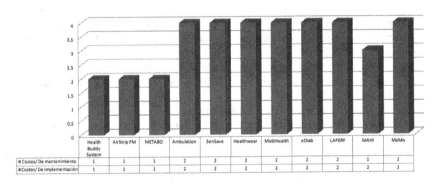

Fig. 11. Costs of the analyzed applications.

5 Conclusions

This paper presented the different contributions made by some researchers in the field of monitoring of patients, either mobile or some approximation to this type. A number of evaluation criteria have been defined to determine the level of integration, composition and functioning which has each proposal, to find deficiencies and to better understand the scope of development of our. The criteria were assessed objectively, based on the specifications of each research. Some of the documented proposals not explained retail distribution of its elements, which makes us think, that they were as development intentions. We can note although there are many research that have been developed, all were developed focusing on particular settings, to solve a situation. This can be seen that some researches have an imperative to lifetime, which limits the concept of "multi-monitoring" that we are seeking in this article. This leads us to develop a software architecture based on the framework that is not dependent on a field of study in particular, but it can be adjusted to different areas. We seek with this facilitate multiple monitoring, integrating different types of diseases or conditions, and that can be monitored by various mobile devices and biometric.

Acknowledgments. The first author is member of the National Research Investigator award (SNI) from the SENACYT as a National Research I.

References

1. Kitchenham, B.: Procedures for Performing Systematic Reviews. Joint Technical Report Software Engineering Group, Department of Computer Science Keele University, United King and Empirical Software Engineering, National ICT Australia Ltd, Australia (2014)
2. BOSCH: Health buddy system (2011). http://www.bosch-telehealth.com. Accessed 2012
3. AirStrip, T.: AirStrip patient monitoring (2011). http://www.airstriptech.com/
4. WellDoc: WellDoc health platform (2011). http://www.welldoc.com/Products-and-Services/Our-Products.aspx. Accessed 2012
5. Georga, E., Protopappas, V., et al.: Data mining for blood glucose prediction and knowledge discovery in diabetic patients: the METABO diabetes modeling and management system. In: Engineering in Medicine and Biology Society, EMBC 2009. Annual International Conference of the IEEE (2009)
6. Ryder, J., Longstaff, B., et al.: Ambulation: a tool for monitoring mobility patterns over time using mobile phones. In: International Conference on Computational Science and Engineering, CSE 2009 (2009)
7. Lorenz, A., Mielke, D., et al.: Personalized mobile health monitoring for elderly. In: 9th International Conference on Human Computer Interaction with Mobile Devices and Services, Singapore. ACM (2007)
8. Chung, W.-Y., Lee, S.-C., et al.: WSN based mobile u-healthcare system with ECG, blood pressure measurement function. In: Engineering in Medicine and Biology Society, EMBS 2008. 30th Annual International Conference of the IEEE (2008)
9. Paradiso, R., Alonso, A., et al.: Remote health monitoring with wearable non-invasive mobile system: the healthwear project. In: Engineering in Medicine and Biology Society, EMBS 2008. 30th Annual International Conference of the IE (2008)
10. Mei, H., Widya, I., et al.: A flexible vital sign representation framework for mobile healthcare. In: Pervasive Healthcare Conference and Workshops 2006, Innsbruck, Austria (2006)
11. Fernández-Luque, L., Sevillano, J.L., Hurtado-Núñez, F.J., Moriana-García, F.J., del Río, F. D., Cascado, D.: eDiab: a system for monitoring, assisting and educating people with diabetes. In: Miesenberger, K., Klaus, J., Zagler, W.L., Karshmer, A.I. (eds.) ICCHP 2006. LNCS, vol. 4061, pp. 1342–1349. Springer, Heidelberg (2006)
12. Tadj, C., Ngantchaha, G.: Context handling in a pervasive computing system framework. In: 3rd International Conference on Mobile Technology, Applications and Systems, Bangkok, Thailand. ACM (2006)
13. Mamykina, L., Mynatt, E.D., et al.: Investigating health management practices of individuals with diabetes. In: SIGCHI Conference on Human Factors in Computing Systems, Montreal, Quebec, Canada. ACM (2006)

A Gesture-Based Interaction Approach for Manipulating Augmented Objects Using Leap Motion

Gustavo López[1(✉)], Luis Quesada[2], and Luis A. Guerrero[1,2]

[1] Centro de Investigaciones en Tecnologías de la Información y Comunicación,
Universidad de Costa Rica, UCR, San Pedro, Costa Rica
gustavo.lopez_h@ucr.ac.cr, luis.guerrero@ecci.ucr.ac.cr
[2] Escuela de Ciencias de la Computación e Informática,
Universidad de Costa Rica, UCR, San Pedro, Costa Rica
luis.quesada@ecci.ucr.ac.cr

Abstract. Ambient Intelligence and Ubiquitous Computing are carrying the world to a reality where almost every object interacts with the environment, either via sensors or actuators, and users must learn how to interact with such systems. This paper presents a gesture-based interaction approach to manipulate such objects. We developed a prototype using a leap motion controller as a hand-tracking device, and a Support Vector Machine as a classifier to distinguish between gestures. Our system was evaluated by 12 users with over 10 commands. We also show a review on gesture-based interaction and compare other proposals with ours.

Keywords: Gesture-Based interaction · Ubiquitous systems · Leap motion

1 Introduction

Ambient Intelligence envisions a world where people are surrounded by intelligent and intuitive interfaces embedded into everyday objects. We call these devices Augmented Objects [1].

With mobile and smart devices in ubiquitous environments, traditional interaction techniques face some challenges. Gestures are currently seen as a promising and natural method to communicate with smart devices [2].

This paper presents an approach to control Augmented Objects using gestures. We propose a set of generic gestures that could be used for interacting with several Augmented Objects. Our set of gestures is based on three characteristics: easy relation between gestures and natural language, technological limitations, and hand motion and posture, to avoid fatigue and pain. To evaluate our gesture proposal, we developed a prototype that transform gestures in commands, and allow remote interaction with Augmented Objects.

Our prototype was developed using a hand tracker called Leap Motion [3], and a Support Vector Machine (SVM). We embedded the leap motion into a specially designed case with visual and auditory feedback. Our prototype works based on the premise that Augmented Objects provide their functionalities via Web Services.

© Springer International Publishing Switzerland 2015
I. Cleland et al. (Eds.): IWAAL 2015, LNCS 9455, pp. 231–243, 2015.
DOI: 10.1007/978-3-319-26410-3_22

We propose a set of gestures that allows users to flexibly and conveniently control multiple devices with simple gestures. However, our system also allows users to create different sets of gestures. We evaluated our system and set of gestures with 12 users and 10 command attempts per user.

The paper is structured as follows: Sect. 2 introduces gesture-based interaction, Leap Motion, SVMs, Augmented Objects, and shows the related work, focused on gesture-based interaction with smart devices. Section 3 details out solution. Section 4 shows our gesture proposal to interact with Augmented Object. Section 5 shows the evaluation performed to test the gesture set and the system prototype. Finally, Sect. 6 shows our conclusion.

2 Background

This section introduces the main concepts regarding gesture-based interaction, the Leap Motion, Support Vector Machines, and Augmented Objects. Moreover a literature review that comprises several gesture-based interaction proposals for Augmented Objects is presented.

2.1 Gesture-Based Interaction

Gestures are an important part of the human-human communication [4]. They are used in everyday life and are usually self-explanatory. The main difference between gestures in Human-Computer Interaction (HCI) and human-human interaction is that in the later, gestures are used to highlight what is being said, rather than the main mean of communication [5].

Several sets of gestures for interacting with smart devices have been presented in literature [6–9]. However, most of the proposed gesture sets were created for ad hoc interaction, (i.e., designed for one specific device).

Gestures for HCI usually have to be learned and remembered by the user and are therefore cognitively demanding. Moreover, computational gesture recognition is not a trivial process.

Gesture recognition is a topic in computer science and language technology, and the goal is to interpret human gestures via mathematical algorithms, process them as signals and use those signals to communicate with computers.

Gesture-based interaction presents several challenges when trying to deploy systems using this paradigm. Some issues such mathematical models, spatial and temporal characteristics of the hands, hand localization and hand tracking, need to be considered. The goal is to unambiguously interpret any user gesture.

Currently, most systems only use symbolic commands based on hand posture and pointing actions [10]. An even bigger problem is that, most commands offered by such systems do not consider hand motion and posture producing fatigue and pain.

With the market release of the Leap Motion device, most of the problems previously described were addressed. The researchers and developers are now focusing on creating system using the Leap Motion capabilities.

2.2   Leap Motion

The Leap Motion Controller senses the movement of a hand placed over it. The scanned area is in the shape of an inverted pyramid with the tip at the central point of the device.

Due to patent restrictions, few details are known about the Leap Motion's inner structure and its basic operational properties. Leap Motion tracks all 10 fingers with a precision of up to 1/100th of a millimeter. Moreover, it tracks hand movements at a rate of over 100 frames per second [3].

Leap Motion employs a right-handed Cartesian coordinate system. Readings are in millimeters. X and Z axis lie horizontally and Y axis is vertical with positive values increasing upwards.

Even though Leap Motion allows tracking of all hand joints, our classification mechanisms only uses 5 joints, the tip of the distal phalanx (Fig. 1) of each finger. For each measured joint we use the coordinates in a 3D space and the direction vector of each distal phalanx.

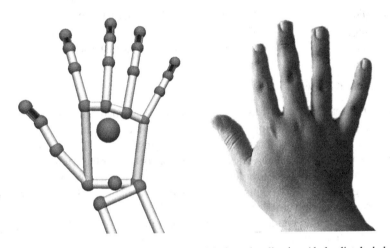

Fig. 1. Bones on the hand using the Leap Motion visualization (dark: distal phalanx)

2.3   Support Vector Machines

Support Vector Machines (SVMs) are supervised learning models that use learning algorithms to recognize patterns for classification or regression [11]. SVMs are based on training examples that allow classification of new observations.

In our prototype we used a supervised learning approach. Our recognition system is based on Scikit-learn's [12] SVM. Even though SVMs were primarily described for two categories classification, the implementation we use (Scikit-learn's C-Support Vector Classification) is capable of performing multi-class classification by using multiple classifiers, i.e., if n = number of classes, then $n*(n-1)/2$ classifiers are constructed.

In SVMs the separation function is defined by the Kernel, there are several types of kernels, (e.g., lineal polynomial, Gaussian). We use the Gaussian Kernel, this decision was based on the fact that we had a larger number of observation than features and the amount of observation was relatively small (i.e., performance was not an issue).

Our SVM implementation uses γ(Gamma) = 0.0001 and C = 100, other parameters required to defined the SVM were default values (see [12]). Gamma is a parameter that controls the width of Gaussian [13]. In our case we use a small gamma to ensure that a given data point has a non-zero kernel value relative to any example in the set of support vectors. Table 1 shows the information of one frame, (i.e., SVM input). All the coordinates and direction vector are rounded to the nearest hundredth.

Table 1. Frame data sample

Parameter finger	Coordinates			Direction vector
	X	Y	Z	
Thumb	−46.474	194.263	50.302	(0.847,−0.118,0.516)
Index	−30.177	224.763	−30.919	(0.320,−0.063,0.945)
Middle	11.632	226.195	−49.157	(0.021,0.013,0.999)
Ring	43.357	223.479	−43.908	(−0.099,0.032,0.994)
Pinky	81.332	216.287	−18.749	(−0.443,0.054,0.894)

2.4   Augmented Objects

Augmented Objects are defined as common objects, provided with additional functionalities through integrated computing or software systems [14]. In this paper we only consider Augmented Objects that were designed following the Human-Object Interaction framework [1]. This framework forces developers to offer the Augmented Object capabilities via Web Services, in order to be consumed by other systems.

Several augmented object examples are available in literature and as retail products. For instance, a bathroom mirror that provides weather forecasting or schedule reminders [15], a ring that tells you the name of the object that you grab [16], or even a pen that creates a digital representation of your handwriting while you write [17].

2.5   A Review of Gesture-Based Interaction for Augmented Objects

Several research papers presented the benefits of using gesture-based interaction with Intelligent Environments, home appliances or even ubiquitous systems.

Yuksel and Adali [2] presented a touch less gesture-based interaction method to interact with ubiquitous devices. Their prototype is based on a wearable controller and it uses Bluetooth to achieve communication between the controller and ubiquitous devices.

A similar work was presented by Hein et al. [20]. Authors presented a free-handed system using a bracelet with an accelerometer embedded. Their system recognizes one hand gestures that do not take longer than a second. However, authors do not present applications for their device.

Lun et al. [7], presented a smart home controller system using gestures. Their solution uses a glove to recognize the user's gestures. Their solution uses flex sensors to detect the user's gestures. They use a Home controller unit that is in charge of controlling the house hold appliances. A similarity between this work and ours is that both can be used to control several devices. Authors state that the system could be improved by substituting the glove with a visual-based gesture translation system. That is our approach to the problem.

Other research papers use different technologies to approach gesture recognition. Moya et al. [21] presented a camera-based gesture instance, Moya, Montero, recognition system for intelligent environments. Their system is composed of a hand detector, a hand tracker, a gesture recognizer, and a mode state machine. Their proposal uses embedded devices with cameras to capture gestures and process them.

Saidinejad et al. [6] presented a Kinect-based gesture recognition system for smart home control. Their work is based on an understanding of a gesture grammar. Their work is still being addressed.

GeeAir [8, 22] is a handheld device for remotely controlling home appliances. GeeAir uses a Nintendo nunchuk as controller. Even though this system uses a special device to recognize commands they present a definition of gesture commands for appliances that are interesting for our work.

Finally, Fernández et al. [23] described a multimodal interfaces approach to interact with Smart Homes. Authors suggest that speech, gestures, movements and other user actions could be used to interact with Smart Homes. Authors used accelerometers of small devices held by the user to recognize gestures. An important characteristic of this approach is that it uses Service Oriented paradigms for communications. This last related work is interesting, because our system could be used to expand Fernandez et al. multimodal interaction architecture.

Table 2 summarizes the review performed in this research. There are three main recognition mechanisms used: wearable technologies, controllers, and image or camera-based mechanisms. Even with the advances with technology, there are still several technological limitations; preventing all gestures to be unambiguously recognized.

Table 2. Literature review summary

Recognition mechanism	Manipulates	Reference
Wearable controller	Ubiquitous devices	[2]
Bracelet	Not stated	[18]
Glove	Smart home	[7]
Cameras	Intelligent environments	[19]
Kinect	Smart home	[6]
Nintendo nunchuk	Home appliances	[8, 20]
Multimodal	Smart home	[21]

Our proposal differs from available systems in the use of Leap Motion technology; moreover, we use augmented objects developed using the same process, ensuring that their capabilities are available via Web Services. Next section details our system proposal.

3 System Overview

We developed a system that allows users to manipulate several augmented objects using hand gestures. Our system is composed by two main components: the system's case (Fig. 2) and the augmented object(s). We assume that all augmented objects provide their functionality via Web Services as they were created using the same construction process [1].

a) Leap Motion   b) System's case   c) Complete System

Fig. 2. System physical components

The system's case is composed of the physical devices (leap motion and feedback components) and the software component. The software component performs several tasks including: (1) gathering frame data from the Leap Motion, (2) cleaning and processing gathered data, (3) applying SVM classification to the cleaned data, (4) performing the classification process, and (5) consuming the corresponding augmented object web service to execute a command and sent feedback.

We defined a classification process that forces the system to classify five consecutive frames as the same before a command is executed. Moreover, after each reading, ten frames are discarded before another one is classified. This decision was based on experimentation; we realized that given the speed of readings, classifying less than five frames could be misinterpreted. The system's workflow is as follows:

1. **The user selects an augmented object he/she wants to control.** The selection of the object can be performed using a physical selector embedded in the case or using a sign language (Costa Rican Sign Language) to spell the name of the object. Levenshtein distance [18] is used to compare the difference between the set of available augmented objects and the one the user spelled.
2. **The user places hand for recognition (base sign indicates that next sign or gesture is a command).** Leap motion controller is very effective recognizing signs and gestures. However, during the implementation and evaluation we detected that, in order to improve recognition an open hand was required. Due to this characteristic we consider a "five" sign as our base (a sign like the one in Fig. 1). When the system recognizes a five sign, it triggers reading and classification of the next recognized gesture.

3. **The user gesture or sign is recorded and classified by the SVM.** For signs: when five consecutive readings are classified as the same, the sign is considered a command. For gestures: with the base sign recognition, data is gathered and the distance between the base sign and the new sign is computed and classified by the SVM.

4. **The selected Augmented Object Web Service is consumed sending the recognized sign command.** To determine the command, a Database is queried for the recognized sign and augmented object. This query returns the command the Web Services will receive. Association between sigs and commands was performed beforehand.

5. **The Augmented Object executes the action and it sends back a confirmation.** This is performed by consuming the Augmented Object web services and waiting for confirmation.

6. **The case feedback devices are used to confirm execution.** Once the augmented object receives and executes the command a confirmation is send to the system and the case provides feedback to the user.

4 Gesture Set Proposal

Besides the proposed system to interact with Augmented Objects, this paper proposes a set of gestures for eight commands: up, down, left, right, turn on, turn off, in, out. Each command can be used to perform different actions in each object. An important characteristic of our gesture set proposal is that is based on three characteristics that signs must comply:

1. Be associated with user's natural language (avoid cognitive load).
2. Consider technological limitations (avoid ambiguous gestures).
3. Should not cause fatigue or pain for the user (ensure that motion and posture are comfortable for the user).

Given that we are using Leap Motion, the technological limitations became apparent immediately. Leap motion uses infrared cameras; therefore, any obstruction between a joint and the Leap Motion obstructs clear readings. We decided to avoid using this kind of gestures.

For motion and posture of hands our set of signs is based on Rempel et al. work [19]. They provide guidelines for the design of hand gestures for HCI. However, they propose gestures based on traditional interactions such as copy, paste, return, menu, etc.

The optimal arm position is with the elbow at a 45 degree angle, avoiding shoulder flexion, given that we do not use arm support. Our proposal uses wrist and forearm side postures.

The time frames for gestures, according to Rempel et al. [19], should not be too high. In our case, the user controls the speed using the base sign that activates classification.

Even though we provide a set of gestures to be used with our system, the set of gestures is customizable, (i.e., users can add, remove or change gestures). Figure 3 shows our gesture set proposal and its general uses. In Fig. 3, left, right, up and down are gestures; in, out and toggle between on and off are signs. All the proposed gestures and signs were selected considering the three factors mentioned above: cognitive load, technological limitations and motion and posture.

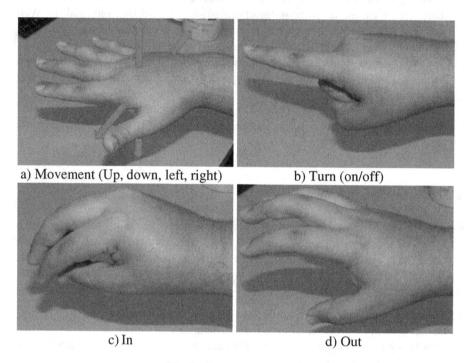

a) Movement (Up, down, left, right)   b) Turn (on/off)

c) In   d) Out

Fig. 3. Gesture set proposal

5 Evaluation

The system was tested in a laboratory setting. Both the system case and the Augmented Objects were placed in the same geographical location. To evaluate our gesture-based interaction approach we used two different Augmented Objects: a webcam and a light switch.

The webcam (Logitech Quick Cam Orbit AF) is a common webcam augmented with mobility capabilities, (i.e., the user controls the camera movements with their hands gestures). The webcam includes servos that allow movement in 2 axes. To implement this camera in our gesture-based system, we created a middleware that uses the software provided by Logitech to manipulate the camera. The middleware is the one that offers its functionality via Web Services that are consumed by our gesture recognition system.

The light switch was augmented with the necessary capabilities to control it remotely, allowing the user to turn on and off the lights with just a hand movement. There are several automatic light switches available in the market; however, to perform this experiment we develop a basic prototype using servos and a traditional light switch.

Figure 4 shows the augmented objects. The results were satisfactory. We were able to control functionalities of both augmented objects using our set of gestures. In case that new gestures are required, user can add them by training the SVM.

Fig. 4. Leap Motion, case, augmented light switch and camera.

The light switch offers two commands: on and off. The camera offers eight commands: 2 axes movement (up, down, left, right), start recording, stop recording, zoom in and zoom out. To control these objects we mapped our gesture set proposal with available functionalities.

The sign execution evaluation was performed with 12 users (3 female and 9 male). One of our participants was left-handed. Each user was asked to perform 10 signs in random order. Results showed that all gestures were recognized with more than 75 % accuracy. Table 3 shows the detailed data gathered during experimentation.

The SVM used by this 12 users only had 30 training observation, all created by one of the researchers. Our experience reveals that more training would make the system achieve better accuracy.

If the results are studied by person, three users got 100 % accuracy, two got 90 % accuracy, two users got 80 % accuracy, four users got 70 % accuracy, and one user got 60 % accuracy. This last result was obtained with the left-handed user.

Users had never seen or used the device. Moreover, none of the users had any experience with sign language or using gestures to manipulate computational devices. When the system failed to recognize a command, users tried again and always got the expected result (i.e., trained users got better performance than untrained users).

Table 3. Evaluation results for 12 participants

Signal	Attempts	Accuracy
In	24	87.5 %
Out	24	79.1 %
Turn on/off	24	83.3 %
Movement	48	79.1 %
Control	120	100 %
Total	240	90.8 %

The fact that users always got the correct answer after the first try leads to think that, some training is required before using the system. User studies are required to further evaluate our gesture-based interaction proposal.

The selection of the Augmented Object, as stated before can be performed by spelling the name of the object. This was tested for the two evaluated Augmented Objects; however, there are several letters that cannot be unambiguously recognized therefore, an alternative mechanism should be incorporated to allow object selection.

Ubiquitous systems will always produce security concerns. Gesture-based interaction and remote control includes even more concerns. Even if the whole gesture recognition process is performed in the embedded system, the embedded system cannot operate directly in the environment or send commands directly to actuators.

With this kind of systems user can control actuators placed anywhere; therefore, authorization is required to reduce risks. In this solution, security is implemented with Web Service credentials, (i.e., only authorized system cases can send commands). However, this issue must be revised and studied in-depth.

6 Discussion and Conclusion

This paper presents a gesture-based interaction approach for manipulating augmented objects. The main difference between this solution and the available in literature is the inclusion of Leap Motion for hand recognition and tracking, and the inclusion of gestures rather than only signs.

A classification method is performed to translate gestures to commands, a SVM is used to classify and a Database stores the corresponding commands for each augmented object. Our solution only considers augmented objects developed in such a manner that their functionality is provided via Web Services.

This research proposes a set of gestures based on three main characteristics: natural language, technological limitations and ergonomics. However, the system was designed to be flexible, (i.e., users can use the gestures that they want).

We tested our system with 12 (3 female and 9 male) users and got results around the 80 % accuracy. It is important to recall that each failed attempt was achieved by the second execution. In the evaluation one left handed user participated and he got the worst results. This is obvious since the SVM was trained by a right handed person.

Another interesting fact is that even though the SVM was trained by a right handed man, both male and female users achieved the same success rate, therefore the training could be performed by a person of a different sex than the actual user.

Certain limitations were found in the system. Technological limitations prevent augmented object selection using sign language, because not all alphabet letters can be unambiguously recognized. Moreover, to add new gestures to the system, a training process for the SVM is required.

The main practical limitation of our approach is of accessibility. The Leap Motion was released a short time ago; therefore, there are still some problems with hand recognition. The main problem has to do with arthropathies (i.e., joint diseases). After we performed our evaluation, the leap motion was tested by a user that suffers arthritis and we had several difficulties. The main difficulty was that the hand was recognized upside down. This finding needs further evaluation and software fixes will probably be required to solve such difficulties. Future work also includes improving the accuracy, and further user testing. Moreover, a comparison of this system with others approaches is required.

Acknowledgments. This work was partially supported by Centro de Investigaciones en Tecnologías de la Información y Comunicación at Universidad de Costa Rica (CITIC-UCR) grand No. 834-B4-159, by Escuela de Ciencias de la Computación e Informática at Universidad de Costa Rica (ECCI-UCR), by Ministerio de Ciencia, Tecnología y Telecomunicaciones (MICITT), and by Consejo Nacional para Investigaciones Científicas y Tecnológicas (CONICIT) of the Government of Costa Rica.

Appendix

The Table shown in this Appendix shows the results of 12 users that tested our system. Results are grouped by sex and leading hand.

User Group	Sign	Attempts	Recognized signs
Female (right handed) N = 3	Movement	12	9
	Turn on/off	6	5
	In	6	5
	Out	6	6
Male (right handed) N = 8	Movement	32	26
	Turn on/off	16	14
	In	16	15
	Out	16	12
Male (left handed) N = 1	Movement	4	3
	Turn on/off	2	1
	In	2	1
	Out	2	1

References

1. López, G., López, M., Guerrero, L.A., Bravo, J.: Human-objects interaction: a framework for designing, developing and evaluating augmented objects. Int. J. Hum.-Comput. Inter. **30** (10), 787–801 (2014)
2. Yuksel, K.A., Adali, S.H.: Prototyping input controller for touch-less interaction with ubiquitous environments. In: International Conference on Human Computer Interaction with Mobile Devices and Services (2011)
3. Leap Motion, Inc. www.leapmotion.com
4. Pavlovic, V., Sharma, R., Huang, T.: Visual interpretation of hand gestures for human-computer interaction: a review. IEEE Trans. Pattern Anal. Mach. Intell. **19**(7), 677–695 (1997)
5. Elepfandt, M., Sünderhauf, M.: Multimodal, touchless interaction in spatial augmented reality environments. In: Duffy, V.G. (ed.) ICDHM 2011. LNCS, vol. 6777, pp. 263–271. Springer, Heidelberg (2011)
6. Saidinejad, H., Veronese, F., Comai, S., Salice, F.: Towards a hand-based gestural language for smart-home control using hand shapes and dynamic hand movements. In: Hervás, R., Lee, S., Nugent, C., Bravo, J. (eds.) UCAmI 2014. LNCS, vol. 8867, pp. 268–271. Springer, Heidelberg (2014)
7. Ng, W.L., Ng, C.K., Noordin, N.K., Ali, B.M.: Gesture based automating household appliances. In: Jacko, J.A. (ed.) Human-Computer Interaction, Part II, HCII 2011. LNCS, vol. 6762, pp. 285–293. Springer, Heidelberg (2011)
8. Pan, G., Wu, J., Zhang, D., Wu, Z., Yang, Y., Li, S.: GeeAir: a universal multimodal remote control device for home appliances. Pers. Ubiquit. Comput. **14**(8), 723–735 (2010)
9. Suau, X., Alcoverro, M., Lopez-Mendez, A., Ruiz-Hidalgo, J., Casas, J.: INTAIRACT: joint hand gesture and fingertip classification for touchless interaction. In: Fusiello, A., Murino, V., Cucchiara, R. (eds.) ECCV 2012 Ws/Demos, Part III. LNCS, vol. 7585, pp. 602–606. Springer, Heidelberg (2012)
10. Jaimes, A., Sebe, N.: Multimodal human computer interaction: a survey. In: Sebe, N., Lew, M., Huang, T.S. (eds.) HCI/ICCV 2005. LNCS, vol. 3766, pp. 1–15. Springer, Heidelberg (2005)
11. Cortes, C., Vapnik, V.: Support-vector networks. Mach. Learn. **20**(3), 273–297 (1995)
12. Scikit-Learn, Machine Learning in Python. http://scikit-learn.org/
13. Ben-Hur, A., Weston, J.: Data Mining Techniques for the Life Sciences. Humana Press, Totowa (2010)
14. Ishii, H., Ullmer, B.: Tangible bits: towards seamless interfaces between people, bits and atoms. In: ACM SIGCHI Conference on Human Factors in Computing Systems (1997)
15. Kawsar, F., Fujinami, K., Nakajima, T.: Augmenting everyday life with sentient artefacts. In: Joint Conference on Smart Objects and Ambient Intelligence: Innovative Context-Aware Services: Usages and Technologies (2005)
16. Chung, K., Shilman, M., Merrill, C., Ishii, H.: OnObject: gestural play with tagged everyday objects. In: ACM Symposium on User Interface Software and Technology (2010)
17. Sra, M., Lee, A., Pao, S., Jiang, G., Ishii, H.: Point and share: from paper to whiteboard. In: ACM Symposium on User Interface Software and Technology (2012)
18. Navarro, G.: A guided tour to approximate string matching. ACM Comput. Surv. **33**(1), 31–88 (2001)
19. Rempel, D., Camilleri, M., Lee, D.: The design of hand gestures for human–computer interaction: lessons from sign language interpreters. Int. J. Hum Comput Stud. **72**(10–11), 728–735 (2014)

20. Hein, A., Hoffmeyer, A., Kirste, T.: Utilizing an accelerometric bracelet for ubiquitous gesture-based interaction. In: Stephanidis, C. (ed.) UAHCI 2009, Part II. LNCS, vol. 5615, pp. 519–527. Springer, Heidelberg (2009)
21. Moya, J.M., de Espinosa, A.M., Araujo, Á., de Goyeneche, J.-M., Vallejo, J.C.: Low-cost gesture-based interaction for intelligent environments. In: Omatu, S., Rocha, M.P., Bravo, J., Fernández, F., Corchado, E., Bustillo, A., Corchado, J.M. (eds.) IWANN 2009, Part II. LNCS, vol. 5518, pp. 752–755. Springer, Heidelberg (2009)
22. Wu, J., Pan, G., Li, S., Wu, Z., Zhang, D.: GeeAir: waving in the air to control home appliances. In: Ubiquitous Intelligence Computing and 7th International Conference on Autonomic Trusted Computing (2010)
23. Fernández, M.Á., Peláez, V., López, G., Carus, J.L., Lobato, V.: Multimodal interfaces for the smart home: findings in the process from architectural design to user evaluation. In: Bravo, J., López-de-Ipiña, D., Moya, F. (eds.) UCAmI 2012. LNCS, vol. 7656, pp. 173–180. Springer, Heidelberg (2012)

Human Interaction and Perspectives
in Ambient Assisted Living Solutions

Characterizing Ubiquitous Systems Privacy Issues by Gender and Age

Gustavo López[1(✉)], Gabriela Marín[1,2], and Marta Calderón[2]

[1] Centro de Investigaciones en Tecnologías de la Información y Comunicación,
Universidad de Costa Rica, UCR, San Pedro, Costa Rica
{gustavo.lopez_h, gabriela.marin,
marta.calderon}@ucr.ac.cr
[2] Escuela de Ciencias de la Computación e Informática,
Universidad de Costa Rica, UCR, San Pedro, Costa Rica

Abstract. Characterizing ubiquitous systems privacy issues by gender and age was our goal. We selected two ubiquitous systems: a wearable system (Google Glass) and an embedded in context system (Smart Office). An online survey, with 400+ participants, which included questions about how people perceive privacy issues related to the use of these two different ubiquitous systems, was conducted. Results show that Google Glass generates a higher degree of concern than the Smart Office. Female participants tend to be more worried than male, independently of the ubiquitous system considered. Finally, the youngest participants (16 to 25 years old) are the most concerned about privacy threats, which was unexpected.

Keywords: Ambient intelligence · Privacy · Gender · Age

1 Introduction

In a Ubiquitous Computing world, physical objects are enhanced with computational capabilities. Usually, Ubiquitous Computing is achieved by embedding small electronic devices (sensors and actuators) in everyday objects. Ubiquitous Computing includes a variety of systems: from obvious video-based monitoring systems to, not so obvious, context-aware systems that use users personal information gathered by sensors.

Ubiquitous Computing proliferation produces several concerns. Two of them are security and privacy. Security is often a necessary ingredient to privacy, as it facilitates the control of information flows, and helps to ensure the correctness of data. However, it is possible to have high levels of security but no privacy, or even, some degree of privacy without security.

Privacy is defined as the individuals' ability to control the terms by which their personal information is collected and used [1]. According to Avizienis, "Security is the concurrent existence of (a) availability for authorized users only, (b) confidentiality, and (c) integrity with 'improper' taken as meaning 'unauthorized'" [2].

Research on privacy in the area of Ubiquitous Computing expands in many different directions. However, privacy issues are still open and it appears that feasible and effective solutions are still quite far from being achieved [1].

© Springer International Publishing Switzerland 2015
I. Cleland et al. (Eds.): IWAAL 2015, LNCS 9455, pp. 247–258, 2015.
DOI: 10.1007/978-3-319-26410-3_23

User willingness to lose privacy in order to ease their daily activities may differ among users. The main goal of this research is to provide a characterization, by age and gender, of privacy concerns for ubiquitous systems, in order to understand the user's perspective and create more privacy efficient systems.

We do not intent to provide a technical solution to privacy issues in Ubiquitous Computing. Several research studies focus on this problem. We aim to characterize such privacy issues in order to have a better understanding of user thinking, and use this information to support better approaches when addressing privacy issues in ubiquitous systems.

The next section presents the concepts of ubiquitous computing, privacy and its relation with technology and demographic factors, and privacy in ubiquitous systems. Afterwards, Sects. 3 and 4 shows the followed procedure and results. Finally, Sect. 5 shows a discussion and the conclusion of this paper.

2   Background

In this section we explain concepts related to Ubiquitous Computing and privacy that were used while working on this research.

2.1   Ubiquitous Computing

Mark Weiser coined the term Ubiquitous Computing around 1988. He defines the main characteristics of Ubiquitous Computing as follows [3]: (1) Every computer will be linked to a network, (2) Users do not have to be aware or the linking process, (3) Services are offered at the right time through user-friendly interface and interaction.

Usually ubiquitous systems identify, monitor and track users. Moreover, most ubiquitous systems have at least two of the following characteristics embedded: sensing, actuating, networking, or decision making capabilities. Figure 1 shows an example of the workflow in ubiquitous systems.

Four stages can be clearly identified in Fig. 1: gathering user and context information, processing the gathered data, performing actions in context, and offering information to other systems. Each one of the mentioned stages creates potential threats to privacy as they gather, store or publish user information. For instance, gathered information could be aggregated to determine user location or association. Critical

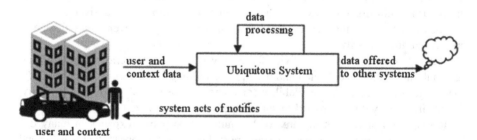

Fig. 1. Ubiquitous system possible workflow

information used for security (e.g., passwords and fingerprints) could be stolen. Unauthorized pictures could be taken and used for different purposes.

It is important to point out that the original purpose of the information could be authorized by the user, but information needs to be protected in order to assure that it is not used for other reasons.

Some attempts to characterize potentially harmful activities exist. For instance, Solove [4] proposes a taxonomy. He groups potentially harmful activities in four sets: information collection, information processing, information dissemination, and invasion. Each stage showed in Fig. 1 can be mapped to one of Solove's sets. The following sections delve into privacy in general, privacy in ubiquitous environments and technology, and demographic factors that affect privacy concerns.

2.2 Privacy

Samuel Warren and Louis Brandeis presented one of the most popular definitions of privacy. They described privacy as "the right to be let alone" [5], a state of solitude and seclusion that would ensure a "general right to the immunity of the person, the right to one's personality" [5].

Another privacy definition was presented by Alan Westin in his book Privacy and Freedom: "Privacy is the claim of individuals, groups, or institutions to determine for themselves when, how, and to what extent information about them is communicated to others" [6].

Clarke [7] identified four different categories of privacy: personal data, communications, experience, and behaviour. Finn *et al.* [8], expanded the first privacy taxonomy, created by Roger Clarke in the mid-1990s, from four to seven categories of privacy: person, behaviour and action, communication, data and image, thoughts and feelings, location and space, and association.

Privacy of person refers to keep privacy of body and characteristics. Privacy of behaviour and action is related to issues such as sexual preferences and religious and political activities. Privacy of communication refers to avoiding the interception of communications by any means. Privacy of data and image is concerned with the degree of control of data and images and the use that other people can exercise. Privacy of thoughts and feelings is oriented to protect people's right not to reveal their thoughts or feelings. Privacy of location and space refers to the right of a person to move in public and semi-public spaces free of tracking and monitoring. Finally, privacy of association includes concerns about people's right to associate with any persons they want, free of surveillance. Undoubtedly, Ubiquitous Computing can threat several of these privacy categories.

2.3 Privacy in Ubiquitous Systems

Solove explains how the user and context data gathering could be used to violate user's privacy with unauthorized surveillance. Data processing could be a threat because it could be used, aggregated, or excluded, or/and used for other reasons that the ones the user agreed with. If the information is shared with other systems, it can be exposed in undesired ways; moreover, it can be distorted or appropriated by others [4].

Ubiquitous Computing have three main properties that come to mind when thinking about privacy: ubiquity, invisibility and sensing. Ubiquity means that computers are everywhere. Invisibility implies that computers not only will be everywhere but they will be invisible to the human eye. The last one, sensing, implies that computers will be able to sense the context, such as temperature, light or noise, but they will also be able to record audio and video, or gather position information from people. In the worst case scenario a person (as user) could be perceived and watched by invisible computers everywhere.

2.4 Privacy, Technology and Demographic Factors

Internet, mobile devices, and Ubiquitous Computing are embedded in user's lives. A conflict between functionality and comfort provided by technology, on the one hand, and threats to privacy, on the other hand, has emerged. However, not everybody perceives this conflict in the same way. Previous studies have shown that some demographic factors influence users' concerns about privacy.

Zukowski and Brown [9] found that age, education and income level are the main demographic factors influencing Internet user's concerns on information privacy. Wang et al. [10] showed that nationality, technical knowledge, gender, age, and frequency of use are predictors of users´ privacy concerns when using systems such as Facebook.

According to Hoy and Milne [11], women are more concerned about others accessing their personal information. Dowd [12] found that young women are concerned about being approached by unknown men through social networks. Lorenzen-Huber et al. [13] mention that elders have naive mental models that make them perceive that risk of losing privacy when using home-base Ubiquitous Computing is less than it actually is.

Gender and age constantly appear among the main factors influencing users' privacy concerns. Therefore, we decided to characterize ubiquitous systems privacy issues by these two factors.

Next section describes how the survey was designed, which ubiquitous systems were used as examples, the participants and main questions of the questionnaire.

3 Procedure

The first step we followed was to decide which ubiquitous systems would be used. We selected two conceptually different systems: a wearable system (Google Glass) and a system embedded in a context (Smart Office).

In order to gather information about how people perceive privacy issues related to the use of two different ubiquitous systems, we designed an on-line questionnaire using Lime Survey. The questionnaire used had five sections. The first section contained questions related to demographic information (age and sex). For each ubiquitous system two sections were included. The first one's purpose was to identify familiarity of participants with the specific technology and willingness to use it. Participants also had the opportunity of watching an embedded video about the system characteristics and functionality. The second part included questions specifically designed to address the seven dimensions presented by Finn et al. [8].

Sections 3.1, 3.2, and 3.3 describe in more detail the ubiquitous systems used, the participants, and the questionnaire designed.

3.1   Ubiquitous Systems Selected

The ubiquitous systems selected for our research, one wearable (Google Glass) and one embedded in context (Smart Office), are described in this section.

Google Glass. Google Glass is a wearable technology with an optical head-mounted display. Google Glass main characteristics are: (1) it allows natural language voice commands, (2) it uses bone conduction transducer as sound mechanism, (3) it has an embedded camera, and (4) it is based on Android operating system [14].

An introductory video of Google Glass was available in the survey. The video was based on "Project Glass: One day..." [15]. The video introduces the main characteristics intended for Google Glass, including: reminders, voice commands, access to social networks, browsing internet, climate information, geo-location, tracking, and route design, videoconference, and camera for taking pictures and videos, all from the user's glasses perspective.

Smart Office. In a smart office, automation includes centralized control of lighting, heating, ventilation and air conditioning, appliances, and security locks of gates and doors, among other functionalities. Smart Office systems include the following types of devices:

1. Sensors to measure or detect factors such as temperature, light, or human presence
2. Dedicated automation controller
3. Actuators such as motorized valves, light switches and servos
4. Wired and wireless buses for communication
5. Interfaces allowing human-machine and/or machine-machine interaction.

An introductory video of the Smart Office was available in the survey. The video was based on "How a smart office functions" [16]. The video shows the main functionalities of a smart office including: building general management (lights, temperature, vents), motion recognition and people identification, and emergency management.

3.2   Participants

Participants in the survey were recruited through social media and e-mail. Any person who wished to participate was allowed to do so. The survey resulted in 427 complete responses and 31 partial (only demographic and Google Glass sections were answered in partial responses).

Of all 458 participants, 63 % (291) were men and 37 % (167) were women. Figure 2 shows age and gender distribution. Students at the School of Computer

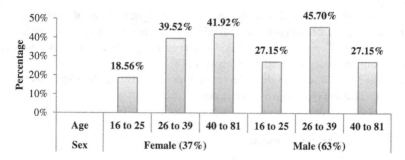

Fig. 2. Distribution by age and gender of the participants

Science were among the first invited. Hence, it is reasonable to expect the sample to be biased towards more male than female respondents.

To characterize our sample we asked participants to know if they were familiar with both Google Glass and the Smart Office. As shown on Table 1, more participants are familiar with Google Glass than with the Smart Office. A clear difference is that male participants are much more familiar of both Google Glass and Smart Office than female participants.

Table 1. Sample familiarity with Google Glass and Smart Office

	Knows Google Glass			Knows Smart Office		
	Male	Female	Total	Male	Female	Total
Yes	230	78	291 (64 %)	158	68	226 (53 %)
No	61	89	167 (36 %)	113	88	201 (47 %)

3.3   Questionnaire

Questions, other than the demographic basic questions and technology familiarity, were related to privacy concerns on ubiquitous systems. Each item was assessed using a five point scale ranked 0 to 4: Not at all (0), Slightly (1), Moderately (2), Very much (3), and Extremely (4). The following questions were asked:

- **Body privacy:** How concerned are you about the possibility of the system copying your body information that could be used to hurt you or steal your identity (fingerprint, iris or vital signs)?
- **Behaviour privacy:** How concerned are you about the presence of the system (used by you or someone else)? Could it affect your behaviour?
- **Communication privacy:** How concerned are you about the possibility of the system facilitating the interception of your communications without your authorization?
- **Image and data privacy:** How concerned are you about the possibility of the system facilitating pictures or videos of you to be taken without your permission?
- **Thoughts and feelings privacy:** How concerned are you about the possibility of the system capturing and/or publishing somehow your thoughts?

- **Location privacy:** How concerned are you about the possibility of your location being known when using the system?
- **Association privacy:** How concerned are you about the possibility of the system publishing the people you are with?
- **External control:** How concerned are you about a hacker taking control over the system's information or functionality without you noticing it?

The first seven questions are inspired in the Seven Types of Privacy proposed by Finn et al. [8]. The last question was included based on the authors' personal privacy concerns and a typical scenario of privacy threat present on movies.

4 Results

With the gathered data we conducted statistical tests. Results of comparing Google Glass vs. Smart Office, in terms of the general degree of concern reported for each system, are presented in Sect. 4.1. Results by gender and age are analyzed with more detail in Sects. 4.2 and 4.3, respectively.

4.1 Google Glass vs. Smart Office

Figure 3 shows that, for the eight privacy categories used, the degree of concern is higher for a wearable technology such as Google Glass, than for the Smart Office. No average falls in the Not at all or the Extremely categories. External control and image are the categories generating the highest degree of concern (close to Very much).

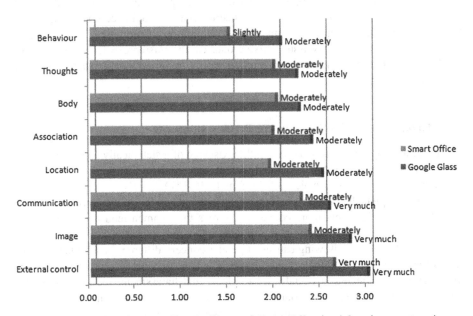

Fig. 3. Comparison between Google Glass and Smart Office in eight privacy categories

We found significant differences between the degree of privacy concern generated by Google Glass and by the Smart Office. To verify the statistical significance of these results, we ran a t-test between the two answer groups (Google Glass and Smart Office). Results confirmed the existence of a statistically significant effect of the ubiquitous system on the perceived value associated with privacy concern (T0 = 5.55; $p < 0.000$; n = 885).

Moreover, we performed a paired t-test to determine if the concerns changed for the same person in each system. Results showed that Google Glass causes more concern than the Smart Office, even for the same respondent (T0 = 11.76; $p < 0.000$; n = 427).

Respondents were the least preoccupied above changes on their behaviour in the presence of these two ubiquitous systems, especially on a structured environment such as the office (Slightly and low Moderately). The Smart Office can be easily related to the job place, where behaviour is determined by what is expected from an employee and not attending rules can bring undesired consequences to him/her. Normally, knowing that he/she is being observed, either by another person or by a machine, conditions his/her behaviour. People are used to control their behaviour according to the circumstances.

People are visibly more concerned about using Google Glass than living/working in smart environments. Results can be explained by the characteristics of the technology in itself, or by the setting where it is supposed to be used. Google glasses are intended for everyday life environments while Smart Office corresponds to a more structured and controlled setting by itself. Google Glass can be invasive in personal life. It can go with you everywhere and be with you at any time. On the other hand, the smart office is can be only invasive during work hours, in a constrained space and time.

It is also very interesting to notice that the question related to external control, category not included in the Seven Types of Privacy proposed by Finn et al. [8], is regarded by the participants as the main concern. Unauthorized access is a real threat. System security plays an important role in Ubiquitous Computing. Even though external control is a security issue, private data can be misrepresented, distorted and disclosed, without the user noticing it. Further work is required to understand the social implications of this issue.

4.2 Gender and Ubiquitous System Privacy Concerns

In a general comparison, results confirm the existence of a statistically significant effect of sex on the perceived value associated with privacy concern (T0 = −4.12; $p < 0.000$; n = 885 in a proportion of male 63.5 %, female 36.5 %).

Figure 4 depicts the concerns by type of system and gender. In the graphic, distance from the center represents more concern. It shows that women tend to be more concerned than men, independently of the ubiquitous system considered.

We can depict the following causes of gender concern differences: (1) Due to more technology familiarity of male than female, (2) Due to women's perceived higher vulnerability than men's, especially related to sexual harassment, (3) Due to gender biased education, where a patriarchal society inculcates women, more than men, principles on their responsibility to ensure a discreet behaviour.

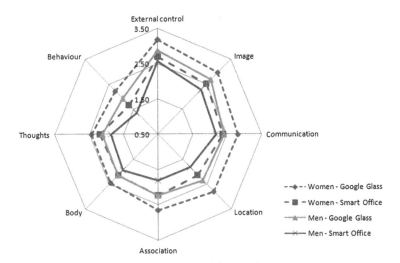

Fig. 4. Comparison between men and women for both systems. Concentric gray lines separate the different categories of answers in the questionnaire: *Slightly* (greater than 0.5 and less than 1.5), *Moderately* (greater than 1.5 and less than 2.5), *Very much* (greater than 2.5 and less than 3.5).

The gathered data can lead to think that Google Glass or similar devices will be more accepted by men than by women.

4.3   Age and Ubiquitous System Privacy Concerns

Population was divided into three groups: young people 16 to 25 (24 %), young adults 26 to 39 (43 %), and mature adults 40 to 81 (33 %). An ANOVA analysis found statistical significance across ages ($F0 = 6.30$; $p = 0.002$; $n = 885$). Moreover, performing individual comparisons (Fisher's test), statistical difference between groups 16 to 25 and 26 to 39 were found. As shown on Fig. 5, lines corresponding to young people and young adults are distant. Mature adults are in the middle.

Young people (16 to 25) are probably more self-conscious of their vulnerabilities. They may also receive more peer pressure or bullying, or are more informed of the technology threats due to education programs. Younger people could also be concerned about external adult surveillance. This would explain their higher degree of privacy concern.

Young adults (26 to 39) tend to be less concerned about privacy issues. They are not victims of social pressure as younger ones, use technology as a working tool, and appreciate its benefits. They have been working with traditional technologies that do not threat their privacy, diminishing their concern on ubiquitous system privacy threats.

Mature adults are very likely less familiar with ubiquitous technologies and, therefore, also less aware about privacy threats than the younger generations. Mature adults are not digital natives (i.e., not born in the Information Age). This leads to a general technology fear.

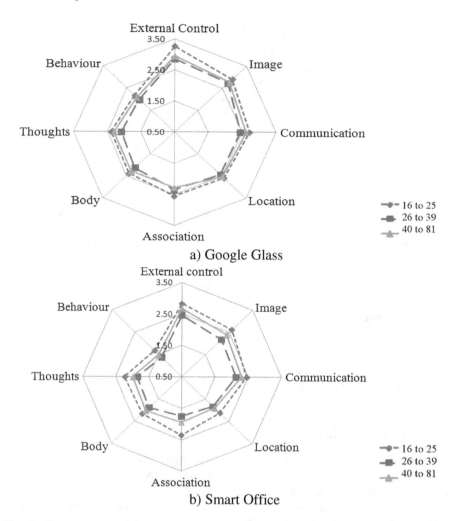

Fig. 5. Comparison among age groups, both systems. Concentric gray lines separate the different categories of answers in the questionnaire: *Slightly* (greater than 0.5 and less than 1.5), *Moderately* (greater than 1.5 and less than 2.5), *Very much* (greater than 2.5 and less than 3.5).

5 Discussion and Conclusions

Our goal was to characterize privacy concerns about ubiquitous systems by age and gender. We received more than 400 responses from people from different age groups, education levels and gender. We focused our research in seven categories of privacy: person, behaviour and action, communication, data and image, thoughts and feelings, location and space, association, and external control. In the survey, each privacy category was assessed using a five point scale ranked from Not at all to Extremely. Participants in the survey rated concern about six out of eight privacy categories as Moderately. The only categories in which participants showed to be very much concerned were external control and image privacy. Behaviour was the category generating the lowest degree of concern, especially when evaluating the Smart Office. This result is very likely due to the fact that people are used to control their behaviour according to the surrounding circumstances.

We found that participants in the survey showed different levels of concern depending on the ubiquitous system characteristics. In particular, they exhibit a higher degree of concern related to the use of a wearable system such as Google Glass than to the presence of an embedded in context system (Smart Office). Concern on privacy breaches may be the cause on participants' differences responses to the question regarding willingness to use the systems.

Figure 6 reflects that less people are willing to use a Google Glass than Smart Office technology. It is interesting to notice that people are willing to use ubiquitous systems despite the risks of privacy breach. This may indicate that people perceive that the benefits received from technology use are more valuable than the risks against their personal privacy. Moreover, women were more concerned overall than men on their privacy, which is consistent with previous studies.

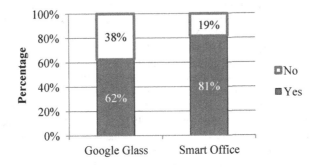

Fig. 6. Participants willingness to use the systems

The group of young people (16 to 25) showed the higher degree of concern. This is a generation with access to computers and Internet almost since they were born. Despite their familiarity with technology, social factors, such as harassment and bullying, may affect their perception of themselves and their privacy concerns.

Future work to find explanation to results found is necessary. Social factors play a role which is not fully understood yet. Moreover, we encourage researchers around the world to conduct this or similar surveys to characterize privacy issues of ubiquitous systems in order to provide a wider understanding of these issues.

Acknowledgements. This work was partially supported by CITIC (Centro de Investigaciones en Tecnologías de la Información y Comunicación) and by ECCI (Escuela de Ciencias de la Computación e Informática) at Universidad de Costa Rica.

References

1. Karyda, M., Gritzalis, S., Park, J.-H.: A critical approach to privacy research in ubiquitous environments – issues and underlying assumptions. In: Denko, M.K., Shih, C., Li, K.-C., Tsao, S.-L., Zeng, Q.-A., Park, S.H., Ko, Y.-B., Hung, S.-H., Park, J.-H. (eds.) EUC-WS 2007. LNCS, vol. 4809, pp. 12–21. Springer, Heidelberg (2007)
2. Avizienis, A., Laprie, J., Randell, B.: Fundamental concepts of dependability. University of Newcastle upon Tyne, Computing Science (2001)
3. Weiser, M.: Ubiquitous computing. Computer 10, 71–72 (1993)
4. Solove, D.J.: A taxonomy of privacy. University of Pennsylvania Law Review (2006)
5. Warren, S., Brandeis, L.: The right to privacy. Harward Law Rev. 4(5), 193–220 (1890)
6. Westin, A.: Privacy and Freedom. Bodley Head, London (1970)
7. Clarke, R.: What's 'Privacy'? Australian Law Reform Commission Workshop (2006)
8. Finn, R., Wright, D., Friedewald, M.: Seven types of privacy. European Data Protection: Coming of Age, pp. 3–32. Springer, Netherlands (2013)
9. Zukowski, T., Brown, I.: Examining the influence of demographic factors on internet users' information privacy concerns. In: Annual Research Conference of the South African Institute of Computer Scientists and Information Technologists on IT Research in Developing Countries, pp. 197–204 (2007)
10. Wang, Y., Norice, G., Cranor, L.F.: Who is concerned about what? A study of American, Chinese and Indian users' privacy concerns on social network sites. In: McCune, J.M., Balacheff, B., Perrig, A., Sadeghi, A.-R., Sasse, A., Beres, Y. (eds.) Trust 2011. LNCS, vol. 6740, pp. 146–153. Springer, Heidelberg (2011)
11. Hoy, M., Milne, G.: Gender differences in privacy-related measures for young adult facebook users. J. Interact. Advertising 10(2), 28–45 (2010)
12. Dowd, M.: Contextualised concerns: the online privacy attitudes of young adults. In: Fischer-Hübner, S., Duquenoy, P., Hansen, M., Leenes, R., Zhang, G. (eds.) Privacy and Identity Management for Life. IFIP AICT, vol. 352, pp. 78–89. Springer, Heidelberg (2011)
13. Lorenzen-Huber, L., Boutain, M., Camp, L., Shankar, K., Connelly, K.: Privacy, technology, and aging: a proposed framework. Ageing Int. 36, 232–252 (2011)
14. Google.: Glass. http://www.google.com/glass. Accessed 18 May 2015
15. Google.: Youtube - Project Glass: One day. https://www.youtube.com/watch?v=9c6W4CCU9M4. Accessed 18 May 2015
16. eVida.: Youtube - How a smart office functions. https://www.youtube.com/watch?v=5V3gjfVB4aw. Accessed 18 May 2015

Do Technology-Related Stimuli Affect Age Estimation?

M.A. Rodrigo Juarez[1(✉)], Jesús Favela[1], and Víctor M. González[2]

[1] Computer Science Department,
Centro de Investigación Científica de Ensenada,
Ensenada, Baja California, Mexico
mijuarez@cicese.edu.mx, favela@cicese.mx
[2] Computer Science Department,
Instituto Tecnológico Autónomo de México, Mexico City, Mexico
victor.gonzalez@itam.mx

Abstract. The potential for ubiquitous ambient technology to assist older adults to sustain an active life, raises questions about whether this can bring transformational effects for users including those related to modifying ageing perception. We aim to investigate the effects that technology related priming has in the perception of ageing via age estimation. Sixty participants, exposed to technology, ageing and neutral related stimuli, were asked to perform a priming activity and to estimate the age of a set of persons depicted in different photographs. We found that neither the estimation of the participants from 'Technology' nor 'Ageing' group differ from the estimation of participants from the 'Neutral' group. Evidence suggests that exposing participants to technology concepts by itself does not alter age perception. However, previous works show that the usage of technology can modify ageing perception. Therefore, we define a longitudinal second experiment in which we will provide different devices to older adults for them to use and through qualitative methods study this phenomenon.

Keywords: Ageing perception · Technology · Priming · Age estimation

1 Introduction

Two of the phenomena that characterize the society of the 21st century are the ageing of society and the increase of technology usage in people's life. According to the United Nations' World Population Ageing 2013 report, the estimated global number of older adults (over 60 years) for 2013 was 841 million people. This number is estimated to increase to 2 billion people in 2050; this will represent 21.1 % of the global population [16]. Regarding the second phenomenon, in Mexico, two of the greatest examples are mobile phone and Internet usage. According to the Mexican Association of Internet (AMIPICI) the number of older adults that could access Internet services from 2007 to 20015 aroused from 2 %[1] to 4 %[2] of the total Internet users.

---

[1] www.amipci.org.mx/estudios/habitos_de_internet/2007_Habitos_Usuarios_Internet_Mx-1.pdf.
[2] www.amipci.org.mx/images/AMIPCI_HABITOS_DEL_INTERNAUTA_MEXICANO_2015.pdf.

© Springer International Publishing Switzerland 2015
I. Cleland et al. (Eds.): IWAAL 2015, LNCS 9455, pp. 259–264, 2015.
DOI: 10.1007/978-3-319-26410-3_24

Consequently, technology is becoming more common in the lives of older adults. Following the evidence of other studies [9] we can see that around the world and in places with good access to information and communications services and networks, the presence of technology goes beyond the desktop and the handheld, and becomes part of the entire space where older adults live, including the living room, the kitchen, the bathroom, etc. Ambient-Assisted Living Technology has gained importance for older adults since it can help them to improve and monitor their health, to prevent accidents and to assist them in their daily life, thus improving the quality of their lives [9]. Among different effects that technology can have in the lives of older adults ranging from the merely practical to the ones that augment and transform their abilities, one wonders whether these alterations on the living would at the end result on changes on the way people will experience ageing, and in general their perception of ageing.

There are different theories that define ageing perception as a construct defined by several dimensions; one important dimension is related to the physical appearance. When we see someone else their facial appearance provides significant cues about health, lifestyle or longevity that helps us to allocate this person within an age range. This estimation of age is highly relevant in social interactions, because it influences the way we feel about the person and how we behave towards them [1]. Therefore any influence in age estimation can produce important behavioural outcomes.

Even though technology usage by elder people is increasing[3], negative stereotypes regarding older adults and technology prevail in society. For example, an extended belief among younger people is that older adults are technologically impaired and technophobic [8]. The fact that designers and developers often fail to consider the older adults' needs is a factor that might contribute to create scenarios where older adults look incompetent when dealing with technologies. Previous studies have shown that older adults appreciate and use technology when it incorporates its needs and worries, which is a predictable result when designers emphasize user-centred design [7]. Consequently we need to understand different dimensions of the relationship between older adults and technology starting from how basic aspects such as people becoming used to the idea of technology being used by older adults.

The main purpose of this research is to show the effects that stimulus related to technology and ageing produce in age estimation. This is important for ubiquitous technology because it would mean that technology could provide a context and a set of tools to improve the behaviour from younger people toward older adults.

2 Previous Work

Although scarce, there is prior research that shows how technology can modify people's perception on ageing. For example Chua et al. [5] found that videogames (particularly group games) help younger people modify their perceptions about older people by creating a scenario that promoted communication and rouse awareness of their capabilities and thus discrediting some stereotypes related to technology.

---

[3] Pew Research Center, April 2014, "Older Adults and Technology Use". Available at: http://www. pewinternet.org/2014/04/03/older-adults-and-technology-use/.

Several studies have considered how the effects of factors, other than technology, influence age perception. These include subjective and objective age, gender, attractiveness and facial ageing-cues and stereotypes. For example, Kotter-Grühn and Hess, in [10] found that: (i) the subjective age (felt age and self-perceived age) of a person is closer to the estimated age (provided by others) than objective age, (ii) objective age does not have an effect on the way other people perceived the ageing process, (iii) finally, they found that people rated as more attractive and fit are perceived as younger by other people. They also found that negative stereotypes do make people feel older and less satisfied with their life [11].

To summarize, there have been numerous studies on how different factors can alter the perception of ageing through its different constructs such as physical appearance, perceived age and age estimation, however technology has not been considered as one of those factors. There have been some studies that relate technology to ageing perception change although as a secondary result. Therefore, this paper tries to fill this void in our understanding of technology and our perception of aging via age estimation. We formulated two hypotheses to be tested: (i) participants exposed to stimuli related to technology will assign lower age ranges to the persons depicted in the photographs than those exposed to neutral stimuli; and (ii) participants exposed to stimuli related to ageing will assign higher age ranges to the persons depicted in the photographs than those exposed to neutral stimuli.

3 Methodology

We conducted an experiment with 60 participants (22 men and 38 women) aged 19–88 years. The participants were recruited from the student and academic body from a research centre and from an academic course for older adults in order to minimize the possible variations from age differences. Each participant was randomly assigned to one of three groups according to the stimuli (words used in the priming activity) to which they would be exposed, so that every group had 20 participants. These groups were: Technology, Ageing and Neutral. The participants were sorted in order to have four participants with age higher than 40 years on each group.

In order to guarantee that the priming would remain unconscious the participants were told a fake objective [3, 14] (studying grammatical, and linguistic skills). Each participant had an individual session in which they completed five activities: a priming activity, a decoy activity, a photography test, a debriefing activity and a personality questionnaire. The priming activity consisted of the 'Sentence Unscrambling Task' [15] in which the participants are given 15 sets of five words (12 of the sets included one priming word whilst the three remaining sets included only neutral words) in order to form a logical sentence using only four words. There was no time limit for this activity in order to guarantee supraliminal priming. Then, in order to reduce the possibility of recalling the priming words in the photography test, we extended the time between the priming and the real test [14] implementing a ten minute decoy activity. We asked the participants to complete 15 sentences choosing the correct word.

For the photography test [10], using a laptop and an online form we showed to the participants, 30 photographs depicting different persons within different ranges of age.

For each photograph the participants had to assign an age range. In order to know the degree of awareness that participants had about the stimuli they were exposed to, we designed a funnel-debriefing questionnaire based on Chartrand and Bargh's questionnaire [4] that asked the participants if they found a common concept among the words, if they figured the real objective of the activities and if they could relate the activities. For the last activity participants had to complete a personality questionnaire in order to guarantee that participants were not prone to sudden or frequent mood changes that might taint the results [12]. We chose to implement the 'Neuroticism' subscale short version of the revised Eysenck Personality Questionnaire for adults (EPQ-BV) [6, 13]. Once the participants completed the questionnaire they were debriefed about the real objective of the experiment.

4 Results

The average score of the participants was 4.4 points ($\sigma = 2.72$), which can be interpreted as 'mildly stable'. Five participants had a score higher than 6, therefore their results were overlooked in the subsequent analysis. Due to this, the number of participants in each group considered in the analysis was: 18 for the 'Neutral' group, 19 for the 'Technology' group and 18 for the 'Ageing' group.

For the analysis of each photograph a Chi-Square Association Test was used to test the relation between the type of stimuli and the age range given to the person depicted. There was no statistical significant difference ($\alpha = 5\%$) between the age ranges given by the participants of the three different groups in any of the 30 photographs.

Following the recommendations from [2], although six of the participants noticed that the words used in the priming were related none of them realized the association between the priming and the objective or between the priming and the photography test, therefore none of the participants was excluded.

5 Discussion

The aim of this research was to identify the effects that the exposure to ageing and technology related stimuli could produce on age estimation.

After analysing the data we can reject both of our hypotheses due to the fact that age estimation from participants of both experimental conditions did not showed statistical significant difference from the estimations of the neutral condition. Considering the conclusions from [10, 11] the results from the ageing related stimuli were unexpected since they found that ageing related stimuli could induce participants to perceive other people as older. This disparity in conclusions could be explained by the valence of the stimuli selected. While they did discern positive and negative stimuli we tried to balance the valence of the words selected in the priming activity. The lack of statistical significant difference from the technology and ageing related stimuli may be due to: technology, by itself, not being a factor that alters the perception of ageing, at least unconsciously, despite the fact that it is related to both, negative and positive stereotypes; from prejudices toward technology; cultural factors; or, considering the results from previous studies, our experimental design was not adequate to measure the effect, e.g., age range in the photography test (5 years i.e., 5–10, 11–15…) was too wide, therefore decreasing the accuracy of the estimation. Despite these results previous research [5] shows that it is possible for technology to affect attitudes and perceptions toward ageing through the usage of technology because it can impact in some of its dimensions such as emotions, learning, satisfaction with life, usefulness to society or promoting physical and mental activity, etc.

Therefore it would be incorrect to conclude from this research that technology has no influence in the perception of ageing, instead we showed the need to address the problem from another point of view. Particularly among older adults, the effects of prejudices toward technology are more important since its pervasiveness means that more aspects of their life are now influenced in a negative way. Therefore, the adoption and usage of technology can be used to mitigate or eliminate this prejudices in order to explore how older adults modify their ageing perception, as a whole, through technology.

We designed a second experiment in which we provided 3 devices, representing different ubiquitous technology paradigms (Personal Informatics, Social Broadcasting, Electronic Paper), to a group of older adults that either attended or did not attend a computing curse (n = 3 for each group). Each participant has been using each one of the devices for two weeks. In order to augment the likelihood that the perception change was due to the use of technology for every device a series of tasks were define so that we could monitor the activity of the participants. At the end of this period we interviewed them. We will analyse the interviews using the Grounded Theory Methodology in order to obtain a theoretical model about this phenomena.

The importance of this second study would lie not only in deepening our understanding about the relation between these two key phenomena, but also in influencing the people's quality of life. If technology can have a positive effect on the perception of ageing, then ambient computing could be used as a mechanism to promote "active ageing" and to increase quality of life. This could produce positive effects such as: improving physical and mental health, enhancing communication and socialization, disposing negative stereotypes about older adults and technology, and helping them maintaining their independence. This can eventually lead to a healthier and more satisfactory life.

References

1. Anzures, G., Ge, L., Wang, Z., Itakura, S., Lee, K.: Culture shapes efficiency of facial age judgments. PLoS ONE **5**(7), e11679 (2010). doi:10.1371/journal.pone.0011679
2. Aronson, E., Wilson, T.D., Brewer, M.B.: Experimentation in social psychology. In: Gilbert, D.T., Fiske, S.T., Lindzey, G. (eds.) The Handbook of Social Psychology, 4th edn, pp. 99–142. McGraw-Hill, New York (1998)
3. Bargh, J.A., Chartrand, T.L.: The mind in the middle: a practical guide to priming and automaticity research. In: Reis, H.T., Judd, C.M. (eds.) Handbook of Research Methods in Social and Personality Psychology, pp. 311–344. Cambridge University Press, Cambridge (2000)

4. Chartrand, T.L., Bargh, J.A.: Automatic activation of impression formation and memorization goals: nonconscious goal priming reproduces effects of explicit task instructions. J. Pers. Soc. Psychol. **71**(3), 464–478 (1996). doi:10.1037/0022-3514.71.3.464

5. Chua, P.-H., Jung, Y., Lwin, M.O., Theng, Y.-L.: Let's play together: effects of video-game play on intergenerational perceptions among youth and elderly participants. Comput. Hum. Behav. **29**(6), 2303–2311 (2013). doi:10.1016/j.chb.2013.04.037

6. Eysenck, S.B.G., Eysenck, H.J., Barrett, P.: A revised version of the psychoticism scale. Pers. Individ. Differ. **6**(1), 21–29 (1985). doi:10.1016/0191-8869(85)90026-1

7. Hope, A., Schwaba, T., Piper, A.M.: Understanding digital and material social communications for older adults. In: Proceedings of the 32nd Annual ACM Conference on Human Factors in Computing Systems - CHI 2014, pp. 3903–3912. ACM Press, New York (2014). doi:10.1145/2556288.2557133

8. Ito, M., O'Day, V.L., Adler, A., Linde, C., Mynatt, E.D.: Making a place for seniors on the Net. ACM SIGCAS Comput. Soc. **31**(3), 15–21 (2001). doi:10.1145/504696.504699

9. Kleinberger, T., Becker, M., Ras, E., Holzinger, A., Müller, P.: Ambient intelligence in assisted living: enable elderly people to handle future interfaces. In: Stephanidis, C. (ed.) UAHCI 2007 (Part II). LNCS, vol. 4555, pp. 103–112. Springer, Heidelberg (2007)

10. Kotter-Gruhn, D., Hess, T.M.: So you think you look young? Matching older adults' subjective ages with age estimations provided by younger, middle-aged, and older adults. Int. J. Behav. Dev. **36**(6), 468–475 (2012). doi:10.1177/0165025412454029

11. Kotter-Grühn, D., Hess, T.M.: The impact of age stereotypes on self-perceptions of aging across the adult lifespan. J. Gerontol. Ser. B Psychol. Sci. Soc. Sci. **67**(5), 563–571 (2012). doi:10.1093/geronb/gbr153

12. Lucas-Carrasco, R., Laidlaw, K., Gómez-Benito, J., Power, M.J.: Reliability and validity of the Attitudes to Ageing Questionnaire (AAQ) in older people in Spain. Int. Psychogeriatr. **25**(03), 490–499 (2013). http://journals.cambridge.org/abstract_S1041610212001809

13. Sato, T.: The Eysenck personality questionnaire brief version: factor structure and reliability. J. Psychol. **139**(6), 545–552 (2005). doi:10.3200/JRLP.139.6.545-552

14. Spaan, P.E.J., Raaijmakers, J.G.W.: Priming effects from young-old to very old age on a word-stem completion task: minimizing explicit contamination. Neuropsychol. Dev. Cogn. Sect. B Aging Neuropsychol. Cogn. **18**(1), 86–107 (2011). doi:10.1080/13825585.2010.511146

15. Srull, T.K., Wyer, R.S.: The role of category accessibility in the interpretation of information about persons: some determinants and implications. J. Pers. Soc. Psychol. **37**(10), 1660 (1979)

16. United Nations Department of Economic and Affairs Population Division. World Population Ageing 2013. New York (2013). doi:ST/ESA/SER.A/348

Experimentation on Emotion Regulation with Single-Colored Images

Marina V. Sokolova[1], Antonio Fernández-Caballero[1]([⊠]), Laura Ros[2],
Luz Fernández-Aguilar[2], and José Miguel Latorre[2]

[1] Instituto de Investigación en Informática de Albacete, Universidad de Castilla-La
Mancha, 02071 Albacete, Spain
Antonio.Fdez@uclm.es
[2] Instituto de Investigación en Discapacidades Neurológicas, Universidad de
Castilla-La Mancha, 02071 Albacete, Spain

Abstract. This paper introduces a series of experiments with the objective of assessing the influence of color in emotion regulation. For this sake, images with one single color or one single dominant color are shown to a set of participants who take part in the experimentation. Firstly, the architecture of the color emotion regulation system is introduced. The methodology for color emotion recognition is based on a novel approach of both direct and indirect emotion evaluation. Then, the experimental setup is discussed together with the testing procedure. The tests are based on questionnaires for emotional state evaluation, color preference and personality. Lastly, the experimental results are described and discussed.

Keywords: Color · Single-colored images · Emotion regulation

1 Introduction

Nowadays, much attention is being paid to emotional well-being of the ageing people [1,2]. In this sense, it is known that the quality of life of older people depends on their emotional interpretation to daily facts and events [3]. Some other relevant aspects in well-being are the everyday social, physical, mental and financial aspects. Although the quality of life can be affected in a negative way by some factors such as specially feeling lonely, poor overall health, self-care capacity limitations, and worry about financial resources, the older adults show high possibilities of emotion regulation. Findings in ageing literature demonstrate that older adults are more effective at regulating emotions in comparison to young adults (e.g. [4,5]), and they are more motivated to suppress interpersonal tensions [6]. These findings also show that color is a parameter that influences on their emotional state. Therefore, color should be well employed in favor of the people of this age group.

Indeed, color is a basic omnipresent factor, which relation with emotion has been demonstrated and discussed in the scientific literature for affective computing [7,8]. Many authors highlight that a certain color can be an additional

© Springer International Publishing Switzerland 2015
I. Cleland et al. (Eds.): IWAAL 2015, LNCS 9455, pp. 265–276, 2015.
DOI: 10.1007/978-3-319-26410-3_25

factor for emotion elicitation and regulation. There are four possible explanations for the associations between color and emotions. They include references to metonymic and metaphoric, thinking, formation of specific emotional reactions for color perception, and sharing connotative structure in the language for color and emotion terms [9].

For instance, some colors are strongly associated with emotions [9,10]. Green is related to envy and relaxation; blue is associated with relaxation and sadness. Red, for example, has both positive and negative impressions, as it is known to be a color of positive activity, dominance and passion. It has also been is associated with arouse, excitement, and stimulation [11]. In Africa, red color is related to anger and triggers more negative emotions [12].

This is why color appears as an excellent tool of emotional modulation. Emotion regulation was initially supposed to be an ability to control the expression of negative emotions, and their suppression. Nevertheless, in terms of affective computing, this can be viewed as a complex phenomenon which widens social competence. It also affects the ability to form and maintain interpersonal relationships, which is of great importance for the health and well-being of ageing adults. Color constantly and imperceptibly affects the emotions of people. A personalized selection of colors would allow to regulate emotions with the aim to enhance positive emotions. Colored environments, where older adults stay, can help in inducing an emotion. The study (experimentation) described in this paper is aimed to discover new relations between color and emotions.

2 Relation Between Color and Emotions

A considerable number of research papers on the evaluation of the relation between color and emotions have been carried out so far. Moreover, the effect of color on the emotional state can be measured indirectly by means of affective semantic words and word combinations [13–15].

A seminal methodology suggests to rate a given word in a scale between two poles, which are semantic terms [16]. After that, factor analysis is used to detect the principal dimensions and the value of each word on the dimensions. With the purpose to study color emotion, factor analysis is usually applied [15]. And, if it fails, independent component analysis is used with intrinsic statistical properties of data such as kurtosis. Factor and correlation analysis (e.g. [13–15,17]) and ANOVA (e.g. [18–20]) are the most widely used classification methods for color-based emotion regulation.

It is important to note that some other findings demonstrate that color features like chroma, hue or lightness cause an impact on emotions [21–23]. Indeed, it has been proved that the chromatic palette contains emotionally charged information, as opposed to the achromatic one [23]. Lightness and chroma of color appear to dominate on most of the color emotion pairs, although the degree of their influence is small in some cases [21]. On the contrary, the hue of a color does not affect the emotional state of the participants of the described test. Similar results that confirm these findings [21] are obtained in another work [11].

Another approach points that older observers show strong preference to colors with higher chroma while younger people prefer achromatic colors [13].

Moreover, with respect to particular colors, a series of experiments conclude that stimulating effects are provoked by pink and yellow color samples; green elicits the feelings of excitement, relaxation and vividness as well as boredom and depression; blue is associated with calmness and coldness; red is stated as tiring and depressive, and together with violet they are named as striking colors [11]. The author of the experiments also finds a positive emotional response to black color for aged adults. In addition, strong colors (especially red) and patterns put the brain into a more excited state and may provoke severe changes in the behavior of introvert persons or people in bad mood [24]. But, the participants in this test feel more positive in the red room than in the blue one, as well as they feel more self-control in a room painted in gray. In another experiment on color emotion [25], the green color attains the most positive emotions, followed by yellow and blue.

3   Color Emotion Recognition

3.1   Methodology for Color Emotion Recognition

At the beginning of the experiment, each participant is due to pass a *Personality Test* with the aim to evaluate the characteristics of his/her personality. Also, an *Emotional State Test* has to be performed before and after each *Color Emotion Test*. Figure 1 shows the sequence in which the color emotion evaluation is carried out. In first place, the emotional state of the participant is evaluated with the Positive and Negative Affect Schedule (PANAS) scales. After that, the proper *Color Emotion Test* is passed. Emotion identification, as it is demonstrated in Fig. 1, is achieved as a result of the outcomes of both tests. The *Personality*

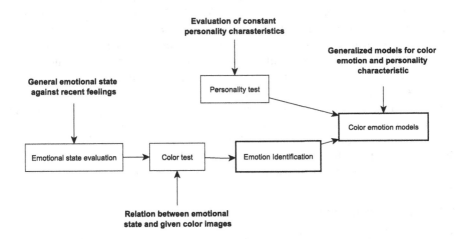

Fig. 1. The overall testing procedure.

Test, namely the NEO Five Factor Inventory, can be carried out before or after the *Color Emotion Test*. Finally, the generalized models for color emotion and personality characteristic are calculated.

PANAS Questionnaire. The Positive and Negative Affect Schedule (PANAS) scales test is a self-reported questionnaire to evaluate emotional states [26]. As aforementioned, this test is used as the *Emotional State Test*. More concretely, PANAS comprises 2 dimensions or factors: one with 10 items related to positive, and another with 10 items related to negative affect. The evaluation is performed with a set of ten positive and ten negative adjectives for every dimension. PANAS enables to evaluate affect changes as it consists of two parts: the first one aims to evaluate mood during the last week, and the last part rates mood in general. The scale is Likert-type, having to choose from 1 ("Strongly disagree") to 5 ("Strongly agree").

NEO-FFI Questionnaire. The NEO Five Factor Inventory (NEO-FFI) is the short version of the questionnaire NEO-PPI [27]. It is an instrument to evaluate the main personality factors. So, it is used in our approach as the *Personality Test*. It consists of 60 items, providing 12 items for each of the following 5 personality dimensions: "Neuroticism", "Extraversion", "Openness to experience", "Conscientiousness", and "Agreeableness". The scale is again Likert-type from 0 ("Totally disagree") to 4 ("Totally agree"). PANAS as well as NEO-FFI are conducted in order to know the effect that mood and personality can have on the *Color Emotion Test*.

Color Emotion Test. The *Color Emotion Test* supposes that a participant observes a single-colored picture during the exposition time, and evaluates his/her impression felt. In this case, really one-colored images as well as images composed of ne dominant color are provided. While a color is perceived, the brain links or associates it with a specific emotion or emotions [17]. This phenomenon is known as color emotion. Thus, an emotion can be described with semantic words, such as "Stressful", "Warm", "Passive" or "Bored". The experiment is inspired by a series of previous research works (e.g. [17,21,22,28–30]). The novelty here is that our proposal has the advantage that it evaluates both direct and indirect information about the effect of color on emotions. On the one hand, indirect information is obtained from the semantic words ("Tension", "Temperature", "Amusement" and "Attractiveness"), whereas direct information is gotten through emotional items ("Joy", "Fear" and "Sadness"). Thus, it is possible to measure the relation between the direct and indirect evaluators.

3.2 Architecture for Color Emotion Regulation

With the aim to embody the proposed experiment, a complete color emotion regulation system (CERS) has been created. The CERS belongs to an organiza-

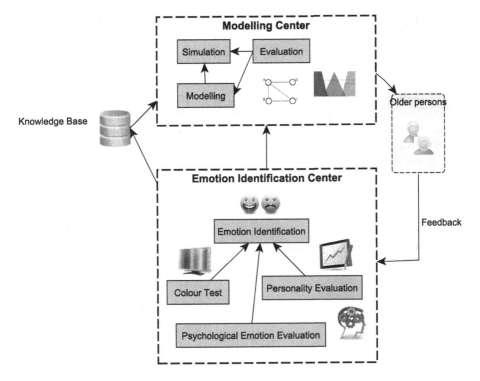

Fig. 2. The architecture of the color emotion regulation system (Color figure online).

tional type, and it is virtually and logically organized into a leveled architecture. It consists of the following modules (see Fig. 2):

- "Emotion Identification Center", which consolidates information from the incoming independent sources. Within this center, data preprocessing, identification, and classification tasks are performed. Here, the initial data are revised to identify errors, outliers, gaps, and duplications. An emotion is identified within this layer, and data are stored in a knowledge base (KB). "Emotion Identification Center" is the module that really interacts with the user and carries out the testing procedure. The three types of tests are performed at this level, including the *Color Emotion Test*, the *Emotional State Test*, and the *Personality Test*. The results of these tests are consolidated, and the resulting emotion is identified.
- "Modeling Center". The aim of this center consists in discovering of models that best describe relations between emotions and colors. Several data mining techniques are used for modeling, including decision trees and fuzzy logic, among others. First, the models are evaluated, and the best ones are selected, and they pass for further processing. Second, the selected models undergo simulations. Lastly, the simulation outcomes are evaluated.

4   Color Emotion Test: Methodology and Results

4.1   Methodology

A preliminary pilot test for 10 persons aged between 65 and 75 years, males and females in equal parts, has been carried out. The experiment is carried out in a room with white-colored walls. Each participant is placed in front of a computer in this room. Figure 3 shows the main menu of the application that the participant interacts with. The sequence of letters *A1-A2-A3* shows the sequence of tasks for a test participant. The task *B* can be carried out apart.

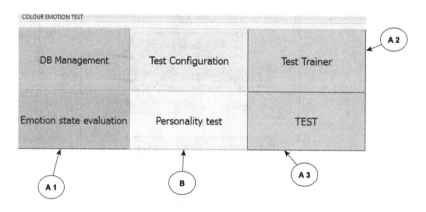

Fig. 3. The main menu of the application.

There are 10 colors that are used in this experimentation: blue, dark blue, brown, green, grey, purple, orange, red, pink, and yellow. The set of colored images is organized in such a way that each of the 10 colors is represented within 3 images, where one image is a plain single-colored one, and the two others are landscapes or images from nature with a marked dominance of a given color (see Fig. 4).

The test starts and goes on as described next:

1. The objectives of the tests are commented to the test participant.
2. After the instructions are given to the participant on how to answer to the *Emotional State Test* questionnaire, he/she starts the test.
3. Next, the participant receives information on how to carry out the *Color Emotion Test*, and he/she tries to answer two questions, doing the trial test with different images from an alternative image set.
4. After the training is over, the participant starts to answer the *Color Emotion Test*. Each participant is asked to judge about each one of 30 single-colored images.

   – A random image is presented during an exposure time of 4.5 s.

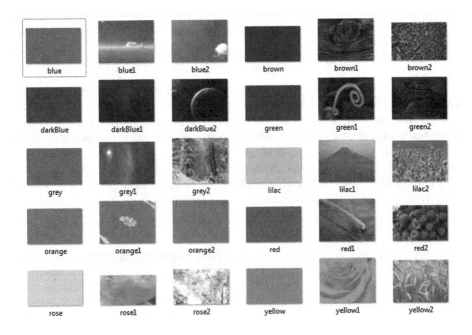

Fig. 4. Color images used in the experiment (Color figure online).

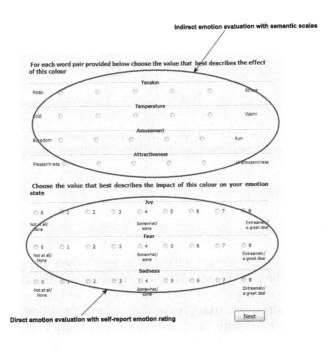

Fig. 5. The questions for emotion evaluation.

– A window with semantic and emotional scales appears (see Fig. 5), and the participant answers the questions by rating semantic words and evaluating emotions.
– The test ends when all the images have been evaluated in this manner.

The whole test duration varies from 30 to 60 min, where the *Emotional State Test* lasts between 5 and 10 min, the trial test between 5 and 15 min, and the *Color Emotion Test* between 20 and 40 min. There are pauses between these three tests, and it is recommended to make a pause every ten minutes while performing the *Color Emotion Test*. As already mentioned, the *Personality Test* can be carried out at any other moment, and it lasts about 30 to 60 min.

Figure 6(a) shows a screen shot with the questions to the NEO-FFI *Personality Test*, and Fig. 6(b) gives a view on a *Emotional State Test* questionnaire window.

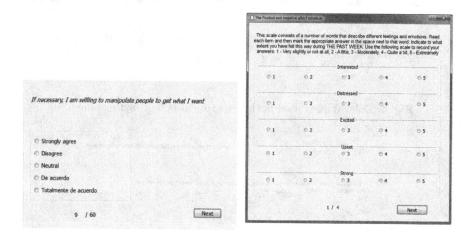

Fig. 6. Screen shots for the NEO-FFI and PANAS questionnaires. (a) Left: *Personality Test* (NEO-FFI) questionnaire window. (b) Right: *Emotional State Test* (PANAS) questionnaire window.

4.2 Results

The experiment outcomes show similarities in single-color perception on the emotional state of the participants. More concretely, semantic scale "Temperature" shows maximum values for colors red and yellow, and grey and red-colored images are rated at the top for the "Tension" scale. Purple, yellow, and pink colors are usually associated with the "Amusement" concept. The semantic scale "Attractiveness" shows that blue and purple colored pictures are preferred, followed by pink and yellow ones.

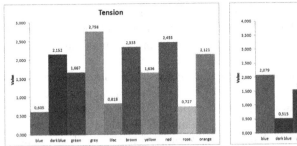
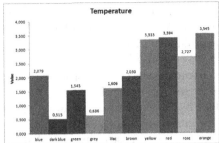
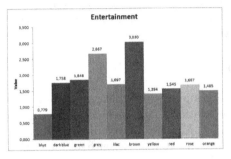
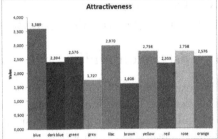

Fig. 7. Ratings for the semantic scales (Color figure online).

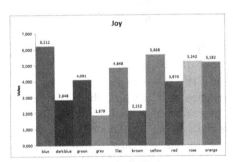

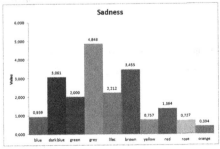

Fig. 8. Ratings for the emotion self-evaluation scales (Color figure online).

Referring to the emotions that have been experienced, the greater part of participants mark their extreme feelings for "Joy" after viewing images in blue, pink, yellow, and orange colors. The greater ranks for "Fear" are obtained for dark blue colored images, and the maximum rates for "Sadness" are obtained for gray colored images.

Figure 7 shows bar charts for the semantic scales. The group of warm colors (red, pink, orange, yellow) and the group of cold colors (gray, green, blue, dark blue) has shown a strong relation to the concept "Temperature" in general.

Figure 8 shows some bar charts for the emotional scales. The blue color (marked as the most pleasant and attractive, receives a major rate for the "Joy" concept together with warm colors. Actually, the concept of "Joy" appears to be multicolored, while "Sadness" and "Fear" are mostly high rated for the cold colors, and very low for the warm colors.

5   Discussion and Conclusions

The results obtained for single-colored images prove that there are strong relations between colors and emotions. These relations have been determined both with indirect and self-reported questionnaires. Moreover, the indirect evaluation with semantic scale "Attractiveness" discovers a strong preference for blue color, and the self-reported rating for blue colored images is highest for the "Joy" concept. In the same way, grey is the most unpleasant color with semantic scale "Attractiveness", and is related to the emotions of "Sadness" and "Fear". Warm colored images are associated with positive emotions, such as "Joy", while they are almost absent in the emotional scales "Sadness" and "Fear", with exception of the red color, which produces "Fear".

The future work has several directions. The first one consists in carrying out more experiments in order to enlarge our database and start data mining. The second way is related to the selection of the test images. As part of plain color images there are landscapes, and images with nature, which may influence not only with color, but with the proper subjective content. And, another directions is in adding additional semantic scales, such as "Dynamics" or "Harmony/Disharmony". Finally, our future plans include to make more experiments for ageing people from different countries, and to compare cultural components of color emotion results.

Acknowledgements. This work was partially supported by Spanish Ministerio de Economía y Competitividad / FEDER under TIN2013-47074-C2-1-R grant.

References

1. Sokolova, M.V., Fernández-Caballero, A., López, M.T., Martínez-Rodrigo, A., Zangróniz, R., Pastor, J.M.: A distributed architecture for multimodal emotion identification. In: Bajo, J., et al. (eds.) Trends in Prac. Appl. of Agents, Multi-Agent Sys. and Sustainability. AISC, vol. 372, pp. 125–132. Springer, Heidelberg (2015)

2. Fernández-Sotos, A., Fernández-Caballero, A., Latorre, J.M.: Elicitation of emotions through music: the influence of note value. In: Vicente, J.M.F., Álvarez-Sánchez, J.R., de la Paz López, F., Toledo-Moreo, F.J., Adeli, H. (eds.) Artificial Computation in Biology and Medicine. LNCS, vol. 9107, pp. 488–497. Springer, Heidelberg (2015)

3. Xavier, F.M.F., Ferraz, M.P.T., Marc, N., Escosteguy, N.U., Moriguchi, E.H.: Elderly people's definition of quality of life. Revista Brasileira de Psiquiatria **25**(1), 31–39 (2003)

4. Gross, J.J., Carstensen, L.L., Pasupathi, M., Tsai, J., Gotestam-Skorpen, C., Hsu, A.Y.C.: Emotion and aging: experience, expression, and control. Psychol. Aging **12**, 590–599 (1997)

5. Scheibe, S., Blanchard-Fields, F.: Effects of regulating emotions on cognitive performance: what is costly for young adults is not so costly for older adults. Psychol. Aging **24**(1), 217–223 (2009)

6. Blanchard-Fields, F., Mienaltowski, A., Seay, R.B.: Age differences in everyday problem-solving effectiveness: older adults select more effective strategies for interpersonal problems. J. Gerontol. Ser. B Psychol. Sci. Soc. Sci. **1**, 61 (2007)

7. Sokolova, M.V., Fernández-Caballero, A., Ros, L., Latorre, J.M., Serrano, J.P.: Evaluation of color preference for emotion regulation. In: Vicente, J.M.F., Álvarez-Sánchez, J.R., de la Paz López, F., Toledo-Moreo, F.J., Adeli, H. (eds.) Artificial Computation in Biology and Medicine. LNCS, vol. 9107, pp. 479–487. Springer, Heidelberg (2015)

8. Sokolova, M.V., Fernández-Caballero, A.: A review on the role of color and light in affective computing. Appl. Sci. **5**(3), 275–293 (2015)

9. Soriano, C., Valenzuela, J.: Emotion and colour across languages: implicit associations in Spanish colour terms. Soc. Sci. Inf. **48**(3), 421–445 (2009)

10. Callejas, A., Acosta, A., Lupiáñez, J.: Green love is ugly: emotions elicited by synesthetic grapheme-color perceptions. Brain Res. **1127**, 99–107 (2007)

11. Manav, B.: Color-emotion associations and color preferences: a case study for residences. Color Res. Appl. **32**(2), 144–150 (2007)

12. Taylor, J., Mbense, T.G.: Red dogs and rotten mealies: how Zulus talk about anger. In: Athansiadou, A., Tabakowska, E. (eds.) Speaking of Emotions: Conceptualization and Expression, pp. 191–226. Mouton de Gruyter, Berlin (1998)

13. Ou, L.C., Luo, M.R., Sun, P.L., Hu, N.C., Chen, H.S.: Age effects on colour emotion, preference, and harmony. Color Res. Appl. **37**(2), 92–105 (2012)

14. Gao, X.P., Xin, J.H., Sato, T., Hansuebsai, A., Scalzo, M., Kajiwara, K., Billger, M.: Analysis of cross-cultural color emotion. Color Res. Appl. **32**(3), 223–229 (2007)

15. Hanada, M.: Analyses of color emotion for color pairs with independent component analysis and factor analysis. Color Res. Appl. **38**(4), 297–308 (2013)

16. Adams, F.M., Osgood, C.E.: A cross-cultural study of the affective meanings of color. J. Cross Cult. Psychol. **4**(2), 135–156 (1973)

17. Solli, M., Lenz, R.: Color emotions for multi-colored images. Color Res. Appl. **36**(3), 210–221 (2011)

18. Küller, R., Ballal, S., Laike, T., Mikellides, B., Tonello, G.: The impact of light and colour on psychological mood: a cross-cultural study of indoor work environments. Ergonomics **49**(14), 1496–1507 (2006)

19. Choi, C.J., Kim, K.S., Kim, C.M., Kim, S.H., Choi, W.S.: Reactivity of heart rate variability after exposure to colored lights in healthy adults with symptoms of anxiety and depression. Int. J. Psychophysiol. **79**(2), 83–88 (2011)

20. Bonnardel, N., Piolat, A., Le Bigot, L.: The impact of colour on website appeal and users' cognitive processes. Displays **32**(2), 69–80 (2011)

21. Xin, J.H., Cheng, K.M., Taylor, G., Sato, T., Hansuebsai, A.: Cross-regional comparison of colour emotions - Part I: quantitative analysis. Color Res. Appl. **29**(6), 451–457 (2004)

22. Xin, J.H., Cheng, K.M., Taylor, G., Sato, T., Hansuebsai, A.: Cross-regional comparison of colour emotions - Part II: qualitative analysis. Color Res. Appl. **29**(6), 458–466 (2004)

23. Jue, J., Kwon, S.M.: Does colour say something about emotions? Laypersons assessments of colour drawings. Arts Psychother. **40**(1), 115–119 (2013)

24. Küller, R., Mikellides, B., Janssens, J.: Color, arousal, and performance - a comparison of three experiments. Color Res. Appl. **34**(2), 141–152 (2009)

25. Kaya, N., Epps, H.H.: Color-emotion associations: past experience and personal preference. In: Proceedings of the 2004 Interim Meeting of the International Color Association, vol. 4, p. 31 (2004)

26. Watson, D., Clark, L.A., Tellegen, A.: Development and validation of brief measures of positive and negative affect: the PANAS scales. J. Pers. Soc. Psychol. **54**(6), 1063 (1988)

27. Costa, P.T., McCrae, R.R.: The revised neo personality inventory (NEO-PI-R). In: Boyle, G.J., Matthews, G., Saklofske, D.H. (eds.) The SAGE Handbook of Personality Theory and Assessment, vol. 2, pp. 179–198. SAGE Publications, London (2008)

28. Ou, L.C., Luo, M.R., Woodcock, A., Wright, A.: A study of colour emotion and colour preference - Part I: colour emotions for single colours. Color Res. Appl. **29**(3), 232–240 (2004)

29. Ou, L.C., Luo, M.R., Woodcock, A., Wright, A.: A study of colour emotion and colour preference - Part II: colour emotions for two-colour combinations. Color Res. Appl. **29**(4), 292–298 (2004)

30. Ou, L.C., Luo, M.R., Woodcock, A., Wright, A.: A study of colour emotion and colour preference - Part III: colour preference modeling. Color Res. Appl. **29**(5), 381–389 (2004)

LED Strips for Color- and Illumination-Based Emotion Regulation at Home

Vicente Ortiz-García-Cervigón[1], Marina V. Sokolova[1],
Rosa María García-Muñoz[2], and Antonio Fernández-Caballero[1,2(✉)]

[1] Instituto de Investigación en Informática de Albacete,
Universidad de Castilla-La Mancha, 02071 Albacete, Spain
[2] Departamento de Sistemas Informáticos,
Universidad de Castilla-La Mancha, 02071 Albacete, Spain
Antonio.Fdez@uclm.es

Abstract. An experimental setup for emotion regulation at home is introduced in this paper. The experimentation starts from the premise that changes in the ambience in terms of illumination and color are able to produce alterations in inhabitants' emotional state. The proposal uses RGB LED strips that are regulable in color and intensity to control the ambience. The full details of the assembly of a circuit that includes a micro-controller and a number of strips are provided. Afterwards, a novel approach for complex color emotion evaluation based on lexical semantic scales and self-evaluation is discussed. Then, the experimental results of a pilot test with 27 participants are discussed.

Keywords: LED strip · Color · Illumination · Emotion regulation · Experimental evaluation

1 Introduction

Light is one of the principal environmental factors that influence on a user. Therefore, its affective impact has been widely researched and reported. Exposure to bright light and luminance distribution affect our mood. This is why, many researchers believe that light can be used to alter/improve emotional states. It is known that regulation of biochemical and hormonal rhythms is amongst the positive effects of light on humans. In this sense, a paper [1] investigates how changes in light exposure are related to the quality of life and social and emotional functioning. The authors find out some strong associations capable of improving these issues. Also, a seminal work has proved the time-course and durability of antidepressant effects of bright light in winter on depressive patients [2]. Exposure to light appears to cause higher clinician ratings of hypo-manic symptoms in patients. In addition, the findings of an experiment for light therapy combined with high-density negative air ionization for the patients with seasonal affective disorder show moderate efficacy of light therapy [3].

Color is another factor which is constantly present in any environment. Moreover, the evidences of the influence of color upon human emotions has been

© Springer International Publishing Switzerland 2015
I. Cleland et al. (Eds.): IWAAL 2015, LNCS 9455, pp. 277–287, 2015.
DOI: 10.1007/978-3-319-26410-3_26

discussed in a number of publications (e.g. [4–7]). Many authors highlight that certain colors are highly influencing for emotion elicitation and regulation. The four possible explanations to color and emotion association, which include references to metonymic and metaphoric thinking, formation of specific emotional reactions for color perception, and sharing connotative structure in the language for color and emotion terms, have been validated [8]. For instance, an experiment was aimed to discover possible relations between colors (and color groups) and emotional changes in participants [9]. The author offered some interesting outcomes, which allow to relate color with emotions. In another experiment, muscle strength reduces within 2.7 s for inmates in prisons which stay during limited time periods in specially painted in bubble-gum pink (Baker-Miller pink) cells [10]. It is important to mention that it has been demonstrated that color characteristics like chroma, hue or lightness also make an impact on emotions [11–13]. Indeed, the chromatic palette contains emotionally charged information as opposed to the achromatic one [13]. Lightness and chroma of color appear to dominate on most of the color emotion pairs in a report [11], although the degree of its influence is small in some cases.

This paper provides a description of the combination of color and light due to their double influence on emotion regulation. Thus, we introduce an experiment aimed to evaluate the influence of colored light on the emotional state of humans [14] by using LED strips in a room.

2 Light/Color and LED Strips

Lighting LED-based solutions have received recognition due to a series of qualities that place them as a leader technology in their area. Illumination based on LED enables obtaining a palette of colors from the basic RGB (red, green and blue) colors and white. Obviously, the quantity of white color determines the maximum intensity, which corresponds to a purely white light (and a maximum value of lumens). Thus, any other color than white has less lumen, but also consumes less energy. An advantage of LED strips is that they provide a way to organize a uniform colored lighting with the possibility to establish separate color zones on demand, and to control them.

With respect to the experiment, LED strips are used thanks to the following characteristics which make them optimal for their use at home: energy saving capabilities and environmental efficiency. Moreover, they are flexible, cuttable, and controllable. That is why they can be installed and easily removed along the perimeters of a room to fit the current needs. To sum up, they are an optimal tool to create the exactly needed lighting effect.

The proposed experimentation with LED strips supposes that each participant observes a colored light from a LED strip during a given exposure time. Afterwards, he/she evaluates the impression received. During the time a color is perceived, the brain links or associates it with a specific emotion or emotions [15]. This phenomenon is known as color emotion. Thus, an emotion can be described with semantic words, such as "stressful", "warm", "passive" or "bored". The experiment has

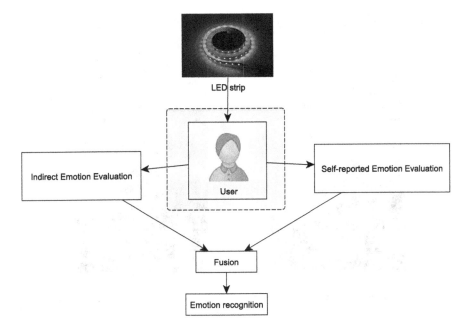

Fig. 1. LED-based induced emotion recognition.

some common features with some previous research works (e.g. [11,12,15]), but provides the advantage to evaluate both direct (self-reported) and indirect information about the effect of color on emotions (as shown in Fig. 1).

On the one hand, the indirect information is obtained from semantic words ("Tension", "Temperature", "Amusement" and "Attractiveness"), whereas direct information is gotten through emotional items ("Joy", "Fear" and "Sadness"). Thus, it is possible to measure the relation between the direct and indirect evaluators with a "Fusion" module.

3   Experimental Setup

The idea of this experiment is to control the illumination of a standard room with dimensions of 5×5 m. Additionally, the LED strips have to vary their color and intensity with the aim of influencing on the emotions felt by the subjects under study. It is also required that the interval of color change is up to 255, and the intensity of light can change up to 4 levels.

The experiment is carried out in a white-painted room, which is equipped with two RGB LED flexible strips. Each LED strip is 5 m long and holds 60 LEDs per meter. Each strip has three access pins for colors in terms of RGB, and one pin for power supply. The strips are fixed along the perimeter of the ceiling and the floor of the room in order to obtain a uniform colored light (see Fig. 2).

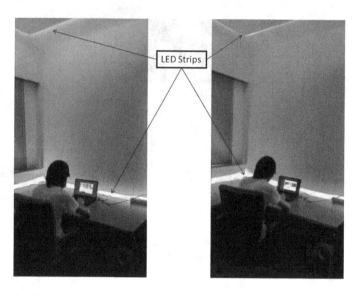

Fig. 2. General view of the experimental placement (Color figure online).

Although LED strips are constructed to work in the RGB color model, it has been decided to transform it to the HSV (hue, saturation, value) model. Indeed, the HSV model facilitates the choice of the color characteristics. The color itself is codified with a hue component, the saturation describes the "whiteness" of the color, and, finally, value is related to the lightness of a given color, and can be changed without losing the chosen color or saturation.

It has been decided to control the LED strips with the *Arduino* micro-controller board due to its simplicity and versatility on the one hand, and its strong executive power and reliability, on the other hand. As the objective is to change the color and illumination by means of the micro-controller, the pulse-width modulation (PWM) outputs of *Arduino* are used in combination with three transistors. This combination enables power supply to each color channel, and it is the most flexible to perform pilot tests. *Arduino* receives the information about the color from a computer through the USB serial port. Moreover, the micro-controller determines a required color as a mixture of the three basic color components. At the same time, it is expandable and programmable to add proper functions.

The LED strips are connected to a central computer through a module as shown in Fig. 3. Here, LED strips are connected to the micro-controller *Arduino* and to the power supply device.

The program code that controls the *Arduino* board is given next:

```
//library RGB from: https://github.com/ratkins/RGBConverter
#include <RGBConverter.h>
```

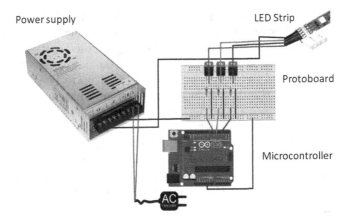

Power supply

LED Strip

Protoboard

Microcontroller

AC

Fig. 3. Schema of the electronic setup.

```
//Color pins
int pinR=3;
int pinG=5;
int pinB=6;
double dataHSB[]={50,1,10};
byte dataRGB \cite{bib3};

RGBConverter myRGBConverter;

void setup(){
 pinMode(pinR,OUTPUT);
 pinMode(pinG,OUTPUT);
 pinMode(pinB,OUTPUT);
 Serial.begin(9600);
}

void loop(){
 while (Serial.available() >=3) {
  for(int i = 0 ; i <= 2; i++){
   dataHSB[i] = Serial.read();
  }
  Serial.flush();
 }

 myRGBConverter.hsvToRgb(2*dataHSB[0]/360, dataHSB[1]/100,
dataHSB[2]/100, dataRGB);
 analogWrite(pinR,dataRGB[0]);
 analogWrite(pinG,dataRGB[1]);
 analogWrite(pinB,dataRGB[2]);
}
```

Firstly, as you can see in the program code, the library *RGBConverter.h* is included to convert between RGB and HSV. The pins which contain the colors and the object to convert are declared. The *setup()* method states that the pins are to be the output, and determines the speed of the output. *Arduino* and the computer are connected by means of the USB serial port. The *loop()* method continuously checks if the data is available. The information is read byte by byte, and the three values are set for hue, saturation and value. Actually, the hue (color) value is measured in degrees and varies from 0 to 360.

Finally, the values are converted into RGB using the *hsvToRgb()* method that displays each of the three values. Then, each of the three pins connects to the *Arduino* through the *analogWrite()* method. Once the program is loaded in the micro-controller's memory, the latter starts the execution.

4   Color and Light Emotion Test

With the aim to discover how the combination of color and intensity from LED strips influence on emotions, a pilot experiment is developed. The experiment consists in inviting subjects to carry out the visual assessments being placed into a room with the installed color and light intensity assembled system (described above). During the visual experiment, the participants are exposed to the following colored lights: red, orange, yellow, pink, green, blue, violet, and white. During the exposure to each color, the subject is offered to describe his/her feelings by answering some questions of a computer-based questionnaire.

There are two types of questions to be answered. Firstly, the test participants are asked to express their feeling about the colored light by selecting a semantic word from emotion-related word pairs, and by indicating its intensity. The semantic scales and word pairs are the following ones: "Tension: relaxed/tense", "Temperature: warm/cold", "Amusement: boring/stimulating", and "Attractiveness: pleasant/unpleasant". In order to ease the interface, each scale is divided into five intervals, and a given participant can only pick one of them, which corresponds to the intensity of the emotion. The second semantic scales and word pairs serve to evaluate what a participant feels while being exposed to the light [16], and these scales are the following ones: "Joy", "Fear", and "Sadness".

5   The Pilot Test

A preliminary pilot test for 27 persons has been carried out. The participants are aged from 18 until 55 years, both males and females, and include people with full secondary and high education. The experiment is carried out in a dark room (no light) with white-colored walls. Each participant is placed in front of the testing computer. The relation between the colored light and emotion is performed with help of a software application.

Each participant is asked to judge about each one of the eight colored lights (see Table 1).

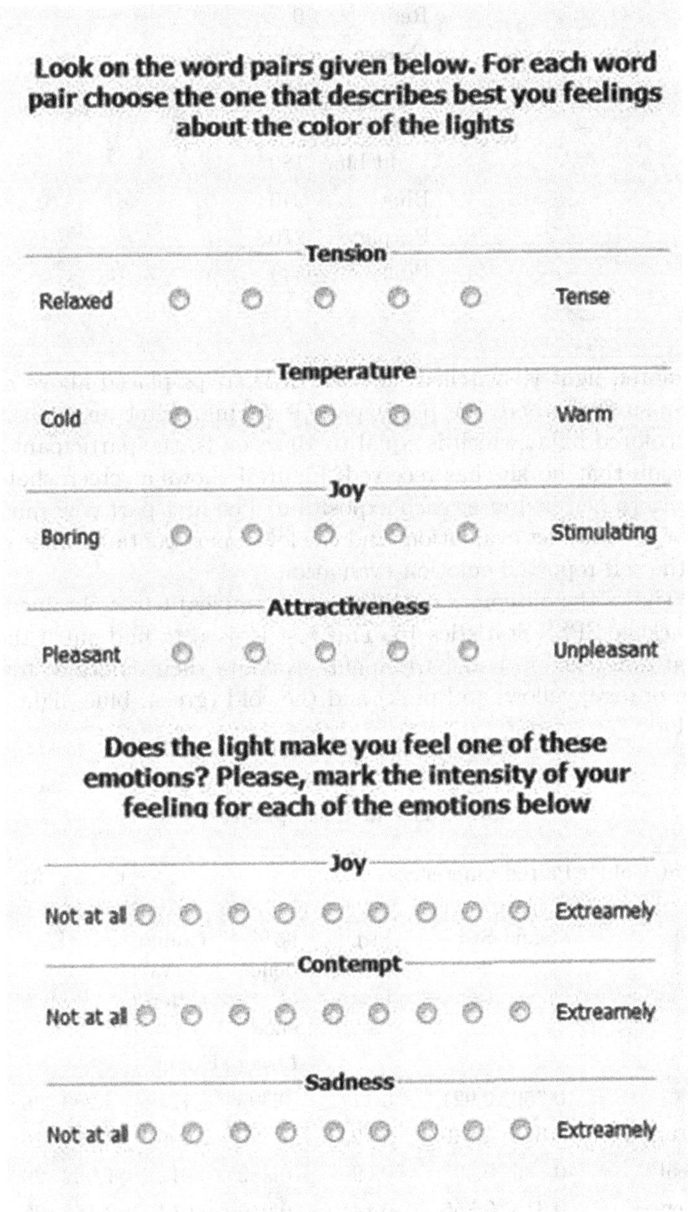

Look on the word pairs given below. For each word pair choose the one that describes best you feelings about the color of the lights

──────────────────────────── Tension ────────────────────────────

Relaxed ⊙ ⊙ ⊙ ⊙ ⊙ Tense

──────────────────────── Temperature ────────────────────────

Cold ⊙ ⊙ ⊙ ⊙ ⊙ Warm

────────────────────────────── Joy ──────────────────────────────

Boring ⊙ ⊙ ⊙ ⊙ ⊙ Stimulating

──────────────────────── Attractiveness ────────────────────────

Pleasant ⊙ ⊙ ⊙ ⊙ ⊙ Unpleasant

Does the light make you feel one of these emotions? Please, mark the intensity of your feeling for each of the emotions below

────────────────────────────── Joy ──────────────────────────────

Not at all ⊙ ⊙ ⊙ ⊙ ⊙ ⊙ ⊙ ⊙ ⊙ Extreamely

──────────────────────────── Contempt ────────────────────────────

Not at all ⊙ ⊙ ⊙ ⊙ ⊙ ⊙ ⊙ ⊙ ⊙ Extreamely

──────────────────────────── Sadness ────────────────────────────

Not at all ⊙ ⊙ ⊙ ⊙ ⊙ ⊙ ⊙ ⊙ ⊙ Extreamely

Fig. 4. Questionnaire.

Table 1. Colored lights used in the test

Color	Hue
Red	0
Orange	20
Yellow	60
Green	120
Light blue	180
Blue	240
Purple	270
Pink	330

Each colored light is switched on both LED strips placed above and below the working surface where the participant is sitting. After an exposition time to a given colored light, which is equal to 10 seconds, the participant evaluates the impression that he/she has received. Figure 4 shows a screen shot with the questionnaire to be filled after each exposition. The first part contains semantic concepts for the indirect evaluation, and the lower part contains three emotional scales for the self-reported emotion evaluation.

Table 2 shows the outcomes of the paired (samples) t-test obtained with the software package SPSS Statistics 15. This test is used to find out if there exists a significant difference in how participants evaluate their emotions towards the warm (red, orange, yellow, and pink) and the cold (green, blue, light blue, and purple) colors.

Table 2. Paired samples test.

Pair "Warm/Cold"	Paired differences					t	fd	Sig. (2-tailed)
	Mean	Std. deviation	Std. error mean	95 % Confidence interval of the difference				
				Lower	Upper			
"Tension"	0.759	0.921	0.177	0.395	1.124	4.283	26	0.000
"Temperature"	1.843	0.640	0.123	1.589	2.096	14.964	26	0.000
"Amusement"	-0.185	0.498	0.096	-0.382	0.012	-1.932	26	0.064
"Attractiveness"	0.315	0.755	0.145	0.016	0.614	2.166	26	0.040
"Joy"	0.093	1.017	0.195	-0.309	0.495	0.473	26	0.640
"Fear"	-0.092	1.282	0.247	-0.599	0.415	-0.375	26	0.711
"Sadness"	-0.454	1.125	0.216	-0.898	-0.009	-2.096		0.046

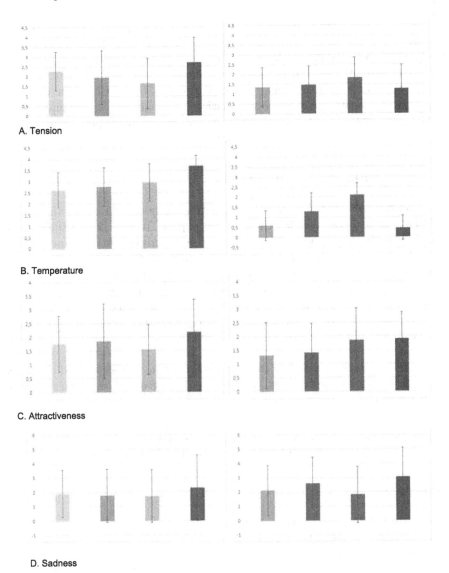

A. Tension

B. Temperature

C. Attractiveness

D. Sadness

Fig. 5. Bar charts for the semantics concepts significant at a level of 0.05. The "C. Attractiveness" shows less attractiveness (Color figure online).

In more detail, the scales that are found significant at a level of 0.05 are:

- "Tension" with a mean of 2.176 for warm and 1.417 for cold colors.
- "Temperature" with a mean of 3.00 for warm and 1.154 for cold colors.
- "Attractiveness" with a mean of 1.852 for warm and 1.537 for cold colors.
- "Sadness" with a mean of 1.639 for warm and 2.093 for cold colors.

Figure 5 shows bar charts for these semantic concepts. Given the normal distribution of the experimental data for each "Warm" and "Cold" color group, the difference between these groups is evident. Thus, "warm" colors are perceived as more *tensed, warmer*, but *less pleasant* than the ones from the "cold" group. Indeed, this last conclusion can be due to the fact that LEDs offer a strong lighting, which results to be too intense with red, orange, yellow, and pink colors. The experimental outcomes show similarities in colored light perception on the emotional state both for males and females.

6   Discussion and Conclusions

An experimental setup for emotion regulation at home, based on the use of RGB LED strips, has been described in this paper. The selection of the components and materials for assembly, as well as the description of the experimental setup, has been provided in detail. The following statistical evaluation of the experimental results have proved the relation between colored light and emotional responses. In this sense, warm colors are rated as more tensed, hot, and less preferable for lighting. Meanwhile, cold colors are rated as more pleasant. With respect to the "Joy" concept, both color groups receive similar evaluations, which can be explained as a particular characteristic of the colors offered by LED strips.

The future steps to complete this experiment would include an additional set of experiments for more complex evaluations of colored light emotion detection and regulation.

Acknowledgements. This work was partially supported by Spanish Ministerio de Economía y Competitividad/FEDER under TIN2013-47074-C2-1-R grant.

References

1. Grandner, M.A., Kripke, D.F., Langer, R.D.: Light exposure is related to social and emotional functioning and to quality of life in older women. Psychiatry Res. **143**(1), 35–42 (2006)
2. Bauer, M.S., Kurtz, J.W., Rubin, L.B., Marcus, J.G.: Mood and behavioral effects of four-week light treatment in winter depressives and controls. J. Psychiatr. Res. **28**(2), 135–145 (1994)
3. Harleman, M.: Colour emotion in full-scale rooms. In: Proceedings of the Interim Meeting of the International Color Association, 3 November, Porto Alegre, Brazil, vol. 5, pp. 223–226 (2004)
4. Sokolova, M.V., Fernández-Caballero, A., Ros, L., Latorre, J.M., Serrano, J.P.: Evaluation of color preference for emotion regulation. In: Vicente, J.M.F., Álvarez-Sánchez, J.R., de la Paz López, F., Toledo-Moreo, F.J., Adeli, H. (eds.) Artificial Computation in Biology and Medicine. LNCS, vol. 9107, pp. 479–487. Springer, Heidelberg (2015)
5. Sokolova, M.V., Fernández-Caballero, A.: A review on the role of color and light in affective computing. Appl. Sci. **5**(3), 275–293 (2015)

6. Sokolova, M.V., Fernández-Caballero, A., López, M.T., Martínez-Rodrigo, A., Zangróniz, R., Pastor, J.M.: A distributed architecture for multimodal emotion identification. In: Bajo, J., Hernández, J.Z., Mathieu, P., Campbell, A., Fernández-Caballero, A., Moreno, M.N., Julián, V., Alonso Betanzos, A., Jiménez-López, M.D., Botti, V. (eds.) Trends in Prac. Appl. of Agents, Multi-Agent Sys. and Sustainability. AISC, vol. 372, pp. 125–132. Springer, Heidelberg (2015)
7. Castillo, J.C., Fernández-Caballero, A., Castro-González, A., Salichs, M.A., López, M.T.: A framework for recognizing and regulating emotions in the elderly. In: Pecchia, L., Chen, L.L., Nugent, C., Bravo, J. (eds.) IWAAL 2014. LNCS, vol. 8868, pp. 320–327. Springer, Heidelberg (2014)
8. Soriano, C., Valenzuela, J.: Emotion and colour across languages: implicit associations in Spanish colour terms. Soc. Sci. Inf. **48**(3), 421–445 (2009)
9. Terman, M., Terman, J.S., Ross, D.C.: A controlled trial of timed bright light and negative air ionization for treatment of winter depression. Arch. Gen. Psychiatry **55**(10), 875–882 (1998)
10. Schauss, A.G.: Tranquilizing effect of color reduces aggressive behavior and potential violence. J. Orthomolecular Psychiatry **8**(4), 218–221 (1979)
11. Xin, J.H., Cheng, K.M., Taylor, G., Sato, T., Hansuebsai, A.: Cross-regional comparison of color emotions Part I: quantitative analysis. Color Res. Appl. **29**(6), 451–457 (2004)
12. Xin, J.H., Cheng, K.M., Taylor, G., Sato, T., Hansuebsai, A.: Cross-regional comparison of color emotions Part II: qualitative analysis. Color Res. Appl. **29**(6), 458–466 (2004)
13. Jue, J., Kwon, S.M.: Does color say something about emotions? Laypersons' assessments of color drawings. Arts Psychother. **40**(1), 115–119 (2013)
14. Fernández-Caballero, A., Latorre, J.M., Pastor, J.M., Fernández-Sotos, A.: Improvement of the elderly quality of life and care through smart emotion regulation. In: Pecchia, L., Chen, L.L., Nugent, C., Bravo, J. (eds.) IWAAL 2014. LNCS, vol. 8868, pp. 348–355. Springer, Heidelberg (2014)
15. Solli, M., Lenz, R.: Color emotions for multi-colored images. Color Res. Appl. **36**(3), 210–221 (2011)
16. Coan, J.A., Allen, J.J.: Handbook of Emotion Elicitation and Assessment. Oxford University Press, New York (2007)

Landmark-Based Histograms of Oriented Gradients for Facial Emotion Recognition

Pablo Guerrero$^{(\boxtimes)}$, Matías Pavez, Diego Chávez, and Sergio F. Ochoa

Computer Science Department, Universidad de Chile, Santiago, Chile
pguerrer@ing.uchile.cl

Abstract. The automatic recognition of human emotions is used to support several computing paradigms, like affective, positive and pervasive computing. Histograms of oriented gradients (HOG) have been successfully used with such a purpose, by processing facial images. However, the results of using HOG vary depending on the position of the facial components in the image used as input. This paper presents an extension to the HOG method, which was named Landmark-based Histograms of Oriented Gradients (LaHOG), that not only calculates HOG blocks in the whole face, but also in specific positions around selected facial landmarks. In this sense, the new method is more robust than its predecessor. In order to evaluate the capabilities and limitations of this proposal, we used it to recognize emotions in face images from the FACES database. In such a process we used two classification strategies: support vector machines and logistic regression. The results show that the extended method significantly surpasses the performance of HOG in the tested database.

Keywords: Emotion recognition · Facial recognition · Pervasive computing · Emotional computing · Histograms of oriented gradients · Social robotics · Logistic regression · Support vector machines

1 Introduction

Over recent decades, machines have increased their capability of performing complex tasks, being integrated into our world and interacting with humans in a natural fashion. Several new computing paradigms, such as positive, affective and pervasive computing, take advantage of these capabilities. Two regular services used by these systems are the user identification and the automatic emotion recognition, typically using voice or face recognition. The research efforts in this direction are gaining momentum, given they can provide a transversal improvement to systems and services used in several application scenarios, such as monitoring patients, determining driver stress, performing psychological diagnosis and training, diagnosing psychological disorders and stimulating social interactions [14,25]. In this paper we address only one aspect of this challenge; particularly, the emotion recognition using facial gestures.

Some of the most successful strategies for emotion recognition rely on the extraction of histograms of oriented gradients (HOG) from face images

© Springer International Publishing Switzerland 2015
I. Cleland et al. (Eds.): IWAAL 2015, LNCS 9455, pp. 288–299, 2015.
DOI: 10.1007/978-3-319-26410-3_27

[3,7,8,10,16,18]. Particularly, HOG features are retrieved from a window that is centered in the face of the people held in the image. Although the HOG approach has shown to be useful, there is an intrinsic assumption that facial gestures will produce gradient changes in determined regions of the face. This assumption will often hold since facial gestures are strongly related to movements of discriminatory facial components, like the mouth, nose, eyes and eyebrows.

Typically, the face detection process gives an estimated position for the bounding box of a person's face. Considering these bounding boxes, we can assume that the position of the facial components inside the image are quite stable. However, differences in the relative positions of those components reduce the validity of the former assumption. These differences may be due to: (i) discrepancies among the borders of the detected face, (ii) variations in the morphology among faces of different people, and (iii) rotations of the face in the picture.

In this work, we propose an extension to the HOG model to deal with such spatial variations for the emotion recognition problem. The proposed extension uses an existing method for finding landmarks in face images. Then, it uses the positions of these facial landmarks to extract a set of refined HOG features. These features are finally added to the HOG features obtained for the whole face, thus easing the emotions recognition. The proposed method, named Landmark-based Histograms of Oriented Gradients (LaHOG), was evaluated using face images from the FACES database [11]. The obtained results indicate that the additional information retrieved by LaHOG helps increase the accuracy of the emotion recognition process; therefore, the performance of the proposed method is higher than its predecessor. Additionally, two classification strategies were tested and compared in order to have more detailed perspective on the model performance. Researchers of positive, affective or pervasive computing can use this proposal not only to perform emotion detection in facial images, but also to improve their own image-based emotion detection algorithms.

The next section presents and discusses the related work. Sections 3 and 4 introduce the HOG and LaHOG methods respectively. Section 5 shows and discusses the evaluation process and the obtained results. Finally, Sect. 6 presents the conclusions and future work.

2   Related Work

The recognition of human emotions from facial images has been addressed in many studies. The literature in this field is too vast, and reviewing it comprehensively is out of the scope of this paper. The reader is referred to [5,13,21] for a more complete view of the previous works.

Typically, the recognition of emotions from facial images can be divided in three stages: face detection and tracking, feature extraction and classification. Concerning detection and tracking, some works (e.g., [19]) focus on the identification of the so-called *action units* (AUs) [12], which are specific facial muscle movements. A comparison of several classification techniques used to recognizing AUs is available in [4].

There are also methods for face detection and tracking that follow other approaches. For instance, in [22] a *ratio template* is presented to detect faces based on three-dimensional forms. A modified version of this ratio template is used in [2] to track faces in cluttered scenes. Following the same purpose, the *PersonSpotter system* [23] was proposed. This system builds an elastic graph out of a stereo image of frontal faces to perform the recognition. However, one of the most used face detectors for this type of input data is the *Viola-Jones face detector* [26], which performs quick recognitions with high success rates. Concerning the recognition using 3D models, *Candide* [1] is a widely used strategy, as well as the *piecewise Bézier volume deformation* model [24] that also proposes a tracking algorithm.

Concerning the feature extraction methods, Yun et al. [28] show an experimental comparison of some well-known methods, considering their performance. The comparison includes *HOG, Local Binary Paterns, Gabor Filters* and combinations of them. The use of HOG for feature extraction is an strategy followed by several works; for instance, Orrite et al. [18] focus on the selection of features from a HOG vector obtained from the whole image. Similarly, in [8] the authors use a dynamic-size grid with the same purpose, whose dimensions are calculated as a function of the distance between detected eyes. Other works apply a *Pyramid of HOG* (PHOG) on a specific window to perform the feature extraction [3,10,16]. For example, in [3], a PHOG is used in conjunction with Gabor filters over the mouth region in order to detect smiles. Dhall et al. [10] propose the use PHOG and *Local Phase Quantization* features over the whole face in selected frames inside a sequence. Finally, in [16] PHOG is combined with a bag of words based on *Scale-Invariant Feature Transform*.

There are also other methods that use of facial landmarks for feature extraction, and thus to recognize emotion. For instance, in [20] the positions of selected facial landmarks are used to recognize AUs in profile images. In [7], HOG features are extracted from two windows whose coordinates are obtained from detected eyes; one for the eyes and eyebrows and the other for the nose and mouth. In [29], the positions of manually located facial landmarks are used to extract Gabor filters and form a feature vector. In [15], the displacements of the nodes of the Candide grid are used to recognizing emotions and detect AUs.

Regarding the classification stage, there is also a vast literature whose review is out of the scope of this paper. The reader is refered to [17] for a thorough revision of the most used methods. The most commonly used approach is the use of *Support Vector Machines* (SVM). SVM in its original formulation allows the discrimination between two classes that are linearly sepparable. Later, the use of non-linear kernels has made SVM able to perform non-linear separations. Another fairly used approach, which usually gets comparable results to those of SVM, is *Logistic Regression*. Both approaches were originally designed to perform binary classification. However, later enhancements have made them able to perform multi-class classification.

All these proposals have shown to be useful to address one or more stages of the emotion recognition process using facial images. However, the results of these methods vary depending on the position of the facial components in the image. In this paper we present a method that helps deal with such a challenge using HOG as a baseline for emotion detection. Particularly, the main contribution of this proposal is the use of a deformable model of the face, in order to position part-specific HOG windows. To the best of our knowledge, this is the first attempt of recognizing emotions using landmark-centered HOG windows. Additionally, this paper presents an experimental comparison of the performance of several sets of parameters for both emotion recognition methods; i.e., HOG and LaHOG.

3   The Histograms of Oriented Gradients Method

Histograms of Oriented Gradients are a feature extraction method, originally proposed by Dalal and Triggs [9]. The HOG feature vector is extracted from a window and it basically measures the relative importance of the different gradient directions in different regions of the window. With that purpose, the image gradient is densely calculated across the window, and then the window is tiled into cells. For each cell, a number of direction bins are considered in order to count the gradients following that direction. In fact, for neglecting noise and mostly taking into account relevant gradients, for each pixel, the modulus of its gradient is summed to the bin that contains its direction. Neighbor cells are then grouped into blocks and their values are normalized with respect to the block. The blocks are overlapped, and thus each cell typically belongs to several blocks. Cells and blocks are typically designed to be square.

The final feature vector is built by aggregating the normalized bin values present in every cell of every block. Therefore, information from a single cell may appear several times within the feature vector, but associated with different blocks and thus having different normalization values.

This method has several parameters, such as: (i) the size of the cell, $c_s \times c_s$, for which typical values are 6×6 and 8×8 pixels, (ii) the size of the block, $b_s \times b_s$, usually 2×2 or 3×3 cells, (iii) the range of directions considered, whether $0° - 180°$ (unsigned direction) or $0° - 360°$ (signed direction), and (iv) the number of direction bins, n_b, usually 9. Then, the descriptor size, d_s, can be computed as shown in Eq. (1), where w is the width in pixels of the square image in use.

$$d_s = n_b \cdot b_s^2 \cdot \left(\frac{w}{c_s} - b_s + 1 \right)^2 \tag{1}$$

HOG features can be used for emotion recognition in a very straightforward fashion. A first convenient step is to get the HOG window positioned in the face. This is achieved by using a face detection algorithm [26] that gets a square window (scaled to a 144×144 pixel window) that fits the face. HOG features are extracted from this rescaled window. Then, the HOG feature vector is used as an input for a classifier that gives the recognized emotion as an output. This approach is considered as a baseline strategy for our method.

4   The Landmark-Based Histograms of Oriented Gradients Method

The proposed approach intends to overcome the problems that arise from the variations in positions of the relevant face parts in different pictures. To make the feature vector more robust to those variations, the HOG blocks are not only calculated from the whole face window, but also from smaller windows centered in selected face landmarks. Next subsection explains the way to obtain the feature vector and the classifiers used to perform the emotion recognition.

4.1   The Feature Vector

The feature vector is composed of two parts. The first part corresponds to the regular HOG feature vector, extracted from a window containing the whole face as described in Subsect. 3. The second part corresponds to several HOG feature vectors, extracted from smaller windows positioned in selected parts of the face. The method for extracting these HOG vectors involves two sequential steps. During the first step, a number of facial landmarks are extracted from the face picture. For that purpose, we used the method proposed by Yu et al. [27], which is based on a two-stage cascaded deformable shape model and it is highly reliable. Figure 1 shows examples of landmarks extracted in face pictures.

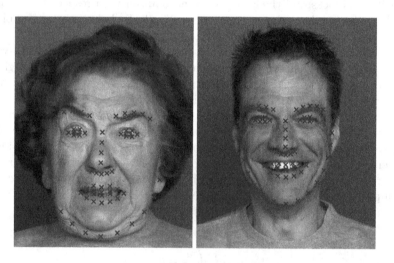

Fig. 1. Landmark extraction examples based on the work of Yu et al. [27].

Then, all the detected landmarks, excepting those of the face border, are selected as centers of relevant face parts. A window containing a single HOG block is considered around the position of each selected landmark. The size of this window is a linear function of some measurement of the face size (more details in Subsect. 5.2). Figure 2 shows the extracted windows for the same faces as before.

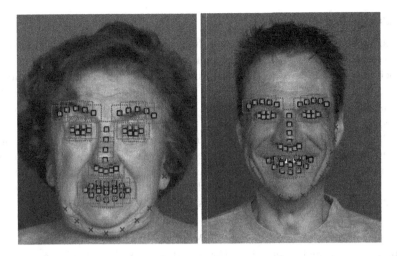

Fig. 2. Examples of selected landmarks and related windows for the images shown in Fig. 1.

4.2   The Classifiers

Two kinds of classifiers were considered to carry out the emotion recognition process. The first one is a Logistic Regression Classifier [17], which is able to deal with multiple classes. The second one is a $\nu-$Support Vector Machine ($\nu-$SVM) classifier, from the LIBSVM library [6], which handles multi-class problems using a *one-against-one* approach. Furthermore, only linear kernels were used for the SVM classifier.

5   Evaluation of LaHOG

The proposed method was compared to the plain use of HOG, in order to determine if the use of landmarks helps improve the emotion recognition process. Next subsections presents the dataset and the parameters used in this evaluation process, as well as the obtained results in this comparison.

5.1   Dataset

The FACES Database [11] was selected as a test bed for the proposed method. It consists of 2,052 face images corresponding to 171 people belonging to three groups: young, middle-age and older. Each picture in the database contains a face expressing one of the six different emotions available: anger, fear, disgust, happiness, sadness and neutrality. For each person and for each emotion, two pictures are available.

5.2   Parameter Selection

There are some parameters of both methods (i.e., HOG and LaHOG) that need to be selected for conducting the comparison process; particularly the cell size c_s, block size b_s, number of orientation bins n_b, and signed/unsigned gradients. We have decided to use $n_b = 9$ and unsigned orientations $(0° - 180°)$ for both methods, since these values have allowed to get good results for similar problems reported in the literature [9].

In the case of HOG, we also had to determine the size of the resized cropped face, and in the case of LaHOG, we specified the width of each landmark centered window. This width is calculated as a fraction of the distance between two specific landmarks: one in the chin and one in the right eye-brow. Then, the window width, w_{LaHOG}, is calculated as follows:

$$w_{LaHOG} = 2\lambda||p_{chin} - p_{r-eyebrow}|| \tag{2}$$

where λ is the scale factor parameter and p_{chin} and $p_{r-eyebrow}$ are the positions of the detected chin and right eyebrow center, respectively. Consequently, all landmark-centered windows are rescaled to $(c_s b_s) \times (c_s b_s)$, and then, HOG descriptors are calculated over each of them. Figure 3 shows the landmarks used when computing w_{LaHOG} and the effect of λ on the landmark window size. The red line represents the distance between both landmarks and the green windows are the result of applying different λ values for a single landmark.

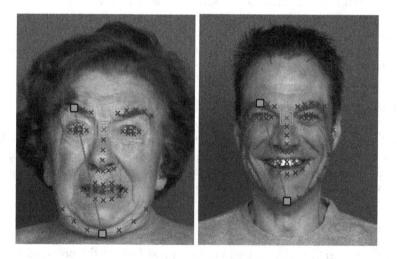

Fig. 3. Examples of window widths as a function of λ. The width of the window is calculated as a fraction of the distance between two landmarks (red line between green squares). The three green squares centered in the landmark (red ex) between the eyes show the window sizes corresponding to $\lambda = \{1/8, 1/12, 1/20\}$ (Color figure online).

In order to select appropriate parameters for each method, we performed prior experiments on the FACES database. The people facial images in the dataset were randomly split into a training (1,200 images) and a test (852 images) subsets. As a result, 1,200 (200 per emotion) images were selected for training and 852 (142 per emotion) for testing. A Logistic Regression classifier was then used to obtain the recognition rates for the selected subsets. In order to get more statistically significant results, this process was repeated 100 times, with a different random dataset permutation each time. Table 1 shows the values assumed by the parameters considered in the evaluation of the baseline method, and their average emotion recognition rates after 100 cycles. The configuration that shown the highest recognition rate for HOG is the following: $\kappa = 144, c_s = 8, b_s = 3$.

Table 1. Set of parameters and their respective average emotion recognition rates for the baseline method

κ	c_s	b_s	HOG[%]
72	6×6	2×2	90.95 ± 1.00
		3×3	91.58 ± 0.95
	8×8	2×2	89.98 ± 1.04
		3×3	90.40 ± 1.04
144	6×6	2×2	91.68 ± 0.96
		3×3	92.34 ± 0.92
	8×8	2×2	91.72 ± 0.95
		3×3	$\mathbf{92.49 \pm 0.95}$
288	6×6	2×2	90.83 ± 1.09
		3×3	91.32 ± 1.06
	8×8	2×2	91.31 ± 1.11
		3×3	91.94 ± 1.02

Table 2 shows the parameters and the respective results for the LaHOG method using, for the whole face feature extraction, the best parameter set found for the baseline method. Therefore, the modified parameters used in this evaluation only correspond to those required to compute the landmark descriptors. The results show that the selected sets of parameters behave similarly, and there are several configuration with an average recognition rate very close to the highest. Nevertheless, we selected the set of parameters that achieved the highest average value: $\lambda = 1/8$, $c_s = 8$ and $b_s = 3$. Additionally, LaHOG gets a higher recognition rate with lower deviation from mean in every tested configuration.

5.3 Analysis of the Evaluation Results

With the purpose of comparing the performance (in terms of emotion recognition) of the two methods, we will now focus on the results obtained when considering the best parameters for each method.

Table 2. Set of parameters and their respective average emotion recognition rates for LaHOG

λ	c_s	b_s	LaHOG[%]
1/8	6 × 6	2 × 2	93.32 ± 0.88
		3 × 3	93.84 ± 0.90
	8 × 8	2 × 2	93.34 ± 0.84
		3 × 3	**93.89 ± 0.89**
1/12	6 × 6	2 × 2	93.21 ± 0.89
		3 × 3	93.68 ± 0.87
	8 × 8	2 × 2	93.27 ± 0.92
		3 × 3	93.78 ± 0.91
1/20	6 × 6	2 × 2	93.06 ± 0.94
		3 × 3	93.46 ± 0.91
	8 × 8	2 × 2	93.11 ± 0.93
		3 × 3	93.57 ± 0.92

The ν–SVM classifier yields an accuracy of 92.68 ± 0.97 % and 93.70 ± 0.94 % for the HOG and the LaHOG methods respectively. Similarly, the Logistic Regression approach yields an accuracy of 92.49 ± 0.95 % and 93.89 ± 0.89 % for these methods, which shows that both classifiers behave similarly. However, due to the high time consumption and large memory usage of the $\nu - SVM$ classifier, we will use the Logistic Regression classifier for the remaining of the paper.

Tables 3 and 4 show the confusion matrices for HOG and LaHOG respectively. Note that LaHOG achieves a higher average recognition rate for each of the tested emotions. If we look in detail the behavior of these methods for each emotion separately, we can see that happiness and fear are the easiest emotions to be recognized. In contrast, sadness and anger get significantly lower recognition rates. Sadness usually gets confused with anger and neutrality, whereas anger gets mostly confused with disgust and sadness. Finally, both disgust and neutrality get confused with anger and sadness most of the time.

Table 3. Confusion Matrix for the HOG Method

	Anger	Disgust	Fear	Happiness	Neutrality	Sadness
Anger	88.65	5.65	0.18	0.15	1.87	3.49
Disgust	3.41	94.58	0.02	0.42	0.08	1.49
Fear	0.06	0.08	95.99	0.01	2.37	1.48
Happiness	0.45	0.13	0.23	99.15	0.04	0.01
Neutrality	3.06	0.31	2.39	0.30	91.32	2.62
Sadness	5.38	1.70	1.49	1.25	4.94	85.23

Table 4. Confusion Matrix for the LaHOG Method

	Anger	Disgust	Fear	Happiness	Neutrality	Sadness
Anger	90.04	5.15	0.18	0.20	1.80	2.62
Disgust	2.88	95.45	0.02	0.31	0.01	1.32
Fear	0.01	0	97.72	0.01	1.46	0.80
Happiness	0.39	0.11	0	99.45	0.04	0.01
Neutrality	1.87	0.03	0.99	0.25	94.17	2.69
Sadness	4.68	1.59	1.17	1.29	4.75	86.52

These results make the proposed method potentially useful for addressing the challenge of monitoring people in several scenarios. Therefore, it could be embedded in ambient assisted living systems, home care solutions and also in health monitoring systems. Considering that the modern medicine addresses the chronic diseases using an integral approach, where the patients' and caregivers' mood are important elements in the caring process, implementations of the proposed emotion recognition method could contribute to support treatments in this area.

6   Conclusions and Future Work

This paper has presented the Landmark-based Histograms of Oriented Gradients (LaHOG) method for emotion recognition using frontal facial images. This method is based on HOG and facial landmark extraction. Several combinations of parameters were evaluated for both HOG and LaHOG. The experimental results obtained using the FACES database show that the performance of the presented method is higher than the baseline method. Although these results are still preliminary, the obtained recognition rates make LaHOG very promising. Considering the classifiers used in the evaluation process, Logistic Regression showed a performance similar to SVM; however, the former used much less computational resources than the latter.

Real-time processing is not achievable by the current implementation of the LaHOG method. Therefore, a very important issue to be addressed in the future is the optimization of the landmark extraction process, in order to extend the range of problems that can be addressed using this solution. One possible strategy to reach this goal is to track the deformable model from one frame to another, for instance, using particle filters.

Another important issue to analyze in this improvement process is the high dimensionality of the feature vector. The use of automatic dimensionality reduction techniques could offer further advantages, in terms of performance and efficiency, to the recognition process.

Aknowledgments. This work has been partially supported by Fondecyt (Chile), grant Nro. 1150252.

References

1. Ahlberg, J.: Candide-3 - an updated parameterized face. Technical report, LiTH-ISY-R-2326, Department of Electrical Engineering, Linkping University, Sweden (2001)
2. Anderson, K., McOwan, P.W.: A real-time automated system for the recognition of human facial expressions. IEEE Trans. Syst. Man Cybern. B Cybern. **36**(1), 96–105 (2006)
3. Bai, Y., Guo, L., Jin, L., Huang, Q.: A novel feature extraction method using pyramid histogram of orientation gradients for smile recognition. In: 2009 16th IEEE International Conference on Image Processing (ICIP), pp. 3305–3308, November 2009
4. Bartlett, M., Littlewort, G., Frank, M., Lainscsek, C., Fasel, I., Movellan, J.: Recognizing facial expression: machine learning and application to spontaneous behavior. In: IEEE Computer Society Conference on Computer Vision and Pattern Recognition, CVPR 2005, vol. 2, pp. 568–573, June 2005
5. Bettadapura, V.: Face expression recognition and analysis: the state of the art. Technical report, College of Computing, Georgia Institute of Technology (2012)
6. Chang, C.C., Lin, C.J.: LIBSVM: a library for support vector machines. ACM Trans. Intell. Syst. Technol. **2**, 1–27 (2011). http://www.csie.ntu.edu.tw/~cjlin/libsvm
7. Chen, J., Chen, Z., Chi, Z., Fu, H.: Facial expression recognition based on facial components detection and hog features. In: Scientific Cooperations International Workshops on Electrical and Computer Engineering Subfields, Istanbul, Turkey, August 2014
8. Dahmane, M., Meunier, J.: Emotion recognition using dynamic grid-based hog features. In: FG, pp. 884–888. IEEE (2011)
9. Dalal, N., Triggs, B.: Histograms of oriented gradients for human detection. In: International Conference on Computer Vision & Pattern Recognition, vol. 2, pp. 886–893, June 2005
10. Dhall, A., Asthana, A., Goecke, R., Gedeon, T.: Emotion recognition using phog and lpq features. In: FG, pp. 878–883. IEEE (2011)
11. Ebner, N.C., Riediger, M., Lindenberger, U.: Faces. a database of facial expressions in young, middle-aged, and older women and men: development and validation. Behav. Res. Meth. **42**(1), 351–362 (2010)
12. Ekman, P., Friesen, W. (eds.): The Facial Action Coding System. Consulting Psychologists Press, Palo Alto (1978)
13. Fasel, B., Luettin, J.: Automatic facial expression analysis: a survey. Pattern Recogn. **36**(1), 259–275 (2003). http://www.sciencedirect.com/science/article/pii/S0031320302000523
14. Kołakowska, A., Landowska, A., Szwoch, M., Szwoch, W., Wróbel, M.R.: Emotion recognition and its applications. In: Hippe, Z.S., Kulikowski, J.L., Mroczek, T., Wtorek, J. (eds.) Human-Computer Systems Interaction: Backgrounds and Applications 3. AISC, vol. 300, pp. 51–62. Springer, Heidelberg (2014)
15. Kotsia, I., Pitas, I.: Facial expression recognition in image sequences using geometric deformation features and support vector machines. IEEE Trans. Image Process. **16**(1), 172–187 (2007)
16. Li, Z., Ichi Imai, J., Kaneko, M.: Facial-component-based bag of words and phog descriptor for facial expression recognition. In: IEEE International Conference on Systems, Man and Cybernetics, SMC 2009, pp. 1353–1358, October 2009

17. Murphy, K.P.: Machine Learning: A Probabilistic Perspective. The MIT Press, Cambridge (2012)
18. Orrite, C., Gañán, A., Rogez, G.: HOG-based decision tree for facial expression classification. In: Araujo, H., Mendonça, A.M., Pinho, A.J., Torres, M.I. (eds.) IbPRIA 2009. LNCS, vol. 5524, pp. 176–183. Springer, Heidelberg (2009)
19. Pantic, M., Patras, I.: Detecting facial actions and their temporal segments in nearly frontal-view face image sequences. In: 2005 IEEE International Conference on Systems, Man and Cybernetics, vol. 4, pp. 3358–3363, October 2005
20. Pantic, M., Patras, I.: Dynamics of facial expression: recognition of facial actions and their temporal segments from face profile image sequences. IEEE Trans. Syst. Man Cybern. Part B Cybern. **36**(2), 433–449 (2006)
21. Pantic, M., Rothkrantz, L.J.M.: Automatic analysis of facial expressions: the state of the art. IEEE Trans. Pattern Anal. Mach. Intell. **22**(12), 1424–1445 (2000). http://dx.doi.org/10.1109/34.895976
22. Sinha, P.: Perceiving and recognizing three-dimensional forms. Ph.D. Thesis, Massachusetts Institute of Technology (1995)
23. Steffens, J., Elagin, E., Neven, H.: Personspotter-fast and robust system for human detection, tracking and recognition. In: Proceedings of the Third IEEE International Conference on Automatic Face and Gesture Recognition, pp. 516–521, April 1998
24. Tao, H., Huang, T.S.: A piecewise Bezier volume deformation model and its applications in facial motion capture. In: Advances in Image Processing and Understanding: A Festschrift for Thomas S. Huang (2002)
25. Tivatansakul, S., Ohkura, M., Puangpontip, S., Achalakul, T.: Emotional healthcare system: emotion detection by facial expressions using japanese database. In: 2014 6th Computer Science and Electronic Engineering Conference (CEEC), pp. 41–46, September 2014
26. Viola, P., Jones, M.J.: Robust real-time face detection. Int. J. Comput. Vis. **57**(2), 137–154 (2004)
27. Yu, X., Huang, J., Zhang, S., Yan, W., Metaxas, D.: Pose-free facial landmark fitting via optimized part mixtures and cascaded deformable shape model. In: 2013 IEEE International Conference on Computer Vision (ICCV), pp. 1944–1951, December 2013
28. Yun, W., Kim, D., Park, C., Kim, J.: Hybrid facial representations for emotion recognition. ETRI J. **35**(6), 1021–1028 (2013)
29. Zheng, W., Zhou, X., Zou, C., Zhao, L.: Facial expression recognition using kernel canonical correlation analysis (KCCA). IEEE Trans. Neural Netw. **17**(1), 233–238 (2006)

Author Index

Printed in the United States
By Bookmasters